The Civilian Lives of U.S. Veterans

The Civilian Lives of U.S. Veterans

Issues and Identities

VOLUME 1

Louis Hicks, Eugenia L. Weiss,
and Jose E. Coll, Editors

*Foreword by Robert A. McDonald,
Secretary of the Department of Veterans Affairs*

PRAEGER™

An Imprint of ABC-CLIO, LLC
Santa Barbara, California • Denver, Colorado

Copyright © 2017 by ABC-CLIO, LLC

All rights reserved. No part of this publication may be reproduced, stored in a retrieval system, or transmitted, in any form or by any means, electronic, mechanical, photocopying, recording, or otherwise, except for the inclusion of brief quotations in a review, without prior permission in writing from the publisher.

Library of Congress Cataloging-in-Publication Data

Names: Hicks, Louis, author. | Weiss, Eugenia L., author. | Coll, Jose E., author.
Title: The civilian lives of U.S. veterans : issues and identities / Louis Hicks, Eugenia L. Weiss, and Jose E. Coll, editors ; foreword by Robert A. McDonald, Secretary of the Department of Veterans Affairs.
Description: Santa Barbara, California : Praeger, an imprint of ABC-CLIO, LLC, [2017] | Includes bibliographical references and index.
Identifiers: LCCN 2016017943 (print) | LCCN 2016018573 (ebook) | ISBN 9781440842788 (set : alk. paper) | ISBN 9781440846809 (volume 1 : alk. paper) | ISBN 9781440846816 (volume 2 : alk. paper) | ISBN 9781440842795 (ebook)
Subjects: LCSH: Veterans—United States. | Veterans—United States—Social conditions. | Veterans—United States—Employment.
Classification: LCC UB357 .H524 2017 (print) | LCC UB357 (ebook) | DDC 305.9/06970973—dc23
LC record available at https://lccn.loc.gov/2016017943

ISBN: 978-1-4408-4278-8 (set)
ISBN: 978-1-4408-4680-9 (vol. 1)
ISBN: 978-1-4408-4681-6 (vol. 2)
EISBN: 978-1-4408-4279-5 (set)

21 20 19 18 17   1 2 3 4 5

This book is also available as an eBook.

Praeger
An Imprint of ABC-CLIO, LLC

ABC-CLIO, LLC
130 Cremona Drive, P.O. Box 1911
Santa Barbara, California 93116-1911
www.abc-clio.com

This book is printed on acid-free paper ∞

Manufactured in the United States of America

This book is dedicated to the military veterans and their families who have proudly served our country with selfless dedication for the greater good of our nation. The editors would like to acknowledge and honor Dr. and Mrs. Somers, who lost their son, Daniel, an Iraq War veteran, to suicide, for their courage and inspiration in helping other veterans and their families through their nonprofit, Operation Engage America, in providing access to care and raising awareness about the needs of the veteran community.

Contents

List of Illustrations   xi

Foreword by Robert A. McDonald   xv

Preface   xvii

VOLUME 1

Chapter One:	Introduction to Veterans' Studies *Louis Hicks, Eugenia L. Weiss, and Jose E. Coll*	1
Chapter Two:	Characteristics of Veterans and Nonveterans within 20th-Century Cohorts in the United States *Janet M. Wilmoth and Andrew S. London*	11
Chapter Three:	The Transition from Active Duty *Daniel Kester and Maureen P. Phillips*	37
Chapter Four:	TAPped Out: A Study of the Department of Defense's Transition Assistance Program *Colleen M. Heflin, Leslie B. Hodges, and Andrew S. London*	61
Chapter Five:	The VA and the Grass Roots *Colin D. Moore*	91

Chapter Six:	The Job Training of Veterans *Bruce D. McDonald III, Myung H. Jin,* *Susan Camilleri, and Vincent Reitano*	113
Chapter Seven:	Veterans in Higher Education *Michael A. Grandillo and John W. M. Magee*	137
Chapter Eight:	Veteran Employment in the 21st Century *Hazel R. Atuel, Mary Keeling,* *Sara M. Kintzle, Anthony M. Hassan,* *and Carl A. Castro*	161
Chapter Nine:	Veterans and Civic Engagement *Fred P. Stone*	181
Chapter Ten:	Veterans as Entrepreneurs *Elizabeth A. Osborn and Louis Hicks*	201
Chapter Eleven:	Veterans as Private Security Contractors *Alison Hawks*	215
Chapter Twelve:	The Preferential Hiring of Military Veterans in the United States *Tim Johnson*	239
Chapter Thirteen:	The Retirement Patterns and Socioeconomic Status of Aging Veterans, 1995–2014 *Christopher R. Tamborini, Patrick Purcell,* *and Anya Olsen*	273
Chapter Fourteen:	Military Expatriates: U.S. Veterans Living Abroad *Yvonne McNulty, Kelly L. Fisher,* *Louis Hicks, and Tim Kane*	305
Chapter Fifteen:	Veterans' Families *Jasmine Strode-Elfant, Paul Hemez,* *Lucky Tedrow, and Jay Teachman*	339

VOLUME 2

Chapter Sixteen:	Veterans' Health *Lisa Leitz*	363

Chapter Seventeen:	The Mental Health of Veterans *Kristi L. Mueller and Jeffrey S. Yarvis*	397
Chapter Eighteen:	The Roles of Veteran Peers in Mental Health Recovery during Transition from Military to Civilian Life *Elisa V. Borah and Stacey Stevens Manser*	431
Chapter Nineteen:	Veterans as the Media Portray Them *Gregory Gross and Eugenia L. Weiss*	455
Chapter Twenty:	Veterans in the Criminal Justice System *Evan R. Seamone and David L. Albright*	481
Chapter Twenty-One:	Veterans and Their Firearms *Daniel Burland*	509
Chapter Twenty-Two:	Suicide among Veterans *Wilbur J. Scott*	531
Chapter Twenty-Three:	Women as Veterans *Molly Clever and Kelly L. Fisher*	553
Chapter Twenty-Four:	What Do We Know about Veteran Status Differences in Social Attitudes? *Andrew S. London, Janet M. Wilmoth, and Cassie Dutton*	577
Chapter Twenty-Five:	Religion and Spirituality in the Veteran Life Course *Michelle Sandhoff*	607
Chapter Twenty-Six:	Immigrants as Veterans *Gina Jackson, Jose E. Coll, and Eugenia L. Weiss*	631
Chapter Twenty-Seven:	Military and Wartime Experiences of Racial and Ethnic Minority Veterans *Nikki R. Wooten, Shanada R. Adams, and Carleigh A. Davis*	649
Chapter Twenty-Eight:	Lesbian, Gay, Bisexual, and Transgender Veterans *Kristen Kavanaugh*	673

Chapter Twenty-Nine:	Housing Veterans: Homelessness and Mortgages *Amy Kate Bailey, Christopher D. Poulos, and Kylee M. Joosten*	693
Chapter Thirty:	Veterans' Expeditions: Tapping the Great Outdoors *Demond Mullins*	719
About the Editors		747
About the Contributors		749
Index		765

Illustrations

Tables

2.1.	Selected Characteristics and Estimated Sizes of Age-18 Cohorts	14
2.2a.	Percentage of Male Veterans Reporting Military Service during Given Service Periods by Age-18 Cohort	16
2.2b.	Percentage of Female Veterans Reporting Military Service during Given Service Periods by Age-18 Cohort	17
2.3.	Sociodemographic, Economic, and Disability Characteristics of Nonveterans and Veterans by Age-18 Cohort among Males	21
2.4.	Sociodemographic, Economic, and Disability Characteristics of Nonveterans and Veterans by Age-18 Cohort among Females	26
3.1.	The Three Phases of Career Development	39
3.2.	Excerpt and Code Count per Interview	49
3.3.	Code Application Process	50
4.1.	Reports of TAP Attendance by Military Branch and Year	71
4.2.	Observed Demographic Characteristics of Eligible Program Participants by Attendance	73
6.1.	Job Training Programs for Veterans	115
7.1.	Educational Attainment of Veterans and Nonveterans, 2014	140
7.2.	Fields of Study Pursued by Veterans, 2002–2013	145
7.3.	Importance of VA Education or Training Benefits by Cohort	147
10.1.	Self-Employed, Unincorporated Veterans by Sex and Period of Service, 2014	206
10.2.	Size of Veteran-Owned Firms in the United States, 2012	207

11.1.	Patriotism as Self-Reported by U.S. Military Veterans Who Are Now Private Security Contractors	221
12.1.	Eligibility Criteria for Preference in the U.S. Federal Government	242
12.2.	Veterans' Preference Policies across the United States	245
12.3.	Key Events in the Emergence of Post–World War II Veterans' Preference	254
13.1a.	Most Recent Military Service and Educational Attainment of Older Male Veterans and Nonveterans by Age, 1995–2014	282
13.1b.	Marital Status and Race/Ethnicity of Older Male Veterans and Nonveterans by Age, 1995–2014	284
13.2a.	Labor Force Participation and Work-Limiting Disability among Older Male Veterans and Nonveterans by Age, 1995–2014	286
13.2b.	Occupation and Industry of Older Male Veterans and Nonveterans by Age, 1995–2014	288
13.3a.	Total Individual Income, Social Security, and Earnings among Older Male Veterans and Nonveterans by Age, 1995–2014	291
13.3b.	Civilian and Military Pensions, Veterans' Benefits, and Public Assistance among Older Male Veterans and Nonveterans by Age, 1995–2014	293
13.4.	Family Income, Poverty, and Reliance on Social Security Income, Older Veterans and Nonveterans by Age, 1995–2014	296
14.1.	Total Deployment of U.S. Military Personnel in Person-Years (Billets), 1950–2015, in 20 Largest Receiving Countries	310
14.2.	U.S. Military Deployed Personnel by 20 Largest Receiving Countries, Cold War Era, 1950–1989	310
14.3.	U.S. Military Deployed Personnel by 20 Largest Receiving Countries, Gulf War I Era, 1990–2001	311
14.4.	U.S. Military Deployed Personnel by 20 Largest Receiving Countries, Post-9/11 Era, 2002–2015	312
14.5.	Sample Characteristics of Expert Commentators	315
14.6.	Characteristics of Participants	316
15.1.	U.S. Veterans by Birth Cohort, Age in 2013, and Historic Era	344
15.2.	Descriptive Statistics for Female Veterans and Nonveterans, by Era, in 2013	346
15.3.	Descriptive Statistics for Male Veterans and Nonveterans, by Era, in 2013	347
15.4.	Differences between Female Veterans and Female Nonveterans in Marital Status, Cohabitation, and Children: Treatment Effects	349
15.5.	Differences between Male Veterans and Male Nonveterans in Marital Status, Cohabitation, and Children: Treatment Effects	351

15.6.	Differences between Female Veterans and Female Nonveterans in Household Type: Treatment Effects	353
15.7.	Differences between Male Veterans and Male Nonveterans in Household Type: Treatment Effects	353
17.1.	Prevalence Rates of Common Mental Health Diagnoses in the U.S. Veteran and Civilian Populations	404
18.1.	Proposed/Draft Certification Curriculum for VA Peer Support Staff	439
18.2.	Veteran Peer Activities as Reported by Peers Involved in the Texas Military Veteran Peer Network	441
20.1.	States and Counties with Specialized Veteran Correctional Housing Units as of September 2015	499
23.1.	Demographic Characteristics of Veteran Population by Gender, 2013	559
23.2.	Economic Characteristics of Veteran Population by Gender, 2013	564
24.1.	Influence of Veteran Status on Confidence in Institutions, Pooled 2010, 2012, and 2014 GSS	584
24.2.	Influence of Veteran Status on Attitudes toward Spending on the Military and Foreign Aid, Pooled 2010, 2012, and 2014 GSS	586
24.3.	Influence of Veteran Status on Patriotic Attitudes, Pooled 2010, 2012, and 2014 GSS	588
24.4.	Influence of Veteran Status on Attitudes about Helping Blacks, Pooled 2010, 2012, and 2014 GSS	589
24.5.	Influence of Veteran Status on Attitudes toward Women and Mothers, Pooled 2010, 2012, and 2014 GSS	592
24.6.	Influence of Veteran Status and Attitudes toward Homosexuals /Homosexuality, Pooled 2010, 2012, and 2014 GSS	594
24.7.	Veteran Status and Attitudes toward Health-Related Issues, Pooled 2010, 2012, and 2014 GSS	596
24.8.	Veteran Status and Attitudes toward Abortion, Pooled 2010, 2012, and 2014 GSS	598
24.9.	Influence of Veteran Status on Attitudes Related to Other Contemporary Social Issues, Pooled 2010, 2012, and 2014 GSS	600
25.1.	Religious Preference and Military Service (General Social Survey, 1974–2014)	614

Figures

2.1.	Lexis Diagram of Age-18 Cohorts in Relation to Periods of U.S. Wars and Military Conflicts	13
2.2.	Percentage of Veterans by Age-18 Cohort and Gender	15

2.3.	Percentage of Veterans Reporting a Service-Connected Disability Rating by Age-18 Cohort and Gender	19
4.1.	Proportion of Service Members that Attended a TAP Workshop by Military Branch, 2007–2012	72
4.2.	Usefulness of Education, Medical, and Housing Information Provided by VA and Job-Related Services Provided by DOL	74
4.3a.	The Most Useful Parts of the Workshop Were . . .	75
4.3b.	The Most Useful Parts of the Workshop Were . . . : Air Force	76
4.3c.	The Most Useful Parts of the Workshop Were . . . : Army	77
4.3d.	The Most Useful Parts of the Workshop Were . . . : Coast Guard	77
4.3e.	The Most Useful Parts of the Workshop Were . . . : Marine Corps	78
4.3f.	The Most Useful Parts of the Workshop Were . . . : Navy	78
4.4.	Improve TAP by . . .	79
22.1.	Durkheim, Pescosolido, and Joiner: How Suicide Occurs	538

Foreword[*]

Robert A. McDonald

The legacy of Veterans' service to our nation and the freedoms they have guaranteed surround us: in public meeting places where we gather and speak openly on any subject; in the many places we gather to worship as we see fit; in the variety of the media we choose to read or watch, written and broadcast by those free to express opinions absent fear of reprisal; in the places we go to cast our votes for those we feel are worthy of governing our country.

We are able to do all of these things because those who wore our nation's uniforms answered the call to service. Through the ebb and flow of history, in times of total war and periods of restless peace, their courage did not waiver; they delivered on the promises of our Constitution.

As we honor our 22 million living Veterans and remember their achievements, we should also consider the challenges and issues they face when they leave uniformed service and reenter American society as civilians. Just as their contributions are unique and enduring, so too are their challenges. Americans of every generation, whether having served in the military or not, have an obligation to understand, and to assist in easing, those challenges.

That obligation was best captured by President Abraham Lincoln in March 1865. As the devastation and killing of the Civil War drew to a close, he reminded the American public, in his second inaugural address, of our duty to care for those "who shall have borne the battle" and their families and survivors. It is from that promise that the Department of Veterans Affairs (VA) draws its inspiring mission. But the VA cannot do it alone.

---

[*]This foreword is a work of the U.S. government and is not subject to copyright protection in the United States. Foreign copyrights may apply.

The chapters in this book shed light on Veterans' lives at work, at home with their families, in public and private organizations and in politics, in challenges to their physical and mental health, as others view them, and in the changing and evolving nature of their demographics in the 21st century.

I hope the broad array of perspectives in this book inspire all its readers to better understand the issues and challenges of our fellow Americans "who have borne the battle."

Preface

The editors would like to thank Jessica Gribble, acquisitions editor at Praeger, for her idea for this book, and for her patience, dedication, and wisdom. We are also grateful to the entire staff at Praeger and ABC-CLIO. They have been unfailingly responsive, thoughtful, and reasonable throughout what can sometimes be a trying process.

Numerous people at St. Mary's College of Maryland helped bring the book along. Isabel Rickman, a senior majoring in sociology, read many of the chapters and improved the writing significantly. Jenna Witman, another sociology student, tracked down materials early on that helped develop the original outline. Lucy Myers and Sandy Robbins of Kent Hall helped produce the manuscript and kept track of the author database and other items. Veronica Arellano Douglas and Conrad Helms, along with the rest of the outstanding staff of the College's excellent library, quickly procured important materials. Professor Charles Holden helped place the voting of veterans into a historical context. Professors Iris Ford and Asif Dowla contributed nuggets of wisdom.

All three of the editors have come to this topic by related routes. One of us (Hicks) left the U.S. military in 1988 and promptly went to college and graduate school on the then-existing version of G.I. education benefits. In graduate school, he was a fish out of water; there were no other veterans in the program at all. While there, sociologists strongly suggested that the young-ish veteran study the military, because "few people are doing that" and "you would have understanding and credibility." And so a direction was set that has continued to the present day with various works.

Outside of Marine Corps base Camp Pendleton, California, Weiss had the honor of serving military veterans and their families as a civilian social worker/psychologist in private practice for almost 18 years. When she began her work, there was little literature on how to successfully engage with and provide effective services for this population, and thus she has made it her life's work and mission to become better educated, conduct research, and train future mental health professionals in the field of veterans' studies.

As a Marine Corps veteran, Coll was a beneficiary of both Chapter 31 Vocational Rehabilitation and Employment (VR&E) and the Chapter 30 Montgomery GI Bill, which allowed him to earn a bachelor's in social work, master's in social work, and PhD in counseling education. This experience has allowed him to develop a keen understanding of the challenges faced by student veterans. Moreover, Coll understands that although earning a degree is an individual act, the attainment and following the path require the support of many, such as professors like Dr. Exum, who has dedicated much of his academic career to exploring how to best serve Vietnam veterans suffering from PTSD; Dr. Beltran, the Korean War veteran, teacher, and mentor who never gave up on the young Coll and unknowingly has been a beacon of perseverance; and Coll's family, Cary, Marcus, Dominik, Nicholas, and Sophia, who continue to charge and conquer any obstacle presented.

Within the many chapters presented in these two volumes, Coll had the opportunity to contribute to a chapter that was past due and represents his own experience in the service—that of "immigrant" soldier. As a Cuban-born citizen, Coll immigrated to the United States during the 1980 Mariel boat lift with his parents, and like many immigrants before him, he too volunteered to serve. This act of service to their adopted nation is not new, as presented in chapter 24, and as our nation continues to combat terror across the globe and immigrants continue to seek safety and prosperity in the United States, they will continue to serve in uniform to support and defend the Constitution of the United States.

We are especially grateful to the hardworking authors of the substantial chapters of this book. They have done a masterful job of producing cogent and succinct overviews of important topics in veterans' affairs on a tight timeline. We thank them one and all. Secretary of the Department of Veterans Affairs Robert McDonald was gracious enough to contribute an inspiring foreword that we are honored to include in this work. Christine Kassar took the fabulous photo of the "8For22" group on the slopes of Denali that appears on the cover of volume 1. Thank you, Chris! We are also grateful to the many people—experts, practitioners, students, and informants—who took the time to explain something about veterans to us. In a volume of this size, it is all but inevitable that some errors will have crept in. We would greatly appreciate learning about these from readers. Finally, we offer our gratitude to our respective families, who endured our innumerable distractions, brief and long, from their lives that we hold so dear. We hope they find the book to have been worth it.

CHAPTER ONE

Introduction to Veterans' Studies

Louis Hicks, Eugenia L. Weiss, and Jose E. Coll

E pluribus unum

Overview

The legacies of war are numerous. Empires are created and destroyed. Industrial and scientific advances are made in the search for military advantage. Cultural exchanges occur as societies collide. Medical breakthroughs respond to the conditions of campaigns and the trauma of battle. Organizational innovations are made to solve pressing strategic and logistical problems under difficult circumstances. War seems to accelerate social change in almost every conceivable way. Some of war's impacts are direct. Some other effects of war—a much less studied group—are mediated by veterans. That is, some of the most important and long-lasting effects of war accompany the return of its participants and the impact they have on their families and societies. Thus, an important result of any war is the creation of veterans: the service members who survived, many of them wounded and disabled. Standing militaries generate a slightly different social status, known somewhat ironically as "peacetime veterans." Veterans stream back into civilian social life, but they are not the same as when they left that status behind. They are changed people, with new ideas, skills, abilities, values, habits, and associations.

Veterans have been coming back into society for millennia. The *Odyssey* is the story of a veteran's return. The Bible likewise contains many stories of veterans. Shakespeare's *Henry V* famously referred to a future veteran:

> This day is called the feast of Crispian:
> He that outlives this day, and comes safe home,
> Will stand a tip-toe when the day is named,
> And rouse him at the name of Crispian.
> He that shall live this day, and see old age,
> Will yearly on the vigil feast his neighbours,
> And say "To-morrow is Saint Crispian":
> Then will he strip his sleeve and show his scars.
> And say "These wounds I had on Crispin's day."
> Old men forget: yet all shall be forgot,
> But he'll remember with advantages
> What feats he did that day.
>
> Henry V, act 4, scene 3

Shakespeare's returning veterans have echoes today in the stories of service members returning from World War II, Korea, Vietnam, deployments in the Cold War, and the more recent wars in the Middle East and elsewhere. A noted American sociologist of the 20th century, Theodore Caplow, dropped out of graduate school to join the U.S. Army in World War II. He served in the Philippines as an "amphibian engineer" and was awarded a Purple Heart. Some weeks after the end of the war, he visited Hiroshima. The sight was never far from his mind during a scholarly career that stretched over the next 60 years. He returned again and again in his research to the problems of nuclear weapons, social conflict, military operations, militarization, and the possibility of "peace games" (Caplow 1947, 1979, 1989, 1998, 2007, 2010; Caplow and Hicks 2002). Veterans who acquire their experience in overseas wars are a major source of the academy's insights into social conflict, politics, war, citizenship, and a host of other topics. Many of the contributors to this volume have been informed and motivated in part by the experiences that made them veterans.

The Scope of Veterans' Studies

The proper subject matter of veterans' studies at the individual level is the study of the social and psychological differences between veterans and nonveterans. If there is no difference, then there's nothing much to study. But there usually are differences, big and small, consequential and trivial. At the level of families, groups, organizations, institutions, and societies, veterans' studies is about how the influx and persistence of veterans in these social groups affects them and their futures, and how these social groups in turn affect veterans.

Every major theme of the social sciences is connected to war's legacy of veterans in society. For example, veterans vote—indeed, they were among the disenfranchised who demanded the vote during the American Revolution and after subsequent wars (Keyssar 2000; Inbody 2016). Veterans run for office. They attend trade schools, colleges, and universities. Veterans change culture. The "Lost Generation" that created so much art, literature, and music in the 1920s became lost during the Great War (Waller 1944, 171–172).

Effects of war that have subsequently been mediated through veterans are important in America today. Two Civil War veterans worried about marksmanship in 1871 founded the National Rifle Association (NRA 2016). Veterans are heavily involved in civic organizations; they lead Boy Scout troops. The G.I. Bill mortgage guarantee funded the building of America's suburbs in the 1950s.

In American history, waves of veterans returning to social life have marked watersheds in the inclusion of previously excluded groups. The long struggles of women, blacks, Hispanics, sexual minorities, and others for civil rights and equal opportunity have found sharp expression in their efforts to receive benefits from the Department of Veterans Affairs (VA) such as education and training, mortgage insurance, and healthcare. Access to such benefits has directly assisted people in these groups and furthered their collective progress, but even more than that, the inclusion of these groups among "those who have borne the battle" has tended to erase invidious distinctions and disprove negative stereotypes. This is not a new story—in the movie *Giant* (Stevens 1956), Elizabeth Taylor demands that a racist doctor treat a sick Hispanic child, Angel Obregon II, who then grows up to fight and die for the United States in World War II—but the process continues to be important to the American experience.

In sociology, the role of the state in caring for veterans has been seen as a model for understanding how politics and states interact generally (Skocpol 1992). In demography, veterans' studies brings up interesting topics, such as the unusually strong awareness of possible locations for migration among soldiers who have been overseas. The migration of veterans inside the United States is a powerful force for the homogenization of regional differences and development of local economies (Hicks and Raney 2003). In political science, the intertwined relationships of the VA, Department of Defense (DoD), congressional committees, veterans' groups, and special interests such as the real estate industry provide an opportunity to see how these connections operate to create policies and impact outcomes.

The veterans of previous wars have been the subject of serious sociological inquiry and commentary. Willard Waller's (1944) magnificent book, *The Veteran Comes Back*, started with a review of the trouble caused by veterans returning from wars as far back as ancient Greece and Rome, progressed through the American Revolutionary War and Civil War, and pronounced that veterans were "America's Gravest Social Problem." He dissected the absurdities of past policies toward veterans: "We allow the tuberculous veteran, ruined by war, to cough out his lungs in the county poor-house; then, years later, perhaps a hundred years later, we pay a pension to a woman who was not born until years after the end of the war. . . . Our policy is pay on account of veterans too much, too late, to the wrong person" (1944, 15). What Waller prescribed was a gigantic, intelligently designed program of rehabilitation, support, assimilation, education, and training. To a great degree, the G.I. Bill (Servicemen's Readjustment Act of 1944) was a successful attempt to overcome the failures that Waller had so carefully described. However, it is amazing how contemporary Waller's book sounds today, with the problems of homelessness, unemployment, suicide, medical care delays, mental health issues, and criminal entanglements among our veteran population.

The aging of the Vietnam-era veterans in recent years has occasioned serious scholarly study of these and other groups of veterans (e.g., Camacho 2007). A helpful starting point for anyone trying to get "up to speed" on veterans' studies is Camacho and Atwood's (2007) overview of 24 articles about veterans published in *Armed Forces & Society* between 1974 and 2006. The concentration of an aging and declining veteran population in rural areas has been examined by Teachman (2012), who noted that this was a tangible measure of an oft-commented-on trend of separation between the military and civilian spheres of American society. The definition and usage of "veteran" has also come under academic scrutiny (Dandeker et al. 2006; Burdett et al. 2012).

The Progress of Veterans' Studies

Veterans' studies is somewhat analogous to women's studies, Hispanic studies, Asian studies, African studies, and so forth. These fields began as tiny acorns of interest that grew over time into impressive trees of knowledge. Marc D. Brodsky, an archivist at Virginia Tech, and Bruce E. Pencek, a librarian at Virginia Tech (2013, 142), recently reviewed the apparent early beginnings of veterans' studies as a distinct academic field that involves particular "subjects, disciplines, methods, and constituencies." They framed their paper in terms of whether libraries are ready to provide the resources for such a field. They noted that the typical institutions of an academic field, "regular conferences, journals, academic programs," are not yet present, but propose that developing these things may not be far in the future.

There are clear signs that a field is coalescing, like a star forming from a giant gas cloud. There are centers for veterans' affairs or studies (at Syracuse University, the University of Utah, the University of Southern California, and Virginia Tech). Some of these have impressive lists of corporate and foundation sponsors, who apparently feel that such centers constitute part of the nation's effort to support veterans. Each center seems to contain within it the tension between instrumental and fundamental questions about veterans. That is, they have programs to help veterans succeed in college (e.g., the Veterans Alliance at Texas State University), but also run research programs designed to generate knowledge about veterans and society. A far greater number of colleges and universities have veterans' centers, variously named, that are designed primarily to help veterans navigate the undergraduate and graduate experience (e.g., the University Veterans Coalition at the University of Nevada, Reno [2016]).

A veterans' studies group at Virginia Tech has been very active in laying the foundation for the field. A series of conferences called "Veterans in Society" have been convened at Virginia Tech (2015) in April 2013, April 2014, and November 2015. The same group is also organizing a National Endowment for the Humanities (NEH) Summer Institute for College and University Teachers called "Veterans in Society: Ambiguities & Representations" (scheduled for July 2016).

Possibly the first undergraduate academic minor in veterans' studies was started by Travis L. Martin at Eastern Kentucky University in Richmond (EKU Veteran Studies Program 2016). The minor is designed to educate "nonveterans and veterans alike about veteran issues." The university also offers a certificate in veterans' studies and a concentration (smaller than the minor, so not equivalent to a major) in veterans' studies. There is also a minor in veterans' studies at the University of Missouri–St. Louis (2016). As of this writing, there does not seem to be a major in veterans' studies at any regionally accredited college or university in the United States.

Further evidence of the formation of the field is the planned appearance in summer 2016 of the inaugural issue of the online, open-access *Journal of Veterans Studies* from Virginia Tech (n.d.). At present there is only one journal on AcademicSearch with the word "veteran" or "veterans" in the title: *The Journal of Military and Veterans' Health*. (Another journal with a similar name, *The Journal of Military, Veteran and Family Health*, has recently been started by the Canadian Institute for Military and Veteran Health Research [2016]). By way of contrast, there are about 70 journals with the word "women" or "women's" in the title. Fifty journals have the word "Asian" in the title. (There are 20 with the word "military" in the title.) A few other journals, such as the University of Southern California's *Journal of Military Behavioral Health*, do include veterans as an important coverage area.

There is not yet an association of veterans' studies," but it may merely be a matter of time, or maybe technology, until there is one. There is a group that maintains a Web site devoted to veterans' studies in rhetoric, composition, and literacy studies (2016). At academia.edu there is a group devoted to veterans' studies that has only six followers as of this writing, but the day is young.

Data Sources and Gray Literature

One difference between studying veterans and other groups will be the amount of gray literature involved. "Gray" literature exists in a kind of limbo between standard publishing and self-publishing. In standard publishing, books are produced by firms that are in the bookselling business, either for profit, like Wadsworth and Routledge, or not for profit, like Oxford University Press and Sage. In standard publishing, serials are journals and magazines that are sold to libraries and individuals by subscription. Often the publisher of a serial is more closely connected to the authors and editors, as is the case with the journals of scholarly associations, such as the *American Sociological Review*, published by the American Sociological Association. However, the authors and editors are typically members rather than employees of the association. In self-publishing, all these distinctions collapse: blogs are serials whose author, editor, and publisher may be one person. Self-published books may be edited by someone paid by the author, but the closeness of the finished product to the author remains clear.

In gray literature, these relationships are different. Typically, formal organizations, such as government agencies and advocacy groups, "publish" a tremendous number of monographs, reports, analyses, working papers, talking points, and other documents. These cannot be ignored by scholars interested in the field—despite their often obvious bias—because such organizations are often privy to data and understanding that may well be unmatched elsewhere. Just because the material is free and isn't part of a traditional publishing house's list does not mean it is unimportant.

This is particularly true for materials on veterans. In the United States, there isn't a cabinet department devoted to any of the other categories of people about whom scholarly fields have developed (such as Asian studies or Hispanic studies). There is, however, a Department of Veterans Affairs, which has a tremendous amount of data about veterans and an institutional expertise about veterans that has no equal. It is not surprising, then, that much of the basic research on veterans is done by the VA and think tanks such as RAND. Some of this material is published through traditional outlets, such as books and journal articles, but a lot of it is submitted to Congress or placed on the organizations' Web sites.

It remains to be seen if this difference in the proportion of gray literature involved in studying veterans will be consequential for the direction of the field. It is generally true that much of the basic work in the social sciences in the United States is done by agencies like the Census Bureau, the Bureau of Labor Statistics, and the Bureau of Justice Statistics. In this sense, the VA's National Center for Veterans Analysis and Statistics is one more government agency with great sophistication and voluminous data, which self-publishes what it chooses to make available to the outside world. But the importance of the government's social scientific efforts may be greater for the study of veterans than it is for, say, the study of minority groups or social attitudes.

Like organizations and institutions, fields of study carry the marks of the period of their birth far into the future. Restaurants have à la carte menus because the first restaurants with menus were in Paris. Legal scholars have to learn a lot of Latin. Sociologists who study stratification and attitudes using the General Social Survey still speak of "PAPRES16," a legacy from a time when variable names in computer programs had a fixed maximum length of eight characters. Veterans' studies is coalescing in a hyperconnected age. Scholars can access the oral histories of veterans online. Surveys are conducted using SurveyMonkey. It remains to be seen how a new field like veterans' studies will make use of these tools, and how the field will in turn be shaped by their use, in a way that may be different from established fields that are adapting new information technology to existing questions and methods.

The Method of Veterans' Studies

The formation of any new field of study in the social sciences is an occasion for reconsideration of methods of data collection and analysis. Like other recently formed fields, veterans' studies is an omnivore, employing a wide variety of methods developed in many different disciplines. For example, in this volume the various authors have used participant observation, sample surveys, content analysis, and structured interviews. The analysis of data in this volume is also broad, from simple tabulations to logistic regression models.

A new field can be a point of departure for a new set of practices about how to generate, establish, and promulgate knowledge by incorporating ideas that have appeared in existing fields but have not yet become standard there. In this volume, we as editors have tried to be sensitive to many methodological concerns. Throughout the presentation of numerical data, we have tried not to present more digits than are actually significant. This is particularly true with survey data, which are subject to a plethora of errors, including unavoidable sampling error. The "faux precision" that can be seen in so many published articles in the social sciences can be set aside as veterans' studies moves forward. We also have tried to avoid "model-shopping" and "significance-hunting," other, more sophisticated problems that are also common in social science research (Young 2009). We have tried to approach our topics from multiple angles where possible, given the constraints of time and length.

In the future, veterans' studies may also be a location for the development of new theoretical paradigms. For example, the return of veterans to their societies could be studied as a movement of social time that engenders social conflict, as in Black's (2011) theoretical paradigm of pure sociology. Similarly, life course perspectives can be brought to bear on the interruption of lives by military service (e.g., Wilmoth and London 2013). Others have suggested a military transition theory that outlines a transition trajectory from military service to civilian life, with implications for veteran well-being, community reintegration, and functioning (Castro, Kintzle, and Hassan 2015).

Theory and Practice

As in other new study areas, many of the researchers involved in veterans' studies cannot be accused of having a purely academic interest in the topic. On the contrary, a large number of them are motivated by decidedly practical impulses to help veterans and their families, businesses, communities, and so forth. Thus, a considerable number of the contributors to this volume are practitioners of one form or another, such as psychotherapists, lawyers, and consultants. They have worked to prevent veteran suicides, improve the criminal justice system, increase the degree completion rate of veterans in higher education, and help veterans make wiser career decisions. Even the more traditional academics whose writing is included in this volume can often be seen as motivated by a goal of ameliorating conditions that they see as unjust and shameful. We look forward to watching and participating in the further development of veterans' studies.

References

Black, Donald. 2011. *Moral Time*. New York: Oxford University Press.

Brodsky, Marc D., and Bruce E. Pencek. 2013. "Is the Library Ready for an Emerging Field? The Case of Veterans Studies." *Proceedings of the Charleston Library Conference*, 142–147. dx.doi.org/10.5703/1288284315249.

Burdett, Howard, Charlotte Woodhead, Amy C. Iversen, Simon Wessely, Christopher Dandeker, and Nicola T. Fear. 2012. "'Are You a Veteran?' Understanding the Term 'Veteran' among UK Ex-Service Personnel: A Research Note." *Armed Forces & Society* 39 (4): 751–759.

Camacho, Paul R. 2007. "Special Issue: Veterans and Veterans' Issues." *Armed Forces & Society* 33 (3): 313–454.

Camacho, Paul R., and Paul L. Atwood. 2007. "A Review of the Literature on Veterans Published in *Armed Forces & Society*, 1974–2006." *Armed Forces & Society* 33 (3): 351–381.

Canadian Institute for Military and Veteran Health Research. 2016. https://cimvhr.ca. Accessed February 22, 2016.

Caplow, Theodore. 1947. "Rumors in War." *Social Forces* 25 (3): 298–302.

Caplow, Theodore. 1979. "The Contradiction Between World Order and Disarmament." *Washington Quarterly* 2 (3): 90–96.

Caplow, Theodore. 1989. *Peace Games*. Middletown, CT: Wesleyan University Press.

Caplow, Theodore. 1998. "A Model for the Partition and Consolidation of National States." *International Review of Sociology* 8 (2): 173–181.

Caplow, Theodore. 2007. *Forbidden Wars: The Unwritten Rules That Keep Us Safe*. Lanham, MD: University Press of America.

Caplow, Theodore. 2010. *Armageddon Postponed: A Different View of Nuclear Weapons*. Lanham, MD: Hamilton Books.

Caplow, Theodore, and Louis Hicks. 2002. *Systems of War and Peace*. 2nd ed. Lanham, MD: University Press of America.

Castro, Carl A., Sara Kintzle, and Anthony Hassan. 2015. *The State of the American Veteran: The Orange County Veterans Study*. Los Angeles: University of Southern California Center for Innovation and Research on Veterans & Military Families.

Dandeker, Christopher, Simon Wessely, Amy Iversen, and John Ross. 2006. "What's in a Name? Defining and Caring for 'Veterans': The United Kingdom in International Perspective." *Armed Forces & Society* 32 (2): 161–177.

EKU Veterans Studies Program. 2016. Eastern Kentucky University. http://vetstudies.eku.edu. Accessed February 4, 2016.

Hicks, Louis, and Curt Raney. 2003. "The Social Impact of Military Growth in St. Mary's County, Maryland, 1940–1995." *Armed Forces & Society* 29 (3): 353–371.

Inbody, Donald S. 2016. *The Soldier Vote: War, Politics, and the Ballot in America.* New York: Palgrave Macmillan.

Keyssar, Alexander. 2000. *The Right to Vote: The Contested History of Democracy in the United States.* New York: Basic Books

National Rifle Association (NRA). 2016. "A Brief History of the NRA." https://home.nra.org/about-the-nra/. Accessed February 4, 2016.

Skocpol, Theda. 1992. *Protecting Soldiers and Mothers: The Political Origins of Social Policy in the United States.* Cambridge, MA: Belknap.

Stevens, George. 1956. *Giant.* Warner Bros.

Teachman, Jay. 2012. "A Note on Disappearing Veterans." *Armed Forces & Society* 39 (4): 740–750.

University of Missouri–St. Louis. 2016. "Department of Military and Veterans Studies." http://www.umsl.edu/~mvs/index.html. Accessed February 16, 2016.

University of Nevada, Reno. 2016. "University Veterans Coalition." http://www.unr.edu/uvc. Accessed February 16, 2016.

"Veterans Studies in Rhetoric, Composition, and Literacy Studies." 2016. http://veteransstudies.org/aboutvs. Accessed February 16, 2016.

[Virginia Tech]. n.d. "About the Journal." *Journal of Veterans Studies.* http://veteransstudies.org/journal/index.php?journal=jvs&page=about. Accessed February 5, 2016.

[Virginia Tech]. 2015. "Veterans in Society." https://veteransinsociety.wordpress.com/veterans-in-society-vis-2015/. Accessed February 4, 2016.

Waller, Willard. 1944. *The Veteran Comes Back.* New York: Dryden Press.

Wilmoth, Janet M., and Andrew S. London, eds. 2013. *Life-Course Perspectives on Military Service.* New York: Routledge.

Young, Cristobal. 2009. "Model Uncertainty in Sociological Research: An Application to Religion and Economic Growth." *American Sociological Review* 74 (3): 380–397.

CHAPTER TWO

Characteristics of Veterans and Nonveterans within 20th-Century Cohorts in the United States

Janet M. Wilmoth and Andrew S. London

Introduction

Cohorts born in the United States during the 20th century experienced a series of wars and military conflicts that shaped how members' lives unfolded. Those born during the first half of the century shouldered the burden of World War I (WWI), World War II (WWII), and the Korean War, while those born at midcentury came of age during the Vietnam War.[1] Cohorts born in the third quarter of the 20th century were eligible to serve in the All-Volunteer Force (AVF), which in recent years has been engaged in the Gulf War and Operations Iraqi Freedom (OIF), Enduring Freedom (OEF), and New Dawn (OND), as well as a myriad of other, smaller operations in the post-9/11 period. The purpose of this chapter is to provide an overview of military service among 20th-century cohorts that are defined in relation to periods of U.S. wars, military conflicts, and historical eras. We first estimate the percentage of each cohort that was a surviving veteran in 2013, and among these veterans, the percentage reporting military service during given service periods and the percentage with a service-connected disability rating. Then, within each cohort, we compare the sociodemographic, economic, and disability characteristics of veterans and nonveterans. Given that during most of the 20th century the conditions under which women were able to serve in the military were different than the conditions that influenced men's participation, all analyses are stratified by gender.

The analyses presented in this chapter draw on data from the 2013 American Community Survey (ACS), which is conducted annually by the U.S. Census Bureau and includes a range of individual- and household-level indicators. The ACS covers over 1.2 million men, of whom more than 214,000 had served in the military, and nearly 1.3 million women, of whom more than 17,000 had served in the military. We focus on analyzing the ACS measures of military service status, period of service, and service-connected disability, as well as gender, age, race, Hispanic ethnicity, foreign-born status, marital status, education, employment status, household income, poverty status, use of the Supplemental Nutritional Assistance Program (SNAP), home ownership, and disability. For the purposes of our analysis, active-duty personnel are included in the veteran category, whereas those who report that they are in the National Guard or reserves but have never served on active duty are included in the nonveteran category. All estimates presented in this chapter are weighted using the person weights provided in the ACS.

This chapter extends prior analyses of veterans based on the ACS data (e.g., Department of Veterans Affairs 2015) by examining inter- and intra-cohort variation. We define cohorts in terms of the historical time period in which they turned age 18 (for an in-depth discussion of the rationale for doing so, as well as alternative approaches to defining cohorts, see Wilmoth et al. forthcoming). Defining cohort membership in terms of when individuals turned 18 enables us to distinguish mutually exclusive categories that include nonveterans and veterans on the basis of their common historical relationship to specific wars and exposure to related cultural influences during a formative stage of the life course. Conceptually, these age-18 cohorts capture the general historical context in which cohort members initially became eligible for military service and allow us to compare the characteristics of cohort members who served on active duty to those who did not. It is important to keep in mind that the findings we report are conditioned on individuals being alive in 2013 and therefore represent the current characteristics of surviving cohort members.

Military Service among 20th-Century Cohorts in the United States

We use eight age-18 cohorts in our analysis: pre-WWII, WWII, Korean War, post–Korean War, Vietnam War, early AVF, Gulf War, and post-9/11. Figure 2.1 presents a lexis diagram that arrays each cohort by periods of wars and military conflicts, and demonstrates each cohort's historical

Characteristics of Veterans and Nonveterans within 20th-Century Cohorts   13

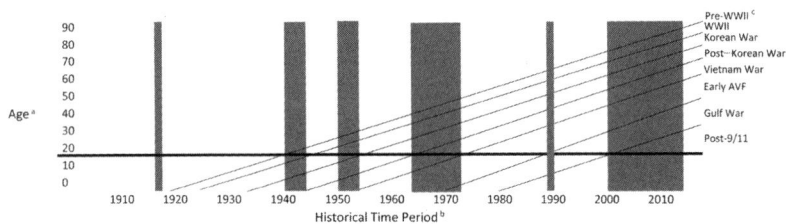

[a] Age 18 indicated by black horizontal line.

[b] Periods of U.S. wars and military conflicts are shown in dark grey. According to the U.S. Code of Federal Regulations (2014) the periods of wars and military conflicts are as follows: WWI = 4/6/1917–11/11/1918; WWII = 12/7/1941–12/31/1946; Korean War = 6/27/1950–1/31/1955; Vietnam War = 8/5/1964–5/7/1975; Gulf War = 8/2/1990–4/6/1991; Post-9/11 = 10/7/2001–End date to be determined.

[c] Cohorts are demarcated by the black diagonal lines. See Table 2.1 for exact birth years and age-18 years for each cohort.

Figure 2.1. Lexis Diagram of Age-18 Cohorts in Relation to Periods of U.S. Wars and Military Conflicts.

location in relation to chronological age. Table 2.1 details the birth years, years turned age 18, and current ages of each cohort's members.

Using the ACS, we estimate that there were over 18.5 million male veterans and nearly 1.7 million female veterans in 2013.[2] Among males, there are a substantial number of veterans in each cohort, with the largest number (over 4.7 million) in the Vietnam War cohort. Among females, the largest number of veterans (nearly 569,000) is in the early AVF cohort. Figure 2.2 presents the percentage of veterans in each of the eight age-18 cohorts by gender. The first panel indicates that the majority of men in each of the oldest three cohorts served in the military, with over 70 percent of the men in the WWII cohort indicating that they are veterans. The percent veteran for men systematically declines across the subsequent cohorts and drops to a low of 5 percent among those in the post-9/11 cohort. The second panel demonstrates the low but relatively steady percentage of women serving in the military across cohorts. The veteran percentage for women ranges from 1 to 2 percent for all cohorts.

Periods of Service and Service-Connected Disability among Veterans

Tables 2.2a and 2.2b present the percentage of veterans reporting military service during given service periods for each cohort. The ACS time periods shown in tables 2.2a and 2.2b generally correspond to the U.S. *Code of Federal Regulations* (2014) periods of war, which are set by the U.S. Congress and used by the Department of Veterans Affairs to determine eligibility for service-related pensions and benefits. Given that the peak ages of military service range from 18 to 29, and some individuals have military

Table 2.1. Selected Characteristics and Estimated Sizes of Age-18 Cohorts.

Age-18 Cohort	Age-18 Years	Birth Years	Age in 2013	No. Male Veterans	No. Male Nonveterans	No. Female Veterans	No. Female Nonveterans	Total No.
Pre-WWII	<1941	<1923	90>	432,869	215,605	38,251	1,555,999	2,242,724
WWII	1942–1946	1924–1928	85–89	948,806	402,880	33,824	2,339,226	3,724,736
Korean War[a]	1947–1954	1929–1936	77–84	2,406,628	1,838,950	63,892	5,776,696	10,086,166
Post–Korean War	1955–1964	1937–1946	67–76	3,823,519	6,222,558	111,170	11,560,108	21,717,355
Vietnam War	1965–1975	1947–1957	56–66	4,747,094	15,287,890	311,377	21,379,206	41,725,567
Early AVF	1976–1990	1958–1972	41–55	3,660,966	28,288,776	568,567	32,326,233	64,844,542
Gulf War[b]	1991–2001	1973–1983	30–40	1,621,492	21,034,257	325,028	22,298,453	45,279,230
Post-9/11	2002>	1984>	<29	1,212,631	25,819,673	242,907	25,731,691	53,006,902

[a]The Korean War cohort also includes those who turned 18 during the post-WWII years from 1947 to 1949.
[b]The Gulf War cohort also includes those who turned 18 after the 1991 cease fire until the start of the post-9/11 period.

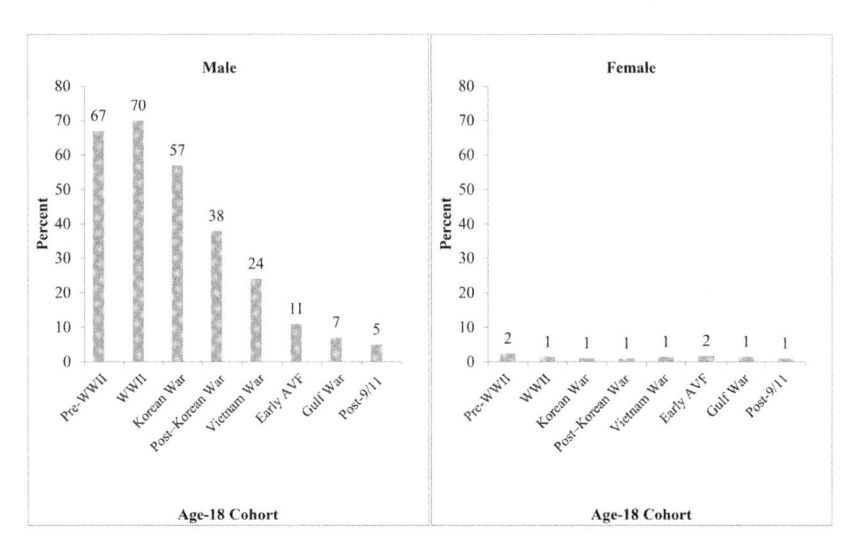

Characteristics of Veterans and Nonveterans within 20th-Century Cohorts 15

Figure 2.2. Percentage of Veterans by Age-18 Cohort and Gender.

service careers lasting 20 years or longer, it is possible for individuals in a given cohort to serve during successive wars or historically contiguous periods of war and peace. The ACS respondents were asked to report all applicable periods of service.

Among male veterans, shown in table 2.2a, 92 percent of the pre-WWII cohort indicated that they served during WWII. This is not surprising given that the mobilization effort for WWII required the service of men who were in their twenties and thirties. Over 11 percent of the pre-WWII cohort men also reported serving in the Korean War, and 3 percent report service during the Vietnam War. While some of those who served in WWII and Korea were 20-year, career military personnel, the select group of long-serving men who served in WWII, the Korean War, and the Vietnam War almost certainly had careers in the armed forces. A large percentage of male veterans in the WWII cohort (82 percent) actually served in WWII, and a relatively large percentage served during the Korean War (21 percent) and the Vietnam War (4 percent). The majority (70 percent) of male veterans in the post-WWII and Korean War cohorts served during the Korean War, with a substantial percentage (36 percent) reporting service during the 1955–1964 period and the Vietnam War (11 percent). Male veterans in the post–Korean War cohort primarily served during 1955–1964 (48 percent) and the Vietnam War (63 percent), but many also served during the 1975–1990 period (9 percent). The majority of male veterans in the Vietnam War cohort served during the Vietnam War (84 percent), and a

Table 2.2a. Percentage of Male Veterans Reporting Military Service during Given Service Periods by Age-18 Cohort.

Service Period	Pre-WWII	WWII	Korean War	Post–Korean War	Vietnam War	Early AVF	Gulf War	Post-9/11
Nov. 1941 or earlier	8	1	0	0	0	0	0	0
Dec. 1941–Dec. 1946[a]	92	82	3	0	0	0	0	0
Jan. 1947–June 1950	6	13	8	0	0	0	0	0
July 1950–Jan. 1955[b]	11	21	70	3	0	0	0	0
Feb. 1955–July 1964	4	5	36	48	1	0	0	0
Aug. 1964–April 1975[c]	3	4	11	63	84	1	0	0
May 1975–Aug. 1990	0	1	3	9	28	73	1	0
Sep. 1990–Aug. 2001	0	0	0	2	9	47	61	1
Sept. 2001>	0	0	0	0	2	20	65	100

N = 214,242.
[a]World War II
[b]Korean War
[c]Vietnam War

Table 2.2b. Percentage of Female Veterans Reporting Military Service during Given Service Periods by Age-18 Cohort.

Service Period	Pre-WWII	WWII	Korean War	Post–Korean War	Vietnam War	Early AVF	Gulf War	Post-9/11
Nov. 1941 or earlier	7	0	0	0	0	0	0	0
Dec. 1941–Dec. 1946[a]	89	66	7	0	0	0	0	0
Jan. 1947–June 1950	4	11	8	0	0	0	0	0
July 1950–Jan. 1955[b]	9	28	62	5	0	0	0	0
Feb. 1955–July 1964	3	6	29	51	0	0	0	0
Aug. 1964–Apr. 1 1975[c]	2	3	11	49	55	1	0	0
May 1975–Aug. 1990	0	1	4	11	55	69	1	0
Sept. 1990–Aug. 2001	0	1	0	4	20	50	62	1
Sept. 2001>	0	0	0	1	5	22	65	100

N =17,654.
[a]World War II
[b]Korean War
[c]Vietnam War

large percentage also served during the 1975–1990 (28 percent) and 1990–2001 (9 percent) periods. Veterans in the early AVF cohort primarily report service during the 1975–1990 (73 percent) and 1990–2001 (47 percent) periods, although a substantial percentage (20 percent) also report service after 2001. For male veterans in the Gulf War cohort, approximately two-thirds report service during 1990–2001 (61 percent) and since 2001 (65 percent). Finally, almost all of the male veterans in the youngest post-9/11 cohort report serving since 2001 (almost 100 percent).

As shown in table 2.2b, the periods of military service patterns among female veterans are generally similar to those of male veterans, with the majority reporting service during the historical time period in which they turned age 18. However, there are two notable exceptions. The first exception is among female veterans in the post–Korean War cohort, who are more likely than male veterans to report service during the 1955–1964 period (51 percent), but less likely than male veterans to report service during the Vietnam War (49 percent). The second exception is among female veterans in the Vietnam War cohort, who are less likely than veteran males to report service during the Vietnam War (55 percent) and more likely than male veterans to report service during the 1975–1990 period (55 percent). Therefore, in both of these midcentury cohorts, female veterans were more likely to serve in periods leading up to or following a war, while male veterans were more likely to serve during war.

Figure 2.3 presents the percentage of veterans reporting that they have a service-connected disability rating, by age-18 cohort. The panel on the left presents results for men and indicates that the percentage with a service-connected disability rating varies substantially across cohorts. Approximately one-tenth to one-sixth of male veterans in the oldest four cohorts reported having a service-connected disability rating, with the highest rate (16 percent) in the pre-WWII cohort and the lowest rate (11 percent) in the Korean War cohort. The percentage of male veterans reporting a service-connected disability is substantially higher among the Vietnam War (22 percent), early AVF (19 percent), and Gulf War (21 percent) cohorts. The youngest post-9/11 cohort has a low percentage with a service-connected disability rating (12 percent), which is likely because this cohort's veteran category includes a high percentage of active-duty personnel (33 percent of male veterans).

As shown in the right-hand panel of figure 2.3, for female veterans, the same general intercohort pattern holds. However, there are some noteworthy nuances that merit comment. First, the percentage of female veterans reporting a service-connected disability in each of the four oldest cohorts is lower than it is among male veterans; however, it is surprisingly high

Characteristics of Veterans and Nonveterans within 20th-Century Cohorts 19

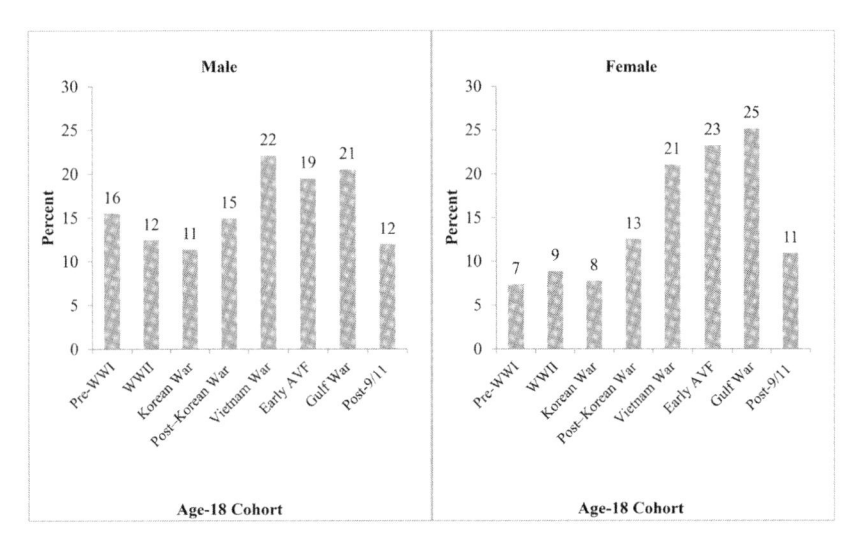

Figure 2.3. Percentage of Veterans Reporting a Service-Connected Disability Rating by Age-18 Cohort and Gender.

(e.g., 9 percent among the WWII cohort and 21 percent among the Post-Korean War cohort), given that women in these cohorts were restricted in their roles as service members and explicitly barred from combat positions by the Women's Armed Services Integration Act of 1948. The exclusion of women from combat positions was only rescinded in 2013, although the armed forces were given until January 1, 2016, to fully implement the new policy (Department of Defense 2013). Second, in light of the combat exclusion for women, it is interesting that the percentage of female veterans reporting a service-connected disability rating in the Vietnam War (21 percent) and post-9/11 (11 percent) cohorts is almost the same as it is for male veteran in those cohorts (22 percent and 12 percent, respectively). Finally, the percentage of female veterans reporting a service-connected disability rating among the early AVF (23 percent) and Gulf War (25 percent) cohorts is actually higher than it is among male veterans in those two cohorts (19 percent and 21 percent, respectively).

Characteristics of Nonveterans and Veterans in Each Cohort

Males

Table 2.3 presents the sociodemographic, economic, and disability characteristics of male nonveterans and veterans by cohort. The table includes six indicators of sociodemographic characteristics: age, race, Hispanic ethnicity, foreign born, marital status, and education. In most cohorts, male veterans and nonveterans are approximately the same age. The only exceptions are the Vietnam War cohort and the post-9/11 cohort, in which veterans are two and three years older, respectively. This is most likely due to historical circumstances that resulted in individuals who turned 18 earlier during the range of years for these cohorts being more likely to serve in the military than individuals who turned 18 in later years. In terms of race, male veterans in every cohort are more likely than male nonveterans to be white than nonwhite. In the pre-WWII cohort, 93 percent of male veterans are white, compared to only 77 percent among the post-9/11 cohort. African American representation among male veterans is highest in the three most recent cohorts, ranging from 12 percent to 17 percent. Although Hispanic representation among male veterans increases substantially across cohorts, from a low of 3 percent for the WWII cohort to a high of 14 percent among the post-9/11 cohort, Hispanics are underrepresented among male veterans compared to male nonveterans in all cohorts. Similarly, in all cohorts, the foreign-born are underrepresented among male veterans compared to male nonveterans, with the highest percentage foreign-born among male veterans (6 percent) being in the Gulf War to post-9/11 cohort. Across all of the cohorts but one (i.e., Vietnam War), male veterans have a higher percentage of being married than male nonveterans. The differences between male veterans and nonveterans are particularly noticeable in the youngest post-9/11 cohort, in which 37 percent of male veterans are married compared to 14 percent of male nonveterans. Male veterans in the three oldest cohorts are less likely to be divorced/separated than male nonveterans, but among all of the subsequent cohorts, male veterans are more likely to be divorced/separated than male nonveterans. The difference is particularly noticeable in the youngest post-9/11 cohort, in which 9 percent of male veterans are divorced/separated compared to 2 percent of male nonveterans. Male veterans across all cohorts are more likely than male nonveterans to have some college education, but the percentage having a college education is only higher among male veterans compared to male nonveterans in pre-WWII, WWII, and Korean War cohorts. This may be due to the features of the G.I. Bill, which have changed over time (see the discussion section for additional information), or because these older cohorts have had more time to return for additional education in midlife.

Table 2.3 contains five indicators of economic characteristics: employment status, income, poverty status, SNAP use, and home ownership. In terms of employment, male veterans in the youngest two cohorts (Gulf War and post-9/11) are more likely than male nonveterans to be employed

Table 2.3. Sociodemographic, Economic, and Disability Characteristics of Nonveterans and Veterans by Age-18 Cohort among Males.

	Pre-WWII		WWII		Korean War		Post–Korean War		Vietnam War		Early AVF		Gulf War		Post-9/11	
	Nonvet	Vet	Nonvet	Vet	Nonvet	Vet	Nonvet	Vet	Nonvet	Vet	Nonvet	Vet	Nonvet	Vet	Nonvet	Vet
Age (mean)	93	93	87	87	80	80	71	71	60	62	48	49	35	35	23	26
Race (%)																
White	79	93	79	93	80	92	82	90	80	84	76	77	71	76	69	77
Black	9	5	9	4	9	6	9	7	10	12	11	17	12	14	14	12
Native Am.	1	0	0	0	1	0	1	1	1	1	1	1	1	1	1	1
Asian	7	2	8	1	7	1	6	1	5	1	6	2	7	3	6	3
Other	3	1	3	1	2	0	2	1	3	1	5	1	7	3	7	3
Multiple	1	1	1	1	1	1	1	1	1	1	1	2	2	3	4	4
Hispanic (%)	13	3	13	3	11	3	10	4	11	5	16	8	22	12	22	14
Foreign-born (%)	30	4	29	3	24	2	18	3	17	3	20	4	23	6	13	4
Marital status (%)																
Married	42	45	58	61	69	70	74	74	69	69	63	64	53	62	14	37
Divorced or separated	6	5	8	6	9	9	13	14	18	21	18	23	10	17	2	9
Widowed	47	47	30	31	18	18	8	8	3	4	1	1	0	0	0	0
Never married	6	3	6	3	5	3	6	4	11	7	18	12	36	21	85	55

(Continued)

Table 2.3. Continued

	Age-18 Cohort																
	Pre-WWII		WWII		Korean War		Post–Korean War		Vietnam War		Early AVF		Gulf War		Post-9/11	
	Nonvet	Vet	Nonvet	Vet	Nonvet	Vet	Nonvet	Vet	Nonvet	Vet	Nonvet	Vet	Nonvet	Vet	Nonvet	Vet
Education (%)																
< High school	37	19	35	18	30	12	19	6	12	5	13	3	13	1	13	1
High school	34	41	34	38	35	41	35	41	34	40	38	38	35	32	41	50
Some college	11	13	11	14	11	18	15	24	20	31	21	32	22	40	29	38
College >	18	27	20	29	25	30	31	29	34	25	29	26	30	27	16	11
Employment status (%)																
Employed	3	2	4	4	10	9	24	22	63	48	80	79	82	84	64	84
Unemployed	0	0	0	0	1	0	1	1	4	4	5	5	6	6	11	6
Not in labor force	97	97	96	96	90	91	75	77	33	48	14	16	12	10	25	10
Income (%)																
Negative or missing	16	8	9	5	4	2	2	1	2	2	2	2	4	2	8	22
0–27,000	43	41	47	41	45	37	33	29	24	24	21	17	22	16	28	22
27,001–66,600	19	25	20	28	24	32	27	31	22	26	22	22	25	28	24	27
66,601–110,000	12	14	13	14	15	17	20	22	24	26	26	28	27	32	22	18
110,001+	11	13	10	13	12	12	18	17	28	22	29	30	23	22	19	11
Poverty (%)	27	13	20	10	14	7	10	6	11	9	13	10	15	9	25	28
SNAP use (%)	9	3	9	3	10	4	9	5	10	9	12	11	16	10	16	9

Owns home (%)																
Owns free and clear	44	57	52	62	54	62	46	47	30	31	17	14	10	8	11	5
Owns with mortgage/loan	15	14	18	16	24	23	36	39	49	50	54	56	44	47	35	23
Cash rent	22	19	18	15	16	11	15	11	18	17	25	26	40	42	44	49
No cash rent or group quarters	17	10	13	7	7	4	4	3	3	3	4	4	5	4	10	24
Any disability (%)	79	76	66	63	47	47	29	32	19	28	12	16	7	10	7	8
Memory	35	26	25	19	14	11	7	6	6	8	5	6	4	6	5	4
Ambulatory	60	54	44	40	29	25	16	16	11	16	6	8	2	4	1	1
Indep. Living	56	47	38	30	19	16	9	7	6	7	4	4	3	3	3	1
Self-care	38	29	24	18	12	9	6	5	4	5	2	3	1	1	1	1
Hearing	47	47	35	37	24	28	14	18	6	12	3	5	1	3	1	3
Vision	25	20	15	11	9	8	5	5	4	4	2	3	1	1	2	1

N = 1,204,599. Italics indicate nonsignificant p>.05 percentage differences between veterans and nonveterans within cohorts. Some small differences are statistically significant because of the large sample size. Distributions may not sum to 100% due to rounding error.

and less likely to be unemployed or not in the labor force. The higher employment rates are most likely due to the fact that our veteran category includes active-duty personnel who are all classified as currently employed in the ACS. In all of the pre-WWII through early AVF cohorts except WWII, a lower percentage of male veterans than male nonveterans are employed. The veteran status employment gap is most pronounced in the Vietnam War cohort, in which 48 percent of veterans are employed compared to 63 percent of nonveterans. Male veterans tend to be faring well compared to male nonveterans in terms of income. Among the pre-WWII, WWII, Korean War, and early AVF cohorts, male veterans are more likely than male nonveterans to be in the three highest income categories. In the post–Korean War, Vietnam War, and Gulf War cohorts, higher percentages of male veterans than nonveterans are in the third and fourth highest income categories. Among those who report income in the post-9/11 cohort, male veterans are less likely than male nonveterans to be the lowest and the two highest categories. Across all cohorts except the post 9/11 cohort, male veterans are less likely to be below the poverty line than male nonveterans. The largest poverty difference is among the pre-WWII cohort, in which 27 percent of male nonveterans are in poverty compared to 13 percent of male veterans. Across all cohorts, male veterans are less likely to report SNAP use than male nonveterans. For example, among the post-9/11 cohort, 16 percent of male nonveterans report SNAP use compared to 9 percent of male veterans. Male veterans in the pre-WWII through the Vietnam War cohorts are more likely than male nonveterans to report owning a home free and clear. The largest difference between male veterans and nonveterans in free and clear home ownership is among the pre-WWII cohort (veterans = 57 percent, nonveterans = 44 percent). Among the early AVF and Gulf War to post-9/11 cohorts, male veterans are less likely than male nonveterans to own a home free and clear, but slightly more likely to own a home with a mortgage/loan. The rates of home ownership among male veterans in the post-9/11 cohort are low compared to male nonveterans because a high percentage of veterans report having no cash rent or living in group quarters, which may be due to the relatively large number of active-duty personnel in this cohort.

Table 2.3 contains seven indicators of disability: any (of the six reported disabilities), memory, ambulatory, independent living, self-care, hearing, and vision. Although the prevalence of disability systematically increases across cohorts due to age-related disability, there are substantial disability differences between veterans and nonveterans within cohorts. Among the pre-WWII and WWII cohorts, a lower percentage of male veterans are disabled (76 percent and 63 percent respectively) compared to male nonveterans (79 percent and 66 percent respectively); the one exception is hearing disability, in which veterans and nonveterans in the two oldest cohorts are not significantly different. Male veterans in the post-WWII and Korean War cohort are not significantly different in terms of the likelihood of any disability, but they are less likely to have a memory, ambulatory, independent living, self-care, or a vision disability than male nonveterans and more likely than male nonveterans to have a hearing disability. The pattern in the post–Korean War cohort is similar, with male veterans being less likely than male nonveterans to have a memory, independent living, self-care, or vision disability; however, in this cohort, male veterans are more likely than male nonveterans to have a hearing disability or any disability. The male veteran disability advantage shifts dramatically for the Vietnam War and early AVF cohorts, in which male veterans are more likely than male nonveterans to report each type of disability (except for vision disability among the Vietnam War cohort). Overall, in the Vietnam War cohort, 28 percent of the male veterans report any disability compared to 19 percent of male nonveterans, and in the early AVF cohort, 16 percent of male veterans report any disability compared to 12 percent of male nonveterans. Male veterans in the Gulf War cohort are more likely than male nonveterans to report a memory, ambulatory, and hearing disability. Overall, in that cohort, 10 percent of male veterans report any disability, compared to 7 percent of male nonveterans. In the post-9/11 cohort, male veterans are more likely than male nonveterans to report an ambulatory disability, or a hearing disability, but are less likely to report a memory disability, independent living disability, or self-care disability. Approximately 8 percent of male veterans in this youngest cohort report any disability, compared to 7 percent of male nonveterans.

Females

Table 2.4 presents the sociodemographic, economic, and disability characteristics of female nonveterans and veterans by cohort. Female veterans are similar in age to female nonveterans except for the post-9/11 cohort, in which veterans are three years older than nonveterans. It is noteworthy that this is the same age difference observed between male veterans and nonveterans in the post-9/11 cohort. Among the four oldest cohorts, female veterans are more likely than female nonveterans to be white, but the reverse is the case among the youngest four cohorts. For example, among the Vietnam War cohort, 46 percent of female veterans are white compared to 79 percent of the nonveterans. The percentage of female veterans who are black has risen across cohorts, from a low of 2 percent

Table 2.4. Sociodemographic, Economic, and Disability Characteristics of Nonveterans and Veterans by Age-18 Cohort among Females.

	Age-18 Cohort																	
	Pre-WWII		WWII		Korean War		Post–Korean War		Vietnam War		Early AVF		Gulf War		Post-9/11	
	Nonvet	Vet	Nonvet	Vet	Nonvet	Vet	Nonvet	Vet	Nonvet	Vet	Nonvet	Vet	Nonvet	Vet	Nonvet	Vet
Age (mean)	93	93	87	87	80	80	71	71	61	60	48	49	35	35	23	26
Race (%)																
White	87	95	87	96	85	88	82	85	79	46	75	67	70	65	69	64
Black	8	2	8	2	9	8	10	10	11	17	13	26	14	23	15	22
Native Am.	0	1	0	1	0	2	1	1	1	1	1	1	1	1	1	1
Asian	3	1	3	1	4	1	4	2	5	2	6	2	7	3	6	4
Other	1	0	1	0	1	0	2	1	2	1	4	2	6	3	6	4
Multiple	1	1	1	0	1	2	1	1	1	2	2	3	3	5	4	6
Hispanic (%)	6	2	6	1	7	3	8	5	9	6	14	7	20	12	20	17
Foreign born (%)	11	5	12	4	14	3	14	5	14	4	19	5	22	6	12	5
Marital status (%)																
Married	8	13	19	27	35	49	52	50	60	50	62	53	58	54	21	39
Divorced/Separated	7	5	8	17	12	13	17	23	22	31	22	31	14	26	4	14
Widowed	81	72	69	51	50	31	25	17	9	8	3	3	1	1	0	1
Never married	5	10	4	5	4	8	5	9	8	12	14	13	27	20	76	47

Education (%)																
< High School	28	6	24	11	21	10	15	5	10	2	10	2	10	1	9	1
High School	48	40	50	42	49	51	45	48	39	27	34	24	27	17	35	36
Some College	12	24	13	26	15	18	19	23	23	33	26	37	26	44	34	45
College >	13	30	14	21	16	22	21	25	28	38	31	37	37	38	22	18
Employment status (%)																
Employed	1	1	2	6	5	9	16	15	51	51	71	74	70	73	62	79
Unemployed	0	0	0	0	0	0	1	1	3	3	5	5	6	6	9	5
Not in Labor Force	99	99	98	94	95	91	83	84	46	46	25	22	24	21	29	16
Income (%)																
Negative or missing	19	13	10	8	5	2	2	2	1	1	1	1	1	1	6	17
0–27,000	48	47	54	49	52	47	41	41	29	26	24	20	20	21	32	24
27,001–66,600	16	19	18	20	22	25	27	27	25	24	22	23	23	29	24	26
66,601–110,000	9	11	10	10	12	14	17	19	23	25	25	26	26	26	21	21
110,001+	9	10	9	13	10	12	13	11	23	24	28	30	30	23	17	12
Poverty (%)	29	21	21	20	16	13	12	11	11	11	13	10	18	11	29	26
SNAP use (%)	7	3	8	3	10	6	11	10	12	12	15	11	21	14	21	11
Owns home (%)																
Owns free and clear	30	44	50	49	53	54	46	41	31	26	17	14	9	6	10	5
Owns with mortgage/loan	15	12	16	20	22	23	34	38	48	50	55	57	47	44	34	22
Cash rent	34	29	22	21	18	19	17	18	19	21	27	28	42	47	49	53
No cash rent or group quarters	22	15	12	10	7	4	3	3	2	2	2	2	2	3	8	20

(*Continued*)

Table 2.4. Continued

| | Age-18 Cohort |||||||||||||||||
| | Pre-WWII || WWII || Korean War || Post–Korean War || Vietnam War || Early AVF || Gulf War || Post-9/11 ||
	Nonvet	Vet	Nonvet	Vet	Nonvet	Vet	Nonvet	Vet	Nonvet	Vet	Nonvet	Vet	Nonvet	Vet	Nonvet	Vet
Any Disability (%)	84	74	68	66	48	51	28	33	20	25	12	16	7	10	5	6
Memory	38	29	25	19	14	12	7	6	6	8	5	7	3	4	3	3
Ambulatory	66	58	50	49	34	33	20	23	14	16	7	10	4	4	1	2
Indep. Living	67	54	46	36	26	24	11	12	7	8	5	5	3	3	2	1
Self-care	45	32	27	21	15	10	6	7	4	5	3	3	1	1	1	1
Hearing	41	43	27	30	15	19	7	11	3	6	2	3	1	1	1	1
Vision	23	18	15	15	9	10	5	5	4	5	3	3	1	2	1	1

N = 1,296,135. Italics indicate nonsignificant p > .05 percentage distribution differences between veterans and nonveterans within cohorts. Some small differences are statistically significant because of the large sample size. Distributions may not sum to 100 percent due to rounding error.

for the WWII cohort to a high of 26 percent among the early AVF cohort. The percentage of female veterans who are Hispanic also increases across cohorts, from a low of 1 percent among the WWII cohort to a high of 17 percent among the post-9/11 cohort. However, for all cohorts, female veterans are less likely than female nonveterans to be Hispanic. Female veterans are also less likely than female nonveterans to be foreign-born. In the pre-WWII, WWII, and Korean War cohorts, female veterans are more likely to be married than female nonveterans, but in the post–Korean War through Gulf War cohorts, female veterans are less likely to be married than female nonveterans. In all but the pre-WWII cohort, female veterans are more likely to be divorced/separated than nonveterans. The differences in marital status are quite large for the youngest post-9/11 cohort, in which female veterans are more likely than female nonveterans to be married (39 percent versus 21 percent) and divorced/separated (14 percent versus 4 percent). Across all of the cohorts, female veterans are more likely than female nonveterans to have some college education and, with the exception of the post-9/11 cohort, to have a college degree.

In terms of the economic indicators, female veterans in the WWII, post-WWII, and Korean War, early AVF, Gulf War, and post-9/11 cohorts are more likely than female nonveterans to be employed. Across these cohorts, the employment difference between female veterans and nonveterans is approximately 3 to 4 percent, except for the post-9/11 cohort in which 62 percent of female nonveterans are employed compared to 79 percent of female veterans. Similar to the employment results for men in this cohort, this difference is likely due to the inclusion of active-duty personnel in the veteran category (24 percent of the female veterans). There are no significant differences in the employment status distributions between female veterans and nonveterans in the pre-WWII, post–Korean War, and Vietnam War cohorts. There are also no significant differences in the income distributions between female veterans and nonveterans in the WWII and post–Korean War cohorts. In the pre-WWII, Korean War, Vietnam War, and early AVF cohorts, compared to female nonveterans, female veterans are less likely to be in the lowest income quartile and more likely to be in the top two income quartiles. Female veterans in the Gulf War cohort are not faring as well given that they are more likely than nonveterans to be in the bottom two income quartiles. In comparison, female veterans in the post-9/11 cohort are less likely than female nonveterans to be in the lowest and highest income quartiles (i.e., they are more likely to be in the middle two income quartiles). Female veterans are less likely to be below the poverty line than female nonveterans in all cohorts except WWII, post–Korean War, and Vietnam

War. The largest difference in poverty is among the pre-WWII cohort, in which 29 percent of female nonveterans are in poverty compared to 21 percent of female veterans. There are no significant differences in SNAP use among female veterans and nonveterans in the post–Korean War and Vietnam War cohorts. In all other cohorts, female veterans are less likely to use SNAP than female nonveterans. The veteran status gap in SNAP use is most pronounced in the post-9/11 cohort, in which 21 percent of female nonveterans report SNAP use compared to 11 percent of female veterans. Female veterans (44 percent) in the oldest pre-WWII cohort are much more likely to own their home free and clear than female nonveterans (30 percent). There are no significant veteran status differences in home ownership for females in the WWII cohort. Female veterans in the Korean War cohort have a slight advantage in terms of home ownership, both free and clear and with a mortgage/loan, relative to female nonveterans. In the post–Korean War, Vietnam War, and early AVF cohorts, female veterans are less likely than female nonveterans to own their home free and clear, but are more likely to own with a mortgage/loan. Home ownership is relatively low among female veterans in the Gulf War and post-9/11 cohorts. Despite the observed differences in home ownership across cohorts, in all of the cohorts except the WWII cohort, female veterans are more likely than female nonveterans to be living in a place that requires cash rent. Rates of living in a place that has no cash rent or group quarters is also lower among female veterans than nonveterans in all of the cohorts except the post-9/11 cohort.

In terms of disability, in the oldest three cohorts, female veterans tend to have lower levels of disability than female nonveterans. This is particularly noticeable in the pre-WWII cohort, in which female veterans are less likely than female nonveterans to have every type of disability except a hearing disability. Overall, in the pre-WWII cohort, 84 percent of female nonveterans report any disability compared to 74 percent of female veterans. In the WWII cohort, there are no significant differences in the percentage reporting any disability by veteran status; approximately two-thirds have any disability. However, female veterans are significantly less likely than female nonveterans to have a memory, independent living, and self-care disability. In the Korean War cohort, there are also no significant differences in any disability, with approximately one-half reporting any disability; however, female veterans are significantly less likely than female nonveterans to have self-care and hearing disabilities. In contrast to the oldest three cohorts, female veterans in the subsequent four cohorts tend to have higher levels of disability than female nonveterans. The differences between female veterans and nonveterans in these cohorts range from a high of 5 percent among the Vietnam War cohort (in which 25 percent of veterans and 30 percent of nonveterans have any disability respectively) to a low of 3 percent in the Gulf War cohort (in which 10 percent of veterans and 7 percent of nonveterans have any disability respectively). Each of these cohorts has a unique pattern of specific types of disability that contribute to the higher level of any disability among female veterans; only the independent living disability category is significantly higher among female veterans than nonveterans across these cohorts. There are few significant veteran status differences in disability rates in the post-9/11 cohort; female veterans are only slightly more likely than female nonveterans to have an ambulatory disability (2 percent versus 1 percent).

Discussion

Across 20th-century cohorts, there are substantial differences in the prevalence of military service and the characteristics of veterans compared to nonveterans. Military service was a normative part of the transition to adulthood for men who were born during the first part of the 20th century (Wilmoth and London 2016). Consequently, the majority of men in the pre-WWII, WWII, and Korean War cohorts report being veterans. Rates of service-connected disability among veteran men in these oldest cohorts are relatively low and, overall, older male veterans seem to have benefited from their service. Men in the post–Korean War cohort are less likely to have served in the military than prior cohorts. While the rates of service-connected disability among male veterans in this cohort are similar to prior cohorts, the male veterans in this cohort are not uniformly more advantaged than their male peers who did not serve in the military. Compared to previous cohorts, rates of military service were lower among men in the Vietnam War cohort and, among those who served, a higher percentage report having a service-connected disability. Furthermore, the male veterans in the Vietnam War cohort appear to be more disadvantaged than veterans from prior cohorts. Men in the early AVF and Gulf War cohorts were less likely to serve in the military than men in the Vietnam War cohort. Among those who did serve in these more recent cohorts, rates of service-connected disability are similar to the Vietnam War cohort veterans. Compared to male nonveterans in these cohorts, male veterans are advantaged in some respects and disadvantaged in other respects. The lowest rates of military service among men are in the post-9/11 cohort, and those men who did report service in this cohort have relatively low rates of service-connected disability, possibly because a high percentage of them are still on active duty. Similar to the prior two cohorts, the male veterans in the post-9/11 cohort are doing better than nonveterans on some indicators, but worse on others. Therefore, the advantages that accumulated to male veterans in older cohorts do not appear to be manifesting among male veterans in the younger cohorts. However, it remains to be seen whether additional veteran status differences will emerge among men in the younger cohorts as they age.

Although the levels of service are substantially lower among women than men in all of the cohorts, similar to the pattern evident among men, female veterans in the oldest cohorts appear to be more advantaged than female nonveterans. However, it should be noted that, compared to men, there are more non-significant differences between female veterans and nonveterans. The small percentage of women in the pre-WWII, WWII, and Korean War cohorts who served have relatively low rates of service-connected disability and are doing better than female nonveterans on a variety of sociodemographic, economic, and disability indicators. Military service continued to be relatively rare among women in the Vietnam War cohort, but those who served have higher rates of service-connected disability than female veterans in prior cohorts. Similar to the pattern among men, females in this cohort were not uniformly benefited by their service. This pattern of advantage in some areas but not others is evident in the Vietnam War, early AVF, and Gulf War cohorts. Rates of service-connected disability are quite high among females in these cohorts, and are even higher than the rates among men for the latter two cohorts. Given this, it is not surprising that female veterans in these cohorts are more likely than nonveterans to have a disability. In addition, female veterans in these cohorts exhibit some advantages and disadvantages relative to nonveterans. This is also the case for female veterans in the post-9/11 cohort. Overall, similar to the pattern observed among men, female veterans in these younger cohorts do not appear to be positioned to accumulate the benefits of military service that were experienced by female veterans in the older cohorts. It will be interesting to see how the characteristics of female veterans change among the post-9/11 and subsequent cohorts given that all military occupations, including combat roles, have been opened to women (Department of Defense 2015).

Collectively, our analysis suggests there are statistically significant and substantively meaningful differences between veterans and nonveterans across 20th-century cohorts. Men and women from older cohorts who served in the military generally appear to be more advantaged than their nonveteran cohort members. Among cohorts who came of age in the middle and latter part of the 20th century, veterans are advantaged on some indicators and disadvantaged on other indicators depending on cohort membership and gender. The intercohort shift in characteristics of veterans relative to nonveterans may be due in part to changes over time in the features and uptake of the G.I. Bill, which provides veterans with educational, housing, and health benefits (Kelty and Segal 2013). There is consistent evidence that the G.I. Bill facilitated educational attainment, occupational status, and economic well-being among men in the WWII and Korean War cohorts (Elman, Wray, and Xi 2014; Mettler 2005; Sampson and Laub 1996). However, veterans from the post–Korean War cohort were not able to take full advantage of G.I. Bill benefits during young adulthood because it was not in effect from 1955 to 1965, and veterans who served during those years were not retroactively covered until the program was reinstated in 1966 (Bennett and McDonald, 2013). This probably contributed to the erosion of the veterans' advantage that we observed in the post–Korean War cohort. Although veterans from the Vietnam War cohort had access to G.I. Bill benefits, reintegration into civilian life after this contentious war was difficult, and there is substantial evidence that Vietnam War veterans have had worse educational, occupational, marital, and health outcomes than prior cohorts (Wilmoth and London 2016). Changes were made to the G.I. Bill in 1984 that have eroded the value of the educational benefits, although the benefits were updated in 2008 in an effort to make postsecondary education more affordable for post-9/11 service members and veterans (Bennett and McDonald 2013). Given this, the youngest cohort of veterans may experience gains over their lives that are similar to those of the oldest cohorts.

The observed intracohort veteran status differences could be due to factors such as service-related experiences (e.g., exposure to combat), military policies (e.g., enlistment criteria, combat assignment, tour of duty rotations), unobserved early life-course characteristics that influenced selection into military service (e.g., early-life socioeconomic disadvantage), other individual-level mid- to late-life characteristics (e.g., occupation, marital status, health behaviors and conditions), and selective mortality during young adulthood through midlife. The sources of the observed veteran status variation within cohorts cannot be determined with the ACS and in fact are quite difficult to identify with statistical modeling given the limitations of existing data. Although many nationally representative data sets contain measures of veteran status, most have very limited information about military service experiences (Wilmoth and London 2016). Furthermore, studies need to include a range of preservice characteristics and adulthood mortality to sufficiently control for selection (Wolf, Wing, and Lopoo 2013). Despite these data and methodological challenges, researchers should continue to try to document inter- and intracohort differences between veterans and nonveterans, as well as to isolate the mechanisms through which military service shapes individual lives and cohort change. Doing so will provide policy makers and practitioners with accurate information that can be used to effectively meet the unique needs of each cohort as they age through the life course.

Notes

1. For consistency, we use the commonly used term "Vietnam War," but it is important to note that this military engagement was the "Vietnam conflict" according to the U.S. *Code of Federal Regulations* (2014).

2. These are likely to be lower bound estimates, given that they are based on self-reported measures of active-duty military service. The National Center for Veterans Analysis and Statistics (2015), which generates estimates that are based on data from the Department of Veterans Affairs, the Department of Defense, the Census Bureau, the Internal Revenue Service, and the Social Security Administration, reported a total of 20,298,098 male veterans and 2,001,252 female veterans in 2013.

References

Bennett, Pamela R., and Katrina B. McDonald. 2013. "Military Service as a Pathway to Early Socioeconomic Achievement for Disadvantaged Groups." In *Life-Course Perspectives on Military Service*, edited by Janet M. Wilmoth and Andrew S. London, 119–143. New York: Routledge.

Code of Federal Regulations. 2014. Pensions, Bonuses, and Veterans' Relief, title 38, §3.2, Periods of war. Accessed December 7, 2015. http://www.ecfr.gov/cgi-bin/text-idx?rgn=div5&node=38:1.0.1.1.4#se38.1.3_12.

Department of Defense. 2013. "Defense Department Rescinds Direct Combat Exclusion Rule; Services to Expand Integration of Women into Previously Restricted Occupations and Units." News release 037-13, January 24. Accessed October 20, 2015. http://archive.defense.gov/releases/release.aspx?releaseid=15784.

Department of Defense. 2015. "Carter Opens All Military Occupation Positions to Women." December 3. Accessed December 7, 2015. http://www.defense.gov/News-Article-View/Article/632536/carter-opens-all-military-occupations-positions-to-women.

Department of Veterans Affairs. 2015. *Profile of Veterans: 2013*. July. Accessed December 23, 2015. http://www.va.gov/vetdata/docs/SpecialReports/Profile_of_Veterans_2013.pdf.

Elman, Cheryl, Linda A. Wray, and Juan Xi. 2014. "Fundamental Resource Dis/advantages, Youth Health, and Adult Educational Outcomes." *Social Science Research* 43: 108–126.

Kelty, Ryan, and David R. Segal. 2013. "The Military as a Transforming Influence: Integration into or Isolation from Normal Adult Roles?" In *Life-Course Perspectives on Military Service*, edited by Janet M. Wilmoth and Andrew S. London, 19–47. New York: Routledge.

Mettler, Suzanne. 2005. *Soldiers to Citizens: The G.I. Bill and the Making of the Greatest Generation*. New York: Oxford University Press.

National Center for Veterans Analysis and Statistics. 2015. Veteran Population Projection Model 2014 (VetPop2014). Accessed October 8, 2015. http://www.va.gov/vetdata/Veteran_Population.asp.

Sampson, Robert J., and John H. Laub. 1996. "Socioeconomic Achievement in the Life Course of Disadvantaged Men: Military Service as a Turning Point, Circa 1940–1965." *American Sociological Review* 61 (3): 347–367.

Wilmoth, Janet M., Scott Landes, Andrew S. London, and Alair MacLean. Forthcoming. "Appendix A: Recommendations Regarding the Measurement of Periods of Military Service and Corresponding Age-18 Cohorts." In *Long-term Outcomes of Military Service: Perspectives on Health and Wellbeing*, edited by Avron Spiro III, Richard A. Settersten Jr., and Carolyn M. Aldwin. Washington, DC: American Psychological Association Press.

Wilmoth, Janet M., and Andrew S. London. 2016. "The Influence of Military Service on Aging." In *Handbook of Aging and the Social Sciences*, 8th ed., edited by Linda K. George and Kenneth F. Ferraro, 227–250. Waltham, MA: Elsevier.

Wolf, Douglas A., Coady Wing, and Leonard M. Lopoo. 2013. "Methodological Problems in Determining the Consequences of Military Service. In *Life-Course Perspectives on Military Service*, edited by Janet M. Wilmoth and Andrew S. London, 254–274. New York: Routledge.

CHAPTER THREE

The Transition from Active Duty

Daniel Kester and Maureen P. Phillips

Introduction

This chapter reports on a qualitative study of 12 veterans, which illuminates the challenges veterans face when transitioning from active duty to the civilian labor force. Our results shed light on the decision-making processes of veterans in the context of postsecondary and adult education programs (PSAEs). We found, generally, that Department of Defense (DoD) transition efforts were considered by veterans to be meager and largely ineffective. We also were able to explicate some important factors surrounding veterans' success, or lack thereof, in transitioning from active duty to some form of schooling, and then on to the civilian labor force.

According to the Defense Manpower Data Center (2016), as of November 30, 2015, there were 1.3 million people on active duty from the four DoD armed services. Another 816,000 people were in the reserves—many of them having served on active duty in the Global War on Terrorism (GWOT), Operation Iraqi Freedom (OIF), Operation Enduring Freedom (OEF), and Operation New Dawn (OND). However, inside the DoD a service-wide reduction in force structure is under way as a result of budget constraints and a purported commitment to draw down from wars in the Middle East. President Barack Obama announced the withdrawal of troops from Afghanistan in December 2009 and from Iraq in October 2011. Since then, many military members have been thrust into reintegration and the transition to the civilian workforce. Many of these new veterans, forced out unwillingly and with short notice, find themselves making uninformed decisions regarding civilian careers and outside of existing military transition programs. Many civilian businesses seek out veterans because of their well-established self-discipline and structured training, and this has encouraged the development of a wide variety of support efforts and literally thousands of Web sites devoted to linking veterans with available job openings. One of the most prominent is Heroes-to-Hire, or H2H.com. Decisions about postmilitary careers are important to American veterans' long-term success, and research demonstrates that the best results follow specific phases in the career development process, which this chapter describes and discusses.

Historically, the G.I. Bill has enabled veterans to be acknowledged for the sacrifice they've made and, whether enthusiastically or problematically, they have been welcomed back into the U.S. economy at the end of their service (Altschuler and Blumin 2009). Following the 1970s and the exponential growth of community colleges and other programs designed to support veterans' educational attainment, it became increasingly important to understand veterans' postservice career development process, as the study discussed in this chapter also sought to do.

Phillips and Jome (2005, 128) argue that to fully succeed in finding meaningful work, "individuals need to acquire self-knowledge and knowledge about the world of work." Accordingly, until a veteran has accomplished due diligence toward occupational and/or self-awareness, he or she is not fully prepared to make a career decision; nevertheless, existing programs rush veterans through the process without much opportunity for either self-reflection or critical understanding of the "world of work" in the civilian economy. For example, the military's Transition Assistance Program (TAP) is a mandatory two-week exit program through which members are funneled at the end of their service enlistment, but TAP includes no self-reflection module about career development or interest, nor any effort to help the service member understand the economic or educational context into which he or she will shortly enter (Veterans' Employment and Training Service 2016). This study found that a lack of awareness about these contexts had long-term effects on veterans' successful integration.

Career Decision-Making Theory

Scholars in a variety of disciplines agree that career decisions are complex and multilayered (Amir and Gait 2006). Career decision-making theories attempt to reduce the number of choices and predict the best fit for the person making decisions about his or her most appropriate occupation. Theories about career decision-making practices address both the content of decision choices and the process of decision making (Walsh and Savickas 2005, 6). The career development process generally consists of three phases: the pre-decision phase; the decision phase; and finally, the post-decision phase. Phase 1, or the pre-decision phase, provides the decision maker with sufficient readiness, or necessary information, to make a career decision. Different people use different styles to make career decisions, which is the concern of phase 2, the actual career decision-making process. In phase 3, all of the post-decision tasks necessary to secure employment, such as résumé writing, interviewing, and searching for a job, take place. Table 3.1 shows the linear aspect of the career development process. Until the decider has accomplished due diligence toward occupational and/or self-awareness, he or she is not fully prepared to make a decision about a career path or educational program of study.

While it is possible to bypass phases 1 and 2 and proceed directly to seeking employment, less than optimal results are likely to occur. Yet most of the major resources presently available to transitioning veterans are concerned only with post-decision activities. The abundance of automated job sites for veterans may be more a reflection of the ease with which such sites can be created than of their value to veterans. In the end, effective career counseling services need a more costly, one-on-one approach requiring human involvement. Understandably, post-discharge, reintegrating veterans are reluctant to incur the expense of career counseling services, because the need for them arises just as they are losing the security of their service positions.

Nevertheless, it is important to help place these individuals on career paths with a greater chance for long-term success, as opposed to merely taking the first available job they encounter. Separating military members require career counseling that includes the full continuum of assistance, from initial career readiness to job placement. Currently, little is known about the career decision-making process of service members when they are in transition from military life into post-secondary and adult education, but this is especially critical to understand in the present economy.

Table 3.1. The Three Phases of Career Development.

Phase 1	Phase 2	Phase 3
Pre–Decision Making	Decision Making	Résumé Writing
Self-Awareness	Decision-Making Process	Interview Skills
Occupational Awareness		Job Search Skills

Source: Walsh and Savickas (2005).

Career planning and readiness, and more specifically a focus on career decision making, could help veterans substantially.

The first career choice is critical to long-term career success. Indeed, making a poor choice in a first career following military service can have dire consequences. According to Brown (2002, 58–59), "Occupational choice and attainment are shaped by community labor market conditions. These are particularly important at the time of labor force entry, as initial placements influence subsequent occupational career trajectories."

First-term veterans, meaning those who complete one term of enlistment and then leave active duty, are often making their initial civilian labor force entry. Yet there remains a significant gap in the literature that qualitatively studies the career decision making of this group. Veterans leave active duty with access to significant educational benefits to assist with a career transition. However, a better understanding of the career decisions of veterans in this context can help veterans make better labor force decisions, enable educational institutions to better understand the unique needs and skills of these nontraditional students, and also help academic institutions offer more effective academic and career training programs. An increase in understanding across these domains has high potential for both veterans' success and the recovery of the U.S. economy.

For example, veteran students need support to know how to properly use their G.I. Bill benefits during this crucial transition period. At present, many of them leap into an academic program without a full understanding of either the educational or labor environments. One small mistake in the use of benefits can result in the repayment of a substantial debt, a predicament that has often thrown veterans out of the campus environment and into the civilian economy unprepared. The most common mistake that students make is taking classes not included in their program of study. This results in the repayment of tuition, and in many cases, Basic Allowance for Housing (BAH) benefits, which can be even more costly than tuition. The consequence is wasted benefits, lower success rates, and long-term negative outcomes for veterans.

Academic Programs, Campus Veterans Centers, and Veteran Success

The study described in this chapter specifically focused on enlisted military members who separated after only one term of service, typically following a four-year enlistment. Equipped with abundant VA educational benefits, the veterans have many options available for entering into post-secondary education or job retraining programs. The Post-9/11 G.I. Bill is only one example of the educational benefits granted to military members who have served on active duty. A veteran who served over three years of active duty or has a service-related disability is entitled to 100 percent tuition at participating educational institutions for 36 months, longer if the student is part-time, and with an additional allowance for books (Department of Veterans Affairs 2016).

The G.I. Bill is a high-value benefit that must be used wisely by veterans in order for them to obtain a college degree in the short amount of time allotted by its terms and conditions. It also makes sense to spend the benefit only after becoming informed. In the end, the veteran must balance the short-term temptation to use the benefit in a way that supplements living expenses—as we found many study subjects doing—with the long-term benefits of completing a college degree or certificate program that will lead to meaningful, lasting employment.

For example, veterans need to understand that because the tuition benefit is based on time rather than money, it may be financially smarter for a veteran to pay out of pocket for lower-priced community college courses and save their G.I. Bill benefits for higher-priced university enrollment. The VA will pay for 36 months of benefits, regardless of whether this means a $70-per-credit community college course or a university course costing four times as much. Veterans, having been heavily focused on their military careers, generally do not have the perspective to understand the distinctions between academic program offerings, the VA's complex benefits tracking process, the vagaries of the civilian economy, or the higher education system overall. Veterans often enter postsecondary and adult education programs to further their skills in a field for which they were trained in the military. Other veterans use the opportunity to make a fresh start. In either case, support-program staff and veterans' centers at academic institutions can become better prepared for influxes of returning veterans by paying particular attention to veterans' lack of awareness about the academic context and by assuming a lack of career self-awareness among veterans. The scale and urgency of the ongoing reduction in force structure and the availability of tuition benefits make this issue timely and worthy of additional research, particularly about the shift in cultural identity experienced by the veterans, which we discuss below.

Study Design

We conducted semistructured, one-on-one interviews lasting 20 to 30 minutes at the veterans' center at a large community college in the southwestern United States. The sample consisted of 12 military veterans. Ten of the veterans were male and two were female. All four uniformed services were represented: four respondents from the U.S Navy, four from the U.S. Marine Corps, two from the U.S. Army, and two from the U.S. Air Force. The interviews consisted of open-ended questions designed to elicit rich data in terms of the general experiences of veterans during this transition, including the decision-making process and the factors considered when making postservice work path choices. The interviewed sample consisted of one-term, former military members only. A basic demographic data collection instrument was used to record information such as name, rank, years of service, current military career, gender, educational level, the screening question, and contact information. Participation in the case study was strictly voluntary, and institutional review board approval by the guiding academic institution was granted in advance of data collection in February 2014. Coding and analysis of the interview data was done using Dedoose software. The analysis centered on emergent themes related to self-awareness, occupational knowledge, decision-making awareness, and descriptions of the transition process.

Ironically, it was notable that there were only two Air Force participants, despite the fact that a large active-duty U.S. Air Force and Air National Guard base are in the community where the study took place. In terms of age, we found many older veterans still in the community college system attempting to transition into a new career, sometimes 20 or more years after separation from service. This was unexpected, but it resulted in some interesting outcomes. The female proportion of study participants (17 percent) is close to the proportion of today's active-duty military (about 15 percent women).

Veteran Profiles

The following short biographical sketches introduce the veterans who participated in our study. We have given them pseudonyms to protect their identities.

Adam

Adam was a male in his twenties who joined the Marine Corps because he lacked direction in life and had no interest in attending postsecondary education. The military provided him with the direction he was seeking. He served in Iraq and Afghanistan and is interested in a postmilitary career in federal law enforcement. He completed career assessments in the military and in college, but only felt that they confirmed what he already knew. He was realistic and has a good attitude about the career development process and is capable of finding career information when he feels he needs it. Unfortunately, even though he was aware that his PSAE institution had available career information, he never asked for it. Adam's transition was tumultuous. As part of an elite reconnaissance team in the Marine Corps, he seemed frustrated that civilians didn't understand his military achievements and treated him as any other student or new hire. On top of that, the military provided very little in the way of support during his separation from the service. The military offered Adam classes on résumé writing and courses designed around applying for unemployment and VA benefits, but offered no framework for career decision-making strategies. His PSAE institution also never reached out to him, nor did he seek help from it. Adam's family provided support during his transition, and he now has a very solid plan to graduate and move on to the university to get his qualifications to become a federal law enforcement officer.

Brian

A navy veteran in his fifties, Brian was initially firmly decided on pursuing the field of education. He described enjoying what he saw as parallels between the ministry and teaching. His interests came by way of his skills, derived from feedback from his friends and family about his teaching and ministry abilities. Brian admitted taking several career tests but did not find any value in the results. He is confident that he could fall back on his navy medical training, but did not relish that line of work, especially when dealing with difficult problems such as working with injured children. Conversely, he expressed awareness of employment that he would not consider, including sanitation jobs or working as a transit bus driver. Brian felt there was insufficient information available to make his career choice. As one of the older veterans we interviewed, his attitude may provide some insight into the progress made in the period since the Vietnam conflict. Brian described transitioning into the civilian workforce as being "like a fish out of water." The military did not offer him much support. Due to a poor final reference from his military supervisor, an arduous transition was made even more problematic. Brian was one of many participants who mentioned that a major stumbling block for veterans is the ability to translate their skills used in the military to what employers need in the civilian workforce. Although his self-reported readiness rating was deemed confident and high, his narrative revealed a different profile for career maturity. This interview revealed that for some veterans, G.I. Bill benefits are sometimes not actually used for the benefit of degree completion but rather as a means of financial subsistence during career indecision.

Craig

A navy veteran in his forties, Craig was interested in cooking and opening his own restaurant. He understood that the employment situation was dire, and he was attempting to overcome his many challenges by graduating with dual degrees in culinary arts and business administration at the community college. It was immediately evident that Craig's military career was very strained. He had been discharged without notice in 1988 and had nothing positive to say about his short navy career. Twenty-six years later, he was still trying to find his way. Craig was using Pell grants and student loans to finance his education. He drew transitional support, as many veterans do, from the Veterans Center. Like Brian, he radiated a lot of confidence about his future; this confidence may be exaggerated, as his narrative described a lack of support, substantial obstacles, and a poor understanding about how to make a career decision.

Diane

Diane, a female in her fifties, joined the military with aspirations of becoming the first female nuclear technician on a navy aircraft carrier. At that time, women were not allowed on combatant ships, so she changed her career plans to join the rapidly growing field of computers and communications. She found career assessments to be valuable, improving her confidence as she was proven to be very competent in many different fields. However, Diane did not contemplate making a civilian career decision until after her separation from the military. She admits, as many respondents did, that she was comforted by the stability of the military. She stated that she didn't realize just how content she was in the military. She alleged that the military rushed her out and provided little support. She did, however, have a good grasp of her interests, values, and occupational information. In addition, she attributed much of her success to the fellow veterans at the campus Veterans Center and the camaraderie she found there. Like many people who are capable in several competencies, Diane seemed to have trouble focusing. She mentioned many options for her future and admitted that she wanted to make the best decision possible "no matter how long it takes."

Ethan

Ethan was a male in his twenties and a first-term army veteran. He had recently married a woman who was entering active duty in the navy. Her training and follow-on assignment locations were unknown. Ethan scored very high on career testing and expressed a wide range of interests. Like many veterans, he was comfortable with the predictable military lifestyle and didn't consider what he would do when he separated until it happened. Ethan came from a family with a long history of military service. He said that the army was not very helpful in his transition, and the TAP program only offered classes about writing a résumé. He did not attempt to request any help from his PSAE institution when he arrived. Because his wife financially supports the family, and they would be moving to a location where she would soon be stationed, he may not have been ready or in a position to make a career decision. Besides his stated interests in brewing beer, working on cars, and building furniture—which sounded more like hobbies—Ethan also stated that he was willing to look "as long as it takes" to find a career. He also felt that he needed to do "a lot more research" before he could make a career choice.

Frank

Frank, a male navy veteran in his thirties, came from a long line of educators and declared that he was interested in becoming a teacher of American government. This interest was sparked by a combination of family history, an inspiring college professor, and the idea of having summers off with his family. Although Frank wanted to remain in the navy, he was forced to leave the military due to a reduction in force structure. He waited about one month to start making a career decision after he separated from the military and eventually decided to attend college to get a teaching degree. In addition, he considered careers in firefighting or police work. Frank estimated that he spent about one month researching careers. Frank admitted that separating was not easy, especially for someone who had seen combat. On the other hand, he enjoyed his freedom and maintained a very positive attitude. He expressed culture shock about leaving a life of such structure and entering a new life not knowing what to expect, a consistent theme among the veterans we interviewed. He felt that the PSAE process was overly cumbersome and that there was no one to advocate for veterans on campus.

Gary

An air force veteran in his twenties, Gary appeared to be an extremely intelligent young man but bitter about being involuntarily separated from the service. At the same time, he made it clear that the military was not a good fit for him. He stated that as a result of his separation he believed he had somehow found his true calling: creative writing. He had scored high on the career testing and had many career options available to him upon entering service. After initial military testing, he decided to go into the mechanical field and worked on engines and generators. As Gary explained it, a person's tested aptitude doesn't necessarily equate to interest in actually performing such duties. The only thing he credits the military with is helping him to understand what he does *not* like to do, which was also a common theme in the interviews. Gary had a difficult time in his transition because, he said, the air force offered him little help. His PSAE was encouraging once he was able to find the appropriate people and resources. Gary's stated dream would be the life of a creative writer, but he was realistic and expressed an understanding about how difficult it would be to make a living through writing alone. Thus, he was considering a path as a high school writing or English teacher. He was proactive and started looking into a career decision almost a year before he separated from the air force. Still, the separation was difficult. He was forced to sell his car and live on unemployment benefits at a time when he said most people had a hard time even relating to him as a veteran.

Heather

Heather served an enlistment in the army. Now in her fifties, she emphatically stated that her career interests had always been nontraditional. If it was traditionally a man's job, she wanted to do it. Of all the people in the study, Heather declared no doubt whatsoever about what she wanted to do. She wanted to be an auto mechanic. Heather also had a difficult time during her exit from the military. She didn't want to leave the army and received limited help when she separated. She tried to reenter the military as an aircraft mechanic but described having had too many life issues at the time, including the care of children. At the time of the interview, she was working toward completing an associate's degree in automotive technology.

Ian

A disabled air force veteran in his thirties, Ian's situation was unique and provided important insight into the vocational rehabilitation process provided by the VA. Ian was provided with one-on-one career development assistance in contrast to the less comprehensive TAP program provided to the other veterans interviewed. Ian was an aircraft bomb loader who suffered a mishap that ended in a severe back injury when he was crushed under a trailer. He was heavily medicated for a few months and afterward suffered through severe withdrawal from opiate pain medications. Eventually, he was able to take advantage of a tremendous amount of support from his friends, family, coworkers, and the VA. He was the only veteran in the study who had support from all three categories—the military, the college, and family—and he also scored the highest in terms of readiness and total career awareness. While he expressed appreciation for the support provided by the VA transition program, he did not express such appreciation about the air force. He stated, "They drag you in with flowers and candy and shunt you out in the backend and don't really worry about what they've done or what your life is going to be like." This was also a judgment shared by many study participants. With assistance from vocational counselors, Ian decided that he was going to work in the computer science industry in information technology. He was informed about the certifications and education required and had already started the process prior to his interview. He had also been networking with IT professionals and had a path selected to transfer to a four-year university after graduation from community college.

Jeff

Jeff was a Marine Corps veteran in his forties interested in teaching science. Like Heather, he had always known that he had an intense interest, in his case in the sciences, particularly astronomy. He took various career assessments but admitted they were not able to provide him with any new information. He tried the medical field while in his 20's but after his first cadaver session he soon eliminated medicine as a viable career option. He described his separation from the military as "chaotic." He felt angry that the Marines had let him down upon his separation and spent his immediate post-military days getting drunk and getting into fights. He said that his aggressive behavior and attitude scared the civilians he encountered. After some months of transition, Jeff was able to slowly regain his initial civilian identity and composure. Jeff portrayed a confident and highly intelligent personality. His interests were strong and he was one of those in the study who made his career choice intuitively, using "gut instinct" and "subconscious research." This could, however, have also been a sign of a decision error or premature foreclosure regarding his career choices.

Kevin

Kevin was a male Marine Corps veteran in his thirties with a stated career interest in computer engineering. He stated that he had always been interested in computers. He took career assessments and decided that they only solidified what he already recognized in himself and so didn't find them useful. He had explored careers but only within the computer field. Interestingly, Kevin kept all of the materials he received from the TAP program in the event he would need them in the future. He admitted it was a lot of paperwork, and that he hadn't gone through it all while participating in the program. He was able to gain support from his family and friends. However, the military didn't provide much help. In fact, Kevin noted that the military understood that they were losing a marine and made it difficult for him to go to appointments. With regard to his PSAE support, he assumed they would have helped if he had sought them out. He didn't because he felt that he was already decided. Kevin had a healthy attitude about his transition and was happy to regain his freedom. He had a supportive family and even bragged that his mother still did his laundry for him. He found himself growing his hair long and not shaving for months, while at the same time still getting up at 5:00 a.m. to run. Finally, toward the end of his transition period, he expressed that he had asked himself why he was doing these things, revealing self-reflection about his process. This expresses the deeply ingrained military identity held after many years of military service. He seemed very confident and had a clearly expressed plan to complete his education at the community college level and transfer to the university to gain employment as a computer engineer. Kevin also expressed happiness with his career path choice.

Lee

Lee was a male Marine Corps veteran in his thirties interested in helping others. He was leaning toward teaching as a result of some positive feedback he had received when he was asked to teach a weapons course. He was also interested in law enforcement or firefighting. His transition was more difficult than he initially expected. As an infantryman, he had difficulty translating his military experience into civilian job skills. Lee realized that his experience as a 21-year-old corporal, managing a platoon of younger marines and every aspect of barracks life, including finance and logistics, was a marketable skill set. He was still looking for a life of meaning and purpose, which he hoped to find in the field of firefighting, law enforcement, or teaching. He expressed that he still needed to do more career research before he would find the best fit but was willing to take a job in any of these areas should they open for him. He indicated that the TAP program was beneficial in his view, but he didn't have the same positive experience with his PSAE institution. The Veterans Center provided a level of comfort and camaraderie for Lee.

The Interviews

In order to examine the veterans' career decision-making maturity, the interview transcripts were thoroughly reviewed and indicative excerpts were highlighted. The excerpts were chosen either because they pertained to one of the assigned codes or because they represented a dominant theme. Each code was weighted "1" for a positive response and "0" for a negative or neutral response. Themes were also collected as memos and ranked by frequency.

There were a total of 12 15- to 30-minute audiotaped interviews with transcribed lengths of 6,049 to 19,522 words each, for a total of 141,837 words. From these interviews 235 total excerpts were highlighted, a mean of 20 excerpts per interview, a low of 14 to a high of 24, as depicted in table 3.2.

Codes were labeled in 208 of the 235 excerpts, while the others were identified as themes. The code frequency per interview ranged from a low of 10 to a high of 26, and a mean of 20 codes per interview. Code application indicates which codes were applied for each study participant. Table 3.3 depicts the process and outcome of applying codes to the data, sorted by values related to decision making, readiness, self-awareness, and transitional support.

Table 3.2. Excerpt and Code Count per Interview.

Name	Excerpts	Codes
Ethan	23	12
Frank	22	24
Lee	21	14
Ian	21	28
Diane	21	18
Kevin	19	18
Adam	19	24
Jeff	18	20
Craig	17	20
Brian	17	10
Gary	16	10
Heather	14	12

Table 3.3. Code Application Process.

	Decision Making	Process	Self-Assessment	Readiness	Attitude	Occupational Competence	Self-Awareness	Interests	Career Testing	Transitional Support	Family	Military	PSAE	TOTALS
Lee	2	2		2	2		1	1		2	1		1	14
Kevin	2	1	1	4	2	2	2	2		1	1			18
Jeff	3	1	2	3	2	1	2	1	1	2			2	20
Ian	4	2	2	4	2	2	1	1		4	2	1	1	26
Heather	2	1	1	3	2	1	1	1						12
Gary	1	1		2	1	1	1	1		1			1	10
Frank	2	1	1	5	3	2	3	3		2	1	1		24
Ethan	3		3	1	1		1	1		1	1			12
Diane	2	1	1	2	1	1	3	2	1	2	2			18
Craig	3	1	2	3	2	1	3	3		1	1			20
Brian				2	1	1	3	3						10
Adam	2	1	1	7	4	3	2	2		1	1			24
TOTAL	26	12	14	38	23	15	23	21	2	17	10	2	5	

Code weight is a description of how each code was used in total from all 12 interviews. Multiple code applications can be used in each area; for instance, if a participant made positive comments about career exploration more than once, each excerpt was coded as a "1." This could result in a single area with between two and four applications of the same code strengthening that area. Notice that the major categories are a sum of the subcategories and are not coded. For instance, Adam scored a total of 7 in the major category of career readiness, a sum of a score of 4 in attitude and a 3 in occupational competence. Occupational competence was a measure of due diligence toward exploring career information.

A high-level overview of the chart indicates a very low positive response toward the military in terms of transition attitude. Nearly all the participants were adamant that the military was little to no help in their transition. This was true in every branch of service and reflects negatively on the DoD transition programs. Career testing instruments also scored very low. Only two participants said they were useful in assisting them in determining a career path or decision; instead, the majority of the participants said that the testing only confirmed what they already knew about themselves.

Analysis of participants' responses to the interview questions centered on the following subquestions:

- What was the level of career self-awareness?
- Was career testing helpful?
- What was the level of occupational awareness?
- What support was available for the transition?
- What was their attitude toward transition and occupational exploration?
- What were their decision-making components and process?
- What decision-making pitfalls were experienced, if any?

In terms of decision-making ability, most participants were not able to articulate a formal decision process. Many seemed to be preoccupied with basic transition and survival needs. The subcategory of "self-assessment" was added as a code after the interviews indicated a wide discrepancy between participants' beliefs that they were decided and the narrative, which indicated otherwise. Many declared themselves as decided upon a career when in fact they were still in the career decision process, sometimes at the very beginning. Interestingly, many indicated their career decision was made by various intuitive means.

Readiness was determined as the sum of the subcategories regarding attitude about participation in the career process and occupational competence. This analytical approach is derived from Strong's construct of career maturity (Linnemeyer and Brown 2010, 617). It is believed that a positive attitude toward career exploration and knowledge about career information are two key indicators that a person is ready to make a career decision. Readiness varied greatly among the study participants, from a low of 1 excerpt to a high of 7. It is notable that the top three scores in readiness also scored the highest overall. Participants scored higher in attitude than in occupational competence, however. The latter category rated low overall, indicating a lack of knowledge necessary to make a comprehensive career decision. This should be examined against the participants' own self-perceptions of decidedness to understand the balance between willingness to explore and the belief that one has no need to explore.

Self-awareness measurements were derived from the categories related to interests and testing. Most respondents seemed to be aware of their interests, as indicated in 21 excerpts, but very few attributed this to any type of career testing. Many indicated that they "just knew" what they were interested in pursuing as a career.

Veterans indicated their attitude toward the perceived level of support they received from the military, their PSAE institution, and their family. Only two excerpts of the interviews indicated they were happy with the level of support from the military, most with strong attitudes about the subject. PSAE support also scored low, with only five excerpts related to positive experiences. However, it is important to make the distinction that the low score was due to the fact that the study participants did not seek help, not because it was unavailable. Finally, the vast majority of support came from family and friends, a total of 10 excerpts. This is also notable and should be taken into consideration in the development of future programs and policies.

Themes

Themes began to emerge after thorough reading of the coded data and were treated as excerpts and analyzed separately. The excerpts, explained below starting with those scoring highest, included military life issues, culture shock issues during transition, and transition difficulties that involved intuition-based decision making:

Military Life Issues

The highest number of linked excerpts related to life in the military. One of the questions asked in the interview examined the likelihood that the veteran would consider returning to military service. This question received a very high response, even for those who didn't have the option to reenlist. The veterans looked back nostalgically on their military service, with its sense of security and predictability. Many told stories about how routine life was: they woke up at the same time each day; regularly exercised individually and in cohesive groups; ate the same food with the same people; and had predictable work schedules, entertainment, and pay. They described how they didn't realize how anesthetized they had become in the structure of the military until they transitioned out. Diane stated, "Actually, I didn't realize how comfortable I was in the military." She compared civilian life to cockroaches, "every bug for themselves."

Conversely, several felt cheated by the service when they were separated. The veterans stated that they were caught off guard or by surprise, and some felt betrayed or angry. Jeff responded to the transition and lack of support this way: "It's unhealthy; you have to depend on yourself. Become very suspicious, you become very defensive, and I had bitterness. How could the Marine Corps let me down? I gave my life to the Marine Corps." However, the veterans were also able to separate the years of service from the experience of separation. Positive narrative was often expressed about military service as a whole, while negative comments were expressed about the transition from active duty.

Culture Shock

"Culture shock" was a descriptive phrase used consistently by the study participants. The veterans expressed awareness that they had had no point of reference for cultural transition, which is an issue that clearly requires further study. While they were young first-term enlistees, indoctrination into the military through the unique intensity of basic training came to be foundational to the veterans' understanding of any sort of work life. By design, this also became a source of a new identity for them, shaped to suit the particular needs of the military. First-term enlistees spent between four and six years of their earliest work life in military uniform occupying this identity, yet within just a few short days, two weeks at most, they were shuffled out of their service commitments and into civilian life after the enlistment contract ended. They were officially on their own and expected to take care of everything regarding their workplace lives and selves. Workplace culture shock may be the single most ignored gap in the study of veteran transition and reintegration.

Nearly all of the veterans expressed the belief that the DoD-designed transition program they experienced was ineffective in terms of helping with a career decision. Some gave the program credit for post-decision issues such as building résumés or how to conduct a job search, though. A related subtopic also came up often: the veterans consistently had a difficult time translating their skills into civilian language to place on a résumé or use in an interview. This effect was magnified in the army and marines, where there are many noncivilian types of jobs such as infantry soldier.

Two of the study participants were glad to be out of the military and enjoyed their new freedom, even while they described continuing military routines out of habit. The range of attitudes toward the freedom of civilian life was expressed in words such as "hurried," "concerned," "fish out of water," "uneasy"; on the lower end of the scale, one veteran described having spent his transition drunk and getting into fights. Several of the veterans expressed feeling forever changed by what they had seen and done in the military and expressed the belief that most civilians would never be able to understand, nor could the veteran adequately explain it to them.

Decision-Making Difficulties

One of the most telling realizations that evolved from the interviews was that the veterans almost unanimously did not make career decisions until after they had separated from the military. Some thought that they would "fall into" a career and later realized that they did not possess, or were not able to express that they had, the proper qualifications for entry into a career field. The amount of self-awareness and occupational knowledge expressed by the participants was also very low. It is indicative that these veterans revealed no anticipation of the difficulties inherent in transition from the military into the civilian workforce. The transcripts revealed subtle indicators regarding symptoms of decision-making difficulties, as well. Some were blatantly obvious, while others were more difficult to identify. For example, Adam, whose wife had recently joined the active-duty navy, was not aware of where they would be stationed. He was interested in woodworking, brewing beer, and working on his car. His statement that "I want to keep an open mind" revealed that he was, in fact, not ready to make a career decision. In terms of career maturity theory, Adam's stance falls under the category *lack of control* and is linked to his lack of power over external forces. This kind of uncertainty is common during the transition from active duty and even while between jobs or educational programs as a service member tries to find his or her right fit.

Craig was a cook in the navy and made it clear that he was not interested in returning to a service career. Craig stated many things he did not want to do, or was not willing to do, but cooking seemed like the easiest choice for him since he was trained for it in the military. This kind of career decision is referred to as *satisficing*, in which a veteran chooses a career because it meets all the basic requirements and he or she sees no need to look further for a better career.

Diane and Ethan both made statements that they were willing to pursue a career decision for "as long as it takes," an indication of the career decision difficulty called *protracted exploration*, in which a person keeps searching for direction rather than making a decision. Protracted exploration can get a service member who is enrolled in a college program into financial difficulty. Many of them don't realize the financial penalties associated with changing from one program of study to another while receiving G.I. Bill tuition benefits. Pre-discharge, comprehensive career planning, and a more structured approach to decision making about both a career and a college degree path would help veterans and those who are trying to support them during transition and while they attend degree programs.

Gary made a statement that he already knew what he wanted to do for a living, so he didn't need to explore careers. This could be true. Some people do know what they want, even from a very young age. However, it could also be an indication of a career difficulty known as *premature foreclosure*, in which all options are shut out before any real exploration has been done.

Lee seemed to know that his interests lay in the public service fields of teaching, firefighting, or law enforcement. These career paths require very divergent skills and aptitudes, but Lee stated that he had not done the required occupational exploration to find the best match for himself. Lack of occupational information leads to protracted difficulty for veterans and those who are eager to support them, and intuitive decisions like Lee's can result in changes in a veteran's program of study and a consequent waste of time and benefits.

Regarding their level of career self-awareness, the study participants expressed a confident sense of what they might like to do as a career. Some participants responded positively to related probing questions as well, resulting in a sum of 21 positive responses. Upon examining the interview transcripts, however, the data revealed that many respondents were more emphatically aware of careers that they did not like, which is valuable in terms of the career development process, but also related to an immature approach to career path choice.

There was an opinion among participants that the variety of career tests offered to them was not helpful. Only two respondents expressed having had a positive experience with testing. The themes further revealed that a majority already felt that they had a sense of what their interests were before taking any kind of career testing, and those that did take tests felt they only confirmed what they already knew about their interests. Several veterans explained that this information came from the Armed Services Vocational Aptitude Battery (ASVAB). Many of the negative responses to career testing may be due to the fact that it was a mandatory function and the career testing was arranged for them. The veterans expressed confusion about the differences between the ASVAB, career testing, and placement testing, such as the tests in math and English that were required during enrollment at their PSAE institution. As career counselors know, career testing is only as good as its interpretation. It is not known to what extent those interpreting the career test results were trained and qualified to do so, particularly among DoD personnel. Even more concerning is the extent to which career testing results were self-interpreted by the veteran without any assistance.

The Importance of Occupational Awareness

Occupational awareness was measured in terms of the level of occupational competence, or knowledge of careers available. The result for this area was 15 positive responses. However, some individuals were far more knowledgeable about careers than others. There were two respondents who gave no indication of any career exploration whatsoever. In addition, a few obtained their occupational information from sources such as television shows and anecdotal information. Consequently, the awareness level of the interview subjects fell into one of four categories. At the lowest level, *unconscious inefficacy*, they didn't know what they didn't know. At this level of awareness it is impossible to make a good career decision, because one is not fully aware of the choices available. Some respondents were deemed *consciously incompetent*, or aware that they didn't know enough, and at least one respondent thought he had "too much" information to make a career decision. The goal was an awareness level of *consciously competent*. This is the level where people can make good career decisions because they have full awareness—they know what they don't know. A final stage is *unconsciously competent*. At this level the interview subjects are so aware that they don't need to consciously think about the process, such as driving a car with such skill that you are not fully aware of all the things you are doing unconsciously to actually drive the car (Murphy 2006).

Respondents revealed a positive experience with occupational exploration, with a low of 1 response and a high of 4. Career readiness, an indication that a person is equipped to begin making a career decision, is important during transition. Many of the veterans had high expectations of obtaining employment upon reentry into the civilian labor market. Unfortunately, for most this was not the case. Many had unrealistic expectations about starting in management that thwarted their attempts to gain meaningful employment. This issue is related to the culture shock of the reintegrating veteran's experience. Generally speaking, service members exit their careers with an inflated sense of accomplishment, particularly if they've been to war or have otherwise led others through difficult tasks on their way up through the enlisted rank promotion system, which is certainly demanding. This inflated sense of career readiness is understandable, but extrapolating such skills is a true challenge, and many overestimate the lateral moves available to them. Without insight into the range of available careers and a positive attitude toward career exploration, a person is unlikely to make a congruent career decision. Readiness among the study participants ranged widely, between a high of 7 and a low of 1. The reason behind this disparity deserves further study.

Most of the respondents had a very difficult time conceptualizing and articulating their decision-making process. All but one respondent described how they came about their career decisions. Many participants indicated that not much actual time or thought had gone into their decisions. There were a total of 24 positive responses with a high of 4, and one respondent who was unable to articulate his decision-making process at all. Almost half of respondents used some sort of intuitive or visceral decision-making process. Common phrases were used, such as "I just fell into it," or "I took a leap of faith," or "I just knew."

By the end of the interviews, it became apparent that the veterans were self-declaring as "firmly career decided" when, in fact, through the interview process it became evident that they were not. All but three study participants indicated that they were decided upon a career, for a total of 14 positive responses (some responded to probing questions as well). The question asked the participants if they felt that they were finished with the career decision-making process, indicating they had made a decision. Despite later expressions of confusion or assertions that revealed a lack of knowledge about the economy, the veterans expressed confidence that they knew.

The veterans responded emphatically to questions about the kind of support they were given by the military during transition. A total of only two positive responses is revealing of a gap between what veterans feel they need from DoD during their transition and what they actually receive. Moreover, the emotions expressed around this issue were intense. Many of the respondents expressed a sense of betrayal by the military upon separation. Probing questions about the TAP program were also met with mostly negative replies, with the chief complaint being that the program is too short and only includes information about résumés and job searches. The veterans had distinctly different perspectives of the military before and after transition. They expressed a nostalgic connotation of military service during the period of their enlistments, and the majority noted they would have stayed in or would consider going back into the military. However, upon separation they expressed feeling rushed, dismissed, and forgotten.

Postsecondary and adult education transition support was also given low ratings, but for a very different reason. The majority of respondents had a positive view of available campus resources; they just didn't seek out the support provided. Only four respondents rated their academic institution positively. It is interesting that eight respondents did not feel the need to ask for help, even while they expressed frustration with the campus system during the interview. However, the veterans enthusiastically felt that the Veterans' Center at their institution provided a positive environment and sense of camaraderie. In many cases it also provided a way for veterans to help each other through difficult transition concerns, and it also acted as a focal point for the institution to reach out to veterans; this reveals a connectedness with fellow veterans that is absent in their relations with other students on campus. Still, more needs to be done to locate and connect with veterans as soon as they arrive on campus, as many incoming student veterans are unaware of such programs or make negative assumptions about what happens in them. As nontraditional students, veterans carry extra burdens of transitioning from military service and redefining themselves as college students. There is a wide gulf between an embossed-under-duress military identity and the concept of oneself as a college freshman.

Finally, there was a wide range of family support for veterans during transition. There were ten positive responses from eight of the respondents, while four respondents felt that either they had received no support from their family or friends, or that family and friends had actually been a hindrance to them during their transition back to civilian life. All military service branches consider family support as critical to mission success, and base Family Readiness Centers (FRCs) are specifically designed to help ease issues such as deployment stress and other personal hardships when the member is on active duty. However, FRC support ends upon separation, just when it appears to be most needed for reintegration success. Initial transition stress on veterans and their families has far-reaching effects on society as a whole.

Conclusion

A key outcome of this qualitative study is an awareness of just how much the transition period, from exiting one's military enlistment to entry into meaningful civilian work, negatively impacts the career decision-making process. The transition period varied in length according to the individual, as the study participants who were still in college more than 20 years after separation revealed, but there are notable constants in the veteran profiles. Most often out of necessity, veterans draw conclusions about career decisions prior to meaningful investigation or self-reflection. The transition period is marked by confusion, uncertainty, shifting identities, culture shock, unmet expectations, and financial instability, among many other stressors. These things conspire to make a decision, any decision, appear to be the right choice; nevertheless, the sociological and psychological data about veterans' mental and physical health, as well as the inordinately high dropout rate in G.I. Bill–supported college enrollments, strongly support the idea that new, more creative programs should be designed to help veterans reflect on their future before the transition period begins, if not immediately before they enroll in an academic program of study intended to lead them to work.

Veterans talked at length of the many unexpected barriers they encountered upon separation from the military, including longer periods of financial insecurity. These barriers prevented many of them from gaining a solid foothold in the civilian community and obstructed their ability to concentrate on critical objectives such as a conscientious decision about a work or career path, thoughtful consideration of an academic pathway, and even locations for reestablishing a home following the service commitment. It is indicative that, by and large, the interview transcripts revealed that the veterans did not fall into a category of career decision-making maturity, and this immaturity is most often seen when the veteran changes programs of study multiple times. This can lead to an exhaustion of VA benefits before a degree program is completed and before any chance for job placement in that career path is possible. Furthermore, such indecision negates the very purpose of the G.I. Bill and indirectly contributes to veteran homelessness and unemployment.

Finally, it is noteworthy that many of the veterans in this case study expressed interest in postmilitary career fields related to public service, such as teaching, or in paramilitary fields, such as firefighting or law enforcement. PSAEs and civil service employers would do well to acknowledge this career alignment for veterans and make such career choices even more accessible to them. Given that long-term job placement success and college retention rates can depend on veterans' career maturity, it makes sense to create programs that help them develop that maturity—including self-reflection and career exploration modules before an enlistment ends and prior to beginning a G.I. Bill–linked commitment to a college degree program. While the veterans gave low ratings to their educational institutions for career decision-making support, this was also tied to their descriptions of a sense of culture shock and disconnection from campus culture. More needs to be done to help veterans overcome culture shock by overtly and self-reflectively confronting the shift in identity they experience during transition. Academic faculty, institutional staff, and industry managers would also benefit from a formal examination of assumptions about veterans and their approach to career pathways.

References

Altschuler, Glenn, and Stuart Blumin. 2009. *The G.I. Bill: A New Deal for Veterans.* New York: Oxford University Press, 2009.

Amir, Tamar, and Itamar Gati. 2006. "Facets of Career Decision-Making Difficulties." *British Journal of Guidance & Counselling* 34: 483–503.

Brown, Duane. 2002. *Career Choice and Development.* 4th ed. San Francisco, CA: Jossey-Bass.

Defense Manpower Data Center (DMDC). 2016. "DoD Personnel, Workforce Reports, & Publications." Washington, DC: DMDC. Accessed February 2, 2016. https://www.dmdc.osd.mil/appj/dwp/dwp_reports.jsp.

Department of Veterans Affairs. 2016. "VA for Vets. Your Gateway to VA Careers." Accessed January 6, 2016. http://vaforvets.va.gov/.

Linnemeyer, Rachel, and Chrisanthia Brown. 2010. "Career Maturity and Foreclosure in Student Athletes, Fine Arts Students, and General College Students." *Journal of Career Development* 37: 616–633.

Murphy, Marian. 2006. "Conscious Competence: Are You Aware of Your Knowledge Needs?" *Catalyst* November: 50–51.

Phillips, Susan D., and LaRae M. Jome. 2005. "Vocational Choices: What Do We Know? What Do We Need to Know?" In *Handbook of Vocational Psychology: Theory, Research, and Practice*, 3rd ed., edited by W. Bruce Walsh and Mark L. Savickas, 127–154. Mahwah, NJ: Lawrence Erlbaum Associates.

Veterans' Employment and Training Service. 2016. "Transition Assistance Program (TAP) Information." Accessed January 6, 2016. http://www.dol.gov/vets/programs/tap/.

Walsh, W. Bruce, and Mark L. Savickas. 2005. "Current Issues and Innovations in Vocational Psychology." In *Handbook of Vocational Psychology: Theory, Research, and Practice*, 3rd ed., edited by W. Bruce Walsh and Mark L. Savickas, 3–14. Mahwah, NJ: Lawrence Erlbaum Associates.

CHAPTER FOUR

TAPped Out: A Study of the Department of Defense's Transition Assistance Program

Colleen M. Heflin, Leslie B. Hodges, and Andrew S. London

Introduction

During the transition from active-duty service to civilian life, military personnel and their families face a number of challenges, including finding employment, obtaining needed mental and physical healthcare services, securing housing, and applying for civilian social service programs, such as the Supplemental Nutrition Assistance Program (SNAP) or disability assistance. Since the 1990s the Department of Defense (DoD) has offered the Transition Assistance Program (TAP) to all service members prior to their separation from the military. TAP provides advice on job search, job interviews, and résumé preparation, as well as information about veterans' benefits, unemployment benefits, and developing a civilian mindset to help individuals as they transition from military life to civilian life. Recently, the program has been redesigned and a new program—called "Transition GPS" (Goals, Progress, Success)—was phased in during 2014. In order to provide a comparison for future evaluations of the new program, we use data from the Current Population Survey (CPS) to document the strengths and weaknesses of the original TAP.

In 2012 approximately 220,000 individuals left military service, and the DoD estimated that about 800 service members per day would transition to civilian life over the subsequent two to three years (Defense Business Board 2013). During the transition from active-duty service to civilian life, military personnel must come to terms with their civilian identity (Smith and True 2014) and often face a number of challenges in the process, such as finding employment (Burnaska 2008; Foster and Vince 2009; Zoli, Maury, and Fay 2015); reconnecting with family (Institute of Medicine 2010; Smith and True 2014); dealing with substance use issues (Golub and Bennett 2014; Golub et al. 2013; Vazan, Golub, and Bennett 2013); obtaining needed mental and physical healthcare services (Foster and Vince 2009; Heady 2007; Institute of Medicine 2010; RAND 2008; Westat 2010); securing housing (Washington et al. 2010; Westat 2010); and applying for social service programs, such as Social Security Disability Insurance (SSDI) (Wilmoth, London, and Heflin 2015b).

Unemployment among Gulf War–era II (post-9/11 wars) veterans, particularly those aged 20 to 24, is a serious problem (Institute for Veterans and Military Families 2013). In addition, there is evidence that veteran status did not protect veterans who served during recent periods from the economic turmoil of the Great Recession (Bureau of Labor Statistics 2010, 2013; Defense Business Board 2013; Institute for Veterans and Military Families 2013). At the height of the Great Recession in 2009, the unemployment rate for Gulf War–era II veterans was 10 percent, with female veterans who served during this period experiencing nearly 12 percent unemployment. By contrast, the unemployment rates in this period for veterans of other service periods were lower than comparable nonveteran unemployment rates, ranging between 7 and 8 percent depending on the service era, compared to 9 percent for nonveterans (Bureau of Labor Statistics 2010). While the overall unemployment situation has improved for veterans and nonveterans in the economic recovery, the employment situation of Gulf War–era II veterans has remained bleak. The unemployment rate for these veterans peaked at 12 percent in 2011 (Institute for Veterans and Military Families 2013). Young Gulf War–era II veterans aged 20 to 24 are continuing to fare poorly in the labor market, with unemployment rates of 30 percent in 2011 and 21 percent in 2012. The unemployment rate for female Gulf War–era II veterans aged 20 to 24 in 2011 was even higher; 35 percent of women veterans who served during that period were unemployed, compared to 13 percent for nonveteran women of the same age (Institute for Veterans and Military Families 2013).

Since the 1990s the DoD has offered TAP to all service members prior to their separation from the military. When TAP became mandatory for separating service members under the 2011 Veterans Opportunity to Work (VOW) to Hire Heroes Act, an updated program and updated technology, making TAP available online, were needed to reach as many service members as possible. The redesign of the program, Transition GPS, was phased in during 2014.

Despite its lengthy history, there is very little in the extant research literature that analyzes TAP using a nationally representative sample of service members. TAP was in effect for over 20 years and was offered to hundreds of thousands of military personnel. While researchers and policy analysts have spent much time and energy evaluating the effectiveness of Temporary Assistance for Needy Families (TANF), job training, Ticket to Work, and other social service programs, DoD programs have not typically received the same attention from the research community (Government Accountability Office 2012). In order to provide a starting place for future evaluations of the new program, we use nationally representative data from the Current Population Survey (CPS) to document the strengths and weaknesses of TAP as reported by program participants. Using nationally representative data from the August Veteran's Supplement to the CPS from 2007 to 2012, we document participation in and satisfaction with TAP overall and by branch of service. Given the rich evaluative information contained in the Veteran's Supplement, we can identify specific services that were found to be effective, barriers to success identified by program participants, and participants' suggestions for improvement. As a consequence, results of our study will be of interest to those currently implementing the Transition GPS program, veterans, others interested in veterans' affairs, and social welfare researchers more generally.

Background

The History of the Transition Assistance Program

With the end of the Cold War in the early 1990s, the DoD anticipated that budget reductions would require a substantial drawdown of the armed forces. As a consequence, a large number of service members faced involuntary separation and the need to find nonmilitary employment (Ulrich 2012). Previous studies of recently separated service members, particularly Vietnam-era veterans, indicated that they experience difficulty finding employment (Burnaska 2008), as well as readjusting to their families and spouses, managing the financial changes that result from military separation, and accessing benefits and services (Hanssen 2008; Marinaccio 2008; Szelwach et al. 2011). While services existed to help veterans find employment under the Veterans' Reemployment Rights Act of 1974 (revised and strengthened as the Uniformed Services Employment and Reemployment Rights Act in 1994), veterans still faced high unemployment during the period immediately following separation. Burnaska (2008) estimates that in the period between 1991 and 2003, the average unemployment rate for service members who had separated within the prior two years was 10 percent, which was more than twice the rate estimated for veterans who had separated six to eight years earlier (4 percent). TAP was developed to address difficulties service members experienced as they transitioned from military service to civilian life, with the specific aims of decreasing the length of time between separation from the military and employment in the civilian sector, and increasing information and awareness of benefits and services available to separated service members. Ensuring success in the labor market and improving the overall quality of civilian life of recently separated veterans was seen as a necessity for recruitment during the All-Volunteer Force (AVF) era (Sadacca et al.1995; Evans 2012).

Modeled on California's Career Awareness Program (CAP) for service members, TAP was piloted in 1989 and fully authorized in 1991 (U.S. House 1991). One of the more unique features of TAP is the number of governmental agencies that have been involved in developing and implementing programmatic features. Oversight and implementation of TAP was a joint effort by the Department of Labor (DOL), the DoD, and the Department of Veterans Affairs (VA). The Department of Education, the U.S. Small Business Administration, and the Department of Homeland Security have also been involved with TAP (Bascetta 2002). The DoD's Transition to Veterans Program Office (TVPO), the DOL's Veterans Education and Training Services (VETS), and the VA's Veterans Benefits Administration have been responsible for oversight, implementation, and evaluation of TAP's various components, as well as the recent redesign of TAP.

Until 2012, transition assistance took place during the 180-day preseparation period. Transition assistance contained two major components: preseparation counseling, which was offered first and was mandatory for separating service members; and employment and veterans' benefits workshops, which were offered in the three months prior to separation and were optional. Separating service members could also attend a disabled veterans' employment and benefits workshop (D-TAP). Mandatory preseparation counseling provided separating service members with information about the benefits and services available to them during and after the separation period and was intended to address the psychological components of the transition from service (Department of Defense 1994; Coll et al. 2011). The optional TAP employment workshop, conducted by the DoL, assisted service members with résumé writing and provided job-seeking tools and information about local job markets (Scott 2012). Participants also had opportunities to practice interviewing and meet with local business representatives, depending on the installation at which they were separating (Bascetta 2002). The optional TAP veterans' benefits workshop (and D-TAP) provided information about benefits and services available to separated service members and their family members through the VA.

Several factors may have impeded TAP's success early on. First, given the political importance of the issues TAP was designed to address, it is perhaps not surprising that none of the governmental departments wanted to take primary responsibility for TAP (Perkins 2011); responsibility for TAP in the face of ongoing veteran unemployment could be construed as agency underperformance or mission failure. Second, variation by rank and lack of coordination between agencies, military branches, and installations may have compounded difficulties with implementation. The length of TAP workshops, the frequency at which workshops were offered, and the enforcement of preseparation counseling all varied by branch and installation (Bascetta 2002). In addition, there is some evidence that there was not uniform support for TAP among commanding officers within the armed services (General Accounting Office 1994), and that different departments, particularly the DoD, were not always amenable to congressional oversight of TAP (U.S. House 2012).

Finally, each agency may have felt that they did not need to fully implement TAP or invest a considerable amount of time and energy in improving the quality of the program because of other employment services already available to veterans, such as the VA's Vocational Rehabilitation and Educational Assistance Program and the DOL's Veterans' Workforce Investment Program (Bascetta 2002; Government Accountability Office 2012). In 2011 there were six federally administered employment and training programs for veterans with an estimated 880,000 participants and total expenditures of $1.2 billion (Government Accountability Office 2012).

In terms of trying to minimize veterans' unemployment rates, overlapping services may be particularly crucial, because some veterans face greater challenges in finding employment than others due to regional variation in labor markets across the United States, state-level variation in employment services, and rural and urban variation in the availability and quality of services. Studies typically find differences in labor market experiences for women veterans (Kleykamp 2013; Manning et al. 2001; Szelwach et al. 2011), rural veterans (Szelwach et al. 2011), and minority veterans (Greenberg and Rosenheck 2007; Hirsch and Mehay 2002;

Kleykamp 2013), as well as differences in labor market experiences for veterans by region (Kleykamp 2013). The existence of multiple employment programs, run by three different government agencies, translates into access to employment assistance and other transition services before, during, and (at multiple points) after separation. Potentially, this maximizes opportunities to help recently separated veterans secure employment.

On the downside, the number of services available to recently separated service members and their variable implementation have made it difficult to isolate the effect of one single program. It is quite possible that participants would have sought out other sources of transition assistance and job training in the absence of TAP or that the availability of TAP freed up spaces in other training programs for veterans seeking job training (Friedlander, Greenberg, and Robins 1997). Evidence of the program's success would require participation in TAP workshops having an effect on the employment outcomes of recently separated service members beyond what other services and trainings may have had (Heindrich et al. 2013; Orr, Bell, and Klerman 2011). Rigorous impact evaluations of federal job training programs for nonveterans suggest that, on average, these programs do not have large effects on earnings and other employment outcomes (Friedlander, Greenberg, and Robins 1997; Greenberg, Michalopoulos, and Robins 2003).

In light of the number of agencies involved in the implementation and oversight of TAP, variation in implementation across branches and installations, the availability of other job search assistance and training programs for veterans, and the lack of evidence that federal job training programs have strong effects, the DoD, DOL, and VA would have had to weigh the costs of an extensive evaluation that might yield limited or null results. Given these considerations, it is perhaps not surprising that oversight focused on individual bases to ensure that TAP workshops were operating as intended (i.e., process evaluation) rather than on developing a national evaluation strategy to measure the actual effectiveness of the program on veterans' integration into the civilian labor market (i.e., impact or outcome evaluation).

Description of TAP Workshops

Initially, TAP workshops were designed to last three days and take place after service members had received preseparation counseling. In practice, the length of the workshops varied between one and five days depending on military branch and installation. Participants were provided employment assistance, such as help with résumé creation and job searches; information about the labor market in the geographic region where the service member planned to reside; and information about veterans' benefits and eligibility for other federal, state, and local programs.

One major criticism of TAP was that it was "prepackaged" rather than tailored to the individual needs of service members (Wells 1998, 5). The majority of information exchanged at the workshops was done through PowerPoint presentations, which led to the program developing a reputation as "death by PowerPoint" (Faurer et al. 2014, 57; U.S. House 2012, 2). The prepackaged approach, especially in terms of the employment workshop, underestimated how complex and challenging it was to help veterans find employment. That complexity resulted from variation in the education and skill levels of different service members, regional labor market differences, whether the transition from service was expected or unexpected, variation in service members' preservice work experience, and variation in service members' health and well-being at the end of their period of service.

The primary goal of the employment workshop was to help service members successfully transition to the civilian labor market. Identified elements of a successful transition included reducing the length of time between separation and employment, increasing the success of service members in finding long-term (sustained) employment, increasing the success of finding quality employment in terms of level of income or job status, and preventing homelessness (Department of Labor 2010). The individual preseparation counseling component addressed the employment goal by identifying the service member's career goals and providing information about veterans' employment assistance programs (Department of Defense 1994). The DOL employment workshop addressed the employment goal by helping transitioning service members with résumé writing, interviewing skills, networking with potential employers, and information on different job markets and career paths (Bascetta 2002; Scott 2012).

The second component of TAP workshops provided separating service members with information about the benefits and services available to them through the VA. At the VA benefits workshop, separating service members received information about continuing education, finding affordable housing and obtaining home loans, and accessing VA healthcare services. Evidence from the National Survey of Veterans suggests that the workshop was effective in educating separating service members about programs, services, and opportunities for veterans; recent veterans, who served in the military or separated from service in the 1990s and 2000s, are more aware of and knowledgeable about services and benefits than veterans who served during previous eras (Westat 2010).

In 2011, after TAP became mandatory under the VOW to Hire Heroes Act, the DOL, DoD, and VA began an overhaul of the TAP program.

Components of the redesigned program, Transition GPS, were piloted at different sites beginning in 2012, and fully implemented in 2014 (Government Accountability Office 2014; Trutko et al. 2013). One of the major reasons for TAP's overhaul was the need to modernize the program. Components of the program are now available online for service members separating overseas, and the DOL employment and VA benefits workshops now include information about enrolling in eBenefits, using online job-seeking tools, and using social media networks to find employment.

However, the overhaul was also driven by evidence that younger veterans and veterans of recent service eras were struggling in the labor market (Institute for Veterans and Military Families 2013; Kleykamp et al. 2013); service members had difficulty translating their military experience into civilian labor market skills (Military.com 2007; Zoli, Maury, and Fay 2015); substantial numbers of recent veterans were struggling with such conditions as post-traumatic stress disorder (PTSD), mild traumatic brain injury, and depression (Rauch 2014); and service members were often reluctant to seek help for problems during and following transition (Coll, Weiss, and Yarvis 2011). All of these factors suggested a need for moving beyond three days of PowerPoint presentations to a more holistic approach to preparing service members for separation from active duty (U.S. House 2013).

The evidence-based programmatic revisions built into Transition GPS focus on educating service members on how their military skills and values align with skills and values that are needed in the civilian labor market, as well as on developing service members' career readiness and coping strategies for difficulties they may face when transitioning. The revised program does this by requiring that service members create a posttransition budget, participate in continuing counseling, and complete a job application or obtain a job offer, and by educating service members on opportunities, benefits, and postseparation training available to them through the VA and other governmental and nonprofit organizations (Department of Defense 2014b; U.S. House 2013).

Previous Research on TAP

Over the period of TAP's operation, several commissions and task forces have examined the program's implementation and, to a lesser extent, the program's successes. As early as 1996, the Commission on Service Members and Veterans Transition Assistance was created to review existing government programs that provide services to veterans and transitioning service members (Bascetta 2002). As noted above, the bulk of this oversight identified difficulties in implementation of TAP across military branches and barriers to program access for separating service members. Generally, external evaluations of TAP have primarily focused on service member satisfaction at specific military bases.

The econometric studies (Barton et al. 1995; Sadacca et al. 1995; LISBOA 2002) that have evaluated TAP have produced mixed evidence of the program's success. For example, an early impact evaluation using nonexperimental research methods similar to those used in evaluations of federal job training programs found no difference in employment based on TAP participation but reported that separating service members who participated in TAP workshops found employment sooner than separating service members who did not participate in the program (Barton et al. 1995).

It is important to note that results from methodologically rigorous impact studies of DOL job training programs for civilians suggest that we should expect that, under the most ideal evaluation conditions, TAP participation will only have small effects on employment (Friedlander, Greenberg, and Robins 1997; Government Accountability Office 2011; Greenberg, Michalopoulos, and Robins 2003). On the other hand, the results from TAP evaluation studies in 1995 and 2002 are consistent with the findings from other federal job training programs that information about their local job market enhances workers' decision making when it comes to seeking additional training, job searches, and employment offers (Department of Labor 2014). Unfortunately, the lack of systematic evidence of the program's impact will make it more difficult to measure the effectiveness of Transition GPS, especially in terms of assessing whether it is an improvement over the original TAP program.

Similar to our study, previous studies have noted the difficulty in developing a solid strategy for identifying program impacts (LISBOA 2002; Silva 2011) and have primarily documented satisfaction with the program (Barton et al. 1995; Sadacca et al. 1995; LISBOA 2002; Hanssen 2008; Silva 2011; Trutko et al. 2013; Faurer et al. 2014). Evidence that service members found the workshops useful and were satisfied with the quality of transition support they received from TAP participation has emerged from a variety of data sources (most collected for a specific installation or branch), including surveys of separating service members (Barton et al. 1995; Sadacca et al. 1995; Silva 2011; Faurer et al. 2014), interviews with separating service members and TAP instructors (Hanssen 2008), and focus groups (LISBOA 2002). In her study of TAP implementation at a U.S. Air Force base, Hanssen (2008, 25) reports: "TAP's ability to address personal questions and alleviate individual concerns about transition was praised in several written comments." Based on nonrandom survey responses from

350 U.S. Army service members in 2011, Faurer et al. (2014, 56) report that "88% [of respondents] would recommend the TAP program to a fellow veteran."

Although some studies have evaluated satisfaction with TAP, to our knowledge no published study has used nationally representative data to document these basic program contours. This is an important limitation of prior research, given the wide variation in program implementation across location and by military branch. Below we describe our use of the CPS to provide a descriptive analysis of factors related to TAP attendance, satisfaction with TAP, and suggestions for improvement. We explore differences over time and by branch of military service. While these results cannot provide evidence of the program's effectiveness, they provide an important baseline for evaluating the new Transition GPS program. The results will allow future evaluators of the program to examine whether changes to the program have addressed TAP participants' suggestions for improvement and to monitor the degree to which satisfaction with the TAP program has carried over to Transition GPS.

Data and Methods

The CPS is a nationally representative survey of about 50,000 households in the United States that is conducted by the U.S. Census Bureau. Since 1995 the CPS has included a module on veterans in its August interview. This project pools data from 2007, 2009, 2010, 2011, and 2012 (the relevant questions were not asked in 2008). In order to receive the module of questions on TAP, the respondent must be a veteran who separated from the military in 1991 or later.

Results

Participation in TAP

Table 4.1 presents the number of TAP attendees by military branch and year. The annual sample size of TAP attendees is between 633 and 695. Approximately one in three TAP attendees served in the army; one in four served in the navy; one in five served in the air force; and the bulk of the remainder (14 percent) served in the Marine Corps. A very small number served in the Coast Guard. Attendance in the TAP program may have been positively influenced by different branches and installations requiring mandatory participation, but also negatively influenced in cases where service members were separating quickly or at overseas bases.

Table 4.1. Reports of TAP Attendance by Military Branch and Year.

	2007		2009		2010		2011		2012		Total	
	n	%	n	%	n	%	n	%	n	%	n	%
Military Branch	633		681		639		695		649		3,297	
Air Force	152	24	155	23	134	21	154	22	131	20	726	22
Army	205	32	225	33	240	38	226	33	256	40	1,152	35
Coast Guard	14	2	13	2	6	1	11	2	10	2	54	2
Marine Corps	97	15	88	13	89	14	107	15	89	14	470	14
Navy	164	26	194	29	167	26	195	28	157	24	877	27

Source: Current Population Survey 2007–2012.

The relative number of attendees from each branch of the military obscures important differences in TAP participation rates between military branches (see figure 4.1). The navy is the only military branch to have a level of participation above 50 percent (52 percent). The Marine Corps, where participation is officially mandatory, is a close second with 48 percent, followed by the air force at 44 percent. The army, though contributing the most TAP attendees, has the lowest participation rate with just 34 percent of all eligible veterans reporting attendance. The lower level of attendance from the army may be due to the fact that it is the largest service branch, but also offers shorter active-duty enlistment contracts than the air force and Marine Corps (Central Intelligence Agency 2016). The Coast Guard has similarly low levels of participation, at 36 percent. From 2007 to 2009, the number of participants increased (slightly), and then dropped off from 2010 to 2012.

In terms of observed differences in demographic characteristics, TAP participants differ significantly from eligible nonparticipants along a number of dimensions (see table 4.2). TAP participants are slightly more likely to be female. In terms of age, TAP participants are overrepresented in the 25–34 and 45–54 age groups, while eligible nonparticipants are overrepresented in the 35–44 and 55 and older age groups. TAP participants had slightly higher levels of education at the time of the survey than eligible nonparticipants. For example, those with a master's degree or higher comprise a slightly larger share of TAP participants than eligible nonparticipants (12 percent versus 10 percent), while those with only a high school diploma comprise a smaller share of TAP participants than eligible nonparticipants (21 percent versus 29 percent). In terms of racial composition, African Americans comprise a larger share of TAP participants than eligible nonparticipants, with whites having the reverse pattern; the two groups

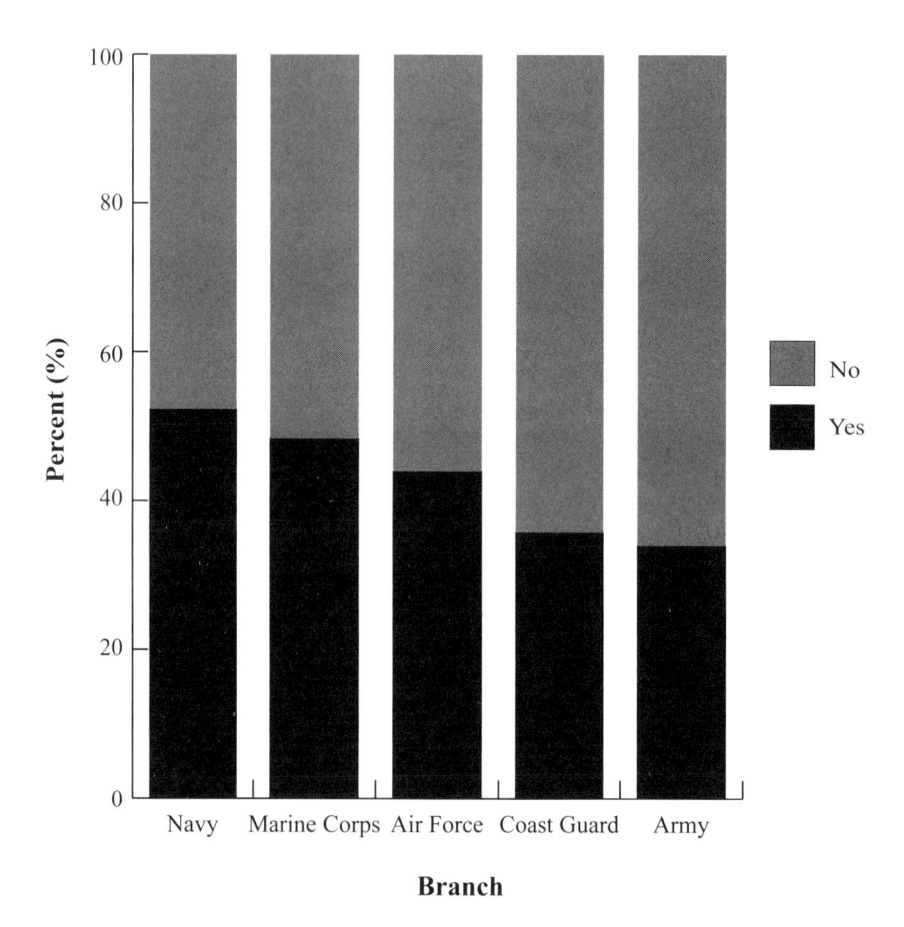

Figure 4.1. Proportion of Service Members that Attended a TAP Workshop by Military Branch, 2007–2012.

have nearly identical percentages of Native Americans, Asians, Hawaiian/Asian Pacific Islander, "other race and ethnicity," and Hispanics. A striking difference between the two groups is that TAP participants are much more likely to have a service-connected disability than nonparticipants (39 percent compared to 17 percent). Finally, TAP participants are more likely to be married and less likely to be never married than nonparticipants. The overrepresentation of married service members among TAP participants is not surprising because, overall, service members are more likely than not to have family obligations and the military uses family-friendly benefits as a recruitment strategy (Cadigan 2006).

Table 4.2. Observed Demographic Characteristics of Eligible Program Participants by Attendance.

		TAP Participants (1)	Eligible Nonparticipants (2)
Gender**	Females	16%	14%
	Males	84%	86%
Age**	Age 17–25	5%	5%
	Age 25–34	31%	24%
	Age 35–44	29%	40%
	Age 45–54	24%	18%
	Age 55 and older	11%	14%
Education***	Less than HS	0%	1%
	HS diploma	21%	29%
	Some college	46%	42%
	Bachelor's degree	21%	18%
	Master's degree or higher	12%	10%
Race***	White	81%	84%
	Black	13%	10%
	American Indian	1%	1%
	Asian	2%	1%
	Hawaiian/API	1%	1%
	Other	3%	3%
Ethnicity	Hispanic	7%	6%
Service-Connected Disability***	Yes	39%	17%
	No	61%	83%
Marital Status***	Married (spouse present)	67%	61%
	Married (spouse absent)	1%	1%
	Widowed	1%	1%
	Divorced	13%	16%
	Separated	2%	3%
	Never married	16%	18%

Column 1 is the percentage of all TAP participants; column 2 is the percentage of all non-TAP participants. Statistical significance of χ^2 distribution reported:
*statistically significant at p<.05.
**statistically significant at p<.01.
***statistically significant at p<.001.
Calculations based on Current Population Survey, 2007–2012.

Satisfaction with TAP Participation

We now turn to results of analyses of participant reports of program usefulness (see figure 4.2). Approximately 73 percent of program participants reported that TAP provided useful information on education, housing, and medical care, which suggests that assistance with basic needs during the transition period was being addressed. Similarly, about 65 percent of participants reported that the information provided on job-related training was useful. As shown in figure 4.2, reports of usefulness of the VA component of the TAP workshops ranged from 83 percent among former Coast Guard service members to 71 percent among former army service members, while reports of usefulness of job-related services ranged from

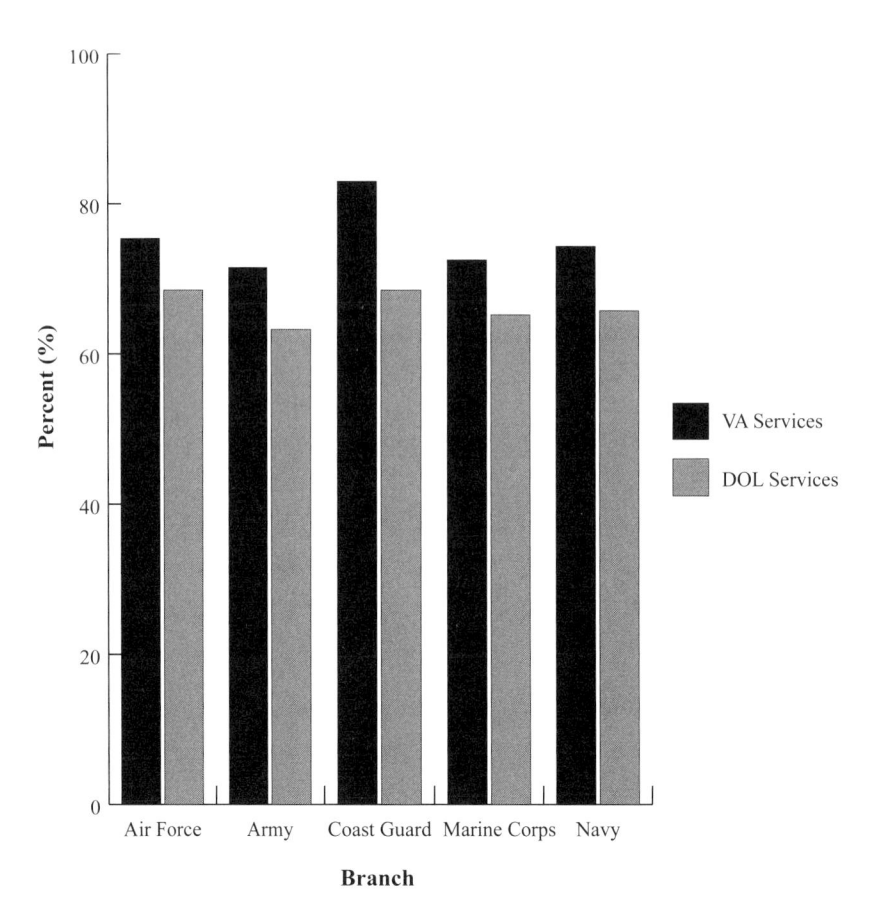

Figure 4.2. Usefulness of Education, Medical, and Housing Information Provided by VA and Job-Related Services Provided by DOL.

TAPped Out

69 percent among former air force and Coast Guard service members to 63 percent among former army service members.

In figures 4.3a–f we present reports of specific program components cited as most useful to participants (results do not add up to 100 percent because service members could report more than one component as

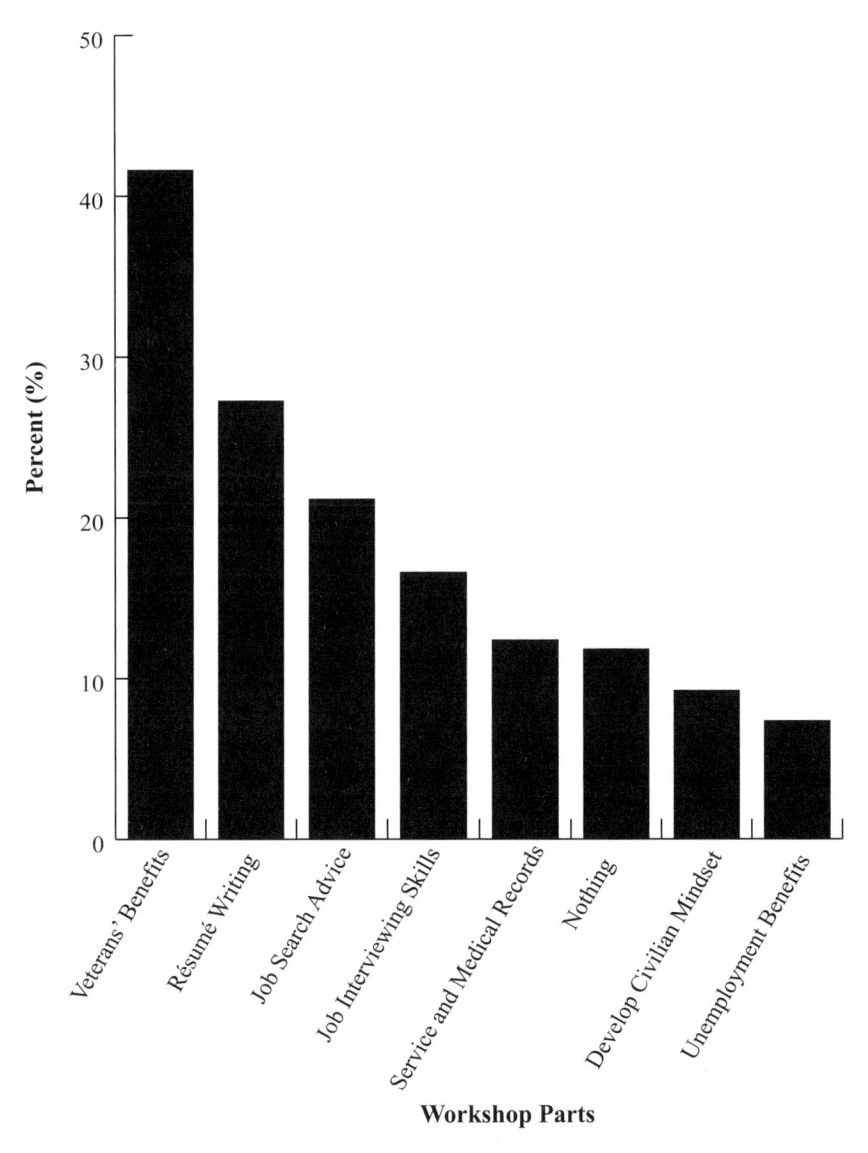

Figure 4.3a. The Most Useful Parts of the Workshop Were . . .

useful). Forty-two percent indicated that information on veterans' benefits was most useful. Specific information related to conducting a job search received much lower levels of endorsement as most useful, with only 27 percent indicating résumé writing, 21 percent indicating job-search behavior and strategies, and 17 percent indicating advice about job interviewing strategies. Approximately 7 percent cited learning about unemployment benefits as the most useful, possibly indicating an expectation of significant challenges ahead in finding employment.

For a significant portion of respondents, the most useful aspects of TAP participation were less tangible or relevant to making a successful transition into the civilian labor force, and some reported no benefit at all. Approximately one in 10 participants indicated that the most useful aspect of the program was learning the importance of making and keeping copies of service and medical records prior to separation. A similar percentage indicated that the most useful aspect of TAP participation was learning about the importance of developing a civilian mind-set. Finally, approximately 12 percent indicated that they did not find any advice or information to be useful.

In terms of variation in the usefulness of different components of the program by branch, over 30 percent of former air force and army service members reported finding information on résumé writing useful, compared to a rate of about 21 percent for other branches. Notably, 25 percent of former Coast Guard service members indicated that information on service and medical records was particularly useful—

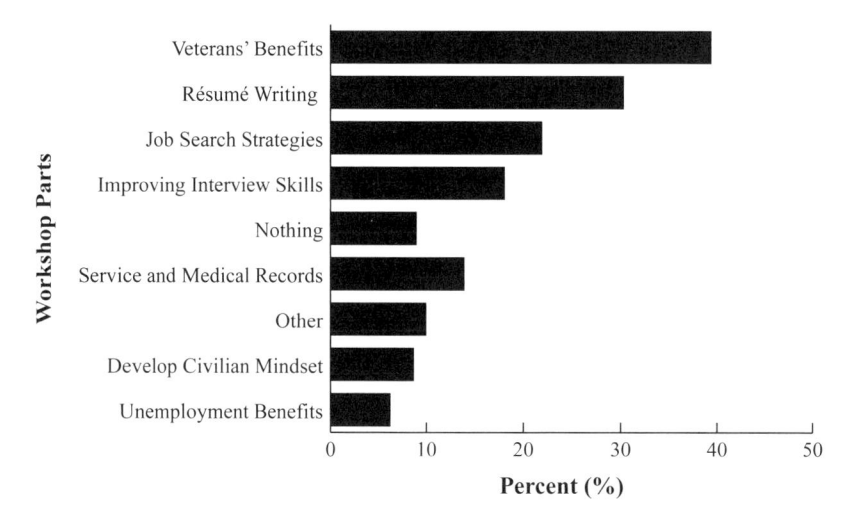

Figure 4.3b. The Most Useful Parts of the Workshop Were . . . : Air Force.

TAPped Out

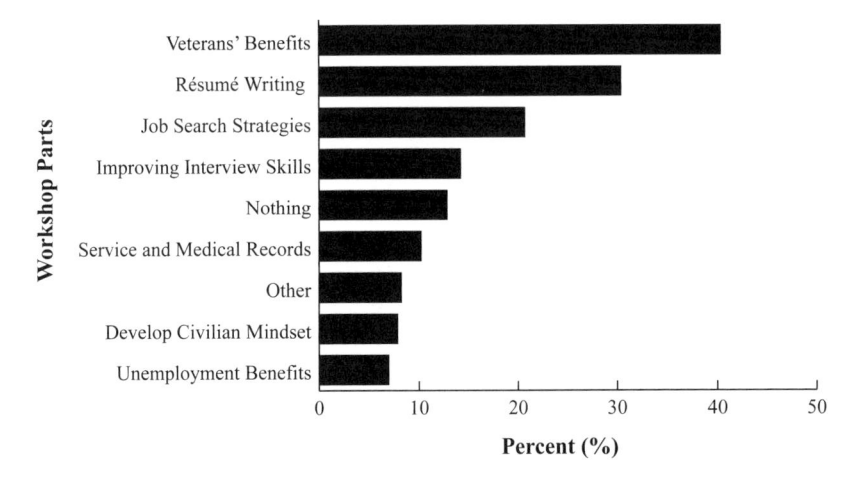

Figure 4.3c. The Most Useful Parts of the Workshop Were . . . : Army.

a much higher percentage than other branches, which varied from 10 to 14 percent finding this information useful. TAP participants who served in the navy reported information on the usefulness of unemployment benefits at higher rates (10 percent compared to between 6 percent and 7 percent for the air force, army, and Marine Corps and 4 percent for the Coast Guard).

When asked about recommending improvements to TAP, 35 percent did not endorse any of the specific possible changes listed in the survey

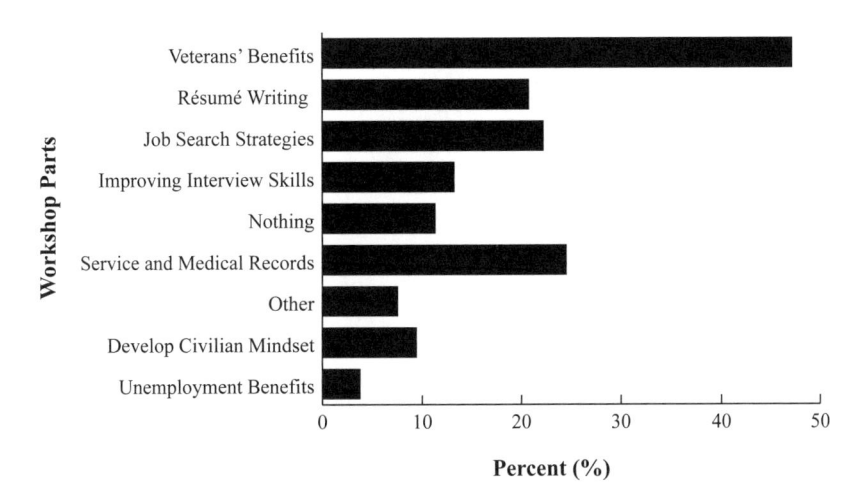

Figure 4.3d. The Most Useful Parts of the Workshop Were . . . : Coast Guard.

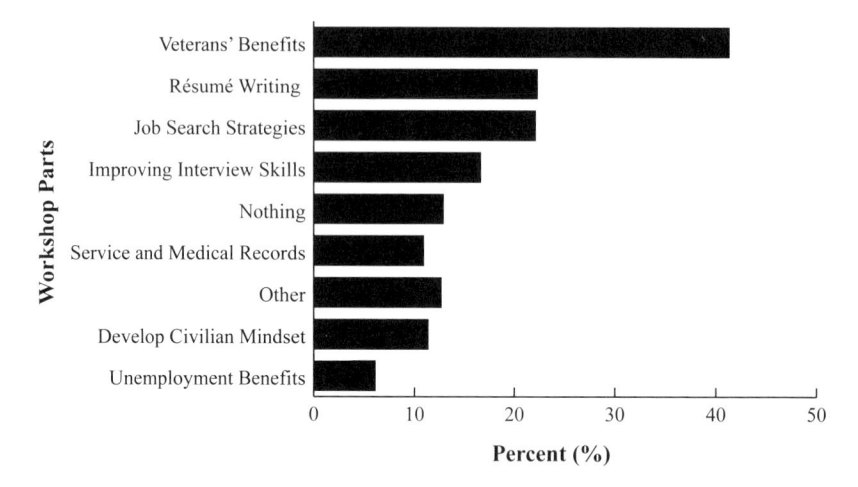

Figure 4.3e. The Most Useful Parts of the Workshop Were . . . : Marine Corps.

and offered no suggestions, while another 25 percent wrote in specific responses to which we did not have access. Based on the responses of participants who offered recommendations, shown in figure 4.4, the endorsed items tended to focus on the format of TAP. Some 11 percent supported the idea of making TAP mandatory, and 8 percent supported lengthening the workshop by a day or two. And 11 percent thought that the timing was an issue and that TAP should be offered six months or more prior to discharge. A similar 12 percent suggested including

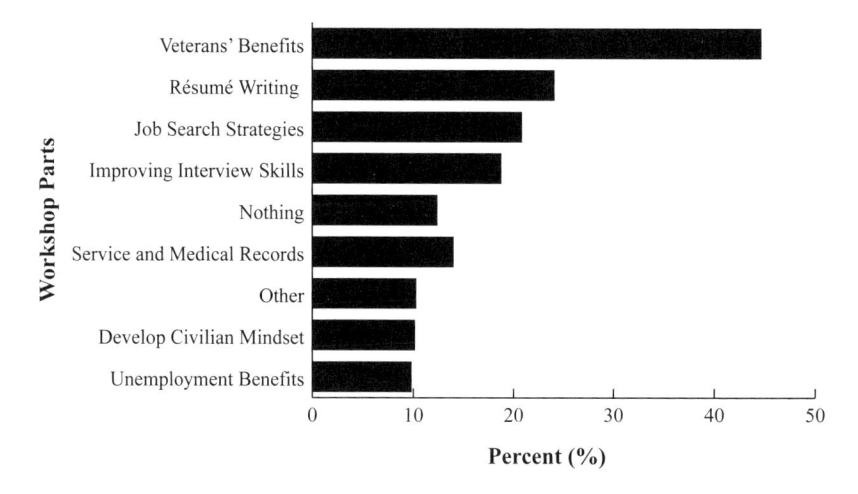

Figure 4.3f. The Most Useful Parts of the Workshop Were . . . : Navy.

TAPped Out

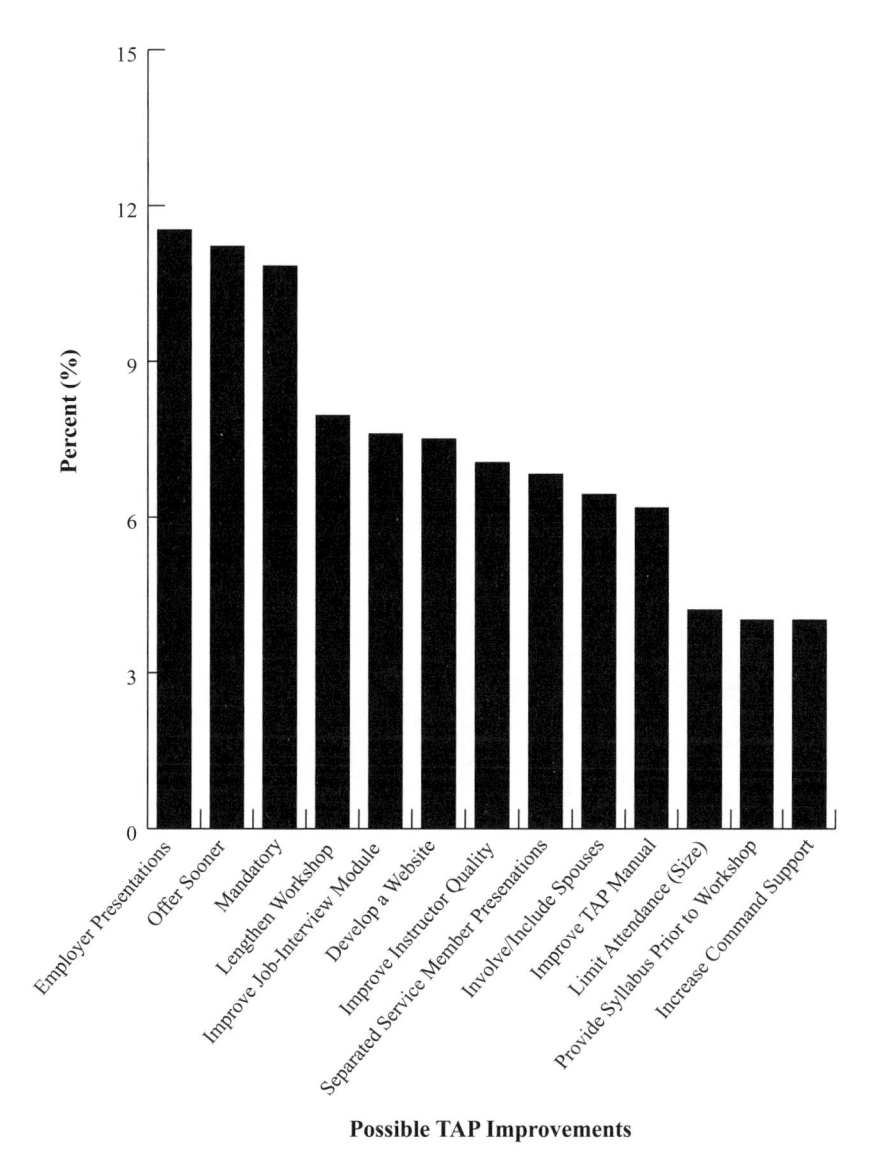

[Bar chart showing Possible TAP Improvements with percentages: Employer Presentations ~11.5%, Offer Sooner ~11.2%, Mandatory ~10.9%, Lengthen Workshop ~8%, Improve Job-Interview Module ~7.6%, Develop a Website ~7.5%, Improve Instructor Quality ~7.1%, Separated Service Member Presentations ~6.8%, Involve/Include Spouses ~6.5%, Improve TAP Manual ~6.2%, Limit Attendance (Size) ~4.3%, Provide Syllabus Prior to Workshop ~4.1%, Increase Command Support ~4.1%]

Possible TAP Improvements

Figure 4.4. Improve TAP by . . .

presentations by employers and (civilian) human resource personnel directly. Approximately 8 percent indicated support for improving the interview skill module, improving the quality of instructors, updating the TAP manual periodically, including presentations by former TAP attendees, and involving spouses in the workshop. Interestingly, only 8 percent indicated support for developing a TAP Web site or videos/CDs for use after the workshop, which is exactly the format that the new program uses. Only limited support (under 5 percent) was received for limiting attendance to under 50 attendees, providing participants with a syllabus prior to attending TAP workshops, and increasing command support for TAP.

Chi-square tests for statistical independence between year and recommendations for improvement reveal that the most common recommendations were less likely over time, perhaps revealing an increase in satisfaction. In addition, significant variation was found by branch of military service. In terms of the recommendations regarding the length of the program, navy and Coast Guard veterans were particularly unlikely to suggest lengthening the workshop, potentially because their workshops were already the longest (as of fiscal year 2001); TAP workshops for the navy and Coast Guard were four days long, whereas the Marine Corps workshops were three to four days long, and the army and air force workshops were, on average, three days long (Bascetta 2002).

Reasons for Nonparticipation

For most branches, more than 50 percent of surveyed service members did not attend a TAP workshop. Eligible nonparticipants were asked why they did not attend. The most common reason reported—cited by 33 percent of respondents who had not participated in TAP—is that the service member already had a job waiting after discharge. Similarly, another 6 percent reported having plans to attend college or a job-training program. Importantly, 27 percent reported having never heard of transition workshops, 5 percent reported that they did not know the date or time of the workshop, and 7 percent indicated that TAP was not offered at their base. Only about 5 percent thought that the workshop would be a waste of time. Importantly, structural barriers to participation do not appear to be a significant problem. Less than 1 percent reported that their commanding officer would not authorize or support attendance, and 1 percent indicated that they could not attend a workshop when it was offered.

Discussion

Since 1991 the military has offered TAP to millions of military personnel to help ease transition to civilian life and employment. Despite the lengthy program history and the volume of participants, very little research in the extant literature has examined program participation and, to some extent, satisfaction. We use nationally representative data from the 2007 to 2012 CPS to examine program participation, reports of program usefulness and suggestions for program improvement from TAP attendees, and reasons for nonattendance among eligible persons who did not attend. Our descriptive results suggest that many veterans value the non-labor-market information provided by TAP, but the employment training is minimal and not considered particularly useful.

One main limitation of this study is the purely descriptive nature of the analysis. However, given that the information presented in table 4.1 demonstrates significant differences in observed characteristics between participants and nonparticipants, which suggests the likely presence of unobserved differences as well, an outcome evaluation would not yield reliable causal results in the absence of a proper identification scheme to deal with selection bias. For example, the observed overrepresentation of female service members and service members with a service-connected disability among TAP users leads us to think that program effectiveness would likely be underestimated if these differences among separated service members who participated in TAP versus those who did not were not taken into account. These groups have been shown to have more difficulty transitioning to the civilian labor market than other groups of veterans, so there is good reason to expect different program effects for these groups than other TAP participants (Department of Labor et al. 2014). In addition, the overrepresentation of service members with master's degrees or higher and those who are married may be evidence of positive selection into program participation that would likely lead to overestimation of program effectiveness if not properly taken into account. Finally, there may be individuals who are highly motivated to take advantage of programs and services throughout their military careers. Because these individuals may be more motivated in their employment efforts, we would expect estimates of TAP participation effects on employment outcomes to be positively biased. The considerable difficulty in isolating program effects from structural variations in implementation across branches of military service, as well as location and variation in observable and unobservable participant characteristics, is a likely reason that existing studies have not produced strong, systematic evidence of TAP's success or lack thereof (Barton et al. 1995; Sadacca et al. 1995).

Our chapter makes a modest contribution to the literature by providing clear documentation regarding program history and intent over TAP's 23-year period of implementation, as well as using nationally representative data over a 6-year period to provide an empirical analysis of the strengths and weaknesses of TAP as reported by veterans themselves.

While it would be better to know the impact of the original TAP program on the labor-force outcomes of recently separated veterans, it is our contention that such an impact study is not possible with available data. However, we feel that a clear understanding of TAP users' perspectives on the program—drawn from nationally representative survey data—can contribute to the development of a systematic evaluation strategy of TAP's successor, Transition GPS.

Directions for Future Research

The absence of a systematic, long-term evaluation of TAP shines light on the need to develop an evaluation strategy for Transition GPS similar to those used to measure the impact of similar programs such as job training programs and prerelease prisoner reentry programs. Designing a robust evaluation strategy would involve ongoing efforts at two stages: process evaluation—how program services are being provided; and impact evaluation—the extent to which participation results in better outcomes for service members making the transition to civilian life. We discuss both of these stages below, drawing on evaluation design and results from DOL employment programs and prisoner reentry programs.

Prior evidence of variation in the implementation of TAP in terms of participation in preseparation counseling, as well as the length of, access to, and information provided at DOL/VA workshops, suggests that researchers may want to consider undertaking a systematic process evaluation of Transition GPS. The aim of such a process evaluation would be to examine the operation and delivery of Transition GPS services, with a specific focus on whether the program redesign has resulted in greater fidelity of implementation across military service branches and whether Transition GPS is meeting the goal of universal participation. A fidelity evaluation could document any adaptations to the curriculum that were occurring. Data collection might involve participant observation, as well as intensive interviews and discussions with the providers of preseparation counseling and the staff tasked with conducting DOL and VA workshops, at a number of bases across military branches and geographic regions.

Process evaluations could also take advantage of enhanced reporting requirements for TAP participation put in place by DoD following the 2011 VOW to Hire Heroes Act, including improved data on the numbers of service members attending TAP, participating in preservice counseling, enrolling in e-benefits through the VA workshop, and completing the Transition GPS program (Sherrill 2014). Analysis using these data could provide insights into which bases and branches may have more or less difficulty in enforcing mandatory participation; whether groups of service members indicate preferences for certain tracks; and whether different programmatic components are selected more often within different branches, at different installations, or among different subgroups of separating service members. Information collected through a process evaluation could be used to identify dissatisfaction with components of the program and ultimately help to reduce the number of participants reporting that none of the workshop components were useful. Finally, the results of a process evaluation would be useful for a subsequent impact evaluation, which would benefit from controlling for variations in implementation, preferences, and attendance across branches and installations.

In addition to ongoing process evaluation, efforts should be made to measure whether the program improves employment outcomes of service members who have transitioned to the civilian sector. Existing impact evaluations of other DOL programs demonstrate how either experimental or quasi-experimental approaches could be used to obtain reliable estimates of the program's success (Bell 2003; Orr et al. 2011). For example, the DOL has recently used randomized controlled trials (RCT) for programs targeting the long-term unemployed, such as the Reemployment Eligibility Assessment (REA)/Reemployment Services (RES) programs, which may be similar in intensity to job services provided at the DOL workshops (Michaelides et al. 2012; Needles, Perez-Johnson, and Dunn 2015). Evaluations using RCT designs can vary the combinations and intensity of services provided to program participants in order to form treatment and comparison groups, rather than restricting access to services for some groups.

Because Transition GPS combines both job training and transition counseling, evaluation strategies and findings from prerelease prisoner reentry programs can also inform the design of future evaluations of Transition GPS. While the population of reentering prisoners varies in meaningful ways from the transitioning veteran population, the hurdles faced during reentry—such as finding housing, reuniting with loved ones, obtaining employment, and alcohol and drug use—may be similar (Seiter and Kadela 2003). Evaluations of prisoner reentry programs suggest that, for prerelease programs, the timing and duration of the program matters, with longer programs appearing to be more effective than shorter programs (Petersilia 2004). In fact, recent summaries of best practices in prisoner reentry programs indicate that many programs have the philosophy that preparing prisoners for reentry to civilian life begins at the point of entering prison (Petersilia 2004). Consistent with this philosophy, the new Transition GPS includes a component called "The Military Life Cycle" transition model, which service members use throughout their military career to align skills they acquire with skills needed in the labor force (Department of Defense 2014a).

In addition, evaluations of prisoner reentry programs have emphasized the importance of accounting for heterogeneity among program participants (Seiter and Kadela 2003; Lynch 2006). Some programs have created a scoring system that identifies the level of risk that a transitioning prisoner faces in terms of the chance of recidivism and then structures services according to the individual's risk level (Seiter and Kadela 2003). Both the former TAP program and the present Transition GPS program have a specific benefits component for veterans with service-connected disabilities, in recognition of the specific difficulties that disabled veterans face in the job market and their risk of poverty and material hardship (London, Heflin, and Wilmoth 2011; Wilmoth, London, and Heflin 2015a). However, rural veterans may experience more difficulty transitioning to civilian life because of limited access to health and employment services (Heady 2007). Women appear to have more difficulty readjusting to family needs and caretaking responsibilities after returning from active duty and may be more likely to experience substance abuse than male veterans (Foster and Vince 2009). The new Transition GPS workshop and curriculum has attempted to meet the challenge of individualizing transition assistance while also providing assistance uniformly across branches and military installations by adopting outcome-based career readiness standards, providing the option of participation in different "tracks" (accessing higher education, career technical training, and entrepreneurship training), and ensuring that *all* separating service members receive preseparation counseling and develop an individual transition plan with the support of a transition staff member (Department of Defense 2014b, 2014c).

Future evaluators of Transition GPS will want to use both stages of the evaluation process to monitor whether the redesigned program is meeting the needs of the diverse population of recently separated service members. A robust national-level impact evaluation of the TAP program would be informative from both policy-making and social improvement standpoints. Currently, there is no direct empirical basis on which to develop a set of expectations about what impact Transition GPS should have on transitioning service members' employment and health outcomes, or, more generally, their well-being. The degree to which transition assistance actually helps separating service members find and sustain quality employment and access to healthcare, financial support for continuing education, and home loans remains largely unknown. However, having a program in place that meets these objectives is essential given the promise of "a life of continued self-improvement" (Faurer et al. 2014, 55). The armed forces rely on this promise for recruitment of new service members, and service members rely on this promise when they make a commitment to serve their country.

References

Barton, M. F., M. S. Davis, S. W. Glasser, N. L. Robb, and R. G. Tutor. 1995. *Transition Assistance Program: Phase III Impact Evaluation*. Prepared for Office of Assistant Secretary for Veterans Employment and Training, Department of Labor. Washington, DC: Systems Research and Applications Corporation and Martin Marietta Energy Systems, Inc.

Bascetta, Cynthia A. 2002. "Military and Veterans' Benefits: Observations on the Transition Assistance Program, Testimony, July 18." *Statement to the U.S. House, Subcommittee on Benefits, Committee on Veterans' Affairs*. GAO-02-914T. Washington, DC: General Accounting Office.

Bascetta, Cynthia A. 2005. "Military and Veterans' Benefits: Improvements Needed in Transition Assistance Services for Reserves and National Guard, Testimony, June 29." *Statement to the U.S. House of Representatives, Subcommittee on Economic Opportunity, Committee on Veterans' Affairs*. GAO-05-844T. Washington, DC: Government Accountability Office.

Bell, Stephen. 2003. *Review of Alternative Methodologies for Employment and Training Program Evaluation*. Washington, DC: Department of Labor, Employment and Training Administration. Accessed November 9, 2015. http://wdr.doleta.gov/research/FullText_Documents/Review%20of%20Alternative%20Methodologies%20for%20Employment%20and%20Training%20Research.pdf.

Bureau of Labor Statistics. 2010. "Employment Situation of Veterans—2009." News release, March 12. Accessed June 11, 2014. http://www.bls.gov/news.release/archives/vet_03122010.pdf.

Bureau of Labor Statistics. 2013. "Employment Situation of Veterans—2012." News release, March 20. Accessed June 11, 2014. http://www.bls.gov/news.release/archives/vet_03202013.pdf.

Burnaska, Kristine. 2008. *Employment Histories Report: Final Compilation Report*. Prepared for Department of Veterans Affairs. Bethesda, MD: Abt Associates, Inc.

Cadigan, John. 2006. "The Impact of Family-Friendly Compensation: An Investigation of Military Personnel Policy." *Review of Public Personnel Administration* 261: 3–20.

Central Intelligence Agency (CIA). 2016. "United States: Military Service Age and Obligation," in *The World Factbook*, February 25. Accessed March 9, 2016. https://www.cia.gov/library/publications/resources/the-world-factbook/geos/us.html.

Coll, Jose E., Eugenia L. Weiss, and Jeffrey S. Yarvis. 2011. "No One Leaves Unchanged: Insights for Civilian Mental Health Care Professionals into the Military Experience and Culture." *Social Work in Health Care* 507: 487–500.

Defense Business Board. 2013. *Employing Our Veterans Part II: Service Member Transition*. Report FY13-01 to the Secretary of Defense. Washington, DC: Defense Business Board.

Defense Department Advisory Committee on Women in the Services (DACOWITS). 2012. *DACOWITS Report*. Washington, DC: DACOWITS.

Department of Defense. 1994. "Instruction: Preparation Counseling for Military Personnel." Number 1332.36, February 14. Washington DC: Department of Defense.

Department of Defense. 2014a. "About DoD TAP." Accessed November 9, 2015. https://www.DoDtap.mil.

Department of Defense. 2014b. "Career Readiness Standards." Accessed November 9, 2015. https://www.DoDtap.mil.

Department of Defense. 2014c. "Individual Transition Plan." Accessed November 9, 2015. https://www.DoDtap.mil/resources

Department of Defense. 2014d. Transition Assistance Program (TAP), TAP101/Overview Info Sheet. Accessed November 9, 2015. https://www.DoDtap.mil/about_DoDTAP.

Department of Labor. 2010. *Veterans Employment & Training Service Annual Report to Congress Fiscal Year 2010*. Washington, DC: Office of the Assistance Secretary for Veterans' Employment and Training, Department of Labor.

Department of Labor, Department of Commerce, Department of Education, and Department of Health and Human Services. 2014. *What Works in Job Training: A Synthesis of the Evidence*. Washington, DC: Department of Labor.

Department of Veterans Affairs. 2005. "Transition Assistance in the VA Military Services Program." Fact sheet. Washington, DC: Office of Public Affairs and Media Relations, Department of Veterans Affairs.

Dyhouse, Tim. 1997. "Job Placement Project Could Revolutionize Military Assistance Transitioning." *VFW: Veterans of Foreign Wars Magazine* 85 (4): 10.

Evans, John T. 2012. *Examining the Re-Design of the Transition Assistance Program (TAP)*. Statement to the U.S. House of Representatives, Committee on Veterans' Affairs, Subcommittee on Economic Opportunity. Hearing, September 20 (Serial No. 112–77). Washington, DC: U.S. Government Printing Office.

Faurer, Judson, Apryl Rogers-Brodersen, and Paul Bailie. 2014. "Managing the Employment of Military Veterans through the Transition Assistance Program (TAP)." *Journal of Business & Economics Research* 12 (1): 55–60.

Foster, Lisa K., and Scott Vince. 2009. *California's Women Veterans: The Challenges and Needs of Those Who Served*. Sacramento: California Research Bureau.

Friedlander, Daniel, David H. Greenberg, and Philip K. Robins. 1997. "Evaluating Government Training Programs for the Economically Disadvantaged." *Journal of Economic Literature* 35: 1809–1855.

General Accounting Office. 1994. "Military Downsizing: Persons Returning to Civilian Life Need More Help from DOD." GAO-94-39. Washington, DC: General Accounting Office.

Golub, Andrew, and Alex S. Bennett. 2014. "Substance Use over the Military-Veteran Life Course: An Analysis of a Sample of OEF/OIF Veterans Returning to Low-income Predominately Minority Communities." *Addictive Behaviors* 39 (2): 449–54.

Golub, Andrew, Peter Vazan, Alexander S. Bennett, and Hilary J. Liberty. 2013. "Unmet Need for Treatment of Substance Use Disorders and Serious Psychological Distress among Veterans: A Nationwide Analysis Using the NSDUH." *Military Medicine* 178 (1): 107–14.

Government Accountability Office. 2011. *Multiple Employment and Training Programs: Providing Information on Colocating Services and Consolidating Administrative Structures Could Promote Efficiencies*. GAO-11-92. Washington, DC: Government Accountability Office.

Government Accountability Office. 2012. *Veterans' Employment and Training: Better Targeting, Coordinating, and Reporting Needed to Enhance Program Effectiveness, Report to Congressional Requesters*. GAO 13-29. Washington, DC: Government Accountability Office.

Government Accountability Office. 2014. *Transitioning Veterans: Improved Oversight Needed to Enhance Implementation of Transition Assistance Program, Report to Congressional Committees*. GAO-14-144. Washington, DC: Government Accountability Office.

Greenberg, David H., Charles Michalopoulos, and Philip K. Robins. 2003. "The Meta-Analysis of Government Sponsored Training Programs." *Industrial and Labor Relations Review* 571: 31–53.

Greenberg, Greg A., and Robert A. Rosenheck. 2007. "Are Male Veterans at Greater Risk for Nonemployment Than Nonveterans?" *Monthly Labor Review* (December): 23–31. http://www.bls.gov/opub/mlr/2007/12/art3full.pdf.

Hanssen, Elizabeth. 2008. "The Effectiveness of the Transition Assistance Program at Hurlburt Field, Florida." Master's thesis, University of Alaska, Anchorage.

Heady, Hilda R. 2007. "Rural Veterans: A Special Concern for Rural Health Advocates." National Rural Health Associates Issue Paper, February. Accessed June 24, 2014. http://www.ruralhealthweb.org.

Heinrich, Carolyn J., Peter R. Mueser, Kenneth R. Troske, Kyung-Seong Jeon, and Daver C. Kahvecioglu. 2013. "Do Public Employment and Training Programs Work?" *IZA Journal of Labor Economics* 2 (1): 1–23.

Hirsch, Barry T., and Stephen L. Mehay. 2002. "Evaluating the Labor Market Performance of Veterans Using a Matched Comparison Group Design." *Journal of Human Resources* 38 (3): 673–700.

Humensky, Jennifer L., Neil Jordan, Kevin T. Stroupe, and Denise M. Hynse. 2013. "How Are Iraq/Afghanistan-Era Veterans Faring in the Labor Market?" *Armed Forces & Society* 39 (1): 158–183.

Institute for Veterans and Military Families. 2013. "The Annual Employment Situation of Veterans 2012." Report, March 2013. Accessed June 11, 2014. http://vets.syr.edu/wp-content/uploads/2013/03/Annual-Employment-Report2012.pdf.

Institute for Veterans and Military Families and Institute for National Security and Counterterrorism. 2011. *A National Veterans Strategy: The Economic, Social and Security Imperative*. Syracuse, NY: Syracuse University.

Institute of Medicine. 2010. *Returning Home from Iraq and Afghanistan: Preliminary Assessment of Readjustment Needs of Veterans, Service Members, and Their Families*. Washington, DC: National Academies Press.

Kleykamp, Meredith. 2013. "Unemployment, Earnings and Enrollment among Post 9/11 Veterans." *Social Science Research* 42: 836–851.

LISBOA, Inc. 2002. *TAP Program Evaluation: Final Report*. JM7-0058/0353-97-70. Prepared for Office of Assistant Secretary for Veterans Employment and Training, Department of Labor. Washington, DC: LISBOA, Inc.

London, Andrew S., Colleen M. Heflin, and Janet M. Wilmoth. 2011. "Work-Related Disability, Veteran Status, and Poverty: Implications for Family Well-Being." *Journal of Poverty* 15: 330–349.

Lynch, James P. 2006. "Prisoner Reentry: Beyond Program Evaluation." *Criminology and Public Policy* 52: 401–412. doi:10.1111/j.1745-9133.2006.00386.x.

Manning, Lory, Brigid O'Farrell, Anne J. Stone, and Vanessa R. Wright. 2001. "Women Veterans' Employment—Issues and Recommendations." WREI Issue Brief. Arlington, VA: Women's Research and Education Institute.

Marinaccio, Janet. 2008. *Veterans Employment Services: A Review of Effective Practices*. Rockville, MD: Goodwill Industries International, Inc.

Michaelides, Marios, Eileen Poe-Yamagata, Jacob Benus, and Dharmendra Tirumalasetti. 2012. *Impact of the Reemployment and Eligibility Assessment REA Initiative in Nevada*. Prepared for the Department of Labor. DoLF091A21507. Columbia, MD: Impaq International.

Military.com. 2007. "Military.com Study Reveals Profound Disconnect between Employers and Transitioning Military Personnel." November 5. Accessed November 9, 2015. http://www.military.com/aboutus/twocolumn/0,15929,PR article110507,00.html.

National Defense Authorization Act for Fiscal Year 1991. Pub. L. No. 101-510, U.S.C. 104 (1990), 1485–1855. Accessed June 3, 2014. http://thomas.loc.gov.

Needles, Karen, Irma Perez-Johnson, and Adam Dunn. 2015. *Implementation of the EUC08 Reemployment Services and Reemployment Eligibility Assessments Program: Findings from Nine States*. Prepared for the Department of Labor. Princeton, NJ: Mathematica Policy Research.

Orr, Larry L., Stephen H. Bell, and Jacob A. Klerman. 2011. "Designing Reliable Impact Evaluations." In *The Workforce Investment Act: Implementation Experiences and Evaluation Findings*, edited by Douglas J. Besharov and Phoebe H. Cottingham, 431–446. Kalamazoo, MI: Upjohn Institute Press.

Ortiz, Ismael. 2012. "Transition Assistance Program (TAP) Employment Workshop Redesign and Implementation." Veterans' Program Letter No. 03-12. Washington, DC: Department of Labor. Accessed June 9, 2014. www.dol.gov/vets.

Perkins, Walter. 2011. "The Military Transition Assistance Program TAP?" *Ezine Articles*, March 31. Accessed March 9, 2016. http://ezinearticles.com/?The-Military-Transition-Assistance-Program-(TAP)?&id=6037168.

Petersilia, Joan. 2004. "What Works in Prisoner Reentry? Reviewing and Questioning the Evidence." *Federal Probation* 682: 4–8.

RAND Corporation. 2008. *Invisible Wounds of War*. Arlington, VA: RAND Corporation.

Rauch, Meredith A. 2014. "Contextual Career Counseling for Transitioning Military Veterans." *Journal of Employment Counseling* 51: 89–96.

Sadacca, Robert, Janice H. Laurence, Ani S. DiFazio, H. John Rauch, and D. Wayne Hintz. 1995. *Outcome Evaluation of the Army Career and Alumni Program's Job Assistance Centers*. Ft. Belvoir, VA: U.S. Army Research Institute for the Behavioral and Social Sciences.

Scott, Christine. 2012. "Veterans Benefits: Federal Employment Assistance." In *Labor Issues and Policies in the U.S.*, edited by John E. Harrison, 117–128. Hauppauge, NY: Nova Science Publishers, Inc.

Seiter, Richard P., and Karen R. Kadela. 2003. "Prisoner Reentry: What Works, What Does Not, and What is Promising." *Crime and Delinquency* 493: 360–388.

Silva, Erin. 2011. "Participation in the Transition Assistance Program and Job Placement Outcomes of U.S. Veterans." Master's thesis, University of Rhode Island.

Smith, R. Tyson, and Gala True. 2014. "Warring Identities: Identity Conflict and the Mental Distress of American Veterans of the Wars in Iraq and Afghanistan." *Society and Mental Health* 4 (2): 147–161.

Stewart, Derek B. 2005. *Military Personnel: Financial Cost and Loss of Critical Skills due to DoD's Homosexual Conduct Policy Cannot Be Completely Estimated*. GAO-05-299. Washington, DC: Government Accountability Office.

Szelwach, Celia R., Jill Steinkogler, Ellen Badger, and Ria Muttukumaru. 2011. "Transitioning to the Civilian Workforce: Issues Impacting the Reentry of Rural Women Veterans." *Journal of Rural Social Sciences* 263: 88–112.

Transition to Veterans Program Office (TVPO). 2013. "Redesigned Transition Assistance Program for Separating Service Members." Interagency Statement of Intent among the Department of Defense, Department of Veterans Affairs, Department of Labor, Department of Education, United States Office of Personnel Management, and United States Small Business Administration. Washington, DC: Department of Defense. prhome.defense.gov/RFM/TVPO.

Trutko, John, Carolyn O'Brien, Burt Barnow, David Balducchi, Dave Darling, Joyce Kaiser, Stephen Wandner, Xiaogang (Bethanie) Wang, and Z. Joan Wang. 2013. *Formative Evaluation of the Veterans' Employment and Training Service's Transition Assistance Program (TAP) Employment Workshop: Findings from Observational Visits; Analysis of Customer Satisfaction Survey; and Options for Future Evaluation of TAP*. Washington, DC: Department of Labor. Accessed June 9, 2014. http://www.dol.gov/asp/evaluation/reports/TAPFormativeEvaluation.pdf.

Ulrich, John. 2012. *Defense Drawdowns: Analysis with Implications*. Strategy Research Project. Carlisle, PA: U.S. Army War College.

U.S. House of Representatives, Committee on Armed Services, Subcommittee on Military Personnel. 2013. *Status of Implementation of the Requirements of the VOW Act and the Recommendations of the Presidential Veterans Employment Initiative Task Force for the DoD Transition Assistance Program—Goals, Plans, and Success (GPS)*. Washington, DC: Government Printing Office.

U.S. House of Representatives, Committee on Veterans' Affairs, Subcommittee on Economic Opportunity. 2012. *Examining the Redesign of the Transition Assistance Program TAP, Hearing, September 20.* Serial No. 112-77. Washington, DC: Government Printing Office.

U.S. House of Representatives, Committee on Veterans' Affairs, Subcommittee on Education Training and Employment. 1991. *Transition Assistance Program, Hearing, July 18 1991 and July 24.* Serial No. 102-18. Washington, DC: Government Printing Office.

Vazan, Peter, Andrew Golub, and Alex S. Bennett. 2013. "Substance Use and Other Mental Health Disorders among Veterans Returning to the Inner City: Prevalence, Correlates, and Rates of Unmet Treatment Need." *Substance Use and Misuse* 4810: 880–893.

Veterans Employment and Training Service (VETS). 2013. "FY 2013 Congressional Budget Justification: Veterans' Employment and Training Service." Washington, DC: Department of Labor.

Washington, Donna L., Elizabeth M. Yano, James McGuire, Vivian Hines, Martin Lee, and Lillian Gelberg. 2010. "Risk Factors for Homelessness among Women Veterans." *Journal of Health Care for the Poor and Underserved* 211: 82–91.

Wells, Theodore John. 1998. "Military Transition Assistance Programs: Identifying the Needs and Values of Dislocated Workers." PhD diss., University of Illinois at Urbana-Champaign.

Westat. 2010. *National Survey of Veterans, Active Duty Service Members, Demobilized National Guard and Reserve Members, Family Members, and Surviving Spouses.* GS-23F-8144H. Washington, DC: Prepared for Department of Veterans Affairs.

Wilmoth, Janet M., Andrew S. London, and Colleen M. Heflin. 2015a. "Economic Well-Being among Older-Adult Households: Variation by Veteran and Disability Status." *Journal of Gerontological Social Work* 58 (4): 399–419.

Wilmoth, Janet M., Andrew S. London, and Colleen M. Heflin. 2015b. "The Use of VA Disability Compensation and Social Security Disability Insurance among Working-aged Veterans." *Disability and Health Journal* 8: 388–396.

Zoli, Corri, Rosalinda Maury, and Daniel Fay. 2015. *Missing Perspectives: Service Members' Transition from Service to Civilian Life—Data-Driven Research to Enact the Promise of the Post-9/11 G.I. Bill.* Syracuse, NY: Institute for Veterans and Military Families, Syracuse University. Accessed November 19, 2015. http://vets.syr.edu/research/highered/.

CHAPTER FIVE

The VA and the Grass Roots

Colin D. Moore

In the administration of American social policy, veterans are unique. Unlike the crazy quilt of agencies that provide support to the poor and the elderly, one massive federal bureaucracy—the Department of Veterans Affairs (VA)—directs virtually all programs for veterans. Since its creation by Herbert Hoover in 1930, the VA has grown to become the second-largest bureaucracy in the United States, with more than 300,000 employees and an operating budget of $164 billion (Department of Veterans Affairs 2015e). The department administers a comprehensive set of services and benefits, including medical care, disability compensation, education, home loan guarantees, life insurance, long-term care, and burial expenses. As a result of its unusual organizational structure, a web of nonprofit organizations, congressional committees, philanthropic foundations, corporations, and state government agencies influences veterans' policies, and those organizations have developed a particularly close relationship with the VA. How can we understand this complex agency? How does this dense network of pressure groups affect the VA's operations? Finally, why does this massive government welfare agency exist in a nation that is often opposed to state-run social programs?

In this chapter I investigate these questions through a survey of the VA's complex organizational ecology. Following Philip Selznick's (1949) landmark analysis of the Tennessee Valley Authority, I examine how various organized interests were co-opted by the VA—brought in to share power and to legitimate the VA as the central figure in veterans' policy—and contributed to its unusual resilience in the face of policy failures and efforts to privatize public services. Co-optation, however, did not cause the VA to become "captured" by one of these groups. As discussed in the following sections, the very strength and diversity of veterans' pressure groups gave the VA a certain measure of autonomy to construct public policy by supporting some factions over others. Yet its organizational success came at a price. Many of the interests that are deeply involved in the formation of veterans' policy, from the academic medical community to the real estate industry, are less concerned with veterans' welfare than with their own financial or organizational goals. While this is hardly unique to veterans' policy, the VA's efforts to appease these important interests have at times made it neglectful of poor, wounded, and younger veterans who are most in need of its services (Klein 1981).

I proceed in eight steps. First, I briefly survey the history and development of the VA from its origins during the Civil War through the postwar years of the G.I. Bill. In the second and third sections I examine the Veterans Health Administration (VHA) and the Veterans Benefits Administration (VBA), the two major departments of the contemporary VA that provide healthcare and financial support services to millions of veterans. The fourth section considers the extensive network of veterans' service organizations (VSOs) and philanthropic groups and their role in influencing policy at the VA. In the fifth through seventh sections the VA's oversight by the House and Senate committees on veterans' affairs is examined, along with the role of the states and other federal agencies in administering veterans' programs. In the final section I discuss how the VA's complex organizational ecology contributes to many of its contemporary policy failures, and I offer some thoughts on future challenges for the agency.

Early History and Development

The United States has always provided some form of assistance to its veterans. The early republic funded medical care for casualties of the American Revolution, while veterans of the Civil War found refuge in the network of National Homes for Disabled and Volunteer Soldiers (Kelly 1997). These early attempts at providing social services for veterans were relatively modest affairs, but they did offer an important lifeline for wounded veterans facing destitution. The most significant state contribution to veterans' welfare in the 19th century came in the form of government pensions. This program began as a way to compensate veterans for war-related injuries, but it was soon expanded to include all Union veterans (veterans of the Confederacy received no federal benefits), eventually becoming the largest government expenditure of the 19th century. By 1893 the United States was spending over 40 percent of its national budget on pensions for nearly one million Union veterans (Skocpol 1992). The generosity of these pensions was due in large part to the Grand Army of the Republic (GAR), the first organized veterans' lobby, which drew political power from its large membership and fierce loyalty to the Republican Party. These pensions undoubtedly supported many soldiers' families, but they also left some Americans skeptical about the value of providing such generous support when it seemed to be based on a corrupt bargain to serve political goals (Skocpol 1992). It was this distrust of veterans' pensions and other financial benefits that would shape veterans' policies after World War I.

Although there was no question that the United States would provide for the wounded soldiers of World War I, few legislators were anxious to re-create the system of Civil War pensions. The result was a small program, known as the Bureau of War Risk Insurance, which provided compensation for veterans' dependents and medical care in various public hospitals (Keene 2001). Able-bodied soldiers, however, received virtually nothing for their service in Europe aside from a train ticket home. A new veterans' organization, the American Legion, was born out of the frustration the new veterans felt about this situation. The Legion, along with the Veterans of Foreign Wars (VFW), pushed for a bonus bill—a direct cash compensation—ostensibly to compensate all veterans for income not made during war (Ortiz 2010). The Veterans Bureau itself took shape during this tumultuous period, and its early activities did not augur well for the future. The VA's first administrator, Col. Charles Forbes, was forced to resign in disgrace after he was found to have embezzled millions of dollars from the new agency (Longman 2007). In response to this scandal, the Veterans Bureau was reorganized as the Veterans Administration in 1930. It later gained cabinet-level status in 1989 and was renamed the Department of Veterans Affairs.

Congress did fund a bonus for veterans of World War I, but it was not due to be paid until 1945—a fact that offered little to comfort to veterans reeling from the Great Depression (Keene 2001, 180). The demand for an early bonus payment became one of the most controversial issues of the day. It led to a dramatic march on the capital in 1932 by disgruntled veterans from across the nation, a group that became known as the Bonus Army (Ortiz 2010). Despite this show of force, veterans did not find relief in Washington; the U.S. Army ejected them from the capital, and Franklin Roosevelt twice vetoed bills to provide immediate payment of the bonus. Congress, which was far more responsive to the plight of millions of veterans throughout the nation, eventually succeeded in overriding Roosevelt's veto and provided immediate bonus payments in 1936 (Ortiz 2010).

Postwar Development

Veterans would receive far more generous treatment after World War II. The experience of the Bonus March and the fear that millions of returning soldiers might face unemployment shaped the design of the Servicemen's Readjustment Act of 1944, better known as the G.I. Bill. This law represented an entirely new approach to veterans' compensation. Veterans no longer received a cash payment in the form of a pension or bonus; rather, they became eligible for programs designed to reintegrate them into American civilian life. It provided business, housing, and farm loans that were guaranteed by the government; money for living expenses and tuition at a college or university of the veteran's choosing; and healthcare for veterans who were wounded or were too poor to pay for their own care. Despite its relatively concise formulation, the G.I. Bill would become one of the most important pieces of social legislation in American history and would dramatically increase the career prospects and living standards of millions of American veterans (Mettler 2005). Yet as transformative as the G.I. Bill was for many veterans, African Americans and other minority veterans often faced discrimination in education and housing policies that made it difficult for them to use their benefits (Herbold 1994).

The extensive nature of the G.I. Bill's programs also led to an expansion of the size and scope of the VA. Some New Deal planners initially conceived of veterans' benefits as part of several national programs that would eventually be extended to all citizens. But as support for the New Deal began to wane, it became clear that this particular expansion of the welfare state would be restricted to veterans—and administered entirely by the VA. Although the VA at the time was poorly equipped to manage this broad array of programs in real estate, employment, and education, most VSOs demanded that the agency be given charge of the entire slate of new social services. Giving the VA sole responsibility, they thought, would make it far easier to guarantee that these services would be provided only to veterans. It was initially unclear how many veterans would take advantage of these opportunities, but the G.I. Bill quickly proved to be enormously popular—and enormously expensive. In fact, the G.I. Bill's education provisions were more costly than the entire Marshall Plan (1948–1951) to rebuild Europe (Frydl 2009).

The VA itself grew in size and importance as it began to manage these new G.I. Bill programs, designed to help all veterans achieve a prosperous middle-class life. Indeed, the existence of the VA made it considerably easier to expand veterans' programs in the future. Furthermore, as the locus of all services provided to veterans, the VA grew in popularity and political power. Although the VSOs remained powerful players in setting veterans' policy, the VA began to acquire its own institutional identity that was not reducible to the preferences of the many pressure groups concerned with veterans' legislation (Frydl 2009). With this historical background in place, we can now turn our attention to the VHA, one of the contemporary VA's two major divisions.

The Veterans Health Administration: Organization and Key Groups

The VHA is the largest division of the Department of Veterans Affairs. Growing from 54 hospitals as a division of the newly consolidated Veterans Administration in 1930 to its current 151 medical centers and 827 outpatient clinics, it is now the largest integrated healthcare system in the United States and among the largest in the world. Unlike other public American healthcare systems, such as Medicare and Medicaid, the VA is entirely owned and operated by the federal government. Healthcare is provided almost entirely free of charge to the 9.1 million veterans enrolled in the system, who receive comprehensive medical and dental care at the VA's hundreds of outpatient clinics (Bagalman 2014; Panangala 2015).

Two major changes in the structure of the VHA shaped its development in the postwar period. The first occurred after World War II in a move borne out of the need to provide an immediate boost to the quality of medical care given to veterans. Under the leadership of Gen. Omar Bradley, the VA created an unusual partnership with academic teaching hospitals. For its part, the VA agreed to build new hospitals near medical schools and to provide positions for faculty and medical residents, while medical schools agreed to help provide desperately needed staff at the new VA hospitals. The VSOs were initially skeptical about this development and feared that veterans would receive experimental care, or would only be admitted if they were found to have ailments that academic physicians deemed "medically interesting" (Moore 2015). Their opposition, however, did not lead to the defeat of this proposal, which quickly gained the support of medical schools and the top leadership at the VA.

This partnership became crucial to the success of academic medicine in the United States, and it resulted in medical schools becoming a major political ally of the VA. Today, it is difficult to imagine medical education and research in the absence of this partnership. Nearly 70 percent of all American physicians receive at least part of their training—as students or residents—at the VA (Department of Veterans Affairs 2015d). In 2013 alone, the VA supported over 40,000 residents, while nearly three in four VA staff clinicians hold an appointment at one of the affiliated medical schools (Heisler and Bagalman 2014). The VA is the second-largest federal payer of medical training, spending between $1.2 and $1.8 billion each year since 2010 (Heisler and Bagalman 2014). As this first transformative moment shows, by collaborating with academic medicine, the VA gained a politically powerful ally that was willing to defend it as a separate, government-run healthcare system.

The second major change in the structure of the VA occurred during its reorganization in the late 1990s. In 1996 President Bill Clinton signed the Veterans' Health Care Eligibility Reform Act (Public Law 104-262), which liberalized eligibility requirements and dramatically increased the number of middle-class veterans with access to VA healthcare. Formerly, care at VA facilities had been limited to veterans with service-connected injuries or to those veterans who were considered destitute. The 1996 changes established a priority group system for enrollment in the VA that allowed a broader, relatively wealthier set of veterans to seek medical care at VA facilities.

Under the current system, veterans in the first priority groups all have service-connected disabilities with ratings from 10 to 50 percent. These veterans usually receive immediate access to the VA system. Veterans with no service-connected injuries are placed in the next four priority groups, with the lowest priority groups (7–8) reserved for middle-income veterans with no service-connected injuries. To gain access to the VA system, veterans must have an income below the current threshold of about $40,000 for veterans with one dependent (Department of Veterans Affairs 2015a). In recent years, exceptions have been made for returning combat veterans from the wars in Iraq and Afghanistan that allow veterans to enroll without demonstrating financial need for up to five years. The result of these changes in eligibility, as well as the influx of veterans returning from Iraq and Afghanistan, has been a tremendous increase in the number of veterans enrolled in the VA. Although the total veteran population has declined by 17 percent over the last decade, the VA-enrolled veteran population has ballooned by 78 percent (Bagalman 2014). Despite these changes, the VA appears to be outperforming Medicare *and* private health providers in terms of cost and quality (Jha et al. 2003). Indeed, the story of the VA's expansion seems to indicate that a health system organized and managed by the federal government can deliver high-quality healthcare for those veterans enrolled in the system.

Why did this change come about? This question offers us an opportunity to see how the VA's grass roots influenced policy change. Prior to the 1996 reform of eligibility requirements, the VA faced an organizational crisis. As World War II veterans began to pass away, the VA was increasingly unable to fill its hospital beds. This problem was coupled with the fact that many older Americans had moved away from the Northeast to the Sunbelt states like Arizona and Florida (Longman 2007). Furthermore, the VA remained primarily an acute care hospital system, in which care was delivered almost entirely in VA medical centers, even as much of American medicine had begun to move to a community care model. In part, this was the result of its alliance with academic medical centers, which left VA care to be delivered primarily in large, urban medical centers, making it increasingly unable to serve veterans in rural areas or the rapidly developing states in the South. Moreover, the physicians on staff were primarily specialists, who were less interested in shifting the VA's focus to outpatient comprehensive care (Young 2001). Many in the VA had long recognized the need to make changes, and they were sensitive to the criticism lodged against them by prominent members of Congress, who were frustrated by the lack of access to VA facilities that many of their constituents faced.

The slow decline of the VA and the rise of external threats reached a crisis during the debate over a national healthcare system under President Clinton. At the time, both the new VA administrator, Jesse Brown, a combat-injured Marine and a former VSO official, and Rep. Sonny Montgomery (D-MS), the new chair of the House Committee on Veterans' Affairs, had planned large expansions of the VA healthcare system. Both Brown and Montgomery aggressively promoted the VA's plans to offer veterans a chance to "buy in" to the veterans system using private insurance or Medicaid funds (McAllister 1993). Even major VSOs were convinced that Clinton's arrival in office would herald major changes to veterans' healthcare, and there was no doubt among Clinton officials that veterans would be a crucial constituency to appease during the healthcare debate (Moore 2015).

The VSOs did not entirely disagree with this assessment, but they remained suspicious of plans that would open VA facilities to large numbers of nonveterans, a proposal made during the previous administration (Carswell 1992). Medical schools were not entirely supportive, either. Most academic hospitals were concerned that a focus on comprehensive care would threaten funding at the VA medical centers. To be sure, options for transforming the VA were limited by its foundational relationship with the academic medical community—one that had become impossible to disentangle without threatening the viability of the more than 100 American medical schools with VA affiliations. But VA officials found in this potential crisis an opportunity to shock the VSO constituent groups and medical schools into compromise and in the process to vastly expand their organization's size by changing eligibility requirements and opening access to all veterans. As one VA official presented the problem, "Two approaches could be pursued to increase the workload of VA hospitals and prevent or delay their closure. First, actions could be taken to attract a larger market share of the veteran population to the VA system, since now only about 20 percent of veterans have ever used VA care.... The second approach ... would be to authorize VA hospitals to treat dependents or other non-veterans on a reimbursable basis" (Baine 1996, 2). This proposal, of course, was anathema to the VSOs, which had worked to defend the VA as a veterans-only program at all costs. Nor was it the case that the VSOs universally supported eligibility expansion. As Gordon Mansfield, executive director of the Paralyzed Veterans of America (PVA), testified, "PVA believes many VA facility directors will be sorely tempted to reallocate some funding now provided to VA's special programs.... Their tendency is to exchange 'breadth for depth'—that is, to offer basic coverage to more of the veterans in their catchment area rather than offer comprehensive, well-integrated services to fewer" (Mansfield 1996, 170).

Notwithstanding the fears of some VSOs, the plan to reform the VA was signed into law in 1996, with strong Republican support. In fact, the eventual changes to the VA system were remarkably similar to the changes that had previously been proposed to integrate the veterans' health system into the Clinton healthcare plan and to attract more veterans to the VA. What, then, explains the support given to eligibility reform from some of the same Republicans who had blocked healthcare reform? Conservative support for VA reform was largely due to VA officials' ability to construct policy proposals that appealed to the political interests of congressional Republicans. The promise of hundreds of new VA clinics served as the common carrier for this policy innovation. In other words, Republican support for the VA's proposed conversion into an integrated primary care medical system was not due to the VA's reputation for medical competence, which was still rather poor before the late 1990s modernization, or pressure from outside interests, but to the tantalizing opportunity for new distributive benefits that committee Republicans found impossible to resist.

Not only did a shift to outpatient care solve a medical problem, it also solved a political problem for the VA and made its proposals extremely attractive to Republicans. One result of the VA's earlier decision to build hospitals next to medical centers meant that by the mid-1990s, with a few notable exceptions, its hospitals were located in urban areas serving urban, Democratic districts. Shifting the VA's focus to outpatient care not only made it more attractive to veterans; it also authorized the VA to expand its facilities into nearly every congressional district. Such changes were attractive to Republicans, because many rural districts and newly expanding communities in the South and Southwest had long been underserved by the VA's urban hospitals.

Along with this shift in enrollment priorities and a shift to outpatient care came new leadership. Dr. Kenneth Kizer was appointed to lead the VHA in 1994 during this transitional period, and he ushered in a variety of innovations, including more support for electronic medical records. Perhaps most controversial was his decision to shift VA management away from Washington to a series of regional networks that would link major VA medical centers with the network of community outpatient clinics that were then being constructed throughout the nation. In many cases, these new districts encompassed several states, a fact that frustrated many members of Congress, including Senator John D. Rockefeller IV, the powerful chair of the Senate Committee on Veterans' Affairs, who saw his own state of West Virginia split into five different regional districts—a move that also afforded the VA some further independence from Congress (Longman 2007).

This brief overview of the VHA reveals the political power of the many pressure groups concerned with veterans' healthcare, but it also demonstrates that the VA is not "captured" by its grass roots. The co-optation of academic medical centers surely contributed to the VA's organizational power over many years, but it also may have contributed to the VA's neglect of the changing needs of many veterans. The most recent shift to outpatient care was not necessarily supported by the VSOs or the academic medical community. The primary force behind the change was the VA itself, which saw its own long-term viability threatened by the possibility of national healthcare reform and the hostility it faced from congressional Republicans. Although there can be no doubt that veterans' policy is shaped in key ways by its network of grassroots organizations, the bureaucracy exercised considerable autonomy in the post–World War II era as it formed partnerships with academic hospitals and during the 1990s as it transformed itself into an integrated healthcare system.

Veterans Benefits Administration: Organization and Key Groups

The VBA which today manages a vast array of educational and benefit programs for veterans through its 300 veterans' centers and 56 regional offices, has been a core component of the VA since the VBA's formation in 1930. Many of the current programs, from pensions for disabled veterans to mortgage assistance, grew out of the initial set of benefits provided by the G.I. Bill. These programs continue to provide significant assistance to millions of veterans at various stages of their lives. In addition, as the number and scope of programs has expanded, new interests have emerged and become deeply invested in the administration of certain veterans' programs.

One significant legacy of the G.I. Bill is the VA-insured home loan program, which often allows veterans to purchase homes with no down payment at all and contributed to an explosion of housing construction after World War II (Frydl 2009). Since it was first enacted in 1944, the VA has guaranteed 21 million loans, making it a major player in the real estate industry. In 2013 alone, the VA guaranteed 630,000 new mortgages—and 90 percent of these homes were purchased with no money down (Prevost 2014). The program is generous enough to be beneficial to veterans of all income groups. The current mortgage limit for a VA loan ranges from $417,500 in less expensive areas to $1,094,625 in the most costly real estate markets (Prevost 2014).

It will come as no surprise that the real estate industry is among the biggest supporters of the VA's mortgage policies. The National Association of Realtors, for example, provides vigorous support for mortgage guarantees and recently lobbied Congress for an increase in the maximum guaranteed loan (National Association of Realtors 2015). As with medicine, then, the VA's involvement in real estate evinces its ability to co-opt new industries as its programmatic reach expands.

Undoubtedly the most significant program to come out of the 1944 G.I. Bill was its education benefit. At the time, few legislators realized how many former service members would take advantage of this initiative or how important it would be in their lives. Although it is often thought of today as the signature policy of the G.I. Bill, some universities were not initially in favor of federal support for veterans to attend college. The presidents of two of the nation's most famous universities, James Conant of Harvard and Robert Hutchins of the University of Chicago, opposed it, fearing that it would force American universities to admit unprepared students who were attracted to this opportunity because they were unable to find gainful employment elsewhere (Olson 1974).

Despite some initial opposition, most colleges and universities soon came to welcome this additional federal support, which offered significant opportunities for university expansion. Indeed, most universities were so anxious to attract veterans that they began to modify admissions policies and to offer remedial or refresher courses to accommodate returning soldiers who had no high school diploma (Olson 1974). The benefit of these education programs can hardly be overstated. In all, over 2.2 million veterans of World War II attended college under the G.I. Bill. Not only did these millions of veterans receive an advanced education that would have been impossible for them to afford without the G.I. Bill, the experience of attending college and receiving this support from the VA also led them to become the most civically minded generation in American history (Mettler 2005).

The education provisions of the G.I. Bill led the VA to become a key funder of higher education (Olson 1974). Consequently, colleges and universities, much like academic medical centers, became major players in the formation of veterans' policy. Despite some disputes over the costs of tuition, the G.I. Bill allowed universities to support larger faculties and graduate programs—and this led them to support the VA and to lobby Congress to continue the generous tuition benefits for later generations of veterans. The G.I. Bill, in other words, led universities to become yet another interest co-opted by the VA. Yet as we will see, their interests would occasionally conflict with those of the VSOs and the VA's other grassroots supporters.

Today, the education benefit is an essential tool to fund higher education and to provide the wherewithal for thousands of veterans to attend college. The post-9/11 G.I. Bill, which became effective in August 2009, is similar to past benefits. It provides for in-state tuition (or $19,000 for private colleges and universities) and a monthly housing allowance for 36 months of education (Dortch 2014). In 2013 the VA spent $10.2 billion to support 754,529 veterans in postsecondary education and training programs (Dortch 2014). Recently the VA has established the Yellow Ribbon G.I. Educational Enhancement Program to cover situations in which tuition and fees are not fully covered by G.I. Bill benefits. In these cases, the VA will split the difference with private universities between tuition and the maximum VA benefit, allowing most veterans to attend the school of their choice.

Despite the tremendous success of this program, the VA-educational partnership has long been haunted by a history of abuse by unscrupulous schools offering worthless degrees. One historian estimates that nearly $14.5 billion spent on the educational provisions of the original postwar G.I. Bill went to fraudulent programs or training hoaxes (Frydl 2009, 8). Although such blatant abuse is rare today, recent controversies have arisen over the role of for-profit colleges and the quality of education that many veterans receive. Consequently, some members of Congress have proposed restricting the revenue that private for-profit colleges and universities may earn from federal funds to no more than 90 percent (Dortch 2014).

Unlike education, disability benefits have a far more controversial history, one that reflects the same fear of corruption or abuse that has haunted veterans' benefits since the Civil War. In the post-Vietnam era, one of the VA's most contentious decisions was whether or not disability pensions ought to be granted to those service members exposed to Agent Orange, an herbicide sprayed over the jungles of Vietnam. Initially, many of the claims made by these veterans were denied because their symptoms appeared years or decades after their exposure. Congress held several hearings from the late 1970s through the 1980s on the issue of Agent Orange. After years of debate, a series of laws was enacted granting disability payments to many of these veterans under the presumption that their exposure to this chemical was responsible for their diseases (Agent Orange Act of 1991, Public Law 102-4).

The Agent Orange cases created a flashpoint between the VA and the VSOs—and represented a significant victory for the VSOs. In many cases, veterans today merely need to demonstrate exposure to the chemical and do not need to show that their specific disease was caused by their service (Panangala 2014). The Agent Orange controversy also reveals the complex process through which different stakeholders contribute to such disability decisions, which usually involve Congress, the VA, the prestigious Institute of Medicine, and many VSOs (Panangala 2014). In this case, the role of VSOs in advocating for these veterans was crucial, because the VA, Congress, and much of the medical establishment were initially skeptical of many veterans' claims that their exposure to Agent Orange caused their illnesses.

In more recent years, the VA has been criticized for being too quick to grant disability benefits to veterans returning from Iraq and Afghanistan. Since 2001, for example, the overall cost of disability pensions has almost tripled to nearly $60 billion, and some have claimed that the program's generosity discourages veterans from seeking work (Philipps 2015). The most controversial part of this program is the "Individual Unemployability" provision, which allows veterans to receive full disability compensation even when the VA has rated their service-connected disabilities below 100 percent. To qualify for this program, a veteran's disabilities must leave him or her unable to be permanently employed. In addition, the veteran must have one service-connected disability with a 60 percent rating or two disabilities with a combined rating of at least 70 percent (Department of Veterans Affairs 2015b). Even some veterans have criticized the current system for being open to abuse and fraud. According to these veterans, an overly permissive disability program will provoke a backlash from the public when the cost becomes too high or when significant fraud or abuse is exposed (Harbaugh 2015).

Veterans' Service Organizations and Philanthropic Groups

Interest groups are fundamental to all areas of American politics, but they play a particularly important role in veterans' politics. To be sure, many industries have close ties to their funding and regulatory agencies, but veterans' organizations are embedded into the very organizational structure of the VA itself. Many of the oldest and most established groups have congressional charters that give them official status as places to assist veterans in making disability claims or gaining access to the healthcare system. Yet the VSOs are not a unified bloc, and they have not necessarily "captured" the VA despite their close relationship to its bureaucracy. In part, this is because they are not the only interests involved in veterans' policy (see the earlier discussion of the healthcare industry, universities, and the real estate industry), but also because the VSOs—which number in the hundreds—represent a broad spectrum of interests, generations, demographic profiles, and ideological perspectives (Department of Veterans Affairs 2014a). For example, should wounded veterans get priority treatment at VA hospitals? How well does the VA serve women or minorities? Should the VA concentrate its resources on the needs of older, retired veterans or younger veterans who need help buying a home and attending college? Each VSO is likely to have a slightly different answer to even these very basic questions about veterans' policy.

Traditional VSOs, led by the American Legion and the Veterans of Foreign Wars, have long focused on a broad expansion of benefits for all veterans. As previous sections have detailed, they have worked to maintain the VA as a separate, veterans-only agency, and have pushed for generous benefits in education, healthcare, and disability pensions. At the same time, however, these stalwarts of veterans' activism have been criticized for being too politically conservative and overly concerned with the needs of the World War II generation. As a result, each generation of veterans has created its own advocacy organizations. The Wounded Warrior Project, for example, focuses specifically on the needs of young veterans in post-9/11 conflicts.

As the military itself has become more diverse, the VSOs have grown to reflect that diversity. Along with traditional organizations that focus on expanding benefits to all veterans, newer VSOs often concentrate on the interests of a specific set of veterans. Some of the most prominent include American Women Veterans, which has concentrated its advocacy efforts on preventing sexual assault in the military. Other VSOs were formed to represent specific racial and ethnic groups, such as the Asian American Veterans Association and Black Veterans of America. Minorities and marginalized groups have made particularly effective use of their VSOs to lobby the military and the VA for changes. For example, well before the military's "Don't Ask, Don't Tell" policy was repealed in 2011, gay and lesbian veterans formed the American Military Partner Association to advocate for the rights of lesbian, gay, bisexual, and transgender (LGBT) soldiers, sailors, marines, and airmen.

While VSOs traditionally come together to defend the most fundamental of veterans' benefits, their interests do conflict at times. For example, the PVA feared the VA's plans to move to an outpatient system of delivering healthcare, which was supported by other VSOs (Mansfield 1996). In other cases, certain VSOs may push an agenda that the others find objectionable, such as the American Military Partner Association's work on securing veterans' benefits for LGBT veterans. In addition to their advocacy for veterans and oversight of the VA, many VSOs have supported a wide variety of philanthropic missions. The issues they focus on reflect a great deal of ideological diversity, from the more conservative VSOs that advocate for a strong national defense to liberal organizations, like the Vietnam Veterans of America, which works to remove landmines throughout the world.

The ultimate effect of this diverse set of organizational interests is quite simple: there is no such thing as a single, unified "veterans' lobby." The networks of VSOs are as diverse and complex as the United States itself. Consequently, the VA retains a certain degree of autonomy from the VSOs, in part because it remains the central node of communication and organization for all veterans' issues.

House and Senate Veterans' Affairs Committees

Along with the diverse set of interest groups, veterans' policy and the VA are unique in another respect: two veterans-specific congressional committees oversee the agency. The move to manage all veterans' issues with one oversight committee in each house of the U.S. Congress was authorized as part of the Legislative Reorganization Act of 1946. After World War II, as the VA grew into a much larger organization handling all services for veterans, the committees in the House and Senate were created to reflect this change. The House and Senate Committees on Veterans' Affairs both recommend all legislation relating to veterans' benefits and have general oversight responsibility for the VA itself. As the House Committee frankly states, "If the Committee finds that the VA is not administering laws as Congress intended, then it is 'corrected' through the hearing process and legislation. We are the voice of Congress for veterans in dealings with the VA" (U.S. House of Representatives, Committee on Veterans' Affairs 2015).

This unique organizational structure has led some observers to conclude that the VA and its congressional committees are part of a classic "iron triangle," which suggests that all aspects of veterans' policies and the VA itself are controlled by the VSOs and the House and Senate committees (Evans

1995). Such accounts often incorrectly assume that the VA merely serves the interests of the members of these committees, who hope to curry favor with the various VSOs and direct spending to their districts. Yet many of the VA's actions are difficult to square with this conventional wisdom. For example, some committee members, most notably Senator Jay Rockefeller of West Virginia, were against aspects of the VA's reorganization plan in the 1990s, but were powerless to stop it (Longman 2007). Even the original decision to ally with academic medical centers was opposed by some members of Congress, who wanted their committees to retain exclusive control over the location of new VA hospitals (Moore 2015). Furthermore, the classic iron triangle model assumes that the committee has one clear and distinct interest, but members of both the House and Senate are often cross-pressured by different VSOs.

Nevertheless, the two committees are often champions of expanded veterans' benefits, and both were sites of significant bipartisan cooperation for much of the post–World War II era. Even in our current era of extreme congressional polarization, Democrats and Republicans have come together to ensure that veterans are getting the benefits and the healthcare that they deserve. In 2014, for example, Senate veterans' committee chair Bernie Sanders (I-VT)—perhaps the most liberal member of the Senate—and House chair Jeff Sessions (R-FL) agreed to a legislative solution after the VA was found to be unable to offer timely appointments to veterans. After a surprisingly quick bipartisan negotiation, Sanders and Sessions agreed to grant the agency a $16.3 billion increase in funding, with $5 billion dedicated to hiring new physicians and staff nurses (Matishak 2014).

Finally, evidence for a true "iron triangle," wherein committee members leave Congress to work for VSOs or other organizations that deal with concerns related to veterans' policy, is rather weak. In fact, as data from the Center for Responsive Politics (2015) suggest, relatively few former members or their staffers seek employment from VSOs or the VA. Although there is evidence that some former staff members have gone to work for companies doing business with the VA, such as TriWest Healthcare Alliance, which administers some Veterans Choice programs, such cases are few and far between (Center for Responsive Politics 2015).

Federalism and the VA: State Agencies

As if veterans' policy were not complicated enough, the VA and many of its programs are also administered in partnership with the 50 states. Sadly, there is a darker legacy of the federated nature of veterans' benefits that comes out of the G.I. Bill provisions after World War II. In some cases, the federated nature of G.I. Bill education and housing benefits stemmed from efforts by southern politicians to deny African Americans benefits (Frydl 2009). Schools that otherwise would not admit African Americans were not forced to do so. Banks that would not lend money to African Americans were allowed to continue that practice (Frydl 2009).

Today, these state-level veterans' agencies provide additional political access points for veterans' interest groups, a fact that has contributed to the lobbying success of veterans, who not only have opportunities to influence veterans' policy at the federal level, but remain important players at the state level. Every state has a corresponding veterans' office, providing services as simple as specialized license plates and as complex as enforcing employment benefits for civil service positions, as well as other special benefits such as grants to remodel the homes of disabled veterans. Some of these services exist in cooperation with federal programs, such as the State Veterans Nursing Home (SVNH) initiative, which provides veterans with long-term care facilities in select states (Panangala 2015). The federated nature of veterans' programs, then, adds 50 important interests to the already crowded universe of veterans' groups.

The VA and Other Federal Agencies

The VA's resources and the scope of its mandate require it to coordinate policies and programs with the Department of Defense (DoD). Although collaboration between these two massive agencies is rarely perfect, both the DoD and the VA have made strides in recent years to improve their efforts, in some cases because changes in the law have required that they do so. For example, disabled service members were once forced to choose between VA disability benefits and their military retirement (Congressional Budget Office 2013). Since a change in the law in 2004, however, they are now eligible for retirement pay *and* VA benefits if they receive a VA disability rating that is greater than 50 percent (Defense Finance and Accounting Service 2015). This is just one example of the complex coordination efforts that are necessary to assure that disabled service members experience a smooth transition into retirement.

In addition to retirement benefits, the VA and the DoD have several joint programs to provide medical services and training, such as coordination around electronic health records, initiatives on amputee care, and mental health research (Department of Defense 2013). The VA has also used its network of hospitals and its extensive research capacity to assist the National Institutes of Health. Recently, both agencies embarked on a five-year study to explore nondrug approaches to chronic pain management at

VA hospitals and their allied academic medical centers (National Institutes of Health 2014).

Finally, through its National Cemetery Administration (NCA), the VA maintains over 3.4 million gravesites at 133 national cemeteries (Department of Veterans Affairs 2015c). The NCA also manages 14 historical cemeteries in partnership with the National Park Service and the American Battle Monuments Commission. Among the most significant of these is the Antietam National Cemetery, where 4,776 Union soldiers from the Battle of Antietam and other Civil War battles in Maryland are buried (National Park Service 2015). The fact that these national parks are also cemeteries requires the VA and the National Park Service to coordinate their visitation and burial policies. The VA's extensive partnerships with these other federal agencies is yet another illustration of the diverse interests that are involved in veterans' programs.

Contemporary Policy Failures and Future Challenges

The vast array of benefits, diverse set of missions, and complex organizational ecology contribute to the VA's political strength and also to its numerous policy failures. Two recent problems highlight these vulnerabilities. The first concerns a huge backlog in disability claims, a problem created, in part, by shifting requirements for eligibility, as well as the number of wounded veterans returning from Iraq and Afghanistan. In response to an outcry from Congress and various VSOs, the VA has made a concerted effort to work through its backlog. Even with additional resources, the VA still had almost 100,000 claims outstanding in August 2015 (Department of Veterans Affairs 2015f), and many of the claims were resolved incorrectly. A recent report concluded that the VA provided nearly $85 million in medical benefits between 2012 and 2014 to veterans who were ineligible (Department of Veterans Affairs 2014b). Despite these problems, much has been done to simplify this process for veterans, and most need only fill out a straightforward form (VA Form 10-10EZ), easily available online, that asks various questions about military service and finances and checks the veteran's record of service.

The VA's more pressing problem is its inability to accommodate all veterans who are eligible for healthcare. In the early 2000s, at the same time the VA was restructuring to attract older, retired veterans in need of comprehensive community care, the wars in Iraq and Afghanistan meant that thousands of wounded veterans were also entering the system. The result of this "perfect storm" was that veterans who were otherwise eligible to receive care had to wait for up to 115 days in some cases. The situation was made even worse by the deceptive practices of some senior officials, who falsified appointment records to hide the facts—a situation that was finally exposed at the Phoenix VA Medical Center in the spring of 2014 (Wagner 2014).

Congress responded to this crisis by providing more funding to hire new physicians and nurses at VA hospitals. It also inaugurated a new Veterans Choice Program, which allows veterans to receive care from non-VA doctors. This program is open to veterans who have been waiting more than 30 days for VA care, live more than 40 miles from a VA medical facility or can demonstrate that traveling to a VA medical facility would impose excessive burdens (Panangala 2015). Although it is still a small program, Veterans Choice may have long-term effects on veterans' healthcare, as the private insurance companies that administer it join the many other interest groups that have a vested interest in the VA. In this way, the advent of Veterans Choice introduces yet another interest into the complex web of organizations surrounding the VA.

Although the Patient Protection and Affordable Care Act (ACA) of 2010 does not affect VA care directly, it does present an opportunity to open the VA system to *all* veterans and their immediate dependents. To pay for this increased enrollment, Congress could embrace a policy that many VSOs have long requested: authorize the VA to bill Medicare and private providers for VA healthcare services. Such a policy would give all veterans access to VA healthcare while maintaining the VA's commitment to medical education and research. It would make the VA a true public option for America's 23.1 million veterans.

Many of the VA's successes, as well as some of its most notable policy failures, can be understood through the unusually diverse array of groups that influence all levels of this complex and organizationally diverse bureaucracy. The VA's own grass roots, in short, have in some cases increased its organizational strength vis-à-vis Congress and competing interests. Many of the examples examined in this chapter have looked at the VA's propensity for co-optation—not only co-optation of many of the traditional veterans' groups, but also its propensity to seek out new constituencies, from academic medical centers and the real estate industry in the 1940s, to a new set of rural and Republican legislators in the 1990s. Although each of these interests plays a central role in the formation of veterans' policy, the sheer diversity of the VA's organizational environment has meant that no lone interest has ever dominated veterans' policy. This has contributed to the VA's remarkable autonomy, allowing it to defend itself against political attacks and to chart its own course. It may also help us understand its surprising resilience in the face of several major policy failures.

Although the VA's ability to co-opt numerous interests means that it is unlikely to be downsized or privatized in the foreseeable future, the very diversity of its grass roots too often leaves it disconnected from the veterans it was designed to serve. Unfortunately, this has increased the perception among some veterans that the VA is more interested in supporting medical research programs and working on its own organizational survival than it is in helping veterans. To regain the trust of veterans, the VA will need to demonstrate that, despite its size and complexity, it is capable of moving swiftly to support veterans in need. Only then will it fulfill its mission—one inspired by Abraham Lincoln's second inaugural address: "To care for him who shall have borne the battle, and for his widow, and his orphan."

References

Bagalman, Erin. 2014. "The Number of Veterans That Use VA Health Care Services: A Fact Sheet." June 3, Congressional Research Service.

Baine, David P. 1996. "Veterans' Health Care: Challenges for the Future." Testimony before the House Committee on Veterans' Affairs. Washington, DC: General Accounting Office.

Carswell, John. 1992. "Health Reform and the VA Medical Care System." *Journal of American Health Policy* 2 (6): 17–21.

Center for Responsive Politics. 2015. "Revolving Door." Accessed August 15, 2015. https://www.opensecrets.org/revolving.

Congressional Budget Office. 2013. "Options for Reducing the Deficit: 2014 to 2023." Accessed November 22, 2015. https://www.cbo.gov/budget-options/2013/44744.

Defense Finance and Accounting Service. 2015. "Concurrent Retirement and Disability Pay." Accessed November 24, 2015. http://www.dfas.mil/retiredmilitary/disability/crdp.html.

Department of Defense. 2013. "DoD and Department of Veterans Affairs (VA) Health Care Resource Sharing Program." Accessed November 24, 2015. http://www.dtic.mil/whs/directives/corres/pdf/601023p.pdf.

Department of Veterans Affairs. 1991. *Report of the Commission on the Future Structure of Veterans Health Care*. Washington, DC: Department of Veterans Affairs.

Department of Veterans Affairs. 2014a. *Directory: Veterans and Military Service Organizations*. Washington, DC: Department of Veterans Affairs.

Department of Veterans Affairs. 2014b. "Follow-Up Audit of 100 Percent Disability Evaluation." June 6. Accessed August 10, 2015. http://www.va.gov/oig/pubs/VAOIG-14-01686-185.pdf.

Department of Veterans Affairs. 2015a. "Annual Income Thresholds—Health Benefits." Accessed August 12, 2015. http://nationalincomelimits.vaftl.us.

Department of Veterans Affairs. 2015b. "Compensation." Accessed August 12, 2015. http://www.benefits.va.gov/compensation/claims-special-individual_unemployability.asp.

Department of Veterans Affairs. 2015c. "Facts about the National Cemetery Administration." Accessed November 15, 2015. http://www.cem.va.gov/cem/docs/factsheets/facts.pdf.

Department of Veterans Affairs. 2015d. "Mission of the Office of Academic Affiliations." Accessed August 20, 2015. http://www.va.gov/oaa/specialfellows/default.asp.

Department of Veterans Affairs. 2015e. "Office of the Budget." Accessed August 20, 2015. http://www.va.gov/budget/products.asp.

Department of Veterans Affairs. 2015f. "Veterans Benefit Administration Reports." Accessed August 10, 2015. http://benefits.va.gov/REPORTS/index.asp.

Dortch, Cassandria. 2014. "The Post-9/11 Veterans Educational Assistance Act of 2008 (Post-9/11 GI Bill): Primer and Issues." *Congressional Research Service*, July 28.

Evans, C. Lawrence. 1995. "Committees and Health Jurisdictions in Congress." In *Intensive Care: How Congress Shapes Health Policy*, edited by Thomas E. Mann and Norman J. Ornstein, 25–51. Washington, DC: American Enterprise Institute and Brookings Institution Press.

Frydl, Kathleen J. 2009. *The GI Bill*. New York: Cambridge University Press.

Harbaugh, Ken. 2015. "The Risk of Over-Thanking Our Veterans." *New York Times*, June 1, A19.

Heisler, Elayne J., and Erin Bagalman. 2014. "The Veterans Health Administration and Medical Education: A Fact Sheet." *Congressional Research Service*, June 6.

Herbold, Hilary. 1994. "Never a Level Playing Field: Blacks and the G.I. Bill." *Journal of Blacks in Higher Education* (Winter): 104–108.

Jha, Ashish K., Jonathan B. Perlin, Kenneth W. Kizer, and R. Adams Dudley. 2003. "Effect of the Transformation of the Veterans Affairs Health Care System on the Quality of Care." *New England Journal of Medicine* 348 (22): 2218–2227.

Keene, Jennifer D. 2001. *Doughboys, the Great War, and the Remaking of America*. Baltimore, MD: Johns Hopkins University Press.

Kelly, Patrick J. 1997. *Creating a National Home: Building the Veterans' Welfare State, 1860–1900*. Cambridge, MA: Harvard University Press.

Klein, Robert. 1981. *Wounded Men, Broken Promises*. New York: Macmillan.

Longman, Phillip. 2007. *Best Care Anywhere: Why VA Health Care Is Better Than Yours*. Sausalito, CA: PoliPointPress.

Mansfield, Gordon. 1996. "Future of the Veterans Health Administration." Testimony before the House Committee on Veterans' Affairs, June 26 and 27. 104th Cong.

Matishak, Martin. 2014. "Obama Signs VA Reform Bill into Law." *The Hill*, August 7.

McAllister, Bill. 1993. "Expanded VA Care System Proposed." *Washington Post*, March 6, A4.

Mettler, Suzanne. 2005. *Soldiers to Citizens: The G.I. Bill and the Making of the Greatest Generation*. New York: Oxford University Press.

Moore, Colin D. 2015. "Innovation without Reputation: How Bureaucrats Saved the Veterans' Health Care System." *Perspectives on Politics* 13 (2): 327–344.

National Association of Realtors. 2015. "Veterans Affairs." Accessed August 25, 2015. http://www.realtor.org/topics/veterans-affairs.

National Institutes of Health. 2014. "NIH and VA Address Pain and Related Conditions in U.S. Military Personnel, Veterans, and Their Families." Accessed November 16, 2015. http://www.nih.gov/news-events/news-releases/nih-va-address-pain-related-conditions-us-military-personnel-veterans-their-families.

National Park Service. 2015. "Antietam National Cemetery." Accessed November 20, 2015. http://www.nps.gov/anti/learn/historyculture/antietam-national-cemetery.htm.

Olson, Keith W. 1974. *The G.I. Bill, the Veterans, and the Colleges*. Lexington: University of Kentucky Press.

Ortiz, Stephan R. 2010. *Beyond the Bonus March and the GI Bill: How Veteran Politics Shaped the New Deal*. New York: New York University Press.

Panangala, Sidath Viranga. 2014. "Veterans Affairs: Presumptive Service Connection and Disability Compensation." *Congressional Research Service*, November 14.

Panangala, Sidath Viranga. 2015. "Health Care for Veterans: Answers to Frequently Asked Questions." *Congressional Research Service*, April 30.

Philipps, Dave. 2015. "Iraq Veteran, Now a West Point Professor, Seeks to Rein in Disability Pay." *New York Times*, January 8, A1.

Prevost, Lisa. 2014. "A Big Year for V.A. Loans." *New York Times*, January 9, RE7.

Selznick, Philip. 1949. *The TVA and the Grass Roots: A Study in the Sociology of Formal Organization*. Berkeley: University of California Press.

Skocpol, Theda. 1992. *Protecting Soldiers and Mothers*. Cambridge, MA: Belknap Press of Harvard University Press.

U.S. House of Representatives, Committee on Veterans' Affairs. 2015. "History and Jurisdiction." Accessed August 14, 2015. https://veterans.house.gov/about/history-jurisdiction.

Veterans Administration. 1946. "Policy in Association of Veterans' Hospitals With Medical Schools." January 30. VA Policy Memorandum No. 2 Accessed March 3, 2014. http://www.va.gov/oaa/Archive/PolicyMemo2.pdf.

Wagner, Dennis. 2014. "Deaths at Phoenix VA Hospital May Be Tied to Delayed Care." *Arizona Republic*, April 10.

Young, Gary J. 2001. "Transforming the Veterans Health Administration: The Revitalization of the VHA." In *Transforming Organizations*, edited by Mark A. Abramson and Paul R. Lawrence, 139–172. Lanham, MD: Rowman & Littlefield.

CHAPTER SIX

The Job Training of Veterans

Bruce D. McDonald III, Myung H. Jin, Susan Camilleri, and Vincent Reitano

Introduction

This chapter focuses on job training programs and services provided to veterans in the United States. Although job training programs are similar to the educational programs that are provided to veterans, there are distinct differences. Whereas educational programs focus on assisting veterans with earning a university degree (Angrist 1993; Smole 2008), job training programs are directed toward preparing veterans to enter the workforce with a vocation or skill (Veterans Benefits Administration 2014). The outcome of such training is typically the receipt of a job certification, such as a mechanic's or nursing license, or journeyman status in a trade or craft, such as carpentry. Many job training programs for veterans also provide basic career skills in such areas as résumé writing, interviewing, and job searching (Veterans Benefits Administration 2015a).

In this chapter we seek to provide a thorough understanding of the job training programs available to veterans by looking at what programs are in existence, how they are organized, and how they are implemented. A number of federal programs provide in-service and postservice assistance to veterans in this capacity. In-service programs are provided by the U.S. Department of Defense (DoD), whose components provide the on-the-job training that service members receive in skills that are both critical to military success and useful to their careers after completion of their service (Borjas and Welch 1986; Cardell et al. 1997; Heo and Eger 2005). The

DoD also provides a transition program that helps service members acclimate to civilian life (Cronk 2012; Transition to Veterans Program Office 2014). Once a service member's term of service is completed, jurisdiction of veterans' job training is handed over to the U.S. Department of Veterans Affairs (VA). The programs overseen by the VA fall into three broad categories: general programs, which focus on the transition into civilian life; programs for veterans with service-connected disabilities, which aim to help veterans overcome their disabilities so as to pursue their desired employment; and competitive grants, which fund employment-oriented programs at the state and local levels (Collins et al. 2014). A summary of the programs covered in this chapter is provided in table 6.1.

As with educational programs, underlying the provision of job training is a dual interest. On the one hand, the DoD utilizes the training and experience service members receive during their service and the opportunities for additional training after the completion of service as an incentive for enlistment (McDonald 2011, 2013). In periods of economic growth, potential candidates for enlistment have more career options, increasing the importance of such incentives. On the other hand, there is a national mood demanding that "we take care of our own" (Obama 2012). This mood includes the belief that offering job training, as with other veterans' services, is the least that the country can do for those who risk their lives for the common good.

While both rationales do have the ring of truth, an examination of the history of the programs reveals that they are more economically driven. Since the end of World War II the United States has undertaken the role of trainer and educator of veterans after the completion of their military service (Angrist 1993; Bound and Turner 2002). Initially, the responsibility was economically driven: too many service members were returning from war, and their reintroduction into the workforce would have overwhelmed the mobilized economy (Bound and Turner 2002). In economic terms, the programs were a success. The nation entered a period of economic growth, and the effects of 16 million veterans being integrated into the civilian labor force were spread out over several years (Olson 1973).

Regardless of intent, the successful employment of veterans has remained a key concern to members of Congress and the broader public (Collins et al. 2014). According to the Bureau of Labor Statistics (2015), the unemployment rate for veterans who served in the U.S. armed forces since September 2001 is higher than that for nonveterans of the same age. In 2014 there were 21.2 million noninstitutionalized veterans in the United States, of whom only 10.7 million (about 50.6 percent) were in the civilian labor force. The remaining 10.5 million veterans remained

The Job Training of Veterans

Table 6.1. Job Training Programs for Veterans.

Program	Provider	Description
Transition Assistance Program (TAP)	DoD	Provides services to exiting service members in the transition to civilian life.
Transition Goals Plans Success (Transition GPS)	DoD	Updates TAP and offered services in cooperation with the U.S. Departments of Veterans Affairs, Labor, and Homeland Security, as well as the Small Business Administration. Program requires all exiting service members to attend.
Vocational Rehabilitation and Employment (VR&E)	VA	Provides funding for training to veterans with service-connected disabilities in pursuit of employment.
Educational Benefits (G.I. Bills)	VA	Provides financial assistance for veterans to pursue vocational and training programs.
Veterans Retraining Assistance Program (VRAP)	VA	Provides financial assistance to veterans not eligible for the G.I. Bill to pursue training in high-demand skills and vocations.
Veterans' Employment and Training Services (VETS)	Labor	Independent agency; coordinates the department's efforts on veteran employment.
Jobs for Veterans State Grant (JVSG)	VA	Administers grants for states to employ veteran-related personnel positions.
Local Veterans Employment Representative (LVER)	VA	Formula grant; funds personnel positions in state government that assist veterans pursuing employment.
Disabled Veterans Outreach Program (DVOP)	VA	Formula grant; funds personnel positions in state government that assist disabled and other high-needs veterans pursuing employment.

outside the labor force for a variety of reasons, including disability, retirement, and individual choice. The ratio of veterans outside the labor force to the entire population far exceeds that of nonveterans, which has led to concerns that the established efforts have been ineffective, thus warranting investigation into what programs are currently available. Ultimately, the efforts for job training are perceived as successful, with nearly 68,000 veterans participating in vocational training activities in 2013 (Office of Public Affairs 2014).

This chapter is structured as follows. Following this introduction to the issue, we turn our attention to the details of service provision. This begins with an overview of the organizations involved in providing veteran job training and the roles and responsibilities they each maintain. Next we focus on the organization and implementation of the in-service programs provided by the DoD, followed by sections on the postservice programs provided by the VA and others. We conclude with a summary of key points on the issue, giving particular attention to the success and failure of veteran training programs in the United States.

Who Provides Training

One of the difficulties faced by veterans in receiving job training is the lack of a consistent, centrally located provider. Primary responsibility for job training lies with the DoD and VA; however, multiple joint initiatives and programs have greatly expanded the number of organizations involved (Transition to Veterans Program Office 2014). While this expansion does provide more opportunities for training, an increase in the number of organizations involved in the provision of public services has been linked to increases in the inefficiencies of the service due to coordination difficulties (Feiock 2007). It may also create uncertainty for veterans about where to turn for the services they need. In this section we discuss which organizations are involved in the provision of job training services.

Informally, the defense sector of the United States has always maintained responsibility for the training of veterans in the form of human capital investments (McDonald 2011). The investments made by this sector are the largest, unified investment in human capital in the country (Bryant and Wilhite 1990). Although not conducted with the explicit intention of supporting postservice employment for service members, the sector has relied on this investment as an incentive for enlistment (McDonald 2013) and as evidence of its efforts dedicated to preparing service members for careers as veterans (Hall et al. 2014). With regard to the latter, the defense sector provides a pathway to a career for service members involved in duties that require the use of advanced technology, as well as for those who participate in the application of directly transferrable skills such as medicine and machinery (Heo and Eger 2005; McDonald and Eger 2010). While such spillovers do exist, the income divide between veterans and nonveterans suggests that the utility of military skills outside the national defense context is greatly overestimated by people working in national defense. Thus, while in-service job training is provided to service members with the intention of its having postservice employment utility, there is little evidence to suggest that these efforts are successful (Bound and Turner 2002; Bryan 2010; McDonald 2011, 2013). In the form of training, the defense sector has provided career counseling and transition assistance to service members at the end of their military service (Transition to Veterans Program Office 2014). Recent changes to the program have made attendance mandatory for exiting service members and have also made the program a collaborative effort across multiple agencies (Collins et al. 2012; Collins et al. 2014).

Formally, the responsibility for postservice veterans' programs lies with the VA. Established in its present form in 1988, the mission of the VA is "to provide benefits and services to Veterans and their families in a responsive, timely, and compassionate manner in recognition of their service to the Nation" (Riley et al. 2014, 1-1). Though some training-related services are provided by the department under the G.I. Bill, its training efforts are primarily coordinated under the Vocational Rehabilitation and Employment (VR&E) program. The VA's direct service provision in job training, however, is limited (Collins et al. 2012). The department focuses the majority of its attention on health-related issues, which has an influence on its job training efforts. Under the VR&E program, the VA directly provides job training assistance to veterans, but only to those with disabilities. The remainder of its efforts fall into basic assistance in career advising, such as training in job search techniques, frequently provided in conjunction with other agencies (Collins et al. 2014).

More direct or in-depth training for nondisabled veterans is coordinated by the VA but is actually performed by a variety of organizations, including federal and state agencies, local governments, nonprofits, and business enterprises. Collaborative efforts have developed around the missions and capacities of federal agencies. The DoD and the VA specialize in national defense and meeting veterans' healthcare needs, respectively. Instead of duplicating efforts to provide a service outside of their expertise, the departments attempt to collaborate to deliver a comprehensive service for the greater good. An example of such collaborative efforts is the basic career and transition advising provided by the DoD's Transition Goals Plans Success (GPS) program, which is supported by the VA, U.S. Departments of Labor, and Homeland Security, as well as the Small Business Administration (Dilger and Lowry 2014).

An example of a federal agency engaging in job training programs for veterans is the U.S. Department of Labor. The department's involvement in veteran training is guided by its focus on employment, as referenced in its mission statement: "[t]o foster, promote, and develop the welfare of the wage earners, job seekers, and retirees of the United States; improve working conditions; advance opportunities for profitable employment; and assure work-related benefits and rights" (Department of Labor 2003). To meet this goal, the department administers several public programs that help individuals receive job training and secure employment. The services offered by these programs include subsidized training and job search assistance and have given priority to veterans since the passage of the Veterans Benefits Act of 2002 (Collins et al. 2012). Other agencies have also participated, on a smaller scale. The U.S. Department of Homeland Security, for example, works with veterans interested in translating their military skills to a civilian, national security context (Homeland Security Careers 2015).

The primary coordinated effort in veterans' job training remains at the federal level, largely because of the national orientation of national security, but also due to the availability of resources. The limited budgets of state and local governments prohibit the financing of many education programs, including those related to job training (Johnson, Oliff, and Williams 2011). Following the "tools of government" approach (see Salamon 2002), the federal government can encourage lower levels of government to provide a service by subsidizing the costs. With the assistance of the U.S. Department of Labor, individual states are able to participate in the job training process with formula grants[1] used to hire personnel who provide assistance to veterans seeking employment, through the Local Veterans Employment Representative (LVER) program (Veterans Benefits Administration 2013b).

While such grants help state and local governments provide services, federal grants frequently come with requirements, such as having to provide the rest of the funding needed for the programs where the newly hired personnel are located (Mikesell 2014). This produces extreme variability from one place to the next in terms of what services are provided locally. This has also opened the door for nonprofit organizations and business enterprises to become more engaged. On the business side, a number of companies have created on-the-job training programs for veterans (Jaffe 2014). These programs employ veterans full-time within the organization while providing them with the training needed to fulfill the job requirements (Urbauer 2013). On the nonprofit side, a growing number of organizations have been established with the aim of helping veterans find employment (Jaffe 2014). Although few provide significant training efforts, many provide assistance in the job search process and advise veterans on how they can best translate their military skills into private employment.

Department of Defense

The DoD, including the branches of military service within it, is tasked with establishing and maintaining the security of the nation (Department of Defense 2015). Since the creation of the Department of War in 1789, the nature of military conflict has changed, and with it the needs of the defense sector to achieve its goal (Davis, Gumpert, and Kugler 1996; Office of the Historian 2015). This transition can be seen in how the training of service members has evolved over time, from the cavalry soldiers, who only needed to ride, shoot, and take orders, to advanced technicians, who must be able to engage on the forefront of cyber warfare. And with these transitions in the training of service members have come additional changes in the utility of military service to veterans after the completion of their service.

As an investment in human capital, military training presents a cost with the expectation of a future benefit. That is, the DoD's investments in training ensure its continued ability to provide the public good of national defense. The distinguishing feature of human capital investments made by the department is that, while the department bears the cost, the service member is the recipient of the long-term benefits (Asch, Hosek, and Warner 2007). The knowledge and skills acquired during service are vested within the individual and cannot be separated from the service member at the completion of his or her service. The DoD uses this long-term benefit as an inducement for military service (Borjas and Welch 1986; Cardell et al. 1997). In the short term, however, the department receives a benefit from its investment in the form of increased productivity in the production of a military good (McDonald 2011).

The broad responsibility for training within the DoD falls to the Under Secretary of Defense for Personnel and Readiness (Office of the Under Secretary for Personnel and Readiness 2015). The under secretary's office is the principal DoD staff agency for all issues relating to human resources, including health systems, family matters, and personnel requirements for weapons support, as well as education and training. Based on recommendations from the individual branches of service and the broader defense community, the under secretary creates the general policies for service member training; however, it is ultimately up to the secretary of defense to approve the policies and the branches to interpret and implement the policies based on their focus and needs.

The DoD does not provide training with the explicit intent of postservice utility; however, the forms of training provided by the military do offer a benefit for veterans. These forms of training include both specific and general on-the-job training. Both Becker (1962) and Sandler and Hartley (1995) acknowledge the importance of the distinction in terms of impact on economic contribution after service. Specific on-the-job training, referred to as *military skills*, includes any training provided that is essential to the workings of the department for the production of national security and is characterized by a lack of utility in the private job market (McDonald 2011). Such training includes little of the systematic subject matter discussed in formal education, perhaps other than physical education and basic healthcare, rather emphasizing the details necessary for national defense.

In an applied sense, new recruits are provided with training in military skills during their initial period of military service. After enlisting in the military, new recruits are sent to a basic training or officer's candidate school, where they receive accession training, defined as the basic soldering skills required for military service (McDonald 2011). While the content of such training is determined by the branch of service and is based on its expectations of need, the primary focus is on transitioning from a civilian to a service member with the intent of creating a base level of capability for the DoD to ensure the department's ability to give orders and fight in the defense of the homeland.

Although these skills are essential to the maintenance of the military and do contribute to the income growth of an individual during service, they are independent of income decisions after service. The contribution of military skills to a veteran's postservice career is determined by how specific the training is, with the prevailing belief being that the more specific the training, the less utility it provides to other firms in the market (Becker 1962; McDonald 2011). For the DoD, the provision of national security is the ideal public good, defined as nonrivalrous and nonexcludable (Holcombe 2006). When specific on-the-job training is provided under the circumstances of a monopsony situation, there is no alternative firm in which a laborer can utilize those skills. Without a market of militaries in the United States, training in military skills would raise the capacity of the sector to ensure national security and defense, but the benefits end there.

For veterans, the training provided that will assist them throughout their civilian careers comes in the form of general on-the-job training. General on-the-job training is any training provided by a firm or industry outside of formal education that is useful to other firms in the market (Becker 1962; Sandler and Hartley 1995). Not only does general training raise the future marginal productivity of laborers for the firm that provides the training, it also increases their marginal productivity for other firms in the market. For the defense sector, this form of training is referred to as *military education* and, as with military skills, includes the skills and knowledge required by service members to fulfill the duties of their assigned positions in the production of the military good. However, unlike military skills, a service member's military education is also useful toward production in the rest of the economy. For example, the defense sector provides training in advanced computer skills, medicine, aircraft piloting, and vehicle repair, all of which can be utilized by veterans for employment after their military service. These investments in training provide income during service and may continue to do so after the completion of service due to the transferability of the skills to the private, public, or nonprofit sectors.

After completing their initial basic training, all service members are sent to some form of advanced individual training (Jensen 1985). This advanced training provides service members with the specifics of their chosen field, that is, the education needed to complete their assigned duty. The types of education offered to service members are determined by their performance on the Armed Services Vocational Aptitude Battery (ASVAB). Administered by the U.S. Military Entrance Processing Command, the ASVAB is a multiple choice test that qualifies service members for the various jobs available, and the results are used to assign service members to advanced training for a job based on the current needs of the particular branch. Upon completion of these training programs, service members are qualified for the position to which they are assigned based on the skills and expertise that they have acquired (called a Military Occupational Specialty [MOS] by the U.S. Army and U.S. Marines, an Air Force Specialty Code [AFSC] by the U.S. Air Force, and a Navy Enlisted Classification [NEC] by the U.S. Navy). Over time, service members may obtain additional qualifications through experience, education, or additional training.

The qualifications provided through military education provide veterans with a postservice career benefit. Active-duty service members who retire or are discharged from military service generally enter the civilian workforce for a second career (Asch, Hosek, and Warner 2007). The utility of the general on-the-job training accumulated through military education is demonstrated by the labor decisions of service members after completion of the first service contract. Service members who receive more military education are more likely to exit the defense sector and pursue employment in the market at higher wages. For example, Air Force pilots often serve as commercial pilots after discharge, and individuals trained as either medical or legal professionals obtain employment in similar fields after military service (McDonald 2011, 2013). In addition to the more educationally advanced training, such as that just mentioned, service members are also trained and qualified in a variety of vocational skills, including automotive repair and computer technology.

Given the large number of veterans who entered the market at the end of World War II, Schickele and Everett (1945) suggested that time spent on military education rather than formal education was not a loss to the productivity of the economy as a whole, but rather a gain for veterans. The general, on-the-job nature of military education suggests that service members return to the market after the completion of service with a set of skills that are both marketable and useful in civilian pursuits. For example, included in the basic training of service members are skills that are essential to military service but reflect the formal education service members could have received in the private sector. These skills include basic algebra, military history and philosophy, and simple vocational and technical skills. The overlap between the skills taught through military education and those offered through higher education is key to the accumulation of human capital, which will benefit service members beyond their tenure in the military.

A classic example of the utility of military education is the role of army engineers during the construction of railroads in the United States. Although the railroads benefited market involvement, they also offered a strategic benefit to the U.S. Army by permitting it to efficiently transport troops and resources around the country (Angevine 2004). As a result, the U.S. Army Corps of Engineers oversaw the development and construction of the nation's railroads. Furthermore, the wealth and possibilities associated with the railroad led to the practice of private firms hiring army engineers away from public service as soon as they gained sufficient knowledge and experience. A modern example is the continuous flow of nuclear technicians trained by the U.S. Navy into the nuclear power plants of civilian electric utility companies. Similar exoduses have occurred over the past 60 years, typically following the development of new technologies by the defense sector (DeGrasse 1983; Redmond and Smith 2000).

From the perspective of the DoD, general training is provided to service members that can be used in a career after the completion of their service (U.S. Army 2015). There is a concern, however, that the qualifications received by individuals during their service do not grant them the appropriate certifications required for employment in the private sector (Flournoy 2014). For example, an airplane mechanic may be qualified to perform maintenance within the U.S. Air Force, but does not automatically receive the Federal Aviation Administration (FAA) certification needed for employment in a similar private sector position as a veteran.

The issue of translating military expertise into civilian qualifications falls primarily to the VA; however, the DoD has formally accepted some responsibility for the job training of veterans with the development of its Transition Assistance Program (TAP) (Transition to Veterans Program Office 2015), which provides preseparation services on issues related to the transition of service members from military to civilian life, including employment counseling. Delivered in coordination with the U.S. Departments of Veterans Affairs, Labor, and Homeland Security, it provides service members with information on how their qualifications correlate with civilian certifications and offers training in job search techniques (Collins et al. 2014). In 2013 the TAP curriculum was redesigned as "Transition GPS" to conform with the Veterans Opportunity to Work (VOW) to Hire Heroes Act of 2011 (Transition to Veterans Program Office 2015). One key feature of the redesign was that participation became mandatory. While the program provides information on postservice careers for service members, it does little to assist the veteran in carrying out the transition. (For more information, see chapter 3.)

Department of Veterans Affairs

Formal responsibility for the provision of services to veterans lies with the VA. Established in its present form in 1988, the VA has a tradition of service dating back to 1921, when the veteran services that were provided across the federal government were consolidated under a single agency, the Veterans Bureau. The specifics of the organization have changed over time, but its focus then, as it is now, was to provide burial, pension, health and disability, and training and education benefits to veterans of the U.S. armed forces (Office of Public Affairs 2006). (See chapter 5.)

To accomplish its mission, the VA is comprised of 14 staff organizations, 7 staff offices, and 3 administrations (Department of Veterans Affairs 2015). The staff organizations and offices provide assistance to the department in its daily management, while the administrations act as the apparatus within the department that provides services to and engages with veterans on a daily basis. While the National Cemetery Administration and the Veterans Health Administration focus on maintaining national cemeteries and providing healthcare and medical assistance, respectively, the Veterans Benefits Administration is responsible for administering the programs of the department that provide financial and other forms of assistance. Included in these benefits are veterans' pensions and home loan guarantees, but also the benefits related to educational, rehabilitation, and employment assistance (Veterans Benefits Administration 2015b).

The first formal training program for veterans in the United States was established with the Vocational Rehabilitation Act of 1918 (Office of Public Affairs 2006). As World War I came to an end, there was concern about the status of returning service members, many of whom were disabled as a result of the conflict. Rather than allowing disabled veterans to return home incapacitated, it was believed that through focused training they would be able to enter the workforce as productive citizens (Bryan 2010). The act placed responsibility for this training under a newly formed Federal Board for Vocational Education, which was consolidated under the Veterans Bureau in 1921 (Office of Public Affairs 2006). The creation of new training programs for veterans has usually been triggered by the involvement of the United States in armed military conflict. In 1943, for example, the World War II Disabled Veterans Rehabilitation Act was passed to extend the vocational rehabilitation services to disabled veterans returning from World War II (Bryan 2010).

Today, the involvement of the VA in job programs falls primarily under its VR&E program (Department of Veterans Affairs 2012a), though the educational funding programs provided by the department (i.e., the G.I. Bill and its variants) also include provisions for financing technical and on-the-job training programs (Department of Veterans Affairs 2012b). In accordance with earlier iterations from 1918 and 1943, the VR&E provides training and career assistance to veterans with disabilities (Department of Veterans Affairs 2012a; Veterans Benefits Administration 2015b); however, rather than providing the training directly, the program provides vocational rehabilitation counselors (VRCs) to work with eligible veterans in developing a career rehabilitation plan. Based on the goals, needs, and skills of the veteran, they are assigned to one of five rehabilitation tracks: (1) reemployment, (2) rapid access to employment, (3) self-employment, (4) employment through long-term services, and (5) independent living services.

The opportunities for training vary by track. For example, those on the "reemployment" plan may only receive basic career counseling, whereas those on "employment through long-term services" may receive more hands-on training and educational assistance. Veterans on the remaining tracks do have access to services, but they are geared toward other directions. Veterans on the rapid access to employment track receive job search assistance, and those on the self-employment track are given entrepreneurship advice. Conversely, independent living services are geared toward helping veterans with severe disabilities master the skills needed to live on their own.

The role of the VRC is to then help veterans implement the track and receive the corresponding benefits. While the VR&E is focused on

The Job Training of Veterans

providing services to veterans with disabilities, some program applicants who do not meet the requirements for participation due to lack of an employment-restricting disability may still be offered basic career counseling in addition to being referred to other resources (Department of Veterans Affairs 2012a).

In addition to the VR&E program, the VA also provides financial support for education to eligible veterans under the G.I. Bill Educational Assistance Programs (Department of Veterans Affairs 2012b). Educational services began under the Servicemen's Readjustment Act of 1944 (commonly known as the G.I. Bill), which aimed to provide educational assistance to avert unemployment, reward military service, and help veterans adjust to civilian life (Collins et al. 2014; Veterans Benefits Administration 2013a). Today, the G.I. Bill Educational Assistance Programs refers to a series of policies that have maintained these goals, including the Post-9/11 G.I. Bill, Montgomery G.I. Bill-Active Duty, and Montgomery G.I. Bill-Selected Reserve.

At the core of G.I. Bill programs is financial support to help cover the cost of tuition and school fees, as well as books, supplies, and housing. Although the common perception is that these programs help veterans attend institutions of higher education in pursuit of a bachelor's, master's, or doctoral degree, they also provide assistance with vocational and training programs, apprenticeships, and other on-the-job training opportunities. This broad availability of educational and training opportunities allows interested veterans to attend a vocational or other non-degree-granting program with the intent of learning a trade.

Contrary to the VR&E program, the G.I. Bill provides services to disabled and nondisabled veterans alike, with program eligibility based on the length and type of military service (Department of Veterans Affairs 2012b). Currently, once veterans are determined to be eligible, they can receive financial assistance for up to 36 months of full-time study or its part-time equivalent. When licensure or certification is needed to practice a trade, financial assistance is provided through the testing process. Financial assistance for pursuing licensure or certification has two impacts: it prepares veterans to enter the labor force in their newly trained field and helps veterans transition the expertise acquired during military service into a postservice career.

While the department has offered other training-related programs over time, for one reason or another, these have ceased to operate. The most recent example is the Veterans Retraining and Assistance Program (VRAP), established as a provision under the VOW to Hire Heroes Act of 2011 (Coy 2012). A temporary program scheduled to end on March 31, 2014,

VRAP sought to provide 12 months of training assistance to older, unemployed veterans who were no longer eligible for benefits under the G.I. Bill. Unlike programs under the G.I. Bill, VRAP limited the type of education and training veterans could pursue to programs at community colleges and technical schools that the U.S. Department of Labor had identified as "high demand" (Collins et al. 2014).

What distinguishes the various programs from one another is how the services are provided. Rather than providing a direct service to veterans, the G.I. Bill and VRAP place the VA in the role of grantor agency that provides funding to veterans, but has minimal involvement in the type of education and training being pursued. This compares to the VR&E program, which also does not provide training services directly, but employs VCRs to work with veterans to determine what kind of training they need and to help them in their pursuit of this training. The role of grantor is common within the VA, as it provides the resources to accomplish its goal while allowing those with the expertise in a given area to carry it out. This is evidenced by the way in which veterans' educational and training grants are handled, as well as by the department's interaction with other agencies and governments.

Other Programs

Primary responsibility for the job training of veterans in the United States lies with the DoD and VA, as previously discussed. Although both agencies provide significant efforts in this area, a number of other organizations have stepped into the position of providing similar services to veterans. This includes federal agencies, but also state and local governments, as well as a variety of nonprofit and business enterprises (Jaffe 2014). These services are often provided in conjunction with the aforementioned departments, but at times are independent. The collaborative activities of multiple organizations are guided by the missions and capacities of those involved, so that veterans receive job training and training assistance from those with the relevant expertise. While the coordination of any collaboration may be overseen by the VA so as to avoid duplication of services, the varied nature of the programs, as well as of those involved in their provision, frequently places the management and fiduciary responsibility directly on those providing the service.

A classic example of interagency collaboration in job training for veterans is the Transition GPS program (Transition to Veterans Program Office 2015). Developed and administered by the DoD, Transition GPS is a military program that focuses on making service members "career-ready" upon discharge. Although the DoD administers the program, it engages other agencies to provide assistance to service members based on the capabilities of the agencies. This includes the VA, which provides information sessions regarding the benefits available to veterans and oversees the application process for those benefits. The U.S. Department of Labor is also involved, providing employment workshops in which service members learn job search skills, such as résumé writing and interview preparation (Transition to Veterans Program Office 2014). To a lesser extent, the Small Business Administration and the U.S. Department of Homeland Security collaborate with Transition GPS to provide career assistance for those interested in entrepreneurship or transitioning into homeland security, respectively (Collins et al. 2014; Dilger and Lowry 2014; Homeland Security Careers 2015). Although the program does provide information regarding the job training resources available to veterans, its involvement in the direct provision of training is minimal.

Another department that contributes to the provision of veterans' services is the U.S. Department of Labor. Its contribution includes assisting other agencies with programming as it relates to labor education and granting veterans priority in their training and service programs (Mikelson et al. 2004). The U.S. Department of Labor also offers support specifically geared toward the training needs of veterans under its Veterans' Employment and Training Services (VETS) program (Davis 2003). VETS is an independent agency within the Department of Labor that was created with the specific intent of assisting veterans' transition from a military to a civilian career (Davis 2003; Veterans' Employment and Training Service 2015). This includes helping veterans receive training and find suitable employment, and actively protecting their employment and reemployment rights. As part of its initiative to assist veterans, VETS administers two formula grants to fund veteran programming at the state level under the direction of the Jobs for Veterans State Grant (JVSG) program (Collins et al. 2014).

The primary grant operated by JVSG is the LVER program (Veterans' Employment and Training Service 2015),[2] which provides formula grants to states for the purpose of hiring personnel to provide employment-related services to veterans. These personnel also act as a resource for veterans, alerting them to the availability of additional employment preparedness services (Veterans Benefits Administration 2013b). This includes referring veterans to the education and training opportunities provided by the Department of Veterans Affairs. In addition, LVER-funded personnel are responsible for community outreach (Mikelson et al. 2004). By reaching out to the community, personnel are able to find new employment opportunities for veterans and develop employment-related workshops that help link the skills of veterans to the needs of the business community. Although the program does not directly provide job training, the engagement of LVER-funded personnel with the community builds mutually beneficial relationships and provides important insight into which skills are in highest demand by employers in the area. Personnel are then able to direct veterans to the resources available to help finance the pursuit of the sought-after skill or craft.

An interesting feature of the LVER program is that while veterans' affairs is a national issue, it provides an opportunity for states to get involved. The impact of unemployment among veterans is felt at the state and local levels, but their limited budgets prohibit the financing of many education programs, including those related to job training (Johnson, Oliff, and Williams 2011). Under certain conditions, such limitations can be overcome. According to Salamon (2002), the tools the federal government has at its disposal are frequently limited to the funding of programs that are carried out at the state or local levels. Within the tools of government approach, the federal government is able to indirectly deliver a service by providing state and local governments with the resources to do so. For service providers, resources are limited, but the opportunity for federal funding can encourage the development of new programs or the expansion of existing ones. This is the case for LVER, in which the Department of Labor funds grants to encourage state-led solutions to improving veterans' employment options.

Grants from the federal government help both state and local governments provide services for veterans, but federal grants frequently come with requirements such as matching funds, which lower governments cannot do during periods of fiscal constraint (Mikesell 2014). This leads to wide variation in the availability and quality of locally provided services. This has resulted in criticism about the management of veterans' programs from the U.S. Congress, government watchdogs, and veterans alike (U.S. House of Representatives 2010; Independent Budget Veterans Service Organizations 2013). In the absence of a consistent service, veterans who reside in economically disadvantaged areas—who are among the most in need of training services—may be the least likely to receive them.

This has also opened the door for nonprofit organizations and private business enterprises to become more engaged in veterans' employment issues. On the business side, companies across the United States have launched veteran hiring initiatives, with some creating on-the-job training programs as well (Hall et al. 2015; Harrell and Berglass 2012). Veteran initiatives commonly involve promises to hire a specified number of veterans. For example, Starbucks promised to hire 10,000 veterans and military spouses, Home Depot committed to 55,000 veteran hires, and Walmart created an initiative to hire any veteran who applies (Jaffe 2014; Starbucks 2013). In more technologically advanced fields, some businesses have established on-the-job training programs that employ veterans fulltime within the organization while providing them the training they need to fulfill the job requirements. Examples include GE, Lockheed Martin, Boeing, and Alcoa (Urbauer 2013). These programs provide good opportunities, but only for a select few, as they are limited in number and typically focus on recruiting veterans who already possess military skills in line with the business's needs, thus minimizing the amount of additional training. Ultimately, the impact of these programs tends to be further diminished due to the geographic constraints of the organization and lack of coordination with the Departments of Veterans Affairs and Labor (Hall et al. 2015).

On the nonprofit side, a growing number of organizations have been established with the aim of helping veterans find employment (Jaffe 2014). Although a few of them provide significant direct training efforts, many provide assistance in the job search process and in how veterans can best translate their military skills into private employment. The growth in nonprofit involvement in veterans' issues is in accordance with the national mood, which emphasizes caring for those who fought to maintain the nation's freedom in a post-9/11 society (Dao 2012). It also stems from a growing dissatisfaction with the performance of the VA. Scandals, such as the recent revelation that veterans were subjected to long waiting periods to receive needed health services, have plagued the department, and many new nonprofits have emerged to fill this gap in service (Cohen 2014).

Nonprofits have increasingly recognized and addressed dissatisfaction with the VA. For example, Goodwill Industries International (2011, 6) acknowledged that "existing supports and infrastructure are ill-equipped to provide all of the resources that many returning service members may need and have earned." Given this reality, Goodwill offers job training and practical experience via internal and external employment opportunities to veterans. Often this assistance provides the necessary link between experiences in combat and experiences in civilian employment, particularly for veterans without relevant vocational or postsecondary education. Services are also modified to fulfill the needs of individual veterans or communities of veterans; for example, the needs of Vietnam veterans for job training, which centered on providing access to training for entry-level positions, differ markedly from those of veterans of the Iraq war, for whom training centers on transitioning military experience into a civilian career.

Nonprofits are engaged in a network of organizations to provide a "web of support" (Werber et al. 2013) for veterans seeking reintegration into civilian life. This is evidenced by Transition 360 Alliance, a network of nonprofits created by the United Services Organization to provide reintegration services including job training (*USO News* 2015). This network acts as a force multiplier, which can address gaps in services by augmenting traditional sources of reintegration support from the VA with the services of intergovernmental, for-profit, and nonprofit organizations (Werber et al. 2013). The services of external organizations such as nonprofits have been deemed "absolutely critical to helping the nation's heroes reintegrate back into society" by military leaders such as Sgt. Maj. Bryan Battaglia (Roulo 2014).

While some may view the rise of nonprofit involvement as direct competition for public programs, the VA has made progress with integrating nonprofits into its mission. This can be seen in the development of the Nonprofit Program Office (NPPO), which oversees collaboration between the department and nonprofits on health-related research (Office of Research and Development 2015). While the creation of this office is promising, it also highlights a persistent challenge in veteran job training: while some attention has been given to employment issues, the vast majority of these organizations are directed toward alleviating homelessness and providing access to healthcare. Therefore, efforts in job training have been sporadic and highly localized, minimizing the VA's ability to adequately address the issue of successfully integrating veterans into the market postservice.

Conclusion

This chapter has sought to provide an understanding of job training programs for veterans in the United States. By introducing the relevant programs within the context of the organizations that provide them, we are better able to understand the missions of the various programs and the decentralized structure within which they operate. While the programs discussed here do not constitute an exhaustive list, they are the ones that veterans are most likely to encounter. Programs absent from this chapter tend to have a limited geographic focus or a narrow scope of mission and delivery, excluding most veterans from taking part in them.

The status of veteran job training in the United States embodies a paradox: while the government and the public encourage veterans to pursue a successful career after the completion of their military service, the tools necessary to do so are not made readily available to them. A common thread among the programs discussed here is referral services. Rather than providing a direct form of training within the organization, many programs redirect veterans elsewhere. Not only does this generate feelings of frustration for veterans, who think they are getting the "runaround," it also contributes to the real possibility that the goal of getting veterans to work is not achieved. After all, the only training-specific program for veterans operated by the federal government was the VRAP, which ended in April 2014.

In addition, the programs that are available have been criticized as ineffective. In a 2010 hearing, the Subcommittee on Economic Opportunity of the U.S. House Committee on Veterans' Affairs (2010) discussed the failure of the VETS program, the U.S. Department of Labor's program that assists veterans' transition from a military to a civilian career, citing examples from the JVSG. These examples focused on the lack of dedication to veterans' issues by the grant-funded personnel and the opportunity for state employees to earn a higher income elsewhere, which resulted in a diminished quality of service and a high rate of turnover among the staff. The recommendation from the hearing was to move the grant-funded positions into the federal personnel system, creating stability and ensuring the ability of personnel to help their constituents.

The dispersal of veterans' services across multiple agencies has also been an issue of complaint. In 2013 the Independent Budget Veterans Service Organization (2013), a watchdog organization comprised of the leading nonprofit organizations focused on veterans' services, argued that the lack of centralization of services under a single agency has created a diseconomy of scale. Too many organizations within the federal system are providing similar services, opening the opportunity for wasted funds due to organizational overlap and uncertainty among veterans about where to turn for help.

The rise of nonprofits also implies criticism of federal services, as they fill gaps within the established system of disparate public programs (Wilson 2013). While a widespread job training program may not be practical for a nonprofit to undertake, organizations such as the U.S. Chamber of Commerce have begun to focus on helping veterans translate their military experience for civilian employers (Jaffe 2014). The question is, are these efforts enough to meet the needs of the veteran population? Services still lack centralization, and an explicit focus on training in the federal government continues to be absent. With the decline in the size of the U.S. armed forces and an economy not yet fully recovered from the Great Recession of 2008–2009, more veterans are entering a competitive civilian job market and will require training if they are to be successful (Faberman and Foster 2013; Holder 2010). In the absence of sufficient federal help, it is anticipated that nonprofits will become the primary providers of training and employment services for veterans in need of assistance as they attempt to successfully reintegrate into the civilian workforce (Wilson 2013).

Notes

1. Formula grants are awarded based on the applicant's meeting a predefined set of requirements rather than through a competitive process.

2. The second grant provided by JVSG is the "Disabled Veterans Outreach Program (DVOP)" (Collins et al. 2014; Mikelson et al. 2004). The focus of the program is similar to that of LVER, but is specifically targeted toward disabled veterans.

References

Angevine, Robert G. 2004. *The Railroad and the State: War, Politics, and Technology in Nineteenth-Century America*. Stanford, CA: Stanford University Press.

Angrist, Joshua D. 1993. "The Effect of Veterans Benefits on Education and Earnings." *Industrial Relations and Labor* 46 (4): 637–652.

Asch, Beth J., James R. Hosek, and John T. Warner. 2007. "New Economics of Manpower in the Post-Cold War Era." In *Handbook of Defense Economics*, edited by Todd Sandler and Keith Hartley, 1075–1138. Amsterdam: Elsevier.

Becker, Gary S. 1962. *Investment in Human Capital: A Theoretical Analysis with Special Reference to Education*. New York: Columbia University Press.

Borjas, George J., and Finis Welch. 1986. "The Post-Service Earnings of Military Retirees." In *Army Manpower Economics*, edited by Curtis L. Gilroy, 295–313. Boulder, CO: Westview Press.

Bound, John, and Sarah Turner. 2002. "Going to War and Going to College: Did World War II and the G.I. Bill Increase Educational Attainment for Returning Veterans?" *Journal of Labor Economics* 20 (4): 784–815.

Bryan, Willie V. 2010. *Sociopolitical Aspects of Disabilities*. 2nd ed. Springfield, IL: Thomas Books.

Bryant, Richard, and Al Wilhite. 1990. "Military Experience and Training Effects on Civilian Wages." *Applied Economics* 22 (1): 69–81.

Bureau of Labor Statistics. 2015. *Employment Situation of Veterans—2014*. Washington, DC: U.S. Department of Labor.

Cardell, S., D. Lamoreau, E. Stromsdorfer, B. Wang, and G. Weeks. 1997. *The Post-Service Earnings of Military Retirees: A Comparison of the 1996 Retired Military Personnel Sample with a Statistically Comparable Sample from the March 1994 Current Population Survey*. Pullman, WA: Washington State University.

Cohen, Rick. 2014. "Shinseki's Out at VA, Time for Nonprofit Sector to Help Fix It." Accessed November 18, 2015. http://nonprofitquarterly.org/2014/05/30/shinseki-s-out-at-va-time-for-nonprofit-sector-to-help-fix-it/.

Collins, Benjamin, David H. Bradley, Cassandria Dortch, Lawrence Kapp, and Christine Scott. 2012. *Employment for Veterans: Trends and Programs*. Washington, DC: Congressional Research Service.

Collins, Benjamin, Robert Jay Dilger, Cassandria Dortch, Lawrence Kapp, Sean Lowry, and Libby Perl. 2014. *Employment for Veterans: Trends and Programs*. Washington, DC: Congressional Research Service.

Coy, Curtis. 2012. "Help VA Spread the Word about VRAP Benefits." *VAntage Point* (blog), May 31. Accessed September 2, 2015. http://www.blogs.va.gov/VAntage/6845/help-va-spread-the-word-about-vrap-benefits/.

Cronk, Terri. 2012. "New Program Aims to Better Help Troops Transition to Civilian Life." *American Forces Press Service*, August 18.

Dao, James. 2012. "In Veterans' Aid, Growth Pains." *New York Times*, November 9, F1.

Davis, E. W. 2003. *The History of Veterans Employment Services*. Denver, CO: National Veterans' Training Institute.

Davis, Paul K., David Gumpert, and Richard Kugler. 1996. *Adaptiveness in National Defense: The Basis of a New Framework*. Santa Monica, CA: RAND Corporation.

DeGrasse, Robert W. 1983. *Military Expansion, Economic Decline: The Impact of Military Spending on U.S. Economic Performance*. Armonk, NY: M.E. Sharpe.

Department of Defense. 2015. "About the Department of Defense (DoD)." Accessed August 29, 2015. http://www.defense.gov/About-DoD.

Department of Labor. 2003. "Our Mission." Accessed August 28, 2015. http://www.dol.gov/opa/aboutdol/mission.htm.

Department of Veterans Affairs. 2012a. *Summary of VA Vocational Rehabilitation and Employment Benefits*. Washington, DC: U.S. Department of Veterans Affairs.

Department of Veterans Affairs. 2012b. *Summary of VA Education Benefits*. Washington, DC: U.S. Department of Veterans Affairs.

Department of Veterans Affairs. 2015. *Functional Organization Manual*. v[ersion] 3.0. Washington, DC: U.S. Department of Veterans Affairs.

Dilger, Robert Jay, and Sean Lowry. 2014. *SBA Veterans Assistance Programs: An Analysis of Contemporary Issues*. Washington, DC: Congressional Research Service.

Faberman, R. Jason, and Taft Foster. 2013. "Unemployment Among Recent Veterans During the Great Recession." *Economic Perspectives* 37 (1): 1–13.

Feiock, Richard C. 2007. "Rational Choice and Regional Governance." *Journal of Urban Affairs* 29 (1): 47–63.

Flournoy, Michele A. 2014. "We Aren't Doing Enough to Help Veterans Transition to Civilian Life." Accessed August 30, 2015. https://www.washingtonpost.com/opinions/we-arent-doing-enough-to-help-veterans-transition-to-civilian-life/2014/04/02/d43189e2-b52a-11e3-b899-20667de76985_story.html.

Goodwill Industries International. 2011. *From Deployment to Employment: Goodwill's Call to Action on Supporting Military Service Members, Veterans, and Their Families*. Rockville, MD: Goodwill Industries International.

Hall, Kimberly Curry, Margaret C. Harrell, Barbara A. Bicksler, Robert Stewart, and Michael P. Fisher. 2014. *Veteran Employment: Lessons from the 100,000 Jobs Mission*. Santa Monica, CA: RAND Corporation.

Hall, Kimberly Curry, Margaret C. Harrell, Barbara A. Bicksler, Robert Stewart, and Michael P. Fisher. 2015. *Connecting Veterans and Employers*. Santa Monica, CA: RAND Corporation.

Harrell, Margaret C., and Nancy Berglass. 2012. *Employing America's Veterans: Perspectives from Business*. Washington, DC: Center for a New American Security.

Heo, Uk, and Robert J. Eger. 2005. "The Security-Prosperity Dilemma in the United States." *Journal of Conflict Resolution* 49 (5): 792–817.

Holcombe, Randall. 2006. *Public Sector Economics: The Role of Government in the American Economy*. Upper Saddle River, NJ: Prentice Hall.

Holder, Kelly Ann. 2010. "Post-9/11 Women Veterans." Paper presented at the Annual Meeting of the Population Association of America, Dallas, TX, April 15–17.

Homeland Security Careers. 2015. "Veterans." U.S. Department of Homeland Security. Accessed August 29, 2015. http://www.dhs.gov/homeland-security-careers/veterans.

Independent Budget Veterans Service Organizations. 2013. *The Independent Budget for the Department of Veterans Affairs*. Washington, DC: The Independent Budget Veterans Service Organizations.

Jaffe, Greg. 2014. "Wanted: Heroes, Trying to Piece Together the Puzzle of Veterans' Unemployment Proves Difficult." *Washington Post*, April 3, A1.

Jensen, Arthur R. 1985. "Armed Services Vocational Aptitude Battery." *Measurement and Evaluation in Counseling and Development* 18 (1): 32–37.

Johnson, Nicholas, Phil Oliff, and Erica Williams. 2011. *An Update on State Budget Cuts*. Washington, DC: Center on Budget and Policy Priorities.

McDonald, Bruce D. 2011. "A Human Capital Model of the Defense-Growth Relationship." PhD diss., Askew School of Public Administration and Policy, Florida State University.

McDonald, Bruce D. 2013. "What We Do and Do Not Know: The Social Implications of Defense." *Political and Military Sociology* 41: 1–18.

McDonald, Bruce D., and Robert J. Eger. 2010. "The Defense-Growth Relationship: An Economic Investigation into Post-Soviet States." *Peace Economics, Peace Science and Public Policy* 16 (1): 1–26.

Mikelson, Kelly S., Nancy Pindus, Demetra Smith Nighingale, Michael Egner, Shinta Herwantoro, and Amber Sears. 2004. *Strategies for Implementing Priority of Service to Veterans in Department of Labor Programs*. Washington, DC: The Urban Institute.

Mikesell, John L. 2014. *Fiscal Administration*. 9th ed. Boston: Wadsworth.

Obama, Barack. 2012. "Remarks by the President on Veterans Day." Washington, DC: Office of the Press Secretary.

Office of Public Affairs. 2006. *VA History in Brief*. Washington, DC: U.S. Department of Veterans Affairs.

Office of Public Affairs. 2014. *North Carolina and the U.S. Department of Veterans Affairs*. Washington, DC: U.S. Department of Veterans Affairs.

Office of Research and Development. 2015. "Nonprofit Program Office." Accessed September 11, 2015. http://www.research.va.gov/programs/nppo/.

Office of the Historian. 2015. "The Establishment of the Department of War." Accessed August 29, 2015. http://history.house.gov/HistoricalHighlight/Detail/35480.

Office of the Under Secretary for Personnel and Readiness. 2015. "About." Accessed August 30, 2015. http://prhome.defense.gov/About.aspx.

Olson, Keith W. 1973. "The G.I. Bill and Higher Education: Success and Surprise." *American Quarterly* 25 (5): 596–610.

Redmond, Kent C., and Thomas M. Smith. 2000. *From Whirlwind to MITRE: The R&D Story of the SAGE Air Defense Computer*. Cambridge, MA: MIT Press.

Riley, Jarnee, Joseph Gasper, Kathyrn Caperna, Helen Liu, Richard Sigman, Mustafa Karakus, and Laurie May. 2014. *Vocational Rehabilitation and Employment Longitudinal Study: Annual Report 2014 for FY2013*. Washington, DC: U.S. Department of Veterans Affairs.

Roulo, Claudette. 2014. "Battaglia: Nonprofits 'Critical' to Helping Troops Reintegrate." Accessed September 22, 2015. http://www.defense.gov/News-Article-View/Article/603529/battaglia-nonprofits-critical-to-helping-troops-reintegrate.

Salamon, Lester M., ed. 2002. *The Tools of Government: A Guide to the New Governance*. Oxford: Oxford University Press.

Sandler, Todd, and Keith Hartley. 1995. *The Economics of Defence*. Cambridge, UK: Cambridge University Press.

Schickele, Rainer, and Glenn Everett. 1945. "The Economic Implications of Universal Military Training." *Annals of the American Academy of Political and Social Sciences* 241 (1): 102–112.

Smole, David P. 2008. *A Brief History of Veterans' Education Benefits and Their Value*. Washington, DC: Congressional Research Service.

Starbucks. 2013. "Military and Spouses—Serve with Us." Accessed September 6, 2015. http://www.starbucks.com/careers/veterans.

Transition to Veterans Program Office. 2014. *Transition Assistance Program*. Washington, DC: U.S. Department of Defense.

Transition to Veterans Program Office. 2015. "About DoD TAP." Accessed August 30, 2015. https://www.dodtap.mil/about_DoDTAP.html.

Urbauer, Kris. 2013. "Get Skills to Work Program Provides Veterans with Career-Building Skills for Advanced Manufacturing." Accessed August 29, 2015. http://www.blogs.va.gov/VAntage/10744/get-skills-to-work-program-provides-veterans-with-career-building-skills-for-advanced-manufacturing/.

U.S. Army. 2015. "Benefits." Accessed August 30, 2015. http://www.goarmy.com/benefits/education-benefits/army-education/career-training-skills.html.

U.S. House of Representatives, Subcommittee on Economic Opportunity of the Committee on Veterans' Affairs. 2010. *Status of Veterans Employment*. April 15. 111th Cong.

USO News. 2015. "With Transition 360 Alliance, USO Seeks to 'Combine the Very Best' to Help Troops Reintegrate into Civilian Life." Accessed September 22, 2015. http://www.uso.org/transition-360-alliance-launch/.

Veterans Benefits Administration. 2013a. "History and Timeline." Accessed September 2, 2015. http://www.benefits.va.gov/gibill/history.asp.

Veterans Benefits Administration. 2013b. "LVER and DVOP Fact Sheet." Washington, DC: U.S. Department of Veterans Affairs.

Veterans Benefits Administration. 2014. "On-the-Job Training and Apprenticeship." Accessed August 23, 2015. http://www.benefits.va.gov/gibill/onthejob_apprenticeship.asp.

Veterans Benefits Administration. 2015a. "Vocational Rehabilitation and Employment (VR&E)." Accessed August 23, 2015. http://www.benefits.va.gov/gibill/onthejob_apprenticeship.asp.

Veterans Benefits Administration. 2015b. "About VBA." Accessed September 1, 2015. http://www.benefits.va.gov/BENEFITS/about.asp.

Veterans' Employment and Training Service. 2015. *Annual Report to Congress: Fiscal Year 2014*. Washington, DC: U.S. Department of Labor.

Werber, Laura, Agnes Gereben Schaefer, Karen Chan Osilla, Elizabeth Wilke, Anny Wong, Joshua Breslau, and Karin E. Kitchens. 2013. *Support for the 21st Century Reserve Force: Insights on Facilitating Successful Reintegration for Citizen Warriors and Their Families*. Santa Monica, CA: RAND Corporation.

Wilson, Catherine E. 2013. "Leadership, Collaboration, and Veterans-Related Nonprofit Organizations." *Journal of Leadership Studies* 7 (1): 48–53.

CHAPTER SEVEN

Veterans in Higher Education

*Michael A. Grandillo and
John W. M. Magee*

Introduction

There is no greater honor than to put one's life on the line in protection of one's country. A nation can be judged by how it treats those less fortunate, or those who give all they have in sacrifice to their nation. Through remarkably effective legislation, veterans who served their country have been and are allowed the chance to embrace a new life. These opportunities, while they have evolved over the years, are still important today.

This chapter surveys the effect of higher education on veterans. It covers government programs, organizations, and activities that support veterans in higher education; the educational differences between veterans and nonveterans; and how veterans impact the institutions of higher education that they encounter. We begin with an overview of the history of the G.I. Bill and how veterans are using this program now. Beyond this historic legislation and its effects, we discuss the enrollment patterns of the various generations of veterans, the levels of education they have accomplished, and the types of degrees that veterans pursue today. Finally, beyond the trends and patterns visible in the enrollment of veterans in higher education, this chapter surveys the current higher educational landscape; the resources that are available to veterans; the impact of Reserve Officers' Training Corps (ROTC) access within campus communities; and the possible future of higher education, such as online learning.

History of the G.I. Bill

The G.I. Bill has been hailed as one of the greatest benefits for our armed service members and a major creator of America's middle class. Enacted in 1944 as the Servicemen's Readjustment Act, this piece of legislation offered World War II veterans the opportunity to reinvent themselves by offering funding to obtain college degrees or vocational/technical training, so they could incorporate new knowledge and skills into civilian life. Ten years after the end of World War II, there were approximately 15,750,000 World War II veterans who had been assimilated back into civilian life. Nearly half of them had enrolled in educational institutions, while others had accepted financial stipends for unemployment and/or other financial benefits (Altschuler and Blumin 2009, 8). Without the passage of the G.I. Bill, a significant number of returning veterans would have been financially prevented from successfully integrating into society. The drafting of this legislation garnered a significant amount of support, but also faced vocal opposition. Conservative critics, while acknowledging the need for financial support and educational development for returning veterans, felt that the cost warranted an expiration date for the program. This would give veterans the opportunity to obtain what they needed, while reducing the burden on the American taxpayer. Liberals, on the other hand, felt that the G.I. Bill should be a permanent benefit for current and future veterans and saw it as similar to other programs commonly referred to as the New Deal (Altschuler and Blumin 2009, 6). Whereas the first G.I. Bill eventually was allowed to expire, it was replaced by successive waves of programs. Nearly 70 years later, the current G.I. Bill has a slightly different name, and there are changes to the policy details. However, it still adheres to the spirit of the original G.I. Bill, which was to offer educational opportunities that can provide a new life to those who risked their lives for the protection of their country.

The original G.I. Bill payouts ended in July 1952 and were replaced by the Veterans Readjustment Assistance Act of 1952 (the Korean War G.I. Bill). This gave the veteran a single stipend that was meant to cover all educational costs. This act encouraged responsible spending, because the veteran could keep the funds not spent on tuition. The next G.I. Bill was enacted in 1966; it expanded the original 90-day minimum service requirement to 180 days. This law was stricter, but still offered critical educational financial support (Department of Veterans Affairs 2005, 18). Later, new laws were enacted that created the Post-Vietnam Era Veteran's Educational Assistance Program (VEAP). This program required a $25–$100 monthly contribution for 12 months from the service member while on active duty (Smole and

Loane 2008, 4). In return, the federal government matched each service members' monthly contribution, up to a maximum of $300 per month. The details varied over time and across various parts of the armed forces. The concept behind VEAP was to save the taxpayers' money, while still allowing a significant educational benefit for veterans.

According to a report submitted by the Congressional Research Service (CRS) to Congress, the Montgomery G.I. Bill—Active Duty (MGIB-AD) and the Montgomery G.I. Bill—Selected Reserve (MGIB-SR) were passed to expand educational assistance to veterans (Smole and Loane 2008). The MGIB-SR added additional eligibility requirements for service members in the reserves. Under the MGIB-SR, service members must complete six years before they are able to collect benefits. The Montgomery G.I. Bill continued VEAP's monthly contribution from active-duty service members, but required the payment to be $100 for a maximum of 12 months. In addition, veterans who wished to collect benefits were required to have received an honorable discharge and to have completed a high school diploma, general education diploma or general educational development (both are names used to describe a "GED"), or 12 credit hours of post-secondary education. MGIB-AD benefits could be used for tuition, fees, books, supplies, and any other expenses associated with enrollment.

The Reserve Educational Assistance Program (REAP) expanded upon the Montgomery G.I. Bill and set percentage benefit amounts for certain levels of service. The Montgomery G.I. Bill stayed in place until the establishment of the post-9/11 G.I. Bill. Finally, the Survivors' and Dependents' Educational Assistance Program (DEA) was established to assist the spouses and children of veterans, by allowing them to access G.I. Bill benefits not used by service members (Smole and Loane 2008, 7).

The Attainment of Higher Education in the Veteran Population

In this section we describe the educational attainment of veterans with regard to postsecondary education. The most global view of the higher education of veterans compared to nonveterans is simply to look at the entire U.S. population of adults aged 25 and older by level of educational attainment, as shown in table 7.1. There are important differences in the education levels of veterans and nonveterans. Nonveterans are considerably more likely to have less than a high school education. Veterans are slightly more likely than nonveterans to have a high school education and no college. The biggest difference is in the category of some college or associate's degree, where veterans are considerably more likely to be found. In the category of bachelor's degree or higher, veterans are slightly underrepresented.

Table 7.1. Educational Attainment of Veterans and Nonveterans, 2014.

	Veterans	Nonveterans
Civilian population, 25 years or older	18,982,128	213,128,198
Less than high school graduate	6.9%	13.7%
High school graduate (includes equivalency)	29.0%	27.6%
Some college or associate's degree	36.9%	28.3%
Bachelor's degree or higher	27.2%	30.3%

Source: American Community Survey 1-Year Estimates, S2101, Veteran Status, 2014.

Looking at the entire population of adults in this way is interesting, but it does have the problem of comparing two groups that have sharply different age distributions. That is, the veterans in table 7.1 are considerably older than the nonveterans. This means that, on average, the veterans completed their education much further in the past, when college attendance was considerably rarer. To take account of this important effect of age, Kelly Ann Holder (2007) of the Census Bureau analyzed the educational attainment of veterans and nonveterans by age groups. One large difference in the age group analysis is that about 27 percent of veterans aged 65 and older (roughly half of all veterans) had completed a bachelor's degree. Only 17 percent of nonveterans aged 65 and older had completed at least a bachelor's degree. This clearly is the result of the G.I. Bill's effects on college completion among veterans of World War II, Korea, and Vietnam eras.

Veterans utilizing G.I. benefits today, within the age group of 18- to 24-year-olds, have nearly identical educational attainment of nonveterans, with a small advantage of 5 percent, with those veterans having some college credit compared to nonveterans (Holder 2007). However, while there is a small gain in obtaining college credit, nonveterans perform 5 percent higher in earning a bachelor's degree overall, compared to veterans in this age group. This changes significantly for 25- to 34-year-olds, where nonveterans perform 8% higher in earning a bachelor's degree than veterans. Whereas nonveterans have higher numbers of bachelor's degree holders for age groups under 54 years, veterans 54 years and older hold a higher number of bachelor's and advanced degrees than nonveterans. The significantly higher number of age 54 and older veteran degree holders can be attributed to a larger range of individuals and also the fact that this age group encompasses veterans involved in the Vietnam War, Korean War, and World War II. Arguably, these generations benefited greatly from the early G.I. Bill offerings of educational financial support, versus the nonveteran population, among which more than 64 percent had a high school education or less, compared with 49 percent of veterans (Holder 2007).

The American Community Survey of 2014 revealed that there are 19,259,717 veterans in the United States (Census Bureau 2014, S2101). A bare majority (51 percent) of these veterans were 18 to 64 years of age. Almost half were 65 or older. About 92 percent of veterans were male and 8 percent female. About 21 percent were classified as minorities. The largest minority group was blacks, at 11.4 percent. Hispanic or Latino was the next largest minority group, at 6 percent. (Hispanics may be of any race, so there is some overlap in these categories.) With the expansion of the Post-9/11 G.I. Bill, the Department of Veterans Affairs (VA) in 2010 allocated $8,317,000,000 toward vocational rehabilitation and education, a 46 percent increase from 2009 (Census Bureau 2011, 341). This provides evidence of the government's commitment to supporting educational pursuits for veterans and its response to the return of a growing number of veterans from Iraq and Afghanistan.

According to the 2015 Veteran Economic Opportunity Report (Department of Veterans Affairs 2015), 225,993 women claimed Post-9/11 G.I. Bill benefits, and 53,530 women currently serving on active duty utilized educational benefits (Department of Veterans Affairs 2015, 71). In addition to serving their country, women veterans consistently outperform nonveteran women in education. However, while the educational level of veteran women is higher than of nonveterans, the unemployment rates of veteran women are also higher than those of nonveteran women. Veteran women who apply their benefits toward education have a lower unemployment rate than nonveteran women (Holder 2007). A higher unemployment rate among veteran women than nonveteran women can be attributed to a large number of veteran women not utilizing G.I. benefits toward completing an education, which results in their having lower qualifications to further careers in the public or private sectors. In assessing degree completion, 19 percent of women veterans completed a bachelor's degree, compared to 15 percent of male veterans. The only area in which male veterans had a higher percentage was those classified as having some high school education or a diploma, with males being at 42 percent versus 26 percent of women. In assessing enrollment and educational achievement, women veterans educationally outperform male veterans (Holder 2007).

In completing degree programs, female veterans outdid their male counterparts by 10 percent, with female veterans completing 101,117 degrees and 79,806 failing to achieve a degree within six years. Male veterans completed 311,019 degrees and 367,355 failed to obtain a degree (Department of Veterans Affairs 2015, 46). There were 34,374 female degree completers aged 20–24 and 23,146 aged 25–29. With female veterans outperforming nonveteran females in degree completions, enrollments, and unemployment rates, there is strong evidence that the G.I. Bill has been instrumental in women veterans' success.

The G.I. Bill and subsequent programs were groundbreaking in showing how a responsible democratic nation supports those who have sacrificed so much. However, not all veterans benefited equally. While many of the program participants built a new life through education, African Americans and women were routinely prevented from fully utilizing the early G.I. Bills' benefits (Eisenmann 2006). It is now recognized that African Americans were purposely prevented from utilizing financial assistance programs for mortgages (see chapter 29). In addition, women who enlisted in military support service programs were denied benefits (see chapter 23).

In 2014 around 21 percent of the entire veteran population was classified as minority (Census Bureau 2014, S2101). One of the great difficulties in assessing veteran minorities in higher education is weak and inaccurate data. This challenge was taken on by the Student Veterans of America, Million Records Project (2014), hosted by Google and other federal and private institutions, to clarify and create precise data tracking for veterans. Previous data had included basic numbers or generalizations that were questionable (Sander 2012).

The Enrollment of Veterans in Higher Education

In this section we describe the current enrollment of veterans in the higher education system, using the latest available data. The G.I. Bill and subsequent programs that supported veterans continue to play an important financial role today. In the post-9/11 world, which includes both the war in Iraq and the war in Afghanistan (the "War on Terror"), veterans still have financial opportunities to continue their undergraduate education. While the laws and regulations have changed with the current G.I. Bills, so has the educational world in America. Whereas returning veterans were once mostly required to be educated through on-campus instruction, today's veterans have a world of options available, including on-campus, satellite, hybrid, and online educational programs. Though these programs have a variety of delivery models, and the quality of the programs and missions of the institutions vary greatly. While veterans may benefit from new educational methods, an increase in awareness of both the excellence of programs and ability to enter successfully into an intended career warrants serious consideration from veterans enrolling and utilizing their benefits.

According to the *Chronicle of Higher Education,* during 2012, 550,000 veterans utilized Post-9/11 G.I. benefits (Sander 2012).

Looking at actual college enrollments, Holder (2007) found that veterans attend college at older ages than nonveterans. Among 18- to 24-year-olds—the so-called traditional-age undergraduate—41 percent of nonveterans were enrolled in college, while only 27 percent of veterans were attending college. While this is a large difference, it is easily explained, as most enrollment-eligible veterans are still serving in the armed forces, either on deployment or active duty, and are not able to dedicate time to a degree program. This can be easily demonstrated by the age group of 25- to 34-year-old veterans having 20 percent of the total enrollment, compared to 11 percent of nonveterans. This trend continues for 35- to 54-year-olds, with veterans having 5 percent of the enrollment, compared to 4 percent of nonveterans. The enrollment tapers off at 55+, with both veterans' and nonveterans' enrollment at just under 1 percent. The census analysis of 2007 demonstrates that mature students (ages 25+) have the highest college enrollment.

In 2007, among 18- to 24-year-old college students, 82 percent of veterans are enrolled in public institutions, versus 75 percent of nonveterans. While veterans have a higher enrollment in public colleges and universities, nonveterans have higher enrollment numbers at private educational institutions of higher learning, with 19 percent of veterans enrolled versus 25 percent of nonveterans. Although these data from the Census Bureau were last updated in 2007, they should demonstrate that private universities of higher learning are deficient in veteran enrollments. This may represent an opportunity for them to recruit veterans to their institutions. In addition to recruitment, it can be argued that there is a lack of resources for veterans on private university campuses relative to public university campuses, which can utilize both taxpayer dollars and other on-campus resources to support veterans. Private universities can compete on faculty-to-student ratio, by offering small class sizes, targeted courses for active-duty service personnel to transfer into civilian life, retention, and maximizing G.I. benefits so veterans can focus on degree completion.

Women have higher enrollments and obtain more degrees than men in most areas and levels of study (Holder 2007). According to a National Center for Veterans Analysis and Statistics (2015b, 5) analysis of American Community Survey data, women make up 8 percent of veterans. Of these female veterans, nearly 20 percent are African Americans, over 8 percent are Hispanic, 2 percent are Asian American, and 66 percent are white, according to the 2010 census. In addition, minority women have a higher percentage of veterans than their minority male counterparts. While the last census states that women only account for 8 percent of the veteran population, they are a growing group. With an increasing population of women serving and women taking on combat and expanded roles in the military, this percentage will undoubtedly increase.

While enrolled at universities, women veterans have higher enrollments in colleges and universities than males. According to Holder (2007), assessing 18- to 24-year-olds, 33 percent of women veterans were enrolled, compared to 26 percent of male veterans. Within the 25- to 34-year-old group a stark contrast occurs, with 30 percent of women veterans enrolled versus 17 percent of male veterans. This trend continues from ages 35 to 54, with veteran women at 11 percent and veteran males at 5 percent. In the 55+ age category the numbers even out, with 1 percent of women veterans and 1 percent of male veterans enrolled. In addition to women veterans having higher enrollments, female veterans aged 25 and older had more college credit or had completed a bachelor's degree than male veterans. Examining the choice of educational institutions of male versus female veterans who utilize G.I. benefits shows that they are equal, with 81 percent of male veterans enrolled in a public institution of higher learning versus 82 percent of women veterans (Holder 2007). This trend continues in private higher educational institutions, with 19 percent of male veterans enrolled, versus 18 percent of female veterans. The only area in which male veterans slightly outperformed female veterans in enrollment was in graduate school at private colleges and universities; however, the difference was tiny. At public universities males have a 1 percent deficiency in public graduate degree programs. Both male and female veterans were within a difference of 1 percent at the private and public graduate level, with a median age of males at 36 years old and females at 33 years old (Holder 2007).

What Veterans Study

The 2015 Veteran Economic Opportunity Report breaks down the following areas of studies, shown in table 7.2. These data emphasize the liberal arts over business and health professions. In assessing earned veteran and nonveteran associate degrees, the trend of liberal arts and sciences, combined with business and nonengineering degrees, is similar to veterans' selections. According to the National Science Foundation (2012, app. table 2–16), 685,666 associate's degrees were conferred in 2009 in the nonscience and engineering category, considerably outnumbering the 47,485 science and engineering degrees. Some 485,772 bachelor's degrees were earned in science and engineering in 2009, versus 1,055,932

Table 7.2. Fields of Study Pursued by Veterans, 2002–2013.

Major Concentration	Number of Veterans	Percentage
Liberal Arts and Sciences, General Studies, and Humanities	57,339	31%
Business, Management, Marketing, and Related Support	35,103	19%
Health Professions and Related Clinical Sciences	19,344	19%
Security and Protective Services	17,570	9%
Engineering Technologies/Technicians	13,820	7%
Computer, Information Sciences, and Support Services	8,816	5%
Mechanic and Repair Technologies/Technicians	7,060	4%
Multi/Interdisciplinary Studies	6,361	3%

Source: Department of Veterans Affairs (2015, 18).

combined nonscience and engineering degrees (National Science Foundation 2012, app. table 2–18). While it is difficult to fully assess veterans' selected majors versus those of nonveterans, it appears that liberal arts and sciences, general studies, and humanities, combined with business and other nonscience and engineering degrees, rank the highest, similar to nonveterans' degrees tracked by the Census Bureau.

Assessing enrollment effects, in 2009 there was a major increase in educational funding for veterans, but enrollment has declined nationally after a significant enrollment boom in 2008–2009 (Fain 2014). Although the recession of 2008 expanded enrollment based on nonveterans' desire to retrain and retool, the economic upturn of recent years has seen a decrease in enrollments. Specifically hard hit are small private liberal arts universities, which don't have access to state and federal funding. However, while universities are undergoing expansion of part-time and online degree programs, the current trend is for veterans to apply for full-time rather than part-time programs (Department of Veterans Affairs 2015b), with some for-profit and not-for-profit entrepreneurial online and extension programs providing direct access to service personnel while they are still in the military.

Though G.I. benefits are provided for any member of the armed services, institutions could assist service members by offering accelerated degree programs. While other branches of the military have lower completion rates, the evidence suggests that the air force provides better access to education and resources. One major advantage is the Air University, which is a regionally accredited community college that provides 68 degree options to air force service members. No other branch of the armed services has an individual institution set up to provide educational degrees for its active-service members at large (Air University 2012). Having a community college dedicated to serving members of the air force explains the higher percentages of associate's-degree-level enrollments and shorter degree completion times in the air force. Other military branches should be encouraged to consider expanding educational access through a means such as this.

Veterans Working in Higher Education

Many veterans have transferred skills, and more important the values of public service, to successful careers after the military in higher education administrative and academic posts. The transition from military to civilian leadership has been evident in a myriad of professions, from corporate boardrooms to political life. For some, the opportunity to transfer the attributes of public service fostered in the military to close association with faculty and staff members and students has been attractive. Many retired and newly discharged military members enter higher education as a new profession.

For example, graduates of the U.S. Military Academy (West Point) have strongly affected higher education in America. They have founded universities such as Norwich and Howard and led them as presidents. Confederate general Robert E. Lee's post–Civil War role as president of Washington College, which would later add his name to its title, led to innovations such as engineering, commercial education, and modern languages being added to the classical curriculum. General Dwight Eisenhower's tenure as president of Columbia proved to be a bridge to the U.S. presidency (Rice and Vigna 2013, 5). Contemporarily, West Point graduate and colonel DeBow Freed, who served as a university president for over 32 years at Ohio Northern University and two other institutions, is an example of a life of service to the nation, promoted as an enduring purpose by the academy and highlighted in *West Point Leadership: Profiles of Courage* (Rice and Vigna 2013). These and many others are examples of veterans employed in higher education who continue to enrich colleges and universities today.

Educational Resources for Veterans

According to the National Survey of Veterans by Westat (2010, 145), around 73 percent of veterans who utilized the G.I. Bill's educational funding found it to be important, as shown in table 7.3. This percentage of those surveyed is nearly in line with those who have completed degree programs. However, not all veterans utilize educational benefits to complete degrees. In the National Survey of Veterans Report, over 36 percent of surveyed National Guard reservists were not aware of internal VA education or training benefits, and 30 percent never considered getting any education or training from the VA. This is an opportunity to begin fixing information chains and providing veterans the opportunity to benefit from educational programs internally and through private and public universities. One frustration in dedicating time to attending colleges and universities is the bureaucracy of institutions, which fail to cater to veteran students and tend to place them in the same category as nonveteran students. While some universities and colleges are ranked higher than others, there is a recognized need for institutions to provide additional and focused orientation training to assist veterans and their transition to higher education (Ackerman, DiRamio, and Mitchell 2009, 8). In addition, because veterans are accustomed to strict military codes of conduct, orders, and social interactions, institutions and some veteran students may find a debriefing style of information beneficial before starting course work.

Table 7.3. Importance of VA Education or Training Benefits by Cohort.

	Percent who have used VA education or training benefits	Percent of those using who indicated that VA benefits were "extremely important" or "very important" in helping meet educational goals preparing to get a better job
All Veterans	37	73
Service Cohorts Nov. 1941 or earlier	33	59
WWII (Dec. 1941 to Dec. 1946)	38	76
Jan 1947 to June 1950	31	78
Korean War	37	70
Feb. 1955 to July 1964	31	63
Vietnam Era (Aug. 1964 to Apr. 1975)	48	69
May 1975 to July 1990	30	74
Aug. 1990 to Aug. 2001	34	83
Sept. 2001 or later	43	90
Females (all ages)	35	87
Black/African American (all ages)	33	77
Hispanic (all ages)	39	84
Young veterans (ages 18–30)	48	95

Source: Westat (2010, table 4.1.8-D).

While this technique would be beneficial for veteran students who are no longer serving in the armed forces, other programs need to be in place for those individuals who are currently serving in the military. Institutions could enroll a greater number of veteran students on their campuses by developing curricula that would operate around service members' current military commitments and provide targeted orientation and student services that cater to a rigorous military schedule. Finally, institutions should put in place policies for coursework for those who are called away from their studies to serve their country, and provide easy suspension and reactivation for courses. Ultimately, for both discharged veterans and active service persons, new resources must be developed to assist those who have served their country.

Military Academies, Federal Service Academies, and ROTC

A variety of academies, colleges, and universities allow candidates who apply to higher educational institutions immediately after high school to attend military institutions, or officer training programs, to obtain a commission in one of the branches of the armed services. These institutions offer four-year baccalaureate degrees along with a commission as an officer in one of the armed services, the Coast Guard, or the maritime service. Others are senior military colleges that offer Reserve Officers' Training Corp (ROTC) programs to obtain a commission as an officer in any branch of the armed services. ROTC was established within a senior military college, but the program option extends to other universities across the country (U.S. Army 2016). (Information about each institution can be found on its Web site.)

United States Military Academy

The best known federal military educational institution in the country is the U.S. Military Academy, commonly known as West Point. The academy is a dedicated institution of higher learning that trains future commissioned officers for the army. Historically, West Point has trained great generals, such as Ulysses S. Grant and Robert E. Lee, and presidents, such as Andrew Jackson and Dwight Eisenhower. From its founding in 1802 until 1976, the academy only trained and educated men. In 1976, after Congress authorized the enrollment of women, the academy accepted female cadets, with 62 graduating in 1980. While the academy has changed over the years, its rigorous educational structure and military leadership focus are maintained today.

According to West Point's current admissions information, the institution has 4,000 cadets currently enrolled. In order to be admitted to the academy, candidates must be between the ages of 17 and 22, with zero dependents or marriages, and not currently pregnant. The academy requires candidates to be in good physical and mental health, requiring a medical examination as part of the process. These requirements are on top of standard academics, college entrance exams (e.g., ACT or SAT scores), and character assessments. The final requirement for all candidates is to be nominated by a member of the House of Representatives, a senator, or the vice president. Upon being admitted to the academy, students' tuition is fully covered by the army, after students agree to be commissioned as officers.

United States Naval Academy

In 1845, four decades after the establishment of West Point, Congress recognized the need for a naval academy. The newly established Naval School opened with 50 midshipmen and 7 professors. The original curriculum included mathematics, military-focused courses, and two liberal arts concentrations. After five years of operations, the Naval School changed its name to the United States Naval Academy. Like West Point, the academy began to admit women in 1976. Today, women are 20 percent of the freshman enrollment at the Naval Academy.

Like West Point and other U.S. military academies, the Naval Academy is highly selective. The maximum age for enrollment is 23, rather than 22. The Naval Academy, like West Point, requires applicants to obtain a recommendation from a member of the House of Representatives or a senator and has similar application guidelines. Upon acceptance the navy will cover all tuition, in exchange for five years' active-duty service in the navy.

United States Coast Guard Academy

Founded in 1876, the U.S. Coast Guard Academy has an unusual history, as the first cohort of cadets did not attend a physical, land-based campus, but operated on a schooner named *Dobbin*. The academy would not open a physical campus on land until 1890. Today the Coast Guard Academy is in New London, Connecticut, and offers a variety of curriculum concentrations, from engineering to the humanities.

Unlike West Point and the Naval Academy, the Coast Guard Academy does not require a congressional nomination or presidential approval. According to the admissions office at the academy, the process is similar to that of selective colleges and universities. Coast Guard Academy is tuition free in exchange for five years' military service; however, students who applied to the academy prior to 2010 were required to pay an entrance fee of $3,000.

United States Air Force Academy

After the establishment of the U.S. Air Force as a separate entity in 1947, discussions about a military academy soon followed. In 1954, with the state of Colorado contributing $1 million for land, the air force established an academy at Colorado Springs, which today enrolls 4,000 students. However, while other military academies operate as a single educational entity, the Air Force Academy incorporates an air force base and houses the 10th Air Wing, with a population of 3,000 military and civilian personnel, surrounded by a community of 25,000 people.

The admission standards are similar to those of West Point and the Naval Academy. Applicants must be U.S. citizens, between the ages of 17 and 23, be unmarried, have no dependents, and be physically fit. The academy also requires an interview to attest to the overall character of the applicant, and utilizes what it calls a "legally authorized nominating entity" in support of a candidate's application; for domestic applicants it is congressional or presidential, for residents of a U.S. territory it is the governor of Puerto Rico or congressional delegate, and for international students it is a nomination from the applicant's country of origin. Though the academy operates in a liberal arts education environment, the ultimate goal is to train future officers to serve in the air force.

United States Merchant Marine Academy

The Merchant Marine Academy is located in Kings Point, New York. A merchant marine is someone who serves the country's marine transportation and defense needs in peace and war. The complexity of this role is evident in the challenging coursework and demanding credit hours, including the heaviest credit requirements of all the federal military academies. In addition, graduates obtain not only a BS degree, but also a U.S. Coast Guard license and an officer's commission in the armed forces. While West Point and the Naval Academy require service in their respective service branches, Merchant Marine Academy graduates have the option of serving five years in the maritime industry, with eight years as an officer in a reserve unit, or five years' active duty in any of the armed forces. Similar to the Coast Guard Academy, nominations from Congress are not required.

Unlike the other military academies, the degree majors are heavily focused on merchant marine concentrations.

Nonfederal Institutions

The federal military academies are not the only higher educational institutions with a military background and curricular components that offer both sponsored tuition and training leading to a commission as a military officer. There are many nonfederal colleges and universities offering these types of opportunities. The oldest of these institutions is Norwich University, which was founded in 1819 as a private military college. Norwich University offers on-campus access to all branches of the armed services and is the birthplace of the ROTC (Norwich University 2016).

Texas A&M is a state university with a deep military background, which houses a military college with separate brigades, wings, or regiments for each of the corresponding armed forces. With a similar military background, the Virginia Polytechnic Institute and State University (2016a, 2016b) (Virginia Tech) hosts a large and active ROTC on campus. While Virginia Tech no longer requires enrollment in the corps, the Virginia Military Institute (VMI), located 80 miles from Virginia Tech, requires all students to actively participate in ROTC; however, unlike at the federal military academies, students are not required to accept commissions into the armed forces (Virginia Military Institute 2016a). Virginia Military Institute has a strong academic and military history, with 11 alumni winning Rhodes scholarships and 7 Medal of Honor recipients (Virginia Military Institute 2016b). The Military College of South Carolina (the Citadel) is structured like VMI (Military College of South Carolina 2016).

Reserve Officers' Training Corps

The ROTC was created to offer tuition scholarships for students enrolled at civilian universities and colleges, with an agreement that graduates would serve for a variety of time periods in one of the branches of the armed services after graduation. The idea and the effect is to transfer some of the curriculum of the service academies into civilian institutions, allowing them to produce much larger cohorts of trained officers than the service academies could hope to educate without dramatic enlargement. Michigan State University, the first land-grant institution in the country, still operates an ROTC program on campus. While students receiving an ROTC scholarship are required to accept a commission into the ROTC service branch, students not intending to be commissioned in the armed forces are allowed to participate in Michigan State University ROTC program with the other cadets and earn college credit for the first two years, but they must pay tuition on their own (Department of Military Science 2015). Other land-grant universities also operate ROTC programs, such as Ohio State University, Pennsylvania State University, and the University of Maryland. While ROTC is prevalent throughout universities in the country, all have different formats and requirements to match the community and culture of the university they are a part of.

The Universities and Colleges That Veterans Attend

Veterans can be found at every type of institution in the galaxy of American higher education, from Ivy League universities to small community colleges. However, they exhibit slightly different enrollment patterns than students as a whole. For example, veterans are more likely to attend public, as opposed to private, universities and colleges.

Public Institutions of Higher Learning

Veterans tend to choose public institutions of higher learning to utilize their G.I. benefits, as opposed to private colleges, community colleges, or for-profit institutions (Census Bureau 2007, 10). One of the greatest benefits is the on-campus experience and community with a wealth of student resources. In addition, publicly funded institutions tend to offer reasonable tuition rates for in-state students and have as their mission to better the public good. Land-grant institutions are intended to make agricultural, technological, and military advancements for the states. Flagship institutions expand major research, while other public institutions fill needs on both larger and smaller scales. These institutions can be attractive to students who wish to immerse themselves in that mission and campus environment; the smaller, private, liberal arts colleges have honorable and precisely focused missions.

Ivy League and Exclusive Private Universities

The admissions acceptance rates at Ivy League and other elite private institutions of higher learning are significantly lower than at public or smaller, private liberal arts institutions. Admission rates are far lower because of the high application standards for prospective students, including high grade point averages (GPA), character interviews, life experience, and other attributes. While there is nothing to preclude veterans from entering these institutions, the standards of admission are typically the same as for nonveterans.

However, in recent years, institutions such as the Posse Foundation have created a multitude of educational program assistance and a network for veterans (Posse Foundation 2015). The foundation's Posse Veterans Program connects veterans with Ivy League and exclusive private universities and provides application resources. Under the program, these networked institutions look beyond high school GPA and assess veterans' military training and life experience when making admissions decisions. The purpose is to increase awareness of dedicated veterans who are prepared to complete a degree, but would otherwise not be reviewed because of their previous military educational background.

Private Liberal Arts Institutions

Private liberal arts universities and colleges play a significant educational role in veterans' education. While the major public universities have their place, most of the small liberal arts universities have deep historical missions that expanded during the 20th century. In Ohio during the early to mid-1900s, Tiffin University dedicated its curricula to training women in clerical and secretarial work; in many ways this allowed Tiffin, as well as other intuitions, to support U.S. efforts in World War II. Expanding the curricula to incorporate these fields resulted in massive enrollment growth and laid the groundwork for the university to be developed into what it is today (Grandillo 2010, 161). This is an example of how smaller universities can dedicate their missions to having a major societal impact.

In assessing private universities today, both the Department of Veterans Affairs and the Census Bureau identify veteran degree completion rates as being the highest in private liberal arts universities. The average veteran's first-degree completion time at private not-for-profit institutions is 4.7 years, compared to 5.8 years at public institutions (Department of Veterans Affairs 2015). This can be attributed to flexible curriculum processes and better student-to-faculty ratios at small, private schools than at large, public universities.

Many of the small, private liberal arts colleges have religious backgrounds. These institutions either continue those missions today or have abandoned those religious cores to embrace a more secularized engagement, with the religious foundation as a historical backdrop. While the maintenance or evolution of these missions is neither right nor wrong, they still serve a purpose today. Veterans can find solace in embracing the choices of many stellar programs in these universities, enjoying smaller class sizes and intimate campus settings. For example, our own institution, Madonna University, embraces a liberal arts core for students, while also implementing the call of Saint Francis by serving and making the world a better place. Both veterans and nonveterans can find noble missions and a call above and beyond, which they can apply to their own lives as they impact communities both domestically and internationally.

Community Colleges

Community colleges have the largest number of veteran enrollments, offering technical degrees and pathways to four-year institutions through articulation agreements (Student Veterans of America 2014, 36). In addition, community colleges offer expanded university centers that bring major four-year institutions to on-campus community colleges. While veterans add an on-campus dynamic to the community, previous military training can benefit the classroom by providing theoretical and practical military insight. A deficiency of community colleges is that some tend to not have a vibrant on-campus student life experience or the same dedication to service learning as four-year institutions, which tend to match the mission of the university to the curricula and on-campus community. This can be attributed to the commuter focus of the community college. While veterans can add to the dynamic of a community college environment, a traditional four-year institution would allow them more educational interaction with the school's community than a community college does.

Not every associate's degree and community college is created equal. Some community colleges, such as Salt Lake Community College (SLCC), have dedicated resources and space for veterans. SLCC provides veterans with a student center where the college can deliver information and dedicate time and resources to veterans (Ahern 2015). The college set aside a physical space for a safe environment and to assist those with post-traumatic stress disorder (PTSD). In addition, SLCC provides mentors, peer advisers, and psychologically trained staff to provide emotional as well as academic support for veterans. This is a great example and a possible model for community colleges for assisting veterans, and should be a call for other institutions to build upon this model or create other models for improved services for veterans, which could then be evaluated for effectiveness.

For-Profit Universities

According to the 2015 Veteran Economic Opportunity Report (Department of Veterans Affairs 2015, 52), the average time for a veteran to complete a degree at a private for-profit institution is 3.3 years. One explanation for the reduced time to degree is that many for-profit institutions offer life experience credits, which leads to a reduction in program completion time (University of Phoenix 2016). Active-duty service members with training certifications and life experience can apply those toward college credit at these institutions. While some private not-for-profit colleges and universities offer this option, the validity and quality of examination of these credits is questionable. In addition, in 2014 the U.S. Department of Education questioned for-profit universities for possible violations of the 90/10 rule, a requirement that for-profit colleges and universities can only get 90 percent of their operating revenue from federal student aid (Stratford 2014). Having veterans enrolled is advantageous, as G.I. educational benefits do not count for the 90/10 rule, which makes them extremely attractive to for-profit recruiters.

Graduating with a degree is a proud moment and should be a celebrated accomplishment. This is even more true for veterans, who have utilized their G.I. Bill benefits at an institution and should have the expectation that their conferred degree will give them future career and educational opportunities. This is unfortunately not the case for some for-profit graduates. One specific case is Bryan Babcock, who testified in front of the Committee on Veterans' Affairs (U.S. House of Representatives, 2013). Babcock, who was pursuing a degree at a for-profit institution of higher learning, was working toward a degree that would open a career in law enforcement. Babcock soon discovered that his degree was not of the same caliber as traditional not-for-profit bachelor's degree programs, and that his credits, and the degree, were not recognized by potential employers. This is a tragic scenario for a veteran, who was duped by clever marketing by a for-profit institution and failed to identify the limitations of his bachelor's degree until after graduation. While for-profit institutions do have a positive side of offerings in the marketplace, there are many stories of regret from both veterans and nonveterans who have attended these institutions. Although not all for-profits operate that way or are riddled with scandal, more information is required from higher educational institutions to inform veterans about the realities of degree programs; this should include all private, public, and for-profit colleges and universities.

Recruitment is an essential function of academic admissions teams in both public and private universities. While every university develops strategic recruiting options, online for-profit universities tend to aggressively market as a major corporation would. Toll-free numbers with instantaneous follow-up are common at major for-profit universities. For-profit institutions are successful at enrolling a little over 10 percent (Student Veterans of America 2014) of the veteran population.

Online and Distance Degree and Educational Access for Veterans

The University of London was granted a charter by Queen Victoria in 1858 to offer distance education to individuals worldwide (University of London 2015). Although correspondence courses are not a new concept, the utilization of the Internet and technology has changed the landscape. Public and private universities have made strides in expanding this mode of education. Though for-profits have been operating over the Internet for a while, public universities are just starting to engage online to expand their degree offerings. Well-known public institutions such as Michigan State University, Pennsylvania State University, Central Michigan University, and even Harvard University, with its Extension School, are offering baccalaureate and graduate degrees in an online or hybrid format. While deployed or active-duty service members previously would have been unable to attend courses far away, these new formats allow access to degrees that was not previously possible. In addition, with reputable institutions adding solid curricula and reputable degrees that cost less than those of for-profit institutions, service members can enroll without having to be discharged. Although online learning can have an isolated atmosphere, veterans and service members can apply their knowledge and experience to the online community and add a dynamic that would be lacking between nonveterans. In addition, many online community degree enrollees have some access to on-campus resources.

Conclusion

The military and higher educational landscapes are changing in this country. Enrollment numbers are soft and fluctuating. Public research universities are developing new brand strategies. Private institutions are bringing nontraditional students into their core missions. For-profit schools are targeting new audiences for accessible degree programs. So too shall veterans continue to play a significant role in the higher education landscape. It is important that higher education institutions continue to develop better degree programs to fulfill the needs of veterans. While nonveterans enjoy access to financial aid, grants, scholarships, and sponsorships, these programs are often modest in comparison to the financial support the G.I. Bill offers veterans for obtaining a better future. This is why institutions of higher learning must continue to develop and honor the precious contribution of veterans and offer the best curricula they can provide. Ensuring a better world for veterans must be a focus for institutions of higher learning. This is required of both private and public institutions, as higher education continues to evolve.

References

Ackerman, Robert, David DiRamio, and Regina L. Garza Mitchell. 2009. "Transitions: Combat Veterans as College Students." *New Directions for Student Services* 126: 5–14.

Ahern, Aaron. 2015. "Salt Lake Community College Veterans Services: A Model of Serving Veterans in Higher Education." *New Directions for Community Colleges* 172 (December 1): 77–86.

Air University. 2012. "Air University Community College of the Air Force 2014–2016 General Catalog Number 20." Revised March 9, 2015. Accessed March 11, 2016. http://www.au.af.mil/au/barnes/ccaf/catalog/2014cat/2014_2016_General_catalog.pdf.

Altschuler, Glenn, and Stuart Blumin. 2009. *The G.I. Bill: A New Deal for Veterans*. New York: Oxford University Press.

Census Bureau. 2007. "The Educational Attainment of Veterans: 2007." Accessed December 15, 2015. https://www.census.gov/hhes/veterans/files/veteransedu cation.pdf.

Census Bureau. 2011. "National Security and Veterans Affairs." *Statistical Abstract of the United States: 2012*. Accessed December 15, 2015. http://www2.census.gov/library/publications/2011/compendia/statab/131ed/tables/defense.pdf.

Census Bureau. 2014. "S2101. Veteran Status 2014 American Community Survey 1-Year Estimates." Washington: DC: Census Bureau. American FactFinder Advanced Search. http://factfinder.census.gov/faces/tableservices/jsf/pages/pro ductview.xhtml?src=bkmk.

Department of Military Science. 2015. Spartan Battalion, Michigan State University. Accessed 2 March 2, 2016. http://armyrotc.msu.edu/.

Department of Veterans Affairs. 2005. "VA History in Brief." Accessed December 15, 2015. http://www.va.gov/opa/publications/archives/docs/history_in_brief.pdf.

Department of Veterans Affairs. 2015. *2015 Veteran Economic Opportunity Report*. Accessed March 2, 2016. http://www.benefits.va.gov/benefits/docs/Veteran EconomicOpportunityReport2015.pdf.

Dethloff, Henry C. 2016. *A Pictorial History of Texas A&M University, 1876–1976*. College Station: Texas A&M University Press.

Eisenmann, Linda. 2006. *Higher Education for Women in Postwar America, 1945–1965*. Baltimore, MD: Johns Hopkins University Press.

Fain, Paul. 2014. "Recession and Completion." *Inside Higher Ed*, November 18. Accessed December 15, 2015. https://www.insidehighered.com/news/2014/11/18/enrollment-numbers-grew-during-recession-graduation-rates-slipped.

Grandillo, Michael A. 2010. *Onward to the Dawn*. St. Louis, MO: Reed Press.

Holder, Kelly Ann. 2007. "The Educational Attainment of Veterans: 2007." Census Bureau. Accessed March 2, 2016. https://www.census.gov/hhes/veterans/files/veteranseducation.pdf.

Kim, Young M., and James S. Cole. "Student Veterans/Service Members' Engagement in College and University Life and Education." American Council on Education; National Survey of Student Engagement. Accessed March 2, 2016. https://www.acenet.edu/news-room/Documents/Student-Veterans-Service-Members-Engagement.pdf.

Military College of South Carolina. 2016. "Requirements for Transfer Students." Accessed January 28, 2016. http://q1.citadel.edu/root/admissions-requirements/admissions-requirements-for-transfer-students.

Morris, Catherine. 2014. "For Profits Under Fire." *Diverse Issues in Higher Education* 31 (20): 16. http://diverseeducation.com/.

National Center for Veterans Analysis and Statistics. 2014. "Veterans Employment 2000 to 2013." Accessed March 2, 2016. http://www.va.gov/vetdata/docs/SpecialReports/Employment_Rates_FINAL.pdf.

National Center for Veterans Analysis and Statistics. 2015a. "Profile of Post-9/11 Veterans: 2013." August. Accessed March 2, 2016. http://www.va.gov/vetdata/docs/SpecialReports/Post_911_Veterans_Profile_2013.pdf.

National Center for Veterans Analysis and Statistics. 2015b. "Profile of Veterans: 2013 Data from the American Community Survey." July. http://www.va.gov/vetdata/docs/SpecialReports/Profile_of_Veterans_2013.pdf.

National Center for Veterans Analysis and Statistics. 2015c. "2013 Minority Veterans Report." August. http://www.va.gov/vetdata/docs/SpecialReports/Minority_Veterans_2013.pdf.

National Conference of State Legislatures. 2015. Accessed December 2015. http://www.ncsl.org/research/education/veterans-and-college.aspx.

National Science Foundation. 2012. "Science and Engineering Indicators 2012." Accessed March 2, 2016. http://www.nsf.gov/statistics/seind12/c2/c2s2.htm.

Norwich University. 2016. "Quick Facts." Accessed January 28, 2016. http://about.norwich.edu/quick-facts/.

Posse Foundation. 2015. "Veterans Posse Program." Accessed March 2, 2016. http://www.possefoundation.org/veterans-posse-program.

Rice, Daniel E., and John Vigna. 2013. *West Point Leadership: Profiles of Courage*. N.p.: Daniel E. Rice.

Sander, Libby. 2012. "The Post-9/11 GI Bill, Explained." *Chronicle of Higher Education*, March 11. Accessed March 2, 2016. http://chronicle.com/article/The-Post-9-11-GI-Bill/131125/.

Smole, David P., and Shannon S. Loane. 2008. "A Brief History of Veterans' Education Benefits and Their Value." *Congressional Research Service*, June 25 Accessed March 2, 2016. https://www.fas.org/sgp/crs/misc/RL34549.pdf.

Stratford, Michael. 2014. "New Fodder for 90/10 Debate." *Inside Higher Ed*, October 13. Accessed March 2, 2016. https://www.insidehighered.com/news

/2014/10/13/more-profit-colleges-would-fail-9010-rule-if-veterans-benefits-are-included-analysis.

Student Veterans of America. 2014. "Million Records Project: A Review of Veteran Achievement in Higher Education." Accessed March 2, 2016. http://studentveterans.org/images/Reingold_Materials/mrp/download-materials/mrp_Full_report.pdf.

University of London. 2015. "International Programs: Our History." Accessed December 27, 2015. http://www.londoninternational.ac.uk/our-global-reputation/our-history.

University of Phoenix. 2016. "Prior Learning Assessment." Accessed January 29, 2016. http://www.phoenix.edu/admissions/prior_learning_assessment.html.

U.S. Army. 2016. "Army ROTC, Ways to Attend." Accessed March 2, 2016. http://www.goarmy.com/rotc/ways-to-attend.html.

U.S. House of Representatives, Committee on Veterans' Affairs. 2013. *Hearing, The Value of Education for Veterans at Public, Private and For-Profit Colleges and Universities.* June 20. 113th Cong., 1st sess. Accessed March 2, 2016. https://www.gpo.gov/fdsys/pkg/CHRG-113hhrg82240/pdf/CHRG-113hhrg82240.pdf.

U.S. Senate, Committee on Health, Education, Labor, and Pensions. 2015. *Hearing, The Federal Investment in For-Profit Education: Are Students Succeeding?* 111th Cong., 2nd sess. https://www.gpo.gov/fdsys/pkg/CHRG-111shrg79648/pdf/CHRG-111shrg79648.pdf.

Veterans Benefits Administration. 2016. "Choosing a School." Accessed March 2, 2016. http://www.benefits.va.gov/GIBILL/choosing_a_school.asp#Degree.

Virginia Military Institute. 2016a. "Admission Requirements." Accessed January 28, 2016. http://admissions.vmi.edu/apply/prepare/requirements/#toggle-id-5.

Virginia Military Institute. 2016b. "History of the Virginia Military Institute." Accessed January 28, 2016. http://www.vmi.edu/uploadedFiles/VMI/Communications_Marketing/Media_Relations/fact_sheets/VMI percent20History percent20Fact percent20Sheet percent202014.pdf.

Virginia Polytechnic Institute and State University. 2016a. "Applying to Virginia Tech." Accessed January 28, 2016. http://www.admiss.vt.edu/apply/what-we-look-for/

Virginia Polytechnic Institute and State University. 2016b. "History and Traditions." Accessed January 28, 2016. https://www.vt.edu/about/traditions/hokie.html

Westat. 2010. "National Survey of Veterans, Active Duty Service Members, Demobilized National Guard and Reserve Members, Family Members, and Surviving Spouses." Accessed March 2, 2016. http://www.va.gov/vetdata/docs/SurveysAndStudies/NVSSurveyFinalWeightedReport.pdf.

CHAPTER EIGHT

Veteran Employment in the 21st Century

*Hazel R. Atuel, Mary Keeling,
Sara M. Kintzle, Anthony M. Hassan,
and Carl A. Castro*

Introduction

From its colonial beginnings onward, the United States has taken responsibility for the welfare of the men and women who have fought its wars. The earliest documentation of these efforts comes to us from the Pequot War, waged by the Plymouth Colony and Massachusetts Bay Colony pilgrims against the Pequot Indians in 1636–1637. At the end of that conflict, the Plymouth pilgrims passed a civil act that provided pensions to wounded soldiers or the families of those who had died in the war (Patterson 2014). Every subsequent war resulted in the passing of more legislation to provide greater compensation and benefits for veterans of different conflicts. Thus, the Revolutionary War has the National Pension Law of 1776 for Revolutionary War veterans, the Civil War has the General Pension Act of 1862 for (Union) Civil War veterans, and so forth.

In the aftermath of World War I, Congress passed the Smith-Sears Veterans Rehabilitation Act of 1918, also known as the Soldier's Rehabilitation Act, to provide vocational rehabilitation to veterans with physical disabilities. The Federal Board of Vocational Education was created to carry out the monumental task of providing services to approximately 204,000 wounded soldiers. This board was later subsumed into the Veterans Bureau, a predecessor of today's Department of Veterans Affairs (Elliott and Leung 2005; Department of Veterans Affairs n.d.).

The nation's entry into World War II brought significant legislative changes to veteran employment, with each piece of legislation addressing the pressing needs of veterans at that time. In 1940 Congress passed the Selective Training and Service Act, which guaranteed full reemployment rights to veterans. The intent of the law was to restore veterans to the same jobs they had held prior to military service or, in cases where the job was no longer available, a similar position (Aaronson 1942). This legislation afforded veterans employment protection and prohibited civilian employers from discriminating against veterans on the basis of military service. This was followed by the Veterans' Preference Act of 1944, which mandated that agencies receiving federal funds give preference to the hiring, appointing, and retaining of veterans in the civilian workforce (Patterson 2014; see chapter 12). These three pieces of legislation—the Soldier's Rehabilitation Act, the Selective Training and Service Act, and the Veterans' Preference Act—make up the legislative foundation of veteran employment and were built upon by subsequent legislation (e.g., Veterans' Readjustment Assistance for Korean War veterans, the Veterans' Readjustment Benefits Act of 1966 for Vietnam Veterans, the Emergency Veterans' Job Training Act of 1983 for Korean and Vietnam War veterans, and the Uniformed Services Employment and Reemployment Rights Act of 1994).

Where does veteran employment stand now? In 2014 the Department of Labor estimated that approximately 21.2 million men and women, or 9 percent of the civilian population, were veterans (Bureau of Labor Statistics 2015). Of these veterans, 48 percent were employed, 5 percent were unemployed, and the remaining 47 percent were not in the labor force because they were retired, or were students, or for some other reason. By contrast, among the 218 million nonveteran men and women, 62 percent were employed, 6 percent were unemployed, and 32 percent were not in the labor force. These estimates suggest that fewer veterans are unemployed compared to their civilian counterparts. The unemployment *rate* among veterans was estimated at 6.6 percent in 2013, lower than the unemployment rate for nonveterans, which was 7.2 percent (Collins et al. 2014).

On the surface, these statistics portray veteran employment as a seemingly simple process and perhaps even a discrete event wherein an active duty service member finishes military service and begins employment in the civilian world. These numbers, however, mask the complex processes underlying veteran employment. Our cursory review of veteran employment legislation both hints at and echoes the challenges faced by veterans through the centuries: civilian employment discrimination and civilian community reintegration difficulties. The fact that every conflict has its own veteran employment–related law indicates that the problem has persisted for a long time. How, then, can 21st-century veterans overcome these challenges? To answer this question, we take a step back, reconceptualize veteran employment from multiple perspectives, and situate veteran employment within civilian society and civilian organizational contexts.

Two decades of research on veteran employment is beginning to uncover individual-level (e.g., psychological) and group-level (e.g., military versus civilian culture) factors that conspire to either ease or impede veterans' successful transition from military to civilian employment. Far from being unidirectional, veteran employment is a bidirectional process reflecting the perspectives of both the veteran employee and civilian employer. From the veteran's point of view, going from military to civilian employment is a transition process that at the individual level entails negotiating military-civilian identities (Cohn 1978; Forces in Mind Trust 2013), navigating the civilian world (Clemens and Milsom 2008), and integrating into the civilian workforce (Prudential Financial 2012) and, ultimately, civilian society. In some cases, accommodating the wounds of war (physical and/or behavioral) is a prerequisite to employment (Tanielian et al. 2008). At the relational level, veterans need to be supported by a network of family and community base (Demers 2011). On the other hand, from the perspective of civilian employers, veteran employment necessitates translating military skills into civilian occupations (Routon 2014) and integrating military culture with civilian culture (e.g., Chicas et al. 2012). The combined findings of research strongly suggest that veteran employment is a dynamic and reciprocal process between the veteran employee and the civilian employer and, furthermore, is undergirded by military, veteran, and civilian support networks.

This chapter aims to (1) contextualize veteran employment as a military-civilian divide; (2) utilize the psychological, implied, and relational contract frameworks to organize the research on veteran employment; and (3) provide directives for future research. It presents an overview of the complex challenges found in veteran employment and sets a research agenda for future studies on veteran employment.

A Greater Understanding of Veteran Employment

The Military-Civilian Divide as Applied to Veteran Employment

From our perspective, the initial step toward an in-depth understanding of veteran employment is to contextualize it as reflecting the military-civilian divide. It has already been argued elsewhere that the military is part and parcel of the diversity that defines a subset of American society (Atuel and De Pedro 2014; Yamada, Atuel, and Weiss 2013). The military is part of the collective "we," but it is different from the rest of "us" (i.e., civilians). It is not the commonalities, but the distinctiveness of the military, that elicits an "us versus them" dichotomy. As applied to veteran employment, the military-civilian divide is manifested in the perseverance of the military identity and military organizational values among veterans.

The Social Identity of Veterans

Crossing over from the military to the civilian workforce is not synonymous with taking on a civilian identity. Unlike their civilian counterparts, veterans' self-concept is derived from their previous military training and occupation (Baruch and Quick 2007, 2009; Brunger, Serrato, and Ogden 2013; Kleykamp 2009; Morin 2011). Past military service has transformed veterans and given them a sense of self that is directly tied to their military experiences. The military has already been described as a "warrior society" in which individuals are trained to be in a constant physical and psychological state of "combat readiness" (Castro and Adler 1999). Whether or not service members engage in actual combat, their primary activities are directed toward preparing for or supporting combat efforts. A growing body of research is already finding support for this "warrior identity" among service members (Daley 1999) and veterans (Lancaster and Hart 2015) alike. In the civilian workplace, past military experience functions as a double-edged sword for veterans: it becomes the basis for defining who they are and who they are not in relation to their civilian peers. In the civilian work environment, the "warrior" identity heightens the cultural differences between veterans and civilians.

The Organizational Values of Veterans

Unlike most civilian jobs, military service is a 24-hour, 7-day-a-week assignment. Service members can be, and have been, called to duty at any time and anywhere they are needed in different parts of the nation and the world. In addition, even while not in uniform, service members are expected to obey military laws, norms, and rules of conduct (Coll, Weiss, and Yarvis 2011). Owing to this special circumstance, the military identity is not "turned off," and perhaps becomes the most salient of all the identities that service members hold (such as gender, race, etc.). On the other hand, civilian jobs are subject to labor laws that for the most part restrict work hours to a certain range (e.g., 8–12 hours a day). Civilian jobs also are embedded within organizations reflecting diverse organizational climates and cultures. Generally speaking, civilian organizations pride themselves on creating a culture of their own to demonstrate leadership innovation (Jung, Chow, and Wu 2003) in the field. Divergence, then, not conformity, is the norm. For veterans, valuing divergence over conformity is anathema to military group cohesion and esprit de corps because it places the individual above the group (Dion 2000; Manning 1991).

When veterans enter the civilian workforce, they begin to confront fundamental differences within themselves in relation to their civilian peers. The perseverance of the military identity and organizational values serve as psychological demarcating lines between veterans and civilians. In some cases, veterans report the civilian employment experience as meaningless, primarily because it does not align with how they see themselves, as "warriors" (Bowling and Sherman 2008). Other veterans perceive creativity, promoted within the civilian workplace, as disorganized or chaotic, and the relative lack of conformity as synonymous with a lack of discipline (Bullock et al. 2009; Buzetta and Rowe 2012). These perceived differences create social distance between veterans and civilians and lower vested interests in civilian careers on the part of veterans. In other words, different identities and organizational values prevent the formation of friendships between veterans and civilians, as well as veterans' long-term civilian career planning (Simpson and Armstrong 2009). As a related consequence, veterans report a sense of isolation from their civilian peers (Hinojosa and Hinojosa 2011) or aimlessness in their careers (Bullock et al. 2009).

Bridging the Military-Civilian Divide as Applied to Veteran Employment

How then do we address this military-civilian divide related to veteran employment? Since veteran employment involves two parties—a veteran employee and a civilian employer—we borrow from organizational theory and research to guide our way forward. Rousseau (1989) conceptualized the employment relationship as reflecting two contracts: a psychological contract and an implied contract. The psychological contract pertains to an *employee's subjective beliefs about the reciprocal obligation* between the employee and the organization, while the implied contract refers to the *patterns of mutual obligation* between the employee and employer. Psychological contracts focus on the employee's experience, whereas implied contracts involve shared norms and expectations between the employee and employer. A study on psychological and implied contracts examined employer-employee dyads and found that mutuality (i.e., agreement regarding one party's specific obligations) and reciprocity (i.e., agreement regarding the reciprocal exchange) are positively related to employee productivity and career advancement (Dabos and Rousseau 2004). That is, when employers and employees have shared understandings of obligations and commitments, employees do more and achieve more, which benefits both parties. These findings also suggest that psychological and implied contracts are not independent of each other; rather, they affect each other, so that mutual obligations (the implied contract) have the potential to shape subjective beliefs (the psychological contract) or vice versa.

Other studies on psychological and implied contracts have examined employment relationships in various contexts (e.g., in the private sector, Turnley and Feldman 1998; in the public sector, Guest and Conway 2002) including the military workforce. For example, Castro and colleagues (2006) applied psychological and implied contracts to shed light on the leadership style (flexible pragmatic versus rigid institutional) best suited to enhance unit performance and the well-being of subordinates. The authors observed that variations in leadership style are associated with variations in implied and psychological contracts. When leaders and subordinates do not agree with the obligations and commitments made within the implied contract, this disagreement informs subordinates' psychological contracts. Simply put, the lack of consensus between leader and subordinates creates a "ripple effect" on both the individual and group levels, with subordinates exhibiting low morale, cohesion, and retention, which in turn affect unit performance.

Following Castro and colleagues (2006), we use the psychological and implied contract framework and extend its application to veteran employment. Moreover, we broaden our understanding by adding a relational contract to the overall conceptual framework. A *relational contract* is the array of social support networks surrounding veterans. Veterans do not exist in a social vacuum. Rather, they are embedded within social networks acquired or formed throughout their lives. These networks include the civilian, military, and veteran groups they belong to. Whether or not veterans choose to associate with any of these groups is beyond the scope of this chapter. Our aim is to merely situate veteran employment within the wider social context. Let us now turn to a definition of each contract as applied to veteran employment and review the empirical base supporting each contract.

The Psychological Contract of Veterans

The psychological contract of veterans pertains to subjective beliefs about reciprocal obligations (Rousseau 1989) within the civilian workplace. It reflects how veterans conceive of commitments made between the self and the civilian employer. It is an individually held, cognitive representation of mutual agreements made within the civilian workforce. The caveat to this contract, however, is that it is shaped by past military service. This is a critical point of departure for the psychological contract of veterans, because their previous military experience informs their expectations of civilian employment. In other words, the "give and take" within military service lays the foundation for the "give and take" between the veteran and the civilian employer.

When veterans transition out of the military, they are coming from an organization considered to be the largest employer in the United States (Department of Defense n.d.). The occupational distribution within the military falls on a broad spectrum representing almost every industry, from agricultural to medical to technological (Today's Military 2015. It is not surprising then that the majority of veterans who transition out of the military are able to find civilian employment (Bureau of Labor Statistics 2014). In 2011 the Department of Labor reported the top four industries employing both male and female veterans, representing various sectors of the economy: government (21 percent male veterans, 30 percent female veterans), manufacturing (14 percent male, 23 percent female), professional (10 percent male, 9 percent female), and retail trade (8 percent male, 8 percent female) (Department of Labor 2011). A closer look at additional data shows different patterns of occupational distribution between male and female veterans (Bureau of Labor Statistics 2014). Of employed male veterans, almost 50 percent held professional (and related), management/business/financial operations, or service occupational roles. Compared to their civilian peers, male veterans were less likely to work in construction. For employed female veterans, almost 70 percent had professional (and related), office/administrative support, or management/business/financial operations occupational roles. Compared to their civilian peers, female veterans were less likely to work in service and sales.

While most veterans transition to the civilian workforce successfully (Morris 2012), other veterans do not make this transition as successfully. For veterans facing difficulties, research has found that a key problem is the relative lack of understanding how the skills, occupational experience, and qualifications gained during military service can be translated into skills, experiences, and qualifications relevant and appropriate to civilian jobs (Kintzle et al. 2015). Additional research indicates difficulties experienced by veterans regarding suitable positions based on how military-specific skills, responsibilities, and experiences can translate to the civilian workplace (Hall et al. 2014; Harrell and Berglass 2012). The ability to match military skills and experiences to civilian job qualifications and requirements has been highlighted as one of the most significant challenges directly related to veteran employment (Faberman and Foster 2013; Hall et al. 2014; Harrell and Berglass 2012). Specifically, the challenges experienced by veterans with résumé writing, interviewing, professional networking, career advancement, and negotiating salaries and benefits are identified in the literature as impacting the ability to translate skills, experiences, and qualifications when making civilian job applications (Prudential Financial 2012).

Employment burdens are compounded among veterans with physical and psychological injuries (Burnett-Zeigler et al. 2011; Elbogen et al. 2012; Horton et al. 2013; O'Connor et al. 2013; Smith 2014). It is reported that veterans facing health challenges as a result of military combat report greater difficulty in finding and maintaining work (Faberman and Foster 2013). In a survey of 1,845 post-9/11 veterans, 65 percent reported having some kind of physical or psychological complaints. Of those with physical and/or psychological health complaints, 23 percent reported being unemployed, compared to 18 percent unemployment among those veterans without any health complaints (Prudential Financial 2012). In these cases, accommodating the physical and/or psychological wounds of war is a prerequisite to employment (Ainspan 2008; Tanielian et al. 2008).

Another line of research is beginning to reveal racial/ethnic differences in the military to civilian employment transition experience. Utilizing data from the 2013 Los Angeles County Veteran Survey (Castro et al. 2014), Atuel and colleagues (2015) examined racial and ethnic differences in job status, yearly income, and job challenges. The overall results showed that black veterans are less likely to have full-time jobs and were earning less than their white counterparts, and that Latino veterans reported greater job challenges than non-Latino white veterans. These results suggest economic disparities, with veterans from underrepresented groups bearing the greatest burden.

For 21st-century veterans, psychological contracts vary as a function of the realities they face when seeking and maintaining employment in the civilian workplace. For most veterans who are employed in the civilian workforce, the military to civilian employment transition appears to be seamless. For this group, perhaps military service provided knowledge and skills that became their capital in gaining and maintaining civilian employment. In addition, perhaps this group of veterans is more physically and psychologically prepared than their veteran peers who are facing employment difficulties (see Kintzle et al. 2015). In this case, the psychological contract could reflect an equitable relationship between the veteran self and the civilian employer. For other veterans, military service seems to put them at a disadvantage at various stages of the employment process.

At the preemployment phase, some veterans report having difficulty navigating the civilian hiring process and translating military-specific skills to civilian occupations (see Kintzle et al. 2015) Once they are employed, a new set of struggles emerges and pertains to opportunities for advancement and higher earnings potential. For veterans facing these employment challenges, the psychological contract is perhaps best described as an inequitable relationship between the veteran employee and the civilian employer. This is because past military experience is found to have little or no bearing in securing and maintaining employment in the civilian work environment. For this group, the knowledge and skills acquired during military service have seemingly limited use in the civilian workplace. Finally, for those who are suffering from physical and/or psychological injuries related to military service, these challenges are more acute, and the prospects for employment are even dimmer. They face fewer opportunities to become employed in the civilian workplace.

The Implied Contract of Veteran Employment

On the other hand, the implied contract of veteran employment refers to the patterns of mutual obligations found in the employee-employer relationship (Rousseau 1989). It is based on shared norms and expectations between the veteran employee and the civilian employer. An implied contract reflects the series of interactions demonstrating commitments made by the veteran employee to the civilian employer and vice versa. From our perspective, the start and end point of the implied contract as applied to veteran employment is the civilian employer. This is because the explicit and implicit rules that govern employee behavior originate from the employer (Rock and Wachter 1996). Although by definition an implied contract is mutual in nature, reciprocity reflects a range of acceptable behavior defined by the employer.

In a RAND study on veteran employment, Hall and colleagues (2014) showed that civilian employers perceived value in hiring veterans. Generally, civilian employers reported veterans to be experienced leaders, able to adapt in a fast-paced environment without stress, demonstrating a strong work ethic, exhibiting integrity and loyalty, and experienced in working with a culturally diverse group or in a global environment. Civilian employers have effective recruitment strategies, activities, and veterans' programs in place that demonstrate best practices for recruitment. However, Hall and colleagues also found that the majority of employers' efforts have been focused more on recruitment and less on retaining veteran employees once they are hired. These existing practices have led to the recommendation that employers should allocate recruitment resources strategically so they can evaluate their current recruitment activities and direct resources to activities showing the greatest results, including veteran performance and career development that are likely to aid retention.

Another study, conducted by the University of Southern California (USC) Center for Innovation and Research on Veterans and Military Families, investigated the employment challenges and risks for unemployment from the perspectives of the civilian employer and of veterans who were utilizing employment services (Kintzle et al. 2015). Most of the veterans in the sample were considered to be in a vulnerable state because they were homeless and received few social supports. The USC study found that the foremost issue reported by both parties is veterans' unpreparedness for civilian employment. What constituted this relative lack of preparation revolved around veterans' (1) unrealistic expectations about the kinds of job opportunities they qualify for, as well as their likely salaries; (2) perceptions of having to "start over" as a civilian; and (3) difficulty in understanding how military experience translates to civilian employment. Another important issue pertains to veterans' unaddressed mental health and substance abuse issues. Most often, PTSD and/or depression and substance abuse problems manifested themselves in several ways in relation to employment. These include the impact on veterans' motivation to find and keep employment and their ability to keep and find success in a job. Another issue refers to veterans' criminal background and/or dishonorable discharge. At times, a criminal background (similar to their civilian counterparts) or a less than honorable discharge engenders hesitancy on the part of the employer to hire veterans along with the lack of available jobs. Finally, there is the existing stigma associated with hiring veterans (Kitzle et al. 2015). Some employers are reluctant to hire veterans because of concerns over issues of mental health, long gaps in employment history, and unwillingness to hire those with a criminal background and/or dishonorable discharge.

Overall, the implied contract on the side of civilian employers could be described as ambivalent. On the one hand, civilian employers acknowledge the value of hiring veterans and see the strengths and positive qualities veterans bring to the workplace. On the other, civilian employers are aware of veterans' shortcomings and many are not willing to take on the liabilities caused by war.

The Relational Contract within Veterans' Social Networks

As previously mentioned, veterans are situated within social networks that have been acquired or formed throughout their lives. Each social network pertains to a group of people representing the trajectory of their military service: preservice (mostly civilians), active duty (mostly service members), and postservice/veteran (mixture of civilians, service members, and veterans). Like any social groups (Wellman and Wortley 1990), these social networks function to provide different types of support (see Cohen and Wills 1985), such as emotional (e.g., providing companionship, Abbey et al. 1985), informational (e.g., providing advice, Cohen 2004), and instrumental (e.g., taking on more household chores, Kawachi and Berkman 2001) support. As applied to veteran employment, all three networks could potentially provide support that overlaps (e.g., military peers, family members, and veteran peers are sources of emotional support), and it is the interactive effect of all three networks that will ensure the success of veterans in the work environment (e.g., Demers 2011). This is why it is imperative to include a relational contract in the veteran employment framework. When veterans progress through each and every step of the employment process, they do so with the support of at least one, in some cases two, or in the ideal world, all three of their social networks. To make this point clearer, let us turn to the types of support provided by the various social networks.

The Military Social Network

Recall that one of the difficulties reported by both veteran employees and civilian employers is the unpreparedness of veterans to enter the civilian workforce (see Kintzle et al. 2015). This relative lack of preparation is mostly attributed to the unrealistic expectations veterans have about civilian employment (with regard to occupational roles and salary). Taking a step back, we find that when service members are getting ready to transition out of the military, they are mandated to complete the Transition Assistance Program (TAP; see chapter 4). As part of the TAP, service members participate in a Department of Labor Employment Workshop that educates them on the logistics of obtaining employment in the civilian workplace. This implies that at the outset, the *military is a source of informational support* for service members transitioning into the civilian work environment. As such, the military can exercise its influence by creating a more realistic picture of civilian employment, one that is perhaps more closely aligned with the expectations of civilian employers (e.g., salary range for a particular occupational role).

The Veteran Social Network

Veteran social networks are the formal and informal infrastructures that have been created and maintained to serve veterans. Formal social networks are embedded within institutions such as the VA, whereas informal social networks are typically community based and grassroots oriented, or could simply be a casual gathering of veterans. *Formal social networks provide both instrumental and informational support* to veterans (e.g., Barber et al. 2008). For example, the VA is charged with implementing several employment training and programs such as On-the Job Training and Apprenticeship. This particular program offers veterans the opportunity to simultaneously learn a trade or skill and receive a salary. At the end of the program, veterans receive a job certification and could potentially be hired by the company where they received their training or did their apprenticeship. On the other hand, *informal social networks predominantly provide emotional support* to veterans. For example, Demers (2011) conducted a qualitative study to examine how veterans reintegrate back into their civilian communities. The results of the study showed that veterans have a strong preference for connecting with other veterans, primarily because other veterans are perceived to be more knowledgeable about what participants are going through during the civilian reintegration process. Demers (2011) interpreted these results to mean that informal social networks can function to aid veterans in reshaping their identities, from military to civilian, and relearning civilian norms.

The Civilian Social Network

The civilian social network is the third and perhaps the most important social system that will provide almost all the social support needed by veterans. Recall the military-civilian divide discussed previously in this chapter. A closer look at this gap shows that this is also a numerical divide, reflecting a military minority and a civilian majority (Yamada, Atuel, and Weiss 2013). If veterans are to thrive in the civilian workplace, they will need to seek support from their civilian social networks, and equally important, people within this particular network will need to start accommodating the unique needs and challenges of veterans. This bidirectional relationship presents several challenges, but the reciprocity that occurs within this network increases the likelihood that veterans will succeed in the workplace.

Military and veteran families have been shown to provide informational, emotional, and instrumental supports (Beardslee et al. 2013; Wadsworth et al. 2013). Within the family unit, each member is dependent on the others for advice (informational support), safety and security (emotional support), and finances (instrumental support) (Cohen 2004). When these types of social support are present within military and veteran families, the family unit develops resilience that is manifested in greater emotional ties, increased communication, and increased closeness (Meredith et al. 2011). As applied to veteran employment, this means that veterans' families play a critical role in buffering the stresses directly related to seeking and maintaining employment in the civilian workplace. The greater the family support, the more veterans are able to withstand the pressures arising from each phase of the employment process.

Ultimately, veteran employment is typically situated within civilian communities. At this broader level, communities have the power to dictate, influence, or even change social norms (Feldman 1984). Social norms are the range of values, beliefs, and behaviors that are deemed acceptable within a particular group (Sherif 1958). Communities also can define lines demarcating who is or is not part of their community (Berman and Phillips 2000). What this means for veteran employment is that *civilian communities can provide normative support* by creating an inclusive environment that honors military service and takes a proactive (instead of reactive) stance in alleviating the unique challenges faced by veterans. As of this writing, community support for veterans, in the form of public-private partnerships or collaboration, is found all over the country. Operating under the auspices of the Office of the Chairman, Joint Chiefs of Staff, the Office of Warrior and Family Support (n.d.) has identified several of these community partnerships or collaborations, all of which have veteran employment as part of their community agenda. Examples are the Illinois Joining Forces, the Nevada Green Zone Initiative, the Augusta Warrior Project, the Charlotte Bridge Home, and the Los Angles Veterans Collaborative.[1] These partnerships or collaborations function to leverage existing resources within the public and private sectors to ensure that veterans have everything they need to successfully integrate back into civilian communities.

Taken together, the psychological contract of the veteran employee; implied contract of the civilian employer; and relational contracts of the military, veteran, and civilian social networks are pathways that can influence the outcome of veteran employment. Far from being independent of each other, these various contracts are interdependent and affect each other. Preliminary evidence of the interrelatedness of these different contracts is emergent in the studies reviewed in this section. In accounting for all these contracts, we are beginning to identify and clarify how these building blocks need to be aligned and strengthened to facilitate a successful military-civilian employment transition not just for some or most, but for all veterans.

Conclusion

For 21st-century veterans, experiences related to the military-civilian employment transition are fraught with challenges. At the policy level, veteran employment legislation has been in place for over a century. It provides employment resources and protects veterans against discrimination on the basis of military service. These laws are apparently sufficient for most veterans, but not for all. This pattern is amplified when we take a closer look at the perspectives of veteran employees and civilian employers. Within this employment dyad, both parties have their own expectations of the other, which at times reflect divergent points of view. For some veterans with physical and/or psychological war-related injuries, the opportunities for employment are almost nonexistent because they are perceived as liabilities within the civilian workforce. In spite of all these challenges, protective factors do exist. But they need to be in place and working in tandem with each other. What we have uncovered and are proposing from a review of the literature pertains to a system of interlocking social networks that provide emotional, informational, and instrumental support to veterans. For the 21st-century veteran, it is this web of social networks that will provide the much-needed support, in the short and long terms, to ensure a successful transition from military to civilian employment.

In surveying the veteran employment terrain, we find the field is still in its infancy. Overall, the research conducted to date is reactive in nature, with studies carried out in rapid response to the pressing military-civilian employment needs of veterans. This reactive nature has led to the lack of a military/veteran-specific theory that serves as a veteran employment roadmap for researchers and practitioners alike. This chapter is a step forward in that direction and presents an initial blueprint for future theory and research to build on.

Note

1. More information is available on their Web sites: Illinois Joining Forces (www.illinoisjoiningforces.org), Nevada Green Zone Initiative (www.veterans.nv.gov/GZI), Augusta Warrior Project (www.augustawarriorproject.org), Charlotte Bridge Home (www.charlottebridgehome.org), and the Los Angles Veterans Collaborative (http://cir.usc.edu).

References

Aaronson, Franklin M. 1942. "Pensions and Compensation to Veterans and Their Dependents." *Social Security Bulletin* 5: 10–24.

Abbey, Antonia, David J. Abramis, and Robert D. Caplan. 1985. "Effects of Different Sources of Social Support and Social Conflict on Emotional Well-Being." *Basic and Applied Social Psychology* 6 (2): 111–129.

Ainspan, Nathan D. 2008. "Finding Employment as a Veteran with a Disability." In *Returning Wars' Wounded, Injured, and Ill: A Reference Handbook*, edited by Nathan D. Ainspan and Walter E. Penk, 102–138. Westport, CT: Praeger Security International.

Atuel, Hazel R., and Kris T. De Pedro. 2014. "Asian-Americans in the Military." In *Asian American Society: An Encyclopedia,* edited by Mary Y. Danico, 678–682. Thousand Oaks, CA: SAGE Publications.

Atuel, Hazel R., Kathleen Ell, Sara Kintzle, Anthony Hassan, and Carl Castro. 2015. "Military to Civilian Employment Transition Experiences of Ethnically Diverse Veterans." Paper presented at the Annual Meeting of the American Psychological Association, Toronto, Canada, August 6–9.

Barber, Jessica A., Robert A. Rosenheck, Moe Armstrong, and Sandra G. Resnick. 2008. "Monitoring the Dissemination of Peer Support in the VA Healthcare System." *Community Mental Health Journal* 44 (6): 433–441.

Baruch, Yehuda, and James Campbell Quick. 2007. "Understanding Second Careers: Lessons from a Study of US Navy Admirals." *Human Resource Management* 46 (4): 471–491.

Baruch, Yehuda, and James Campbell Quick. 2009. "Setting Sail in a New Direction: Career Transitions of US Navy Admirals to the Civilian Sector." *Personnel Review* 38 (3): 270–285.

Beardslee, William R., Lee E. Klosinski, William Saltzman, Catherine Mogil, Susan Pangelinan, Carl P. McKnight, and Patricia Lester. 2013. "Dissemination of Family-Centered Prevention for Military and Veteran Families: Adaptations and Adoption within Community and Military Systems of Care." *Clinical Child and Family Psychology Review* 16 (4): 394–409.

Berman, Yitzhak, and David Phillips. 2000. "Indicators of Social Quality and Social Exclusion at National and Community Level." *Social Indicators Research* 50 (3): 329–350.

Bowling, Ursula B., and Michelle D. Sherman. 2008. "Welcoming Them Home: Supporting Service Members and Their Families in Navigating the Tasks of Reintegration." *Professional Psychology: Research and Practice* 39 (4): 451–458.

Brunger, Helen, Jonathan Serrato, and Jane Ogden. 2013. "'No Man's Land': The Transition to Civilian Life." *Journal of Aggression, Conflict and Peace Research* 5 (2): 86–100.

Bullock, Emily E., Jennifer Braud, Lindsay Andrews, and Jennifer Phillips. 2009. "Career Concerns of Unemployed US War Veterans: Suggestions from a Cognitive Information Processing Approach." *Journal of Employment Counseling* 46 (4): 171–181.

Bureau of Labor Statistics. 2014. "Employment Situation of Veterans." Accessed September 1, 2015. http://www.bls.gov/news.release/pdf/vet.pdf.

Bureau of Labor Statistics. 2015. "Employment of Veterans by Occupation, 2014." Accessed September 1, 2015. http://www.bls.gov/opub/ted/2015/employment-of-veterans-by-occupation-2014.htm.

Burnett-Zeigler, Inger, Marcia Valenstein, Mark Ilgen, Adrian J. Blow, Lisa A. Gorman, and Kara Zivin. 2011. "Civilian Employment among Recently Returning Afghanistan and Iraq National Guard Veterans." *Military Medicine* 176 (6): 639–646.

Buzzetta, Mary, and Shirley Rowe. 2012. "Today's Veterans: Using Cognitive Information Processing (CIP) Approach to Build Upon Their Career Dreams." *Career Convergence Magazine*, November 1. Accessed September 1, 2015. http://www.ncda.org/aws/NCDA/pt/sd/news_article/66290/_self/layout_details/false.

Castro, Carl A., and Amy B. Adler. 1999. "OPTEMPO: Effects on Soldier and Unit Readiness." *Parameters* 29 (3): 86–95.

Castro, Carl A., Sara Kintzle, and Anthony Hassan. 2014. *The State of the American Veteran: The Los Angeles County Veterans Study*. Los Angeles: University of Southern California Center for Innovation and Research on Veterans and Military Families.

Castro, Carl A., Jeffrey L. Thomas, and Amy B. Adler. 2006. "Toward a Liberal Theory of Military Leadership." In *Military Life: The Psychology of Serving in Peace and Combat*, edited by Amy B. Adler, Carl A. Castro, and Thomas W. Britt, 2:192–212. Westport, CT: Praeger Security International.

Chicas, Joseph, Paul Maiden, Hyunsung Oh, D. Young, and Sherrie Wilcox. 2012. *From War to the Workplace: Helping Veterans Transition to Civilian Work Settings*. Los Angeles: University of Southern California Center for Innovation and Research on Veterans and Military Families.

Clemens, Elysia V., and Amy S. Milsom. 2008. "Enlisted Service Members' Transition into the Civilian World of Work: A Cognitive Information Processing Approach." *Career Development Quarterly* 56 (3): 246–256.

Cohen, Sheldon. 2004. "Social Relationships and Health." *American Psychologist* 59 (8): 676–684.

Cohen, Sheldon, and Thomas A. Wills. 1985. "Stress, Social Support, and the Buffering Hypothesis." *Psychological Bulletin* 98 (2): 310–357.

Cohn, Richard M. 1978. "The Effect of Employment Status Change on Self-Attitudes." *Social Psychology* 41 (2): 81–93.

Coll, Jose E., Eugenia L. Weiss, and Jeffrey S. Yarvis. 2011. "No One Leaves Unchanged: Insights for Civilian Mental Health Care Professionals into the Military Experience and Culture." *Social Work in Health Care* 50 (7): 487–500.

Collins, Benjamin, Robert Jay Dilger, Cassandria Dortch, Lawrence Kapp, Sean Lowry, and Libby Perl. 2014. *Employment for Veterans: Trends and Programs*. R42790. Washington, DC: Congressional Research Service. Accessed January 13, 2016. https://www.fas.org/sgp/crs/misc/R42790.pdf.

Dabos, Guillermo E., and Denise M. Rousseau. 2004. "Mutuality and Reciprocity in the Psychological Contracts of Employees and Employers." *Journal of Applied Psychology* 89 (1): 52–72.

Daley, James G. 1999. "Understanding the Military as an Ethnic Identity." In *Social Work Practice in the Military*, edited by James G. Daley, 291–303. Binghamton, NY: Haworth.

Davis, E.W. n.d. "The History of Veterans Employment Services". Accessed September 1, 2015. http://www.nvti.ucdenver.edu/resources/resourceLibrary/pdfs/HistoryofVETS.pdf.

Demers, Anne. 2011. "When Veterans Return: The Role of Community in Reintegration." *Journal of Loss and Trauma* 16 (2): 160–179.

Department of Defense. n.d. "DoD 101: Introductory Overview of the Department of Defense." Accessed September 1, 2015. http://www.defense.gov/About-DoD/DoD-101.

Department of Labor. 2011. "The Veteran Labor Force in the Recovery." Accessed January 13, 2016. http://www.dol.gov/_sec/media/reports/VeteransLaborForce/VeteransLaborForce.pdf

Department of Veterans Affairs. n.d. "VA History in Brief." Accessed January 13, 2016. http://www.va.gov/opa/publications/archives/docs/history_in_brief.pdf.

Dion, Kenneth L. 2000. "Group Cohesion: From 'Field of Forces' to Multidimensional Construct." *Group Dynamics: Theory, Research, and Practice* 4 (1): 7–26.

Elbogen, Eric B., Sally C. Johnson, H. Ryan Wagner, Virginia M. Newton, and Jean C. Beckham. 2012. "Financial Well-Being and Postdeployment Adjustment among Iraq and Afghanistan War Veterans." *Military Medicine* 177 (6): 669–675.

Elliott, Timothy R., and Paul Leung. 2005. "Vocational Rehabilitation: History and Practice." In *Handbook of Vocational Psychology*, edited by W. Bruce Walsh and Mark L. Savickas, 319–343. Mahwah, NJ: Lawrence Erlbaum Associates.

Faberman, R. Jason, and Taft Foster. 2013. "Unemployment among Recent Veterans during the Great Recession." *Economic Perspectives* 37 (1): 1–13.

Feldman, Daniel C. 1984. "The Development and Enforcement of Group Norms." *Academy of Management Review* 9 (1): 47–53.

Forces in Mind Trust. 2013. "The Transition Mapping Study: Understanding the Transition Process for Service Personnel Returning to Civilian Life." Accessed September 1, 2015. http://www.fim-trust.org/wp-content/uploads/2015/01/20130810-TMS-Report.pdf.

Guest, David E., and Neil Conway. 2002. "Communicating the Psychological Contract: An Employer Perspective." *Human Resource Management Journal* 12 (2): 22–38.

Hall, Kimberly Curry, Margaret C. Harrell, Barbara A. Bicksler, Robert Stewart, and Michael P. Fisher. 2014. *Veteran Employment: Lessons from the 100,000 Jobs Mission.* Santa Monica, CA: RAND Corporation.

Harrell, Margaret C., and Nancy Berglass. 2012. *Employing America's Veterans: Perspectives from Businesses.* Washington, DC: Center for a New American Security.

Hinojosa, Ramon, and Melanie Sberna Hinojosa. 2011. "Using Military Friendships to Optimize Postdeployment Reintegration for Male Operation Iraqi Freedom/Operation Enduring Freedom Veterans." *Journal of Rehabilitation Research and Development* 48 (10): 1145–1158.

Horton, Jaime L., Isabel G. Jacobson, Charlene A. Wong, Timothy S. Wells, Edward J. Boyko, Besa Smith, Margaret A. K. Ryan, and Tyler C. Smith. 2013.

"The Impact of Prior Deployment Experience on Civilian Employment after Military Service." *Occupational and Environmental Medicine* 70: 408–417.

Jung, Dong I., Chee Chow, and Anne Wu. 2003. "The Role of Transformational Leadership in Enhancing Organizational Innovation: Hypotheses and Some Preliminary Findings." *Leadership Quarterly* 14 (4): 525–544.

Kawachi, Ichiro, and Lisa F. Berkman. 2001. "Social Ties and Mental Health." *Journal of Urban Health* 78 (3): 458–467.

Kintzle, Sara, Mary Keeling, Elizabeth Xintarianos, Kamil Taylor-Diggs, Chris Munch, Anthony M. Hassan, and Carl A. Castro. 2015. *Exploring the Economic and Employment Challenges facing U.S. Veterans: A Qualitative Study of Volunteers of America Service Providers and Veteran Clients*. Los Angeles: University of Southern California Center for Innovation and Research on Veterans and Military Families.

Kleykamp, Meredith. 2009. "A Great Place to Start? The Effect of Prior Military Service on Hiring." *Armed Forces & Society* 35 (2): 266–285.

Lancaster, Steven L., and Roland P. Hart. 2015. "Military Identity and Psychological Functioning: A Pilot Study." *Military Behavioral Health* 3 (1): 83–87.

Manning, Frederick J. 1991. "Morale, Cohesion, and Esprit De Corps." In *Handbook of Military Psychology*, edited by Reuven Gal and A. David Mangelsdorff, 453–470. New York: John Wiley and Sons.

Meredith, Lisa S., Cathy D. Sherbourne, Sarah J. Gaillot, Lydia Hansell, Hans V. Ritschard, Andrew M. Parker, and Glenda Wrenn. 2011. *Promoting Psychological Resilience in the US Military*. Santa Monica, CA: RAND Corporation.

Morin, Rich. 2011. "The Difficult Transition from Military to Civilian Life." Pew Research Center. Accessed September 1, 2015. http://www.pewsocialtrends.org/2011/12/08/the-difficult-transition-from-military-to-civilian-life/.

Morris, Carol. 2012. *Coming Home: Support for Returning Veterans in Charlotte-Mecklenburg*. Charlotte Bridge Home. Accessed September 1, 2015. http://www.fftc.org/document.doc?id=1831.

O'Connor, Kathryn, Anna Kline, Leon Sawh, Stephanie Rodrigues, William Fisher, Vincent Kane, John Kuhn, Marsha Ellison, and David Smelson. 2013. "Unemployment and Co-Occurring Disorders among Homeless Veterans." *Journal of Dual Diagnosis* 9 (2): 134–138.

Office of Warrior and Family Support. n.d. "Expanding Public-Private Partnerships." Accessed January 13, 2016. http://www.jcs.mil/Portals/36/Documents/CORe/Public_Private_Partnerships_Final.pdf.

Patterson, Stephanie. 2014. "A Historical Overview of Disability and Employment in the United States, 1600 to 1950." *Review of Disability Studies: An International Journal* 7 (3). Accessed January 13, 2016. http://www.rds.hawaii.edu/ojs/index.php/journal/article/view/117.

Prudential Financial. 2012. "Veterans' Employment Challenges: Perceptions and Experiences of Transitioning from Military to Civilian Life." Accessed September 1, 2015. https://www.prudential.com/documents/public/VeteransEmploymentChallenges.pdf.

Rock, Edward B., and Michael L. Wachter. 1996. "The Enforceability of Norms and the Employment Relationship." *University of Pennsylvania Law Review* 144 (5): 1913–1952.

Rousseau, Denise M. 1989. "Psychological and Implied Contracts in Organizations." *Employee Responsibilities and Rights Journal* 2 (2): 121–139.

Routon, P. Wesley. 2014. "The Effects of 21st Century Military Service on Civilian Labor and Educational Outcomes." *Journal of Labor Research* 35: 15–38.

Sherif, Muzafer. 1958. "Group Influences upon the Formation of Norms and Attitudes." In *Readings in Social Psychology*, edited by Eleanor Maccoby, Theodore M. Newcomb, and Eugene L. Hartley, 219–232. New York: Holt, Rinehart and Winston.

Simpson, Amy, and Starla Armstrong. 2009. "From the Military to the Civilian Workforce: Addressing Veteran Career Development Concerns." *Career Planning & Adult Development Journal* 25 (1): 177–187.

Smith, Diane L. 2014. "The Relationship between Employment and Veteran Status, Disability and Gender from 2004–2011 Behavioral Risk Factor Surveillance System (BRFSS)." *Work* 49 (2): 325–334.

Tanielian, Terri, Lisa H. Jaycox, David M. Adamson, M. Audrey Burnam, Rachel M. Burns, Leah B. Caldarone, Robert A. Cox, Elizabeth J. D'Amico, Claudia Diaz, Christine Eibner, Gail Fisher, Todd C. Helmus, Benjamin R. Karney, Beau Kilmer, Grant N. Marshall, Laurie T. Martin, Lisa S. Meredith, Karen N. Metscher, Karen Chan Osilla, Rosalie Liccardo Pacula, Rajeev Ramchand, Jeanne S. Ringel, Terry L. Schell, Jerry M. Sollinger, Mary E. Vaiana, Kayla M. Williams, and Michael R. Yochelson. 2008. *Invisible Wounds of War: Psychological and Cognitive Injuries, their Consequences, and Services to Assist Recovery*. Santa Monica, CA: RAND Corporation.

Today's Military. 2015. "Joining Overview." Accessed June 2, 2016. http://todaysmilitary.com/joining.

Turnley, William H., and Daniel C. Feldman. 1998. "Psychological Contract Violations during Corporate Restructuring." *Human Resource Management* 37 (1): 71–83.

Wadsworth, Shelley MacDermid, Patricia Lester, Christina Marini, Stephen Cozza, Jo Sornborger, Thomas Strouse, and William Beardslee. 2013. "Approaching Family-Focused Systems of Care for Military and Veteran Families." *Military Behavioral Health* 1 (1): 31–40.

Wellman, Barry, and Scot Wortley. 1990. "Different Strokes from Different Folks: Community Ties and Social Support." *American Journal of Sociology* 96 (3): 558–588.

Yamada, Ann-Marie, Hazel R. Atuel, and Eugenia L. Weiss. 2013. "Military Culture and Multicultural Diversity among Military Service Members: Implications for Mental Health Providers." In *Handbook of Multicultural Mental Health: Assessment and Treatment of Diverse Populations*, edited by Freddy A. Paniagua and Ann-Marie Yamada, 389–410. Cambridge, MA: Academic Press.

CHAPTER NINE

Veterans and Civic Engagement

Fred P. Stone

Introduction

At 2:30 a.m., the 1st Platoon gathered to comb the streets of a dangerous neighborhood. Their mission this morning, however, was not to secure the streets of Baghdad by looking for terrorists, as many of them had done during their combat tours. These were the streets of Phoenix, where they sought out homeless veterans who needed help. Over three nights, the platoon registered 75 veterans to receive public assistance and persuaded 40 of them to accept public housing and leave the streets (Rosenberg 2014). The platoon's leader was Rachel Gutierrez, an Operation Iraqi Freedom (OIF) veteran who served five years in the U.S. Army. Gutierrez knows war firsthand and returned from OIF with post-traumatic stress disorder (PTSD) and a host of other mental and physical problems. "I was really depressed," she said (Rosenberg 2014). Leading the 1st Platoon and helping other veterans has given her a sense of purpose and belonging that she missed when she left the military and has helped her to better deal with her own problems (Zoroya 2014).

Gutierrez is typical of many men and women of the U.S. armed forces who have spent years serving in the military and now want to continue to serve as civilians. Compared to nonveterans, they are more likely to be working to solve community problems. They volunteer more hours per year and are more politically engaged than nonveterans (Tivald and Kawashima-Ginsberg 2015). This chapter examines some of the reasons that veterans have a higher level of civic engagement than nonveterans by looking at two elements: volunteering and seeking public office.

Civic Engagement and Military Culture

Civic engagement involves community service, collective action, political involvement, and social change, and consists of "the interactions of citizens with their society and their government" (Adler and Goggin 2005, 241). It is the political, social, and moral engagements that make democracy work (Berger 2009). Serving in the military is arguably the ultimate form of civic engagement (Flanagan and Levine 2010), as military members offer their very lives in protecting and serving their country.

Civic engagement for veterans stems in part from the U.S. military culture that promotes honor, integrity, courage, commitment, loyalty, respect, and devotion to duty (Exum, Coll, and Weiss 2011) and is founded on patriotism and commitment to service to the nation (Janowitz 1971). One of the U.S. Air Force's core values is "Service Before Self" (U.S. Air Force 1997), and the U.S. Army has a long tradition of duty: the commitment to the country and the unit (Janowitz 1971). The OIF/Operation Enduring Freedom (OIF/OEF) Veteran Survey of 779 veterans found 92 percent reported that serving their community was important, and 90 percent thought it was a "basic responsibility of every American" (Yonkman and Bridgeland 2009, 9). Seventy percent of this group had volunteered in their communities while they were on active duty.

Military culture also explains why many veterans seek political office. The military emphasizes leadership development, and many military members think that every organization should be run like the military (Hajjar 2014). This may explain why veterans are more likely than nonveterans to take on leadership roles in community organizations (Tivald and Kawashima-Ginsberg 2015).

The military culture's focus on working together in groups, overcoming difficult problems, and working with diverse populations is another reason that veterans are civically engaged. Civic engagement requires diverse groups of people to come together for a common purpose. While the U.S. military is largely made up of white men, it is one of the most racially diverse organizations in the United States and arguably less segregated by gender than many civilian organizations (Burk and Espinoza 2012; Firestone 1992). For decades, it was the only large organization that routinely placed people of color in positions of power over white men (Sarkesian and Connor 2006). Although the military has been considered homophobic (Dunivin 1994), the repeal of "Don't Ask, Don't Tell" was broadly supported by military members (Department of Defense 2010) and has had few or no negative effects on the military (Belkin et al. 2013).

From a military culture standpoint, it is not surprising that many veterans are civically engaged. Civic engagement is highly compatible with their beliefs about service, leadership, and working in diverse groups.

The Military and Civic Engagement in Uniform

The military culture has increasingly developed a peacekeeper-diplomat focus (Hajjar 2014); as a result, many military members have accrued important civic engagement skills. On peacekeeping missions, they act as agents of community service, collective action, political involvement, and social change and help disaster-stricken communities rebuild by providing water, electricity, shelter, and other support (U.S. Army 2016).

Two Department of Defense doctrine publications directly highlight these missions. Joint Publications 3-57, *Civil-Military Operations* (CMO) (Joint Chiefs of Staff 2013) and 3-29, *Foreign Humanitarian Assistance* (FHA) (Joint Chiefs of Staff 2014), provide guidance for the military to assist nations and local communities. The doctrine for CMO focuses on helping to stabilize and combat counterinsurgencies and other irregular threats, but the activities to accomplish these objectives do not include direct combat. Instead, CMO concentrates on cooperation between the military and civilian administration and providing resources for the populace (Joint Chiefs of Staff 2013, x). The primary goal of these operations is to facilitate military operations, but CMO recognizes that providing aid and support is one of the most effective ways to end hostilities and bring about peace. CMO includes civil administration in friendly areas as well as occupied areas where the military establishes itself as the government, and it provides guidance on how to interact with civilian authorities and coordinate efforts. It is a form of civic engagement in which the military knows that bringing resources to a community and cooperating with local leaders is more effective than establishing onerous military rules and laws.

The CMO activities during OIF/OEF included 34 provincial reconstruction teams (PRT), which helped local governments through construction, governance support, and security. While these teams were primarily composed of civilians, they included military civil affairs teams and other military personnel. The 24 teams in Iraq were almost all led by foreign service officers, who are all civilians employed by the U.S. State Department. But in Afghanistan teams were led by U.S. military commanders. While the teams encountered many challenges, local communities provided generally positive feedback (Abbaszadeh et al. 2008).

While CMO focuses on operations around war, FHA focuses exclusively on humanitarian activities. Its operations are almost always in support of other government agencies and are often conducted in cooperation with the U.S. Agency for International Development or the Department of State. Its objectives are to "save lives, alleviate suffering, and minimize the economic costs of conflict, disasters, and displacement" (Joint Chiefs of Staff 2014, I-1), and its activities include providing food, shelter, medical aid, and clothing along with other services. Humanitarian and civic assistance (HCA), an element of FHA, offers medical and veterinary care, rudimentary transportation systems, sanitation facilities, and other public works.

A few examples of FHA operations are the responses to the 2011 Great East Japan earthquake, 2010 Haiti earthquake, and 2004 tsunami in Southeast Asia. Operation Tomodachi, the U.S. military response to the Great East Japan earthquake, which killed more than 15,000 people, provided 260 tons of humanitarian assistance to the Japanese people, reopened the runways at the Sendai airport, and provided expert consultation on radiation exposure prevention and medical care. The operations included members from all branches of the military, including sailors from the 7th Fleet and airmen from the 374th Airlift Wing at Yokota Air Base in Japan. Joint Task Force-Haiti provided 22,200 personnel to Haiti after an earthquake took the lives of more than 300,000 people (Cecchine et al. 2013). The military worked with 16 World Food Programme sites and collaborated with the Haitian government and nongovernmental organizations. Twelve thousand Department of Defense personnel provided relief during Operation Unified Response to the 2004 tsunami in Southeast Asia (Office of History 2006).

Besides operations overseas, the military also delivers humanitarian and civil support to state and local governments in the United States. The National Guard has 350,000 members from all U.S. states and territories. Among the many civilian-related activities the Guard performs are supporting counterdrug missions, providing emergency management assistance, supplying homeland response forces, and providing firefighting systems.

These humanitarian and peacekeeping missions turn modern-day warriors into social workers—although many military members may not like the label. These missions require members to interact with communities, overcome barriers, and provide support, and they give military members skills and experiences that they can use after they leave the service. Veterans who primarily participated in reconstruction efforts during OIF/OEF volunteered at higher rates when they returned home than veterans who primarily served in combat or medical roles (Yonkman and Bridgeland 2009). Their military experiences primed them for civic engagement. Many military members confess that these types of civic engagement have been some of the most rewarding missions of their military careers.

Theories and Motivations for Volunteering

Veteran volunteers provide an average of 160 hours of service annually, compared to 120 hours for nonveteran volunteers, and 18 percent are involved in civic groups compared to 6 percent of nonveterans (Tivald and Kawashima-Ginsberg 2015). Veterans who are 20 to 49 years of age "have the highest rate of volunteering among all Americans" (Tivald and Kawashima-Ginsberg 2015, 10). More than 27,000 veterans have served in AmeriCorps and Senior Corps (Corporation for National & Community Service 2014).

Volunteering is a way to participate in a community in a meaningful way and make a contribution for the public good (McAllum 2014), but the reasons for volunteering vary. The functional approach argues that volunteers have six types of motivations: values, understanding, social, career, protective, and enhancement (Clary et al. 1998). This section examines each of these motivations in relationship to veterans volunteering.

The motivation of values concerns the desire to help others. Some people have an "altruistic personality" that pushes them to service (Rushton, Chrisjohn, and Fekken 1981). Kishon-Barash, Midlarsky, and Johnson's (1999, 655) review found that Vietnam veterans have a "higher inclination to help others" and that veterans with PTSD displayed a more mature motivation of altruism rather than self-centered reasons for helping. Altruism studies, however, tend to rely on self-reports and may be more a reflection of attitudes than of actions. Thus, it is difficult to know if altruism is the primary reason for the high rates of veteran volunteering.

Another reason veterans volunteer at higher rates is that it gives them the opportunity to use their skills or learn new ones—understanding (Clary et al. 1998). Veterans have a host of skills that can be useful in helping their communities. Ninety-one percent of military jobs are directly related to civilian jobs (Yonkman and Bridgeland 2009). These skills include management, team building, and logistical abilities as well as specific construction, mechanical, or maintenance skills. McCarthy and Tucker (1999) found that students with previous community service experience have more self-efficacy in volunteering and were confident that their contributions made a difference. Similarly, veterans with humanitarian mission experience or applicable job skills may be more likely to believe that they can make a positive contribution to a project or program.

Volunteering also serves as a social function. In the civilian community, this may be an opportunity to be with friends or meet people in the community. For veterans, volunteering may be a way to reconnect with the military. Separating from the military is difficult for many veterans because it means that they are removed not only from their military peers, but also from their identity—an identity that brought them prestige and praise (Janowitz 1971). Volunteering allows veterans to feel that they are giving something back to the people who meant the most to them and to be a part of the military again, at least in spirit. Veterans consistently report that their primary volunteer interests are to work with military members and their families (Yonkman and Bridgeland 2009).

Career benefit is another element of volunteering. In one study, volunteering resulted in an overall 27 percent increase in finding employment and specifically a 4 percent increase for veterans (Spera et al. 2013). The researchers posited that volunteers gain skills that make them more attractive to employers. Many corporations believe that employees involved in community service have higher morale and learn important teamwork skills (McCarthy and Tucker 1999).

The protective function of volunteering focuses on protecting self-esteem. Clary and colleagues (1998) argued that people volunteer for protection from negative views or features of themselves. People may feel guilty about either their lack of contributions to society or their good fortune. Related to protection is enhancement. Unlike the desire to relieve negative emotions, enhancement involves the positive contributions that volunteering makes to one's self esteem. From this perspective, volunteering shows others that a person is good, and his or her sense of self is reinforced by doing good deeds (Clary, Snyder, and Ridge 1992). It means that volunteering meets a person's own needs or desires and is not focused on what others want (Shye 2010). The United States holds the military and military members in high public esteem. Pew Research Center (2013) found 78 percent of people surveyed ranked the military profession as the top occupation in terms of contributing to society. "Thank you for your service" has become a cliché to the point that some veterans are offended by the phrase (Richtel 2015). Many veterans, however, enjoy this attention, and from this perspective, volunteering allows them to continue to be seen as positively contributing to society.

The functional approach is limited in its ability to explain volunteerism, in part because volunteers report a variety of motives that do not show much prior thought. Shye (2010) identified two other factors that better explain veterans volunteering: demographic antecedents and circumstances. Demographic antecedents are the resources needed to volunteer. While many people may have the desire to volunteer, they may not have the time or money to be able to do so. This may explain why many veterans—particularly retirees—volunteer: they have the time and resources to do so. Circumstances are the triggers and opportunities that prompt volunteering and may explain the extent if not the reasons for volunteering. Since September 11, 2001, the United States has increasingly focused on the service of military members and the needs of veterans. There are an estimated 40,000 nonprofit organizations dedicated to serving military members, veterans, and their families and another 400,000 service organizations that provide some services for this group (Charity Watch 2015). This plethora of organizations helping military members, veterans, and their families offers ample opportunities for veterans to volunteer.

All of these elements play a role in veterans' volunteering. While many veterans focus their volunteering on "giving back" to their country and to their fellow service members and their families, other veterans see these activities as a way to make them more employable and bolster their résumés. Some veterans volunteer because they have the time and resources to help, while others take advantage of the many opportunities presented by organizations and groups helping military members, veterans, and their families.

Veterans and Volunteering

This section looks at a few organizations at which veterans are volunteering. Often the organizations that serve veterans are those led by veterans. The Mission Continues (n.d.; TMC) is one of these organizations. It helps veterans adjust to life after leaving the service. It was founded in 2007 by Eric Grietens, a former Navy SEAL and OIF veteran, who was inspired by wounded Marines who expressed a desire to continue to serve their country even if their wounds precluded them from doing so in the military. TMC offers veterans this opportunity through fellowships and the Service Platoon Program. The fellowships are six-month community service awards for post-9/11 veterans to volunteer at a nonprofit organization in their community. Fellows receive a stipend and leadership training. Consistent with the functional theory of volunteering, TMC advertises that "the Fellowship Program is ideal for veterans looking to start a new career, gain practical experience while attending school or for a new way to serve at home" (Mission Continues n.d.). In other words, TMC offers veterans an opportunity for altruism as well as job enhancement. In 2014, fellows provided 100,000 hours of service to nonprofits across the country (Mission Continues n.d.). TMC also brings together teams of veterans in its Service Platoon Program. The program mobilizes veterans as well as active duty, guard, and reserve members to tackle specific problems in their communities. Examples include reducing hunger in the District of Columbia among inner-city youth; solving homelessness in Phoenix, Arizona; and mentoring at-risk youth in Orlando, Florida. Since 2013 almost 3,000 veterans in 30 platoons have volunteered in 25 cities (Tivald and Kawashima-Ginsberg 2015).

Another veteran-inspired organization is Team Rubicon. Founded by two former Marines, Team Rubicon provides emergency response teams of veterans to travel immediately to disasters. The teams "bridge the gap" between the moment the disaster happens and the response of conventional aid (Team Rubicon n.d.). The most notable example of Team Rubicon's efforts was during the 2010 Haitian earthquake, when nearly one million people were made homeless in a matter of minutes. Within three days of the earthquake, a group of eight veterans flew to the Dominican Republic, rented a truck, and headed into Haiti loaded with medical supplies, where "they treated thousands of patients, traveling to camps deemed 'too dangerous' by other aid organizations" (Team Rubicon n.d.). This was the first of dozens of missions that Team Rubicon has deployed in areas ranging from Pakistan, Turkey, and Burma to Missouri, Texas, and Oklahoma.

Team Rubicon supports several elements of the functional theory of volunteering: giving veterans a purpose, altruism, and socializing. Its mission statement is that its "work is motivated solely by the altruistic desire to help those in demonstrable need" (Team Rubicon n.d.), but Team Rubicon likewise allows veterans to work with other veterans in completing a difficult mission, much as they did when they were in the military.

Purple Heart Homes is another example of veterans volunteering to help veterans (Purple Heart Homes n.d.). John Gallina and Dale Beatty, both Purple Heart Medal recipients, created this organization to provide quality housing to disabled veterans. Their Veterans Aging In Place program renovates homes for disabled veterans so that they can have a safe home environment. Purple Heart Homes helps veterans acquire a residence and offers a mentoring program in how to become financially stable and successfully own a home.

Purple Heart Homes demonstrates a number of the elements of volunteering. It offers veterans the opportunity to use their skills—such as giving home ownership advice—in assisting other veterans. It likewise fulfills the social and altruism aspects of volunteering.

Theories of Political Involvement

Veterans have run for political office since the birth of the United States. Twenty-six of forty-four presidents have been veterans. George Washington (1775) famously wrote, "When we assumed the soldier, we did not lay aside the citizen." Like Washington, many veterans today have political ambitions. One survey found that 8 percent of veterans wanted to run for public office (Tivald and Kawashima-Ginsberg 2015). This political ambition is motivated by a number of factors: strategic considerations, ideological motivations, minority status expectations, politicized upbringing, competitive traits, and stage of life (Fox and Lawless 2005).

The strategic considerations are whether or not the potential candidate believes that he or she can win. In a study of U.S. House of Representative races, the perception that one can win an election was the most important predictor of whether or not a person would seek office (Maisel and Stone 2014). Veterans have a lot of reasons to believe that they will win. In the 2014 midterm elections, 164 military veterans were nominated by either Democrats or Republicans for the U.S. House of Representatives, and 20 were nominated for the Senate (Lynn and Neihoff 2014). Although Congress today has fewer veterans than in previous generations, 101 of the 535 members of the 114th Congress are veterans (Manning 2015). This veteran share of Congress is roughly double the proportion of veterans in the adult population of the United States (Tivald and Kawashima-Ginsberg 2015). In short, veterans are well represented in Congress, which may encourage other veterans to run.

Veterans have a number of attributes that increase their electability. The public holds the military in high esteem. A 2015 Gallup poll found that the American public has more trust in the military than any other major institution (Gallup 2015). Seventy-two percent reported a "great deal" or "quite a lot" of trust in the military. Ironically, veterans running for Congress want to join the institution with the lowest level of confidence. In the same poll, Congress scored less than 10 percent confidence. The trust that the public has in military members may be one reason they are elected, but military experience alone does not ensure electability. Professional experience beyond military service appears essential to winning elections (Lynn and Neihoff 2014).

Veterans, moreover, may have ideological reasons for seeking political office. Military members have historically "accepted the values of the liberal democratic state and have no wish to subvert them" (Cimbala 2012, 81). They have a strong commitment to democracy, although, ironically, they have spent years in an organization that is anything but democratic. This commitment to democracy, however, is limited while on active duty, because military members are not the ones who make the most important decisions that affect the military. For example, the decision to go to war may be informed by military leaders, but it is actually made by (democratically elected) politicians. This desire to be the decision makers may be one of the reasons that military members go into politics. They want to shape the policies and programs that affect military members, veterans, and their families. In Congress, veterans are among the strongest advocates for the military. Politicians with military experience have a unique perspective that informs military-related issues (Lynn and Neihoff 2014), and veterans often strive to be seated on relevant committees such as the armed services committees of the House and Senate.

Veterans also have the advantage of being predominantly from the dominant social group: white men. White men continue to hold the most seats in elected bodies in the United States. Although white men make up only 31 percent of the U.S. population, they hold 64 percent of all elected offices (Women Donors Network 2014). In 2013, 69 percent of the active U.S. military was white, and among officers, who are the most likely to be seen as electable, 78 percent were white (Office of the Deputy Assistant Secretary of Defense 2013). From the political ambition theory viewpoint, white male veterans are more likely to be expected to run for office, while minorities and women are not, although other barriers such as sexism and racism discourage these groups from running.

The military culture is founded on a masculine, warrior paradigm that focuses on competing and winning (Dunivin 1994). Many people enter politics because they are ambitious and desire the prestige and power associated with political office. Certainly some veterans are seeking these elements, but there are other elements to ambition beyond self-interest. Many military members feel that the military community is superior to the civilian world. They are repulsed by the selfishness of civilians and feel that the military has something better to offer the United States (Caplow and Hicks 2002). By being in politics, veterans may believe that they are bringing something more to their community and nation. Veterans are acting on the values of selflessness and commitment that they associate with military service.

Moreover, veterans may want to make a difference at the political level because the issues surrounding military service are personal. For example, the high rate of suicide among veterans (Department of Veterans Affairs 2013) may spur the nation to action, but it personally impacts veterans. It is not uncommon to talk to veterans who have had friends who have killed themselves or have struggled with depression and suicidal thoughts. When veterans see homeless men wearing uniforms, they may view them not as society's castaways, but as their brothers-in-arms. More than most, veterans have a special interest in solving the problems facing military members, veterans, and their families.

Being in politics furthermore offers veterans something that they did not have in their military careers—freedom. Military members are restricted in their ability to participate in the political process. While they are strongly encouraged to vote, military members are restricted from many partisan activities, especially while in uniform (Department of Defense 2008). Veterans do vote in higher numbers than civilians and seem more engaged in the political process (Tivald and Kawashima-Ginsberg 2015). Being veterans as opposed to active duty military members, they have more freedom to voice their political views.

Veterans in Politics

The military in theory is apolitical, and military leaders have historically been "above politics" (Janowitz 1971, 233). Some senior military leaders have so strongly endorsed this position that they have not voted. General George Marshall never voted (Cray 1990), and General David Petraeus did not vote after being promoted to Major General (Kels 2008). Bruce Ackerman (2010), professor of law and political science at Yale University, wrote that in the early 20th century, "The overwhelming majority of [U.S. military] officers even refused to vote since this required them to think of themselves as partisans for the time it took to cast a secret ballot. As late as 1976, 55% of the higher ranks (majors and above) continued to identify as independents." He argued that the military has drifted away from its apolitical past, becoming more partisan and more conservative. In 1976, 33 percent of the officer corps identified as Republicans; by 1996, the percentage rose to 67 percent (Ackerman 2010).

Veterans are often identified more with Republicans than with Democrats. They share more demographic characteristics with the former, such as being male, wealthier, and married, and are more likely to consider themselves conservative (Klingler and Chatagnier 2014). Studies of voting patterns, however, have found little evidence that veteran voting patterns are different than those of the general population (Teigen 2007). Still, veterans seeking political office tend to be predominantly Republicans, although this appears to be changing somewhat (Lynn and Neihoff 2014).

The number of veterans in politics has been changing. After World War II, veterans in political office were common, in large part because so many men had served in World War II and would later obtain college degrees under the G.I. Bill. The number of veterans in Congress rose dramatically starting in 1945 and peaked in the 1970s, when veterans made up 73 percent of the 92nd Congress (Manning 2015). The decline in the number of veterans certainly has had an influence. A Gallup (2012) poll found that 80 percent of men between the ages of 85 and 90 were veterans, compared to 12 percent of 25- to 39-year-olds being veterans. The last two World War II veterans in Congress left at the end of 2014 (Gonyea 2014).

Today, a number of notable politicians are veterans. Tammy Duckworth, a U.S. Representative for Illinois, is one of the most recognizable veterans in Congress. She served in the Illinois National Guard and lost her legs and partial use of her right arm after the helicopter she was piloting was hit by an enemy rocket in 2004 during OIF. She lost a bid for a seat in Congress in 2006, but was appointed assistant secretary of veterans affairs by President Barack Obama in 2009. In 2012 she was elected to Congress and has worked extensively to help military members, veterans, and their families. Her combat experience certainly helped her electability. All female veterans serving in Congress have seen combat. Her personal experiences have likewise shaped her political positions. She has worked extensively to improve veterans' access to healthcare and housing (Duckworth 2015)

Martha McSally, a U.S. representative from Arizona, is a retired Air Force colonel and was the first female fighter pilot to fly in combat. She was also the first woman to command a fighter squadron. She unsuccessfully ran for Arizona's 8th Congressional District in 2012, but won the 2nd Congressional District by 161 votes in 2014. She is the first Republican woman to represent Arizona in the House of Representatives and serves on the Armed Services Committee. McSally had a controversial military career, in which she sued the Department of Defense over its policy that required military women stationed in Saudi Arabia to wear abayas. She argued that the policy was demeaning to female service members; in 2002 the U.S. Senate unanimously voted to prohibit the practice. In Congress, she has directly challenged the Department of Defense on its reluctance to allow women to serve in combat roles and its handling of sexual assaults (McSally 2015).

John Kerry, currently the U.S. secretary of state, served for four months in Vietnam, where he was awarded the Silver Star, the Bronze Star, and three Purple Hearts. Upon his return to the United States, Kerry joined the Vietnam Veterans Against the War and famously spoke out against the war at the Fulbright hearings. He continued to work to end the Vietnam War and famously said "How do you ask a man to be last man to die for a mistake?" (Brinkley 2004, 11). He served as the lieutenant governor of Massachusetts as well as U.S. senator from the state. He was the Democratic nominee for president in 2004. Kerry joined the military for the same reason that many men and women do: "It was the right thing to do" (Kristof 2014). Although Kerry had always displayed strong political ambitions, his voluntary enlistment was arguably due to his commitment to service for his country.

Barriers and Obstacles to Civic Engagement

Veterans face a number of obstacles to civic engagement. Ironically, what makes veterans valuable assets in the military can become an obstruction as a civilian. The military culture's emphasis on mission accomplishment and masculinity can be seen as overpowering to nonveterans. Military members are also stigmatized, especially if they are combat veterans. Got Your Six, a campaign that focuses on empowering veterans in their transition to civilian life, found that veterans are often stigmatized as more likely to be homeless and mentally ill (Lieberman and Stewart 2014). Veterans are stereotyped as men with high rates of PTSD who are prone to violence, damaged, and uneducated. While some veterans certainly struggle with problems, these stereotypes—like many stereotypes—are far from the truth. Mr. Marvin from Got Your Six stated that "99 percent of us [veterans] are neither heroic nor broken" (Phillips 2015, A11). These same concerns probably impact civic engagement in terms of being allowed to volunteer and to some degree in seeking political office.

Some veterans struggle with adapting to civilian life. Many veterans are perplexed by contrasts between the civilian and military cultures. One marine reported that "we expect a certain degree of professionalism, a certain degree of respect" that he did not feel as a civilian (Chicas et al. 2012). Like many veterans, he reported that he only felt comfortable around other veterans. While this may explain a desire to volunteer to work with military members, veterans, and their families, it can be an obstacle to other types of civic engagement, such as volunteering for strictly civilian organizations.

The lack of civilian-oriented skills may similarly be a barrier to civic engagement. While many veterans have skills that appear compatible, there are some differences between applying the skills used in the military and those used in the civilian community. Even when the skills are compatible, veterans may feel some sense of trepidation about how civilians run volunteer organizations compared to how the military operates.

Finally, some veterans create their own barriers to civic engagement with a sense of entitlement. They believe that they are entitled not only to jobs, but to jobs that are "worthy" of them and their skills. A Center for Innovation and Research on Veterans & Military Families (CIR) study found that veterans were concerned about the lack of jobs that use their skills and experiences and pay a fair wage (Chicas et al. 2012). While running for political office is more likely to be bolstered by a sense of entitlement, volunteering may be thwarted. Volunteering requires some measure of humility, and many volunteer opportunities are not glamorous.

Veterans pursing political office also encounter a barrier: being a veteran. The Veterans Campaign found that military service was both an asset and a liability for seeking political office (Lynn and Neihoff 2014). While many voters associate military service with integrity, other voters are unfamiliar with the military and even suspicious of it. Candidates' military records have been closely scrutinized and the subject of controversy on the campaign trail. For example, Senator Joni Ernst's military record was questioned because she routinely called herself a combat veteran when in fact she was never fired upon or exposed to improvised explosive devices. Still, her assertion that she was a combat veteran was consistent with the Department of Defense definition, and her unit could have come under attack. These types of distinctions can confuse voters and hurt a veteran's election chances. In general, attacks on veterans' military records have been ineffective unless the incidents are clearly associated with questions of integrity and character (Lynn and Neihoff 2014).

Conclusion

Veterans represent a unique group in the United States who have a strong sense of patriotism and commitment to democracy. Theories of volunteering and seeking political office offer a number of explanations for why veterans are more politically engaged and volunteer more time than civilians. In general, civic engagement for veterans comes from a sense of civic duty, self-interest, or both. Their civic duty interests stem from the military culture and its focus on service. Veterans either believe that they have something unique to offer their communities and their country, or they have simply internalized the values of service and want to provide for the common good. Self-interest can motivate civic engagement as well. This self-interest can be financial, such as acquiring skills for employment, or it can be for the prestige and appreciation that comes with civic engagement. The most likely explanation, however, is that veterans are motivated by a combination of factors. Being a part of the political process and volunteering in their communities offers veterans the chance to make a positive difference for themselves and others and "is a natural progression for those who have served in uniform" (Tivald and Kawashima-Ginsberg 2015, 13).

References

Abbaszadeh, Nima, Mark Crow, Marianne El-Khoury, Jonathan Gandomi, David Kuwayama, Christopher MacPherson, Meghan Nutting, Nealin Parker, and Taya Weiss. 2008. *Provincial Reconstruction Teams: Lessons and Recommendations*.

Princeton, NJ: Princeton University Woodrow Wilson School of Public and International Relations. Accessed January 17, 2016. http://wws.princeton.edu/sites/default/files/content/docs/news/wws591b.pdf.

Ackerman, Bruce. 2010. "An Increasingly Politicized Military." *Los Angeles Times*, June 20. Accessed December 23, 2015. http://articles.latimes.com/print/2010/jun/22/opinion/la-oe-ackerman-mcchrystal-20100623.

Adler, Richard P., and Judy Goggin. 2005. "What Do We Mean by 'Civic Engagement'?" *Journal of Transformative Education* 3 (3): 236–253. doi:10.1177/1541344605276792.

Belkin, Aaron, Morten G. Ender, Nathaniel Frank, Stacie R. Furia, George Lucas, Gary Packard, Steven M. Samuels, Tammy Schultz, and David R. Segal. 2013. "Readiness and DADT repeal: Has the New Policy of Open Service Undermined the Military?" *Armed Forces & Society* 39 (4): 587–601.

Berger, Ben. 2009. "Political Theory, Political Science, and the End of Civic Engagement." *Perspectives on Politics* 7 (2): 335–50. doi:10.1017/S153759270909080X.

Brinkley, Douglas. 2004. *Tour of Duty: John Kerry and the Vietnam War*. New York: William Morrow.

Burk, James, and Evelyn Espinoza. 2012. "Race Relations within the U.S. Military." *Annual Review of Sociology* 38: 401–22.

Caplow, Theodore, and Louis Hicks. 2002. *Systems of War and Peace*. 2nd ed. Lanham, MD: University Press of America.

Cecchine, Gary, Forrest E. Morgan, Michael A. Wermuth, Timothy Jackson, Agnes Gereben Schaefer, and Matthew Stafford. 2013. *The U.S. Military Response to the 2010 Haiti Earthquake: Consideration for Army Leaders*. RAND Corporation, Aroyo Center. Accessed January 17, 2016. http://www.rand.org/content/dam/rand/pubs/research_reports/RR300/RR304/RAND_RR304.pdf.

Charity Watch. 2015. *A Donor's Guide to Serving the Needs of Veterans and the Military*. Accessed December 23, 2015. https://www.charitywatch.org/charitywatch-articles/a-donor-39-s-guide-to-serving-the-needs-of-veterans-and-the-military/150.

Chicas, Joseph, Paul Maiden, Hyunsung Oh, Sherrie Wilcox, and David Young. 2012 (June). "From War to the Workplace: Helping Veterans Transition to Civilian Work Settings." Center for Innovation and Research on Veterans & Military Families (CIR). *CIR Policy Brief*. June. Accessed January 17, 2016. http://cir.usc.edu/wp-content/uploads/2013/10/201206_PB-cover.png.

Cimbala, Stephen J. 2012. *Civil-Military Relations in Perspective: Strategy, Structure and Policy*. Burlington, VT: Ashgate.

Clary, E. Gil, Mark Snyder, and Robert D. Ridge. 1992. "Volunteers' Motivations: A Functional Strategy for the Recruitment, Placement, and Retention of Volunteers." *Nonprofit Management & Leadership* 2 (4): 333–350. doi: 10.1002/nml.4130020403.

Clary, E. Gil, Mark Snyder, Robert D. Ridge, John Copeland, Arthur A. Stukas, Julie Haugen, and Peter Miene. 1998. "Understanding and Assessing the Motivations of Volunteers: A Functional Approach." *Journal of Personality and Social Psychology* 74 (6): 1516–1530. doi:10.1037/0022-3514.74.6.1516.

Corporation for National & Community Service. 2014. "Congressional Budget Justification, Fiscal Year 2014." Accessed January 10, 2016. http://www.nationalservice.gov/sites/default/files/documents/cbj_2014_report.pdf.

Cray, Ed. 1990. *General of the Army George C. Marshall, Soldier and Statesman*. New York: Norton.

Department of Defense. 2008. *Directive 1344.10: Political Activities by Members of the Armed Forces*. Washington, DC: Department of Defense. Accessed January 10, 2016. http://www.dtic.mil/whs/directives/corres/pdf/134410p.pdf.

Department of Defense. 2010. *Report of the Comprehensive Review of the Issues Associated with a Repeal of "Don't Ask, Don't Tell."* Washington, D.C.: Department of Defense. Accessed January 17, 2016. https://archive.org/details/ComprehensiveReviewOfTheIssuesAssociatedWithARepealOfdontAsk.

Department of Veterans Affairs. 2013. *Suicide Data Report, 2012*. 2013 ASI 8608-39. Washington, DC: Department of Veterans Affairs. Accessed January 10, 2016. http://www.va.gov/opa/docs/Suicide-Data-Report-2012-final.pdf.

Duckworth, Tammy. 2015. "About Tammy." Accessed December 31. http://duckworth.house.gov/index.php/about-tammy/biography.

Dunivin, Karen O. 1994. "Military Culture: Change and Continuity." *Armed Forces & Society* 20 (4): 531–547. doi:http://dx.doi.org/10.1177/0095327X9402000403.

Exum, Herbert A., Jose E. Coll, and Eugenia L. Weiss. 2011. *A Civilian Counselor's Primer for Counseling Veterans*. 2nd ed. Deer Park, NY: Linus Publications.

Firestone, Juanita M. 1992. "Occupational Segregation: Comparing the Civilian and Military Work Force." *Armed Forces and Society* 18: 363–81.

Flanagan, Constance, and Peter Levine. 2010. "Civic Engagement and the Transition to Adulthood." *Future of Children* 20 (1): 159–179. doi:10.1353/foc.0.0043.

Fox, Richard L., and Jennifer L. Lawless. 2005. "To Run or Not to Run for Office: Explaining Nascent Political Ambition." *American Journal of Political Science* 49 (3): 642–659. doi:10.1111/j.1540-5907.2005.00147.x.

Gallup. 2012. *In U.S., 24% of Men, 2% of Women Are Veterans*. November 2. http://www.gallup.com/poll/158729/men-women-veterans.aspx.

Gallup. 2015. *Confidence in Institutions*. June 2–7. Accessed January 17, 2016. http://www.gallup.com/poll/1597/confidence-institutions.aspx.

Gonyea, Don. 2014. "Congress Says Goodbye to Its Last World War II Vets." *National Public Radio*, December 9. Accessed January 10, 2016. http://www.npr.org/sections/itsallpolitics/2014/12/09/369663245/congress-says-goodbye-to-its-last-world-war-ii-vets.

Hajjar, Remi M. 2014. "Emergent Postmodern US Military Culture." *Armed Forces & Society* 40 (1): 118–145. doi:10.1177/0095327X12465261.

Janowitz, Morris. 1971. *The Professional Soldier: A Social and Political Portrait*. Glencoe, IL: Free Press.

Joint Chiefs of Staff. 2013. *Civil-Military Operations*. Joint Publication 3–57. Accessed January 10, 2016. http://www.dtic.mil/doctrine/new_pubs/jp3_57.pdf.

Joint Chiefs of Staff. 2014. *Foreign Humanitarian Assistance*. Joint Publication 3–29. Accessed January 10, 2016. http://www.dtic.mil/doctrine/new_pubs/jp3_29.pdf.

Kels, Charles. 2008. "The Nonpartisan Military." *Armed Forces Journal*, August 1. Accessed January 10, 2016. http://www.armedforcesjournal.com/the-nonpartisan-military/.

Kishon-Barash, Ronit, Elizabeth Midlarsky, and David R. Johnson. 1999. "Altruism and the Vietnam War Veteran: The Relationship of Helping to Symptomatology." *Journal of Traumatic Stress* 12 (4): 655–62.

Klingler, Jonathan D., and J. Tyson Chatagnier. 2014. "Are You Doing Your Part? Veterans' Political Attitudes and Heinlein's Conception of Citizenship." *Armed Forces & Society* 40 (4): 673–95.

Kristof, Nicholas D. 2014. "A War Hero or a Phony?" *New York Times*, September 18. Accessed January 17, 2016. http://www.nytimes.com/2004/09/18/opinion/a-war-hero-or-a-phony.html?_r=0.

Lieberman, Drew, and Kathryn Stewart. 2014. *Strengthening Perceptions of America's Post 9/11 Veterans: A Survey Analysis Report*. Greenberg Quinlin Rosner Research: Got Your Six. Accessed January 10, 2016. http://www.gotyour6.org/wp-content/uploads/2014/10/GY6-Survey-Analysis-Report-2014.pdf.

Lynn, Seth, and Crystal Neihoff. 2014. *Field Report 2014: Veterans En Route to the 114th Congress*. Veterans Campaign. Accessed January 10, 2016. http://www.veteranscampaign.org/field-report/.

Maisel, L. Sandy, and Walter J. Stone. 2014. "Candidate Emergence Revisited: The Lingering Effects of Recruitment, Ambition, and Successful Prospects among House Candidates." *Political Science Quarterly* 129 (3): 429–447. doi:10.1002/polq.12217.

Manning, Jennifer E. 2015. "Membership of the 114th Congress: A Profile." Congressional Research Service, CRS Report. Accessed January 10, 2016. https://www.fas.org/sgp/crs/misc/R43869.pdf.

McAllum, Kirstie. 2014. "Meanings of Organizational Volunteering: Diverse Volunteer Pathways." *Management Communication Quarterly* 28 (1): 84–110. doi:10.1177/0893318913517237.

McCarthy, Anne M., and Mary L. Tucker. 1999. "Student Attitudes Toward Service-Learning: Implications for Implementation." *Journal of Management Education* 23 (5): 554–73.

McSally, Martha. 2015. "Biography." Accessed December 31. https://mcsally.house.gov/about/full-biography.

Mission Continues, The. n.d. "Join the Movement." Accessed January 10, 2016. https://www.missioncontinues.org/get-involved/.

Office of History. 2006. *With Compassion and Hope: The Story of Operation Unified Assistance*. Headquarters, Pacific Air Forces. Accessed January 10, 2016. http://www.afhra.af.mil/shared/media/document/AFD-100129-095.pdf.

Office of the Deputy Assistant Secretary of Defense. 2013. *2013 Demographics: Profile of the Military Community*. Washington, D.C. Accessed January 10, 2016.

http://download.militaryonesource.mil/12038/MOS/Reports/2013-Demographics-Report.pdf.

Petraeus, David. 2013. "How We Won in Iraq—and Why All the Hard-Won Gains of the Surge Are in Grave Danger of Being Lost Today." *Foreign Policy* (October 29). Accessed January 10, 2016. http://foreignpolicy.com/2013/10/29/how-we-won-in-iraq/.

Pew Research Center. 2013. *Public Esteem for Military Still High*. Washington, DC: Pew Research Center. Accessed January 10, 2016. http://www.pewforum.org/2013/07/11/public-esteem-for-military-still-high/.

Phillips, Dave. 2015. "Coming Home to Dangerous Stereotypes." *New York Times*, February 15. Accessed January 10, 2016. http://www.nytimes.com/2015/02/06/us/a-veteran-works-to-break-the-broken-hero-stereotype.html?_r=0.

Purple Heart Homes. n.d. Accessed January 10, 2016. http://www.phhusa.org/.

Richtel, Matt. 2015. "Please Don't Thank Me for My Service: News Analysis." *New York Times*, February 22. Accessed January 10, 2016. http://www.nytimes.com/2015/02/22/sunday-review/please-dont-thank-me-for-my-service.html?_r=0.

Rosenberg, Tina. 2014. "Veterans at Home, On a Mission of Compassion." *New York Times*, February 26. Accessed January 10, 2016. http://opinionator.blogs.nytimes.com/2014/02/26/returning-veterans-on-a-mission-of-compassion/?login=email&_r=0.

Rushton, Philippe J., Roland D. Chrisjohn, and G. Cynthia Fekken. 1981. "The Altruistic Personality and the Self-Report Altruism Scale." *Personality and Individual Differences* 2 (4): 293–302.

Sarkesian, Sam Charles, and Robert E. Connor. 2006. *The US Military Profession into the Twenty-First Century: War, Peace and Politics*. 2nd ed. London: Routledge.

Shye, Samuel. 2010. "The Motivation to Volunteer: A Systemic Quality of Life Theory." *Social Indicators Research* 98 (2): 183–200. doi:10.1007/s11205-009-9545-3.

Spera, Christopher, Robin Ghertner, Anthony Nerino, and Adrienne DiTommaso. (2013). *Volunteering as a Pathway to Employment: Does Volunteering Increase Odds of Finding a Job for the Out of Work*. Corporation for National & Community Service. Accessed January 10, 2016. http://www.nationalservice.gov/sites/default/files/upload/employment_research_report.pdf.

Team Rubicon. n.d. "Our Mission." Accessed January 10, 2016. http://www.teamrubiconusa.org/our-mission/.

Teigen, Jeremy M. 2007. "Veterans' Party Identification, Candidate Affect, and Vote Choice in the 2004 U.S. Presidential Election." *Armed Forces & Society* 33 (3): 414–437.

Tivald, Julia, and Kei Kawashima-Ginsberg. 2015. *2015 Veterans Civic Health Index*. Accessed January 10, 2016. https://gotyour6.org/wp-content/uploads/2015/08/Veterans-Civic-Health-Index-2015.pdf.

U.S. Air Force. 1997. *The United States Air Force Core Values*. Accessed January 10, 2016. http://www.e-publishing.af.mil/shared/media/document/AFD-070906-003.pdf.

U.S. Army. 2016. "Humanitarian Relief." Accessed January 10. http://www.army.mil/humanitarian/.

Washington, George. 1775. *The George Washington Papers at the Library of Congress.* Accessed January 17, 2016. http://memory.loc.gov/cgi-bin/query/r?ammem/mgw:@field%28DOCID+@lit%28gw030217%29%29#N0337-226.

Women Donors Network. 2014. "Who Leads Us?" Accessed January 10, 2016. http://www.washingtonpost.com/wp-srv/blogs/WDN-Reflective-Democracy-Campaign-Information-Kit.pdf.

Yonkman, Mary M., and John M. Bridgeland. 2009. *All Volunteer Force: From Military to Civilian Service.* Civic Enterprises. Accessed January 10, 2016. http://www.civicenterprises.net/MediaLibrary/Docs/all_volunteer_force.pdf.

Zoroya, G. 2014. "Veterans Find Their Niche—and Run with It." *USA Today*, June 1. Accessed January 10, 2016. http://www.usatoday.com/story/news/nation/2014/06/01/veterans-afghanistan-iraq-wars-homefront-suicide-gis/9686015/.

CHAPTER TEN

Veterans as Entrepreneurs

Elizabeth A. Osborn and Louis Hicks

Introduction

For over two centuries active-duty service members have been defending the principles of free enterprise when they defend the Constitution of the United States of America. Property rights, including the right to own the means of production, are enshrined in the founding documents of the republic. The U.S. Constitution created a federal government with the power to regulate commerce, bankruptcies, and money. Various parts of the Bill of Rights prohibit restraints on freedom of association, unreasonable seizures of property during investigations, and the taking of "private property for public use, without just compensation." These provisions are all hallmarks of a free enterprise system.

The right to earn wages—freely contracted for—was a crucial point of contention in the American Civil War. Said President Abraham Lincoln in his second inaugural address, "It may seem strange that any men should dare to ask a just God's assistance in wringing their bread from the sweat of other men's faces, but let us judge not, that we be not judged." The Cold War, which involved millions of American service members and billions of dollars of expenditure from 1945 to 1991, was in large part a dispute over whether the leading economies of the world would be organized as capitalist or communist. The ability to go into business for one's self—and to freely hire others as employees—has been important to the American government and military since the very beginning. It is not surprising, then, that U.S. veterans often go to work in private enterprises, and in particular, start and manage thousands of businesses after their active duty service ends.

This chapter describes veterans who start their own businesses after their military service. It includes information about the numbers, characteristics, motivations, and activities of veteran entrepreneurs; the various programs and activities of governments and other agencies to support veteran entrepreneurs; and the effects of veteran entrepreneurs on local, regional, and national scales. Interviews with numerous veteran entrepreneurs illuminate the data found in economic surveys.

Military Service and the Skills of Entrepreneurs

Long before they encounter programs aimed specifically at veterans, most veterans are helped along the way toward entrepreneurship by their active-duty service itself. Many aspects of military service are supportive of the transition to entrepreneurship. This may seem strange to readers who imagine the American military as an authoritarian organization with a fetish for bureaucracy and a culture of selflessness rather than personal profit. And so it is, at least in caricature. But it is also an organization that typically inculcates many skills that can enable veterans to succeed in business. Service members routinely learn organizational skills, strategic and tactical planning skills, record keeping, complex scheduling, information gathering, process controls, inventory management, transportation planning, facilities usage, and a whole host of other relevant abilities. They are exposed to different cultures, both from within the wider American society and, very often, overseas. The military is also an organization that calculates and takes risks, sometimes for huge stakes. It is also, or can be, a supremely rational enterprise that teaches rationality in action, the slow and careful fitting of ways and means to goals and purposes. Finally, the American military has an ethos of personal responsibility, loyalty, honesty, resilience, and hard work—again, all tremendously valuable skills for entrepreneurs.

Service in the American military can also be supportive of later entrepreneurship by providing veterans with the chance to learn skills that are not typically part of the military experience. Service members do not usually learn marketing, business finance, cash management, real estate leasing, commercial law, and the other usual aspects of running a business in America. But they do get the G.I. Bill, and most of the colleges and universities that they attend teach these subjects.

Military service provides even more practical advantages to the budding entrepreneur—a financial cushion from which to launch a business.

Many beginning entrepreneurs among the nonveteran population cobble together their start-up funds from a wide variety of sources: loans and gifts from family and friends; their own personal savings; cash-out refinancing of a principal residence; and, rather infamously in the case of many tech entrepreneurs, outrageous balances on a wallet full of credit cards. Veterans might avail themselves of all these sources, but some of them have additional resources. For example, disabled veterans may receive compensation that can cover their living expenses indefinitely, allowing them to avoid having to pay themselves during the early years of a business, when it is typically cash-starved. Veterans can purchase a home with a low- or no-money-down VA loan, freeing up cash for their business. Military retirees—who are often as young as 40 years old—have an income for life, plus other valuable benefits such as free or nearly free healthcare. This again frees them from the need to spend money on living expenses before the business has fully succeeded. Many veterans leave the military in a great position to start a business.

Government Programs for Veteran Entrepreneurs

The federal government operates a plethora of programs designed to help veterans start and succeed in a small business. This might be said to begin with the Transition Assistance Planning (TAP) program provided to service members and their spouses as they leave active duty. This is a joint program of the armed services, the Department of Defense (DoD), the Department of Labor (DOL), and the Department of Veterans Affairs (VA). Retirees can access the TAP services for the rest of their lives; nonretirees must use the program during the first six months after leaving the service. Spouses' eligibility mirrors that of the service members. Even civilian employees of the DoD can use the program, if they are leaving because of a reduction in force (RIF) or base realignment and closure (BRAC). TAP consists of information, counseling, and workshops covering a wide array of topics: employability assessment, résumé preparation, wardrobe, job search tactics, planning for higher education or occupational training, occupational licensing and certification, health and dental benefits and planning, financial planning, finding a new place to live, and so forth.

TAP includes mention of "self-employed small business ownership" as an alternative to finding a job, and that the Small Business Administration (SBA) can help the veteran explore this possibility. It specifically refers to veterans as "qualified and capable" of becoming entrepreneurs (Department of the Army 2016, 26). In another, longer section (46–61), veterans are particularly encouraged to consider business ownership and provided with detailed information about how to start their own business, including writing a business plan, sources of financing, and the advantages and disadvantages of franchising. The SBA created a "Boots to Business" training track for use inside TAP. This includes an "eight-week, instructor-led online course that offers in-depth instruction on the elements of a business plan and tips and techniques for starting a business" (Small Business Administration 2016a). The veteran is introduced to the SBA's program for veterans, as well as the National Veterans Business Development Corporation (TVC) (charged with "creating and enhancing entrepreneurial business opportunities" for veterans) and the Center for Veterans Enterprise (CVE), which the VA established in 2001 to help "veterans succeed in business," especially with regard to government procurement opportunities.

Beyond TAP, the SBA is the most important support for veterans as entrepreneurs. It runs a large number of programs with wide geographic reach in support of small businesses in America. A special organization in the SBA, the Office of Veterans Business Development, is designed to "maximize, the availability, applicability and usability, of small business programs" for veterans. The office provides training, counseling and mentorship, and oversight of federal procurement programs. There are also Veterans Business Outreach Centers, which are run by organizations that partner with the SBA (Small Business Administration 2016b). For example, Old Dominion University (2016) operates a center that covers Virginia, Delaware, Pennsylvania, and West Virginia.

Beyond government-operated or -funded programs, there are also some commercial resources for veteran entrepreneurs. One commercially owned resource for veteran entrepreneurs is a Web directory of over 24,000 veteran-owned businesses maintained by Veteran Owned Business (2016), which itself is owned by a "proud military veteran."

How Many Veterans Are Entrepreneurs?

The number of veteran entrepreneurs can be estimated in various ways. The Current Population Survey includes information about self-employment and veteran status. In 2010 the 11.8 million veterans who were working or looking for work constituted almost 8 percent of the U.S. labor force (Department of Labor 2011, 1). Roughly equal proportions of male veterans and nonveterans in the labor force—about 8 percent—are self-employed. Among female veterans, self-employment is lower (4 percent) than among female nonveterans. Veterans of World War II, the Korean War, and the Vietnam eras have a relatively high rate of self-employment (11 percent). Veterans of the Gulf War I era have a lower rate of self-employment (4 percent), and veterans of the Gulf War II era (Post-9/11 era) have the lowest rate of all, 2 percent (Department of Labor 2011, 3).

The aging of many veterans out of their prime working years has caused a recent drop in the number of employed veterans. By 2014 the number of employed veterans had dropped to 10.2 million, and veterans made up only 7 percent of the labor force, as shown in table 10.1. In 2014 about 91,000 veterans were self-employed workers (unincorporated) in agriculture and related industries, and another 660,000 veterans were "self-employed workers, unincorporated" in nonagricultural industries.

For our purposes, these data have a significant flaw. Veteran entrepreneurs who have incorporated their businesses are moved into the "wage and salary workers" category and are no longer counted as "self-employed." From a certain point of view this makes sense; veteran entrepreneurs who own stock in their company and run it are nevertheless drawing a salary, and hence are employees of the corporation. However, it means that these numbers underestimate the number of veteran entrepreneurs. and in particular, leave out precisely those veteran start-ups that are successful enough to lead to incorporation.

Another major source of statistical information about veteran entrepreneurs is the Survey of Business Owners conducted by the Census Bureau. The 2012 survey asked a large sample of businesses for information, including the veteran status of the owner. This survey covers most of the private enterprise sector of the American economy. Table 10.2 shows the major features of veteran-owned businesses.

Beyond the 2.5 million veteran-owned businesses found by the Survey of Business Owners, another 587,000 businesses were found that were equally owned by veteran(s) and nonveteran(s). The 2012 survey also includes information about the gender, ethnicity, and race of veteran business owners, the number of their employees, their gross receipts, and the distribution of veteran-owned businesses across the country and across the various sectors of the economy. The Census Bureau (2015) highlighted some key facts about veteran-owned businesses in 2012:

- There were 2.5 million veteran-owned firms nationally in 2012, up from 2.4 million, or 3.0 percent, in 2007. Veteran-owned firms comprised 9.1 percent of all U.S. firms. For comparison, veterans accounted for 8.9 percent of the population in 2012, according to the American Community Survey.
- Of the 50 most populous cities in 2012, Virginia Beach had the highest proportion of veteran-owned businesses, with 15.2 percent.
- California and Texas led all states in the number of veteran-owned firms, with 252,377 and 213,590 firms, respectively.
- Los Angeles County had more veteran-owned firms than any other county in 2012, with 69,608.

Table 10.1. Self-Employed, Unincorporated Veterans by Sex and Period of Service, 2014.

	Veterans						Nonveterans
		Gulf War Era (1990–2014)			WW II, Korean War, and Vietnam Era	Other Service Periods	
	Total	Total	Gulf War Era II	Gulf War Era I			
All Workers							
Total employed (in thousands)	10,171	5,003	2,353	2,650	2,522	2,645	134,589
Self-employed, Agriculture (as percent of total employed)	0.9	0.2	0.2	0.3	2.5	0.8	0.5
Self-employed, Nonagriculture (as percent of total employed)	6.5	3.6	2.8	4.4	11.8	6.7	5.9
Men							
Total employed (in thousands)	8,868	4,157	1,952	2,205	2,432	2,279	68,085
Self-employed, Agriculture (as percent of total employed)	1.1	0.3	0.2	0.3	2.6	0.9	0.7
Self-employed, Nonagriculture (as percent of total employed)	6.8	3.6	2.7	4.4	12.0	7.3	6.6
Women							
Total employed (in thousands)	1,303	847	402	445	90	366	66,494
Self-employed, Agriculture (as percent of total employed)	0.0	0.0	0.0	0.0	0.0	0.1	0.3
Self-employed, Nonagriculture (as percent of total employed)	4.0	3.7	3.0	4.3	7.3	3.7	5.1

Source: Bureau of Labor Statistics (2015, Table 5). Discrepancy in totals caused by rounding.

Table 10.2. Size of Veteran-Owned Firms in the United States, 2012.

Dimension	Veteran-Owned Firms	All Firms
Number of firms with or without paid employees	2,521,682	27,626,360
Sales, receipts, or value of shipments of firms with or without paid employees ($billions of dollars)	1,141	33,536
Number of firms with paid employees	442,485	5,424,458
Sales, receipts, or value of shipments of firms with paid employees ($billions of dollars)	1,048	32,495
Number of paid employees for pay period including March 12, 2012	5,026,272	115,249,007
Annual payroll ($billions of dollars)	195	5,236
Number of firms without paid employees	2,079,197	22,201,902
Sales, receipts, or value of shipments of firms without paid employees ($billions of dollars)	92	1,041

Source: Census Bureau (2012).

Trends in Veteran Ownership of Businesses

Trends in the number of veteran-owned businesses and proportion of all businesses that are veteran-owned are heavily affected by the underlying demographics of veterans. For example, in 2015 almost 46 percent of veterans were age 65 or older (National Center for Veterans Analysis and Statistics 2016), compared to only 19 percent of the entire adult population (Colby and Ortman 2015). As the veteran population aged, relative to the entire population, over the past 20 years, the proportion of the adult population that owned a business declined, from just over 10 percent to just over 5 percent (Kauffman 2016). However, the index of entrepreneurial activity did not show as great a decline: the index was 0.35 percent in 1996 and 0.23 percent in 2013 (Fairlie 2014, 15).

The Effects of Veteran Entrepreneurship

Veteran entrepreneurs have had transformative effects on the places where their energies and talents have found fertile ground in which to take root. These effects are most obvious in locations around large military bases, where many veterans choose to live. In such places, economic and social development is accelerated by the arrival of numerous veterans who go into business (Hicks and Raney 2003).

The Characteristics of Veteran Entrepreneurs

Entrepreneurs, entrepreneurship, and *entrepreneurial spirit* are all commonly used terms, but they are also complex concepts. What is an entrepreneur? The term dates back to the mid-1700s, when Cantillon (1755 [2010]) referred to entrepreneurs as merchants, adventurers, or employers, but it was not until the mid-1900s that Schumpeter (1947) noted that entrepreneurs are innovators. Since then the definition has expanded to label entrepreneurs as the engines of the economy, captains of business, and leaders of social change (Osborn and Slomczynski 2005).

The popular perception is that entrepreneurship is the domain of young people. The reality is that a few young tycoons dominate the news, but data dispute their impact. From 1989 to 2013 the share of households headed by someone under age 30 who had a stake in or owned a privately held business fell from 11 to 4 percent (Slayback 2016). Compare this to the increase in veteran entrepreneurs in the same time frame. It may be the case that local, state, and federal regulations, along with poor economic growth and a lack of experience, may contribute to the differences in the recruitment of entrepreneurs. The data below serve as a partial explanation of the increase in veteran entrepreneurs.

Who are the entrepreneurs? Are they born, or can they be taught? What separates entrepreneurs from nonentrepreneurs? How are entrepreneurs recruited? How do potential entrepreneurs become actual entrepreneurs? Volumes have been written about entrepreneurs from various social strata, geographic locations, and historical periods. Here the obstacles and opportunities for veteran entrepreneurs are examined. Are veteran entrepreneurs a distinct group, with particular characteristics, or do their experiences reflect the experiences of entrepreneurs in general? Does military experience carry through a civilian lifetime? Would veteran entrepreneurs "do it again"? These are just some of the questions that lend insight into the uniqueness of a military experience for veteran entrepreneurs.

The following autobiographical accounts were obtained through in-person, in-depth interviews with veteran entrepreneurs from a range of locations: one area whose major industry is a military base, two big cities, and small towns. The sample population was limited to small to medium-sized businesses (SMEs) with a diverse group of interviewees. It is important to note that this was a sample selected from directories available to the public. Unsuccessful entrepreneurs were not interviewed. Therefore, the analysis should be viewed as how military service plays a role in thriving veteran-owned enterprises. An institutional review board (IRB) proposal was approved by St. Mary's College of Maryland prior to the interviews, and all participants were informed of their right to confidentiality. All names of the respondents and their businesses have been changed or deleted. Responses were analyzed for common themes of family background, entrepreneurial spirit, military history, and business experience.

Military History and Entrepreneurial Family Background

Entrance into the military differed among the respondents; some were drafted and some volunteered for service. Their educational levels also differed, as did their social standing. One factor that was constant across all was the continuing education and on-the-job training they received.

> I was drafted straight out of high school and was assigned to communications training. From there I went to Vietnam and got the nickname "TC" for "Top Cat." I was the boss of four other guys and that taught me a lot. I got a job easily after I got out, and was able to go to Community College. (two small, veteran-owned businesses)

Some people are "pushed" into entrepreneurship, and some are "pulled." Hard times, high unemployment, and low education can force people to look for alternative means of support. Sometimes they are motivated to learn, or they are eager to travel. Sometimes a combination of multiple factors draws them in another direction.

> I was tired of making someone else look good. I wanted to be at the top of the pecking order and I wanted to be the "yes man" to my own dream. (small, woman-owned, veteran-owned business)

Family background has been one of the stronger indicators of whether one does or does not become an entrepreneur. The socialization process can play a significant role in entrepreneurial recruitment. When an entrepreneurial family background intersects with a military history, the impact is enhanced. Ironically, at the start of several interviews the interviewee would report no history of family entrepreneurship. As the interview continued, the interviewee began to recall his early life and remember family business ventures he had previously not identified as entrepreneurship:

> My dad was a laborer but he was also a lawn contractor. I didn't think of him as an entrepreneur but I suppose he was one. He gave me a sense of pride in work. He always told me "you can," don't say, "you can't." My mother was an independent beauty product saleswoman. That too has an entrepreneurial component. (small, veteran-owned, minority business)

One respondent had two businesses, commercial fishing and a restaurant, but he didn't think the family fishing was entrepreneurial. At the end of the interview, he traced fishing back five generations:

> Military service has a long history in my family. My father and brothers all served. Commercial fishing goes back in my family from before we came to the United States. My father had me out working on the boats when I was only two and a half or three. It was my first job. I was scared sometimes. The waves were way over my head. Later I painted boats for my uncle until I was sixteen and was drafted. I didn't think of it as being entrepreneurial. It was what we did. (two small, veteran-owned businesses)

Two women respondents reported there were no entrepreneurial ventures in their family, but both their fathers had been in the military and had promoted entrepreneurial ideals. The first interviewee was supported in her entrepreneurial endeavors at age eight. The second woman used the military to set a new course for her life.

> My dad used to say, "If you do nothing, you are nothing," "Get a pay check," and "Always have a business card." Between the ages of eight and twelve years old I held backyard carnivals to raise money for Children's Hospital. I had surgery when I was very young and it left a big impression on me. I had seven siblings who became my employees. That success set the scene for later speculation. (small, women-owned, veteran-owned business)

> My father was in the service and then worked the family farm. My parents thought school was for lazy people who didn't want to work. My only option for getting off the farm was to join the military. It was a path where I could do something and keep my family happy. (small, women-owned, veteran-owned business)

The Transfer of Military Experience to Entrepreneurship

All the interviewees reinforced the impact of their military experience, from the start-up phase of their businesses through their present status, and in almost every case that impact was highly significant. Military culture, connections, a sense of community, leadership, and trust were important determinants of their success.

Strong social bonds are evident in many groups. Alumni groups, sport teams, communities, and so forth all illustrate the strength of the relationships between members. There are few, however, that rival the connectedness of military personnel. As one interviewee commented:

> It all goes back to the training. You build a sense of camaraderie. The people you train and work with become friends forever. Army friends are different; they have been put to the test. Their life experience is different. (small, women-owned, veteran-owned business)

Symbols and language are principal components of any culture. In the military they represent cultural values that shape the institution and connect members across military branches. Language is such a powerful force that researchers suggest that it may even shape our perceptions of the world (Whorf 1956). Respondents placed high significance on the role of language during, and after, active duty. Language in the military is standardized:

> Vets know military language. They know how every branch of the service works because they all had similar training. When you are in business and you are talking to a vet you can talk about a plane or a tank and they know all about it. They have driven it, or flown it, or taken it apart. (small, veteran-owned, minority business)

> And, everything has an acronym. There is a government acronym for everything. They protect the group dynamics because we are the only ones who understand them. (small, women-owned, veteran-owned business)

For many respondents, business activity was a continuation of what they were doing while in service. Many veterans continue to live and work close to military installations. They rely on their connections and networks that are familiar. Although all were clear that networks are not "pipelines" for veterans, they admitted that if all else were equal, they would hire a veteran. Even among those who did not actively recruit veteran employees, there was an admission that a military experience carries an edge:

> Vets come first. They get extra points on application. When I have to outsource I have to find someone who is trustworthy and I trust military first. I know whom to turn to when my life is on the line and I know whom to turn to when my business is on the line. (small, woman-owned, veteran-owned business)

> I learned to balance egos and handle a lot of paperwork. We had to give endless reports to superiors and that taught me the discipline to keep records for my own business. I did a lot of work on my own and liked the

autonomy. I learned about the legal system and that helped me in my first jobs after I left the service and when I later started my own business. (small, woman-owned, veteran-owned business)

When I was in Vietnam there were no rations available when we came off a twelve-hour shift. A buddy and I bought cases of soda and a refrigerator and sold snacks and soda. It was my first entrepreneurial shot. I am not an aggressive businessman but I want to be my own boss. (two small, veteran-owned businesses)

In my experience the connection between the military complex and the business world comes down to structure and simplicity. On the military side of structure is support for the mission, and a break down of demographics, i.e., race, ethnicity, and gender. On the simplicity side, starting a business was like jumping out of a plane with no parachute but I saw that contractors made more money than servicemen were making doing the same job. I looked back at five points I learned in the military: administration, marketing, operations, logistics, and finance. Starting my own business was like the marine structure on steroids but I believed that any business could work like the military. (small, veteran-owned, minority business)

A particularly interesting military plan that was designed to "draft" young doctors to provide medical coverage in wartime proved to have the latent function of cultivating an entrepreneurial spirit. The "Berry Plan," instituted in 1953, ran through the end of the Vietnam War in 1975 (Berry 1976). Military installations were in dire need of physicians, but a draft would undermine the needs of civilian hospitals. The solution came in the form of a plan that would provide fairly for both institutions. The original plan gave new graduates and young physicians in training three options: (1) join the service of their choice immediately after internship, (2) complete one year of residency following internship and after service return to their residency program, or (3) complete a full residency training in a specialty of their choice. If the physician did not select one of the three options, he or she was risking ordinary selective draft. The plan was later adjusted to a lottery, in which losers were drafted straight to Vietnam and winners were given option 2 above. One surgeon who won option 2 described the opportunity that stimulated his entrepreneurial spirit:

I completed my internship and first year residency when I was called up for duty. The Vietnam War was just ending so I was not sent overseas but rather was stationed in a stateside army hospital. There were three of us just out of residency with no attending to supervise us. We essentially had our own practice. I was doing all kinds of general surgery that I had only been able to assist on during residency. We learned a lot about the art of surgery but also how to run a practice. The time spent in the military engaged my entrepreneurship and honed my leadership skills. It was an invaluable experience that carried through my return to civilian life and a successful private practice. (veteran-owned medical practice)

Conclusion

It is clear that entrepreneurs share common characteristics such as risk taking, innovativeness, and the desire for autonomy. Many have a family history of entrepreneurship that inspires their own spirit. Others follow in the path of role models who may be good friends or icons of business. Most network within their educational institutions, early work connections, clubs, sport groups, or other organizations that provide information, mutual support, or business and financial contacts. They often engage in ongoing education through workshops, on-the-job training, or formal programs. They are recruited from all demographic groups.

What, then, distinguishes veteran entrepreneurs? It is the ubiquitous military experience that fosters the entrepreneurial spirit. Although this is a small sample, the strength of this trend is undeniable. Even for those who failed at times, the training helped them move on to success. As noted in the autobiographical accounts, many veteran entrepreneurs experienced push or pull factors that influenced the decision to enter the military. They, like nonveteran entrepreneurs, came from diverse class, gender, race, and geographic categories, and had varying civilian experiences. However, throughout the accounts, the binding constants for the development of their entrepreneurial spirit were the shared proficiency they gained in practical skills, a strong leadership capability, a mastery of innovation, and the importance of social bonds. These strengths have served them well.

References

Berry, Frank B. 1976. "The Story of 'The Berry Plan.'" *Bulletin of the New York Academy of Medicine* 52 (3): 278–282.

Bureau of Labor Statistics. 2015. *Employment Situation of Veterans—2014*. Accessed January 19, 2016. http://www.bls.gov/news.release/pdf/vet.pdf.

Cantillon, Richard. (1755) 2010. *An Essay on Economic Theory: An English Translation of Richard Cantillon's "Essai sur la Nature du Commerce en Général."* Translated by Chantal Saucier. Edited by Mark Thornton. Auburn, AL: Ludwig von Mises Institute. Accessed June 7, 2016. https://mises.org/library/essay-economic-theory-0.

Census Bureau. 2012. *2012 Survey of Business Owners*. Accessed June 7, 2016. https://www.census.gov/library/publications/2012/econ/2012-sbo.html.

Census Bureau. 2015. "Los Angeles County a Microcosm of Nation's Diverse Collection of Business Owners, Census Bureau Reports." December 15. Release No. CB15-209. Accessed January 20, 2016. https://www.census.gov/newsroom/press-releases/2015/cb15-209.html.

Colby, Sandra L., and Jennifer M. Ortman. 2015. "Projections of the Size and Composition of the U.S. Population: 2014 to 2060." *Current Population Reports* P25-1143. Washington, DC: Census Bureau.

Department of the Army. 2016. "Pre-Separation Guide: Active Component." Accessed January 19, 2016. https://www.acap.army.mil/acap_documents/about_acap/PreSepGuide_AD.pdf.

Department of Labor. 2011. "The Veteran Labor Force in the Recovery." Accessed January 19, 2016. http://www.dol.gov/_sec/media/reports/VeteransLaborForce/VeteransLaborForce.pdf.

Fairlie, Robert W. 2014. *Kaufmann Index of Entrepreneurial Activity, 1996–2013*. Kansas City, MO: Ewing Marion Kauffman Foundation.

Hicks, Louis, and Curt Raney. 2003. "The Social Impact of Military Growth in St. Mary's County, Maryland, 1940–1995." *Armed Forces & Society* 29 (3): 353–371.

Kauffman Foundation. 2016. "Entrepreneurial Demographics, National." Accessed January 20, 2016. http://www.kauffman.org/microsites/kauffman-index/profiles/entrepreneurial-demographics/national?Demographic=VeteranStatus&Report=MainStreet.

National Center for Veterans Analysis and Statistics. 2016. "Factsheet Update 11/18/15." Accessed January 20, 2016. http://www.va.gov/vetdata/docs/pocketcards/fy2016q1.pdf.

Old Dominion University. 2016. "Veterans Business Outreach Center." Accessed January 19, 2016. http://www.odu.edu/partnerships/business/gateway/programs/vboc.

Osborn, Elizabeth, and Kazimierz M. Slomczynski. 2005. *Open for Business: The Persistent Entrepreneurial Class in Poland*. Warsaw, Poland: IFiS Publishers.

Schumpeter, Joseph A. 1947. "The Creative Response in Economic History." *Journal of Economic History* 7: 149–159.

Slayback, Zachary. 2016. "Where Are All of the Young Entrepreneurs?" LinkedIn, January 4. Accessed June 7, 2016. https://www.linkedin.com/pulse/where-all-young-entrepreneurs-zachary-slayback.

Small Business Administration. 2016a. "About Boots to Business." Accessed January 19, 2016. https://www.sba.gov/offices/headquarters/ovbd/resources/160511.

Small Business Administration. 2016b. "Veterans Business Outreach Centers." Accessed January 19, 2016. https://www.sba.gov/tools/local-assistance/vboc.

Veteran Owned Business. 2016. "Veteran Owned Business Project." Accessed January 19, 2016. http://www.veteranownedbusiness.com.

Whorf, Benjamin L. 1956. *Language, Thought, and Reality*. Cambridge, MA: MIT Press.

CHAPTER ELEVEN

Veterans as Private Security Contractors

Alison Hawks

Introduction

This chapter discusses new concepts relevant to the sociological aspects of a specific type of private security contractor: the U.S. military veteran. This segment of the private security industry has become increasingly important as a new part of the labor market for U.S. veterans after 9/11. An acceptable career path, private security contractors are here to stay; the U.S. government has recently acknowledged that it cannot fight wars without them (Schwartz and Church 2013). Peter W. Singer's (2003) *Corporate Warriors* marked the beginning of a comprehensive academic inquiry into the privatization of security after the Cold War. Since Singer's book was published, the growing body of scholarship on the privatization of security includes theoretical applications of international relations theory (Kinsey 2006; Avant 2005), historical narratives of mercenaries (Percy 2007; McFate 2015), civil-military relations (Krahmann 2010; Bruneau 2011), civil-military coordination (Dunigan 2011; Kelty 2005, 2008, 2009; Kelty and Bierman 2013), U.S. foreign policy (Stanger 2014; Kinsey and Erbel 2011), the regulation and accountability of private actors (Dickenson 2011; Abrahamsen Williams 2007; Avant 2005), critical gender studies (Chisholm 2014; Stachowitsch 2013, 2014; Eichler 2013), sociological aspects (Higate 2009, 2011, 2012b, 2012c, 2012d, 2014; Hawks 2014, 2015), and health issues (Feinstein and Botes 2009; Messenger et al. 2012; Dunigan et al. 2013).

Here I use the term *private security contractor* to mean a contractor who is armed as a requirement of a contract, what Singer referred to as the "tip of the spear" (Singer 2003). In 2008, defense contractors in Iraq outnumbered uniformed personnel on the ground by 1.2:1 (173,000 to 146,000 respectively) (Schwartz 2009). However, the majority of these contractors supported coalition forces by performing functions such as base support and logistics and janitorial, cafeteria, and construction work. There were also training and consulting contractors providing services such as training the Iraqi Army (Singer 2003; Kinsey 2006; Avant 2005). Armed private security contractors, contracted to provide protection of either persons ("active" security) or places ("static" security; e.g., guarding a base) constituted the smallest percentage of the total contractor population. The majority of defense contractors provided employment for military veterans, for whom no additional skills or knowledge were needed, and operational experience was almost always required (Berndtsson 2011, 318). These armed defense contracting opportunities offer a physical environment that is similar to one the veteran may have experienced while on active duty. This environmental similarity—in some cases, continuity—presents interesting and unique questions about the military to civilian transition that do not apply to other types of civilian employment. For example, some of the literature on military veterans observes a type of "natural gravitation" to other institutionalized forms of employment after military service (Jolly 1996; Higate 2001). At first glance, working in security contracting may be considered to be one such move. However, the distinct corporate nature and organizational structure of private security companies (PSCs) suggests that an individual may be seeking something more than just continuity of institutional structure in the choice of postmilitary employment. Because of this, career decisions to enter private security contracting after military service challenge traditional approaches to our understanding of military to civilian transition and require additional study.

The precise number of private security contractors working around the world is not known, for several reasons, such as the inadequacy of available databases due to a lack of adequate auditing and transparency by the contract bid holder (e.g., governments, organizations, or individuals). Privacy and security issues in the for-profit PSC industry often limit access by researchers to proprietary data. Contractors can, and do, operate around the world in varying capacities (Singer 2003). Current estimates put Western, English-speaking armed security contractors at around 45,000 (Hawks 2014). Yet despite their small number, more defense contractors than U.S. soldiers have died in the recent wars in Iraq and Afghanistan (Miller 2010).

With their presence on the ground at times indiscernible to host populations (Hammes 2010), security contractors are now an integral and indispensable part of the U.S. military's total force (Schwartz and Church 2013). Despite popular assumptions, armed private security contractors are the smallest sector of the PSC industry. Despite disproportionate media attention on Westerners during the wars in Iraq and Afghanistan, security contracting is not restricted to Western, English-speaking individuals; most security contractors are, in fact, not Westerners (Schwartz and Church 2013). The majority of security contractors in these two conflicts were either local nationals (LNs), such as Iraqis or Afghans, or third-country nationals (TCNs), representing non-Western countries from around the world (Singer 2003). Security contractors are, by the service they provide, now firmly embedded in new wars.

In the recent Iraq and Afghanistan conflicts, the term "security contractor" became a contested label and was often conflated by the term "mercenary." There are several reasons to briefly discuss this important distinction of contractor versus mercenary as it relates to U.S. military veterans-turned-security contractors. Examining the work profiles of private security contractors will better define their work and career paths within the industry, replacing subjective popular myths with empirical evidence regarding a population about which little is known. Using the term "mercenary" to categorize U.S. contractors (of all types and backgrounds) is legally incorrect. As Krahmann (2010, 6) concisely observed, "the difference between the two is the corporate nature and associated legal status, whereas mercenaries operate outside the law." She further, and usefully, highlights the international legal definition of mercenaries:

(1) they are specially recruited locally or abroad in order to fight in an armed conflict;
(2) they take a direct part in the hostilities;
(3) they are motivated to take part in hostilities essentially by the desire for private gain and are promised, by or on behalf of a party of the conflict, material compensation substantially in excess of that promised or paid to combatants of similar ranks and functions in the armed forces of that party;
(4) they are neither a national or party to the conflict nor a resident of territory controlled by a party to the conflict;
(5) they are not a member of the armed forces of a party to the conflict; and,
(6) they have not been sent by a state which is not a party to the conflict on official duty as a member of its armed forces. ("Protocol Additional to Geneva Conventions," cited in Krahmann 2010)

In terms of Iraq and Afghanistan, conditions (2) and (4) of the Protocol rule out any coalition force national being a mercenary, as well as local nationals of the countries engaged in the primary conflict. Rules for the use of force (RUF) further stipulate the legal restrictions for defense contractors to engage in offensive combat (U.S. Joint Forces Command 2010, II-5). However, armed security contractors do retain their inherent right to self-defense in areas of operation. This particular stipulation was used as a defense in a recent criminal case (*United States of America v. Paul A. Slough, et al.*) involving four U.S. private security contractors employed by the PSC Blackwater Worldwide. However, the contractors were found guilty of excessive use of force (Dunsmuir 2015). While the name "Blackwater" became synonymous with the private security industry in much of the popular media, these contractors' behavior is not representative of either private security contractors as a group or the PSC industry as a whole. Industry initiatives, standards, and codes of conduct (e.g., ASIS International 2012) define an industry whose actions represent a legitimate and corporate nature, whereas certain Blackwater contractors demonstrated actions that do not reflect industry values or norms.

By the definition of the Geneva Conventions, U.S. security contractors are not mercenaries. As Krahmann (2010, 3) noted, the condition of "motivation" is difficult to prosecute simultaneously with all of the other conditions. However, empirical evidence of the motivations of U.S. security contractors does exist, and these data directly challenge the notion of "mercenary" as traditionally conceived. In 2011 Franke and von Boemcken published their findings on the values and attitudes of former U.S. law enforcement turned private security contractors. They found the cohort displayed a high degree of patriotism, an observation not historically true of mercenaries, who typically eschew loyalty to a state, organization, or individual (Thompson 1994). Ethically, the Franke and von Boemcken (2011, 11) cohort seems robust:

> Virtually everyone in our sample agreed that it was important to "respect the dignity of all human beings and adhere to relevant international law," "to minimize loss of life and destruction of property," to investigate violations of human rights and humanitarian law, and to take action against unlawful activities.

Most interesting were the data on motivation. Franke and von Boemcken's results ranked the "motivation of earning more money than in my previous job" as the fifth *least important* reason for becoming a private security contractor, six percentage points below the reason "to serve my country."[1] Franke and von Boemcken's data clarify that U.S. private security contractors consider themselves to be professionals, with a specific occupational identity correlated to specific skills and knowledge. This finding challenges much of what has been written to date on private security contractors (Krahmann 2010; Leander 2005) and is not an isolated empirical finding. Higate (2012a), Dunigan (2011), Berndtsson (2011), and I (Hawks 2014, 2015) found professionalism to exist empirically by way of standards and norms among the security contractors themselves, as well as being present in their parent PSCs. We report that professionalism represents the dominant self-description of this population. These findings should shift the discussion away from a "mercenary" archetype. This revised perception of private security contractors is particularly relevant to U.S. military veterans who become private security contractors because they perceive security contracting to be a professional occupation that is a logical career progression after military service. This perspective has several caveats: how well equipped this population believes itself to be for civilian employment, availability of opportunities for civilian employment postcontract, and access to employment that does not require a difficult reintegration to civilian life after military service. Before addressing these four issues, it is important to understand the unique aspects of these private security contractors.

Demographics of U.S. Military Veterans as Private Security Contractors

The data presented here were drawn from a large-scale study of private security contractors, of which this chapter presents one aspect. The survey was sent to approximately 16,000 private security contractors by two security contractor recruitment agencies and one PSC over the course of six months. The survey was distributed by SurveyMonkey, and all participants were anonymous. The response rate was 9.8 percent, which can be considered typical for a low-visibility population.

Of the men and women who completed the survey (n = 1,515), 86 percent had prior military experience. Sixty-five percent had served in the UK armed forces, 16 percent in the U.S. armed forces, and the remaining 19 percent in the militaries of countries other than the United States and United Kingdom. All survey respondents (military and law enforcement) confirmed that they had been or were currently armed private security contractors working overseas. This chapter considers the data for those who previously served in the U.S. military (16 percent of the original sample). In the rest of this chapter, the terms "survey respondents" and "private security contractors" refer to this American subset of the total sample.

This subset (n = 249) is similar in size to Franke and von Boemcken's survey cohort of former U.S. law enforcement turned security contractors (n = 223), from which reliability of the data is inferred. My U.S. cohort consisted of 247 men and 2 women. This survey is the first survey to report any data on female private security contractors. The average age in the sample population was between 41 and 55 years old (61 percent). Most (61 percent) of the sample had completed between 1 and 10 years of military service. Most respondents had served in the U.S. Army (53 percent) or U.S. Navy (12 percent). A majority of respondents (58 percent) had continued their formal education beyond high school. Of the 41 percent that had no college degree or specialty certification, 14 percent had at least completed a high school diploma.

A large plurality (46 percent) reported spending between one and six months in civilian life between leaving the military and becoming a private security contractor. A significant number (42 percent) had reported four years or more in civilian life after exiting the military and before starting security contracting. Over two-thirds of the respondents indicated previous combat experience. Interestingly, 98 percent of those reporting *no* combat experience had been deployed on one or more contracts to Iraq and Afghanistan. This lack of exposure to combat while in the military may influence their perceptions of well-being; this possibility is explored later in the chapter.

Most of the U.S. cohort (93 percent) were noncommissioned officers; the majority (64 percent) had held a rank ranging from corporal (E-4) to staff sergeant (E-6). Of the commissioned officers, 65 percent (n = 17) had been captains (O-3). Military rank is significant when interpreting the data, because it is indicative of levels of skill, knowledge, and experience, perceived by individuals to qualify them as "professional" within a profession. Abbott (1998, 8) defines a profession as "exclusive occupational groups applying somewhat abstract knowledge to particular cases." Friedson states that "'profession,' as opposed to the term 'amateur,' connotes not only earning a living by one's work, but also superior skillfulness, or expertise at doing a professional as opposed to amateurish job" (Friedson 1994, 157). Either of these definitions categorizes this U.S. cohort as professionals, because they possessed the skills, knowledge, and experience of professional soldiers. This chapter does not consider private security contractors to be professional soldiers, but it does argue that based on the data collected, it is reasonable to call private security contractors professionals working within a profession.

Empirical data on rank, when combined with data on the motivations and patriotism of U.S. private security contractors, are persuasive in making a case that these individuals perceive themselves to be professionals and continue to perceive their relationship to the state as similar to what it was when they were active duty soldiers. The continuation of this perceived relationship means that there appears to also be a continuation of the individual's military identity, to the extent that individuals consider themselves to be bound by their sense of patriotism (see table 11.1). Franke and von Boemcken (2011, 5) hypothesized that if private security contractors "resemble the image of the classical mercenary . . . we would not expect them to be overly patriotic or show much concern for ethical behaviour." Table 11.1 shows the data collected from my research, using the same 5-point Likert scale survey as that used by Franke and von Boemcken to assess the "patriotism" of private security contractors.

These data provide empirical evidence that contradicts popular conceptions of private security contractors by showing that a respondent's primary allegiance is to his or her own country (84.5 percent agree). Such data directly challenge traditional notions of applying the term "mercenaries" (defined by the Geneva Conventions Additional Protocol as having

Table 11.1. Patriotism as Self-Reported by U.S. Military Veterans Who Are Now Private Security Contractors.

Patriotism (N = 220; Mean = 3.33)				
		% Agree	% Neutral	% Disagree
P.1	I look upon my work as a security contractor as a "calling" where I can serve my country.	69.0	17.7	13.2
P.2	We should strive for loyalty to our own country before we can afford to consider world brotherhood.	73.2	16.4	10.5
P.3	A citizen should always feel that his or her primary allegiance is to his or her own country.	84.5	8.6	6.8
P.4	All citizens should be willing to fight for their country.	83.6	6.8	9.5
P.5	The strongest indicator of good citizenship is performance of military service in defense of one's country.	60.9	16.8	22.2
P.6	The promotion of patriotism should be an important aim of citizenship education.	81.7	10.0	8.2

no particular loyalty to any one country) to private security contractors. The survey respondents are qualitatively different from the traditional concept of mercenaries. In addition, data from the survey provide additional insights for a more accurate terminology by including additional demographics. Respondents were older, educated, and included females, all with sufficient military experience to confer a sense of professionalism, and expressed motivations similar to those reported for individuals joining militaries (Woodruff, Kelty, and Segal 2006). Further, the data in table 11.1 confirm and extend Franke and von Boemcken's original study, demonstrating the reliability of the data as representative of U.S. private security contractors in general.

Profile of Female U.S. Military Veterans as Private Security Contractors

Fewer than 1 percent of this cohort was female (n = 2),[2] so no meaningful statistical analysis is possible. Female private security contractors have not been previously acknowledged or studied in academic inquiries on the private security contractor population (Vrdoljak 2010), and they are currently an unstudied population. The experiences of the two U.S. military veterans turned private security contractors are discussed below.

Both women had been enlisted soldiers, one with the rank of sergeant (E-5) and the other with the rank of staff sergeant (E-6). They served in the U.S. Army for between 1 and 10 years and had spent 6 or more years in civilian life between leaving the military and becoming security contractors. Neither woman had higher education beyond an associate's degree at the time of the survey. Both indicated they felt they had been unable to transfer skill sets learned in the military into the civilian world. One of the two respondents described her experience thus:

> As a woman, I found the world of security contracting to be a challenge, but one that was not impossible to meet. It gave me a sense of accomplishment to be able to perform just as well as my colleagues in this previously male-dominated field.

The respondent appears to consider the field of private security contracting a reasonable career opportunity for women. Cursory research on professional employment sites such as LinkedIn indicates that there is a robust population of female security contractors, the majority of whom appear to specialize in canine handling as a result of prior military experience. The interviewees' perceptions and their professional grouping on sites like LinkedIn is worth exploring and should be considered for future research.

Within the context of the demographics of the sample cohort, I next address key issues and challenges that influence or impact a veteran's decision to enter security contracting as a profession after military service.

Preparation for Civilian Life and Postcontracting Employability

My data showed that the sample cohort prepared for their military exit predominantly by seeking employment as private security contractors. In terms of transition preparation, most (74 percent) of the sample population followed the military exit guideline of preparing between 12 and 24 months in advance of leaving. Prior research on the transition from military to civilian life has reported that "those who planned had less trouble adjusting to their new lifestyle" (McClure 1999, 317; Fuller and Redfering 1976). Unlike previously published studies, which found that many service members do not plan or prepare until a few months before they exit (e.g., Frank 1993), most (71 percent) of my sample actively sought employment as contractors while serving in the military. Current dogma would predict that this cohort would be more likely to have less trouble adjusting than those who do not plan for postmilitary employment. Interestingly, the environment of private security contracting, unlike most conventional civilian jobs, does not require a challenging adjustment or adaptation from military life. However, a decision to seek post-transition employment as a private security contractor may significantly alter an individual's postcontract employability due to unforeseen negative consequences.

First, becoming a private security contractor immediately after military service will affect eligibility for government-provided transition services. Some benefits, notably the Transition Assistance Program (TAP), are available for 180 days from date of military exit for those who are eligible (retirees have longer eligibility). The loss of this support may be detrimental to successful reentry into civilian life once a contractor decides to exit private security work or completes a contract and has no opportunity to continue in that work sector. Second, most U.S. military veterans who enter private security contracting do not have to extend their current skill sets significantly. The lack of new and updated skills may negatively affect the veteran's market competitiveness when seeking conventional civilian work postcontracting. Veterans may decide to become security contractors for social reasons, for example, wanting to belong in a like-minded group, or to continue using the familiar culture of the military, or looking for recognition of their skills and capabilities. In these examples, becoming a private security contractor reinforces and reaffirms an individual's military identity. This is not necessarily a bad thing, especially if the individual is successful in working in security contracting until reaching retirement. An individual seeking to enter contracting for any of the above reasons may experience great difficulty in the reintegration into conventional civilian life after working for PSCs. Due to a lack of foresight, those who become security contractors immediately after military service may not have engaged with the transition process to the same extent as a veteran who left the military for civilian life (noncontracting). In this case, the veteran will face reintegration challenges without the support of government-provided transition services (at least, for nonretirees) and/or lacking new key skills and capabilities essential to secure alternate civilian employment. In addition, the challenge for such veterans is that the social rewards offered by security contracting that attracted them to the work do not necessarily address the root causes of their potential transition issues. Another hurdle to successful transition to civilian life for these veterans is that the physical locations of security contracting, for example, Iraq and Afghanistan, increase the difficulty of developing civilian social networks that would support and improve the chances of securing alternate civilian employment after private security contracting.

Environment of Private Security Contracting

Private security contracting is a career path that offers the U.S. veteran several cultural advantages. Veterans who deployed previously to the location where they are now contracting are familiar with local conditions and the local work environment. This is a stark difference from other types of civilian employment, for example, working in a bank. Janowitz (1964) described this dilemma as follows: "The military man must stress the distinctiveness of his calling, but the second career problem places emphasis on its non-distinctiveness." In the transition literature, this predicament is termed "role confusion" and/or "role transition," because veterans will likely face confusion and feel disoriented as they struggle to translate their skills and capabilities to civilian employment. Importantly, veterans may not be able to predict the quality and demands of a civilian employment experience as accurately as they could with a security contractor. In the latter case, a transitioning veteran can anticipate similarities in the work to be performed, the vocabulary that will be used, the expectations regarding whom to approach about tasks, and how to achieve goals. This reduced uncertainty about the work environment in security contracting may appeal to many veterans. Veterans' civilian work experiences have been shown to include expectations and expectation management that go little beyond having particular qualifications and that do not prepare veterans for the work environment itself (Forces in Mind Trust 2013, 18).

The cultural similarity of security contracting and active duty military service usually means that an individual is not challenged by difficult changes in work expectations and accountability. However, the nature of PSCs at the operational level may still require a change in perceptions of work and the equivalent of role transfer, due to the lack of military-like rank hierarchy in contracting. For example, security contractors may work in a variety of work group settings. In Iraq, it was common to operate in teams of four, with a designated "team leader" to whom the remaining three were subordinate (Shepherd 2008; Heron 2010). Team leaders may come from a different and possibly lower rank in their previous military life than the other contractors in the team. Consequently, there may be confrontations within the group when an individual must come to terms with taking orders from someone who may have been several ranks below him or her in the military. While prior military experience is a requirement for most security contracting jobs, experience in the field as a contractor counts within the merit-based system common to civilian organizations and corporations. In terms of transition, this may require a brief period of adjustment for incoming private security contractors. This challenge does not appear to be significant enough to cause the individual to stop working on a contract or to exit a security contractor career.

An important aspect relevant to work environment issues is the return to a physical environment in which a veteran with post-traumatic stress disorder (PTSD) had been previously deployed. The current hypothesis is that under such conditions, the environment may protect against PTSD episodes if an individual is able to maintain similar levels of hypervigilance to those experienced when he or she was in military service. A key concern is that such veterans may only exacerbate their mental distress and delay seeking appropriate care that would alleviate their PTSD. A quarter of the contractors surveyed in Dunigan et al.'s (2013) study on the mental health and well-being of contractors in conflict environments met the criteria for PTSD. This hypothesis and the consequences for veterans with PTSD working as contractors are well worth exploring in future research.

Security contractors usually experience short, recurring deployment cycles of 90 days, with 30 days of leave between deployments. This may mean security contractors are away from their families the same amount of time (if not more for those who continuously contract) as when they were active duty soldiers. The ability to control when and how often to deploy may attract those individuals seeking autonomy or control over their choices and use of time (Gowen, Craft, and Zimmermann). Private security contracting allows veterans to exert control over the work environment, which may help stabilize other issues they may be experiencing in their lives.

However, the "circuit"—as private security contracting is called in the industry—is a type of employment that, in the words of one security contractor interviewed, means "there is no security in security." If an individual goes several months between contracts, there is a distinct possibility that he or she will be unable to secure employment on a subsequent contract. For the population of U.S. veterans who become security contractors, this appears to be a high-risk career employment choice in terms of stable income and job security, despite the perceived high front-end salary advantage. In future trends for the U.S. civilian working population, predictions are that there will be less job security overall and more frequent career changes as demographics, cultural trends, and new technologies alter the job market. The ability to maintain lifelong learning and flexibility in work and career choices will become increasingly important (Karoly and Panis 2004).

The role of remuneration in decision making about careers is important when explaining why U.S. veterans become private security contractors. For the sample population under discussion, an average salary of a security contractor operating in Iraq and Afghanistan over the course of the year was approximately US$160,000 (Krahmann 2010). This is a significant leap in apparent remuneration from that of a staff sergeant in the U.S. Army. However, when the various details of government benefits and taxation effects are considered, security contractors do not seem to enjoy such a dramatic advantage. Jocelyn (2008) compared security contractor earnings to that of a staff sergeant using various government pay scales. After factoring in noncash benefits such as healthcare, installation-based benefits, subsistence-in-kind, family housing and barracks, education, and other benefits, the staff sergeant receives a net cash contribution of $69,340 (not including retirement pay accrual, VA compensation and pension, and VA healthcare worth approximately $34,000 per year). In contrast, a contractor may have net cash compensation equivalent to $38,306 after paying (in cash) for benefits such as healthcare, housing, and retirement contributions. Further studies are needed to clarify whether veterans making a career transition are aware of these significant differences in remuneration, compared to that of alternate civilian careers.

Security contracting as a form of postmilitary employment is not as lucrative as it may initially seem. However, the system of payment and various tax-free exemptions have allowed some private security contractors to pay off debts, buy a home, pay for children's education, or contribute to a retirement fund in ways they could not have done had they stayed in the military. For this subset, becoming a security contractor has enhanced their socioeconomic status and quality of living. Needless to say, at the other end of the spectrum, the large monthly checks may also be squandered relatively quickly and may restrict an individual's choice to leave security contracting for alternate civilian employment because he or she cannot afford to do so.

An improved understanding of the attraction of the environment of security contracting for U.S. veterans sheds light on issues experienced in transition and expectations of civilian employment. In addition to the environment, there are powerful social incentives that attract veterans to this form of employment. For those who seek to utilize their military skill sets in a civilian occupation, private security contracting offers an attractive employment option. The environment has much to offer a U.S. veteran in terms of familiarity, reduction of uncertainty, autonomy, and control over one's time, and it can be financially rewarding. Drawbacks to the environment include a role transition that will not facilitate an individual's reintegration to civilian life, because no new skills are developed to make them more competitive for future civilian employment. For some, security contracting may provide financial rewards only in the short term.

There is an element of risk in security contractor employment that needs to be considered by those making the decision. Schooner and Swan (2010) found that armed security contractors were 4.5 times more likely to die than uniformed soldiers. Dunigan (2011, 74–75) observed problems involving a lack of military-civilian coordination that created greater insecurity for security contractors and military personnel. As a consequence, both were less effective, and security contractors became more vulnerable to physical attacks. The inability of host populations to distinguish between a U.S. (or coalition) soldier and a security contractor has historically led to significant security issues (Hammes 2011). Unlike the military, security contractors do not have "backup" in hostile situations. For example, security contractors, when under hostile fire, cannot request a tank or helicopter for assistance that might allow them to survive the situation with fewer casualties. As a result, contractors sometimes work in significantly more vulnerable situations than do uniformed personnel when risk, rather than the task being performed, is considered. Despite these risks, the environmental incentives remain strong, especially when the social incentives offered by security contracting are considered.

Private security contracting for U.S. veterans offers strong social incentives when compared to other types of civilian employment. These incentives appear to address issues reported by veterans during and after their transition from military to civilian life. The first is a coping mechanism used by veterans who struggle with the transition, called "replication" (Harris, Gringart, and Drake 2013; Brunger et al. 2013). This is not to say that those U.S. veterans who become private security contractors went into contracting because they all struggled in their transition. "Replication" for security contractors is less about a psychological struggle per se and more about either a continuation of or return to an identity known and familiar to the veteran. Replication can have positive and negative effects. It can, as Harris, Gringart, and Drake (2013, 309) found, "serve as a buffer against negative aspects of retirement as it requires only small changes to personal behaviour while core aspects of the organization, culture and identity are maintained." However, it may also delay or postpone an individual's engagement with the crucial step of identity reconstruction as a part of the transition process to civilian life.

A social incentive that security contracting offers U.S. veterans is the use of a distinct common language from which the individual can derive a sense of identity. Most Western security contractors have military experience. "Military speak" (usage and vocabulary) is prevalent among security contractors, whether from the operational level on the ground or from the corporate management level at a company's headquarters. Language, in this case, is a powerful social incentive, as it appears to be the precursor to other social incentives, such as a sense of belonging, feeling fulfillment, a sense of purpose, and professionalism. For example, the use of a common language allows the individual to understand others and to be understood. Language has been shown to be a barrier in the reintegration process into civilian life and employment. One veteran described the experience of trying to become acquainted with civilians after military service as a "fundamental difference." He explained that "the civilians have their drinking stories, and 'this chick I met last night' stories, and the veterans' got their 'no shit, there I was' stories. It's kind of like we're a different breed of person after we get back" (Rumann and Hamrick 2010, 446).

Harris, Gringart, and Drake (2013, 106) call this identification through language "linguistic identity." The lack of a common language between the veteran and the civilian can cause a veteran to feel isolated and invisible. Hall (2011, 10) described this separation as "magnified by the language, often spoke in acronyms and other idiosyncratic terms." Veterans who attend university or college after military service gravitate to one another because they find in other veterans not only an understanding and recognition of past experiences, but also a language in which to communicate these experiences (Ramio, Ackerman, and Mitchell 2008; Burnett and Segoria 2009). The common language of the military present in security contracting may provide individuals with the connection they need to hold on to their former military identity. Some may use this connection to deal with the perceived loss of recognition in civilian life. Milowe (1964, 102) stated that those who felt this sense of loss "uniformly faced a plunge from being the whale to being a minnow." Security contracting—in colloquial terms—may allow the individual to continue being a "whale." Interestingly, the majority of this recognition is peer-to-peer among security contractors and does not extend to civilian society as a whole, whose members often see security contractors in a negative light.

Access and Barriers to Care for Health and Well-Being Issues

There has been little research on the mental health and well-being of defense contractors, including armed private security contractors. The latter are a hard-to-reach population for academic studies. The differences in experience, function, and type of contractor, for example, local national (LN) or third-country national (TCN), make these people a difficult population from which to draw a representative sample. Further, data collection on defense contractors by the U.S. government did not begin until 2007, four and six years after Afghanistan and Iraq, respectively, making it difficult to collect reliable data on this population.[3] Irrespective of work assignments and experience, contractors report many of the same experiences as those reported by active duty personnel in Iraq and Afghanistan, including, for example, incoming fire, ambush, kidnapping, mortar attacks, gunshot and shrapnel wounds, witnessing the death of fellow contractors, the consequences of improvised explosive devices (IEDs), seeing civilians wounded and/or killed, and uncovering human remains (Messenger et al. 2012, 861). Dunigan and colleagues (2013) used the similarity of these experiences as reasonable evidence that contractors in conflict environments may also experience the same issues and challenges as do active duty military personnel operating in these same environments. Dunigan's study surveyed a range of contractors deployed to conflict environments, and reported that 25 percent of contractors met criteria for probable PTSD. Moreover, 18 percent screened positive for depression, and 10 percent reported high-risk drinking. By comparison, the respective proportions of U.S. military troops deployed to Iraq or Afghanistan have been estimated at 4–20 percent for PTSD, 5–37 percent for depression, and 5–39 percent for alcohol abuse.

Dunigan et al. (2013, 69) found stigma to be a limiting factor that prevented contractors from seeking care for these problems. Many contractors reported fear of losing the confidence of their colleagues and superiors, and ultimately their jobs. At least half of the sample reported that "concern for future employment was [a] barrier to seeking mental health treatment, and most would be unlikely to report symptoms of a mental health problem to a supervisor or other company official." Messenger et al.'s (2012, 864) findings echo this sentiment in their study, as "most participants were resistant to seeking help for psychological distress and tended to view a career in private security as incompatible with seeking help for psychiatric difficulties." In addition, there are contractors who actively seek care and assistance but who do not receive it. In his investigative report for *ProPublica*, T. Christian Miller (2009a, 21–22) found that between 2002 and 2007, "insurers turned down 60 percent of contractors who claimed to suffer psychological damage, such as post-traumatic stress disorder," even though those contractors reported mental and physical issues, such as loss of limbs, burns, loss of hearing or eyesight, depression, suicidal ideation, and suicide. These contractors were seeking compensation from the Defense Base Act (DBA), a U.S. government mandate for all U.S. government-funded contractors to provide workers with compensation insurance. Systematic denial of DBA claims was subsequently highlighted by a congressional inquiry into the DBA and its insurance provider, American International Group (Miller 2009b).

The relevance of these data to U.S. veterans who become (armed or unarmed) security contractors is twofold. First are the implications of these data for both the individual and the PSC industry. If, as Dunigan et al. (2013) showed, the individual meets diagnostic criteria for PTSD while a contractor, the medical and psychological risks of this form of employment far outweigh those of other forms of civilian employment. The high-risk environment of security contracting may serve as a "protective" environment, requiring a level of hypervigilance that could potentially mask the symptoms of PTSD. Because the security contractor is no longer eligible for the military transition program of services, a contractor exiting this profession may face significant access and barrier to care issues postcontract. The key, and often neglected, issue of home location was highlighted by Risen (2007). The geographic locations of contractors' homes in rural regions or states, or in urban areas of social and health disparities, in the United States means there may be little or no access to high-quality mental health workers and neuroscience expertise.

Another challenge in the future for the PSC industry is the recruitment and retention of an adequate and healthy workforce with prior military experience. The U.S. military is forecast to reduce its force by 40,000 in the coming years. As a consequence, the U.S. government will likely increase its reliance on contractors to support its interests around the world (Schwartz and Church 2013). While it is unlikely the labor market for security contractors will return to that of the 2005 "gold rush" in Iraq, these trends indicate that security contracting will continue to be a post-military employment option for veterans, and that the numbers of qualified veterans seeking security contracting as a career choice will decline.

Security Contracting as a Mechanism to Facilitate Reintegration to Civilian Life

Use of security contracting to facilitate their reentry into civilian life by our sample population appeared to depend on the length of time an individual had spent in civilian life between leaving the military and becoming a private security contractor. For those who spent less than six months in civilian life, the decision to become a security contractor delayed their reintegration into conventional civilian life. Such a decision may have significant implications for this group in improving their post-contracting employability and updating their work skill sets in terms of social integration, cultural acclimation, and relevant emerging technologies in the workplace. These individuals may be slower to build civilian and social networks and remain at unaltered risk for mental health issues (Hatch et al. 2013). Most of the individuals in the sample were not eligible for U.S. government-provided transition support services, such as résumé writing and interview preparation. Thus, becoming a private security contractor immediately after military service (i.e., within six months) may put veterans into a vulnerable position for employment and social civilian integration when they eventually exit security contracting. For military retirees, this is less of an issue. However, due to the nature of the industry, becoming a security contractor may be neither a stable nor a sustainable long-term career choice.

For those veterans who were in civilian life for longer than six months between leaving the military and becoming private security contractors, there is the opportunity to address perceived social issues, such as a sense of belonging, fulfillment, purpose, recognition for skill and ability, and the use of a common language. For this particular cohort, becoming a security contractor is likely to have a positive effect on the individual, while not necessarily addressing the root causes of his or her challenges in integrating into civilian life and society.

Conclusion

This chapter discussed issues relevant to U.S. veterans' decisions to become private security contractors. As a relatively new form of employment in the post-9/11 world, private security contracting is an employment option that has not yet received extensive sociological inquiry. The inclusion of this chapter in this edited volume is a vanguard indicator that research in this area will receive more attention. As the PSC industry continues to adjust to the market, it is reasonable to assume, as the U.S. government has, that private security contracting is a valid and valuable U.S. employment sector. A closer inquiry into this form of employment is essential, as it has significant life-risk implications for the veteran that are absent from most other forms of civilian employment. This chapter discussed the challenges of a career path that does not enhance the competitiveness of the veteran for future alternate civilian jobs (outside of the private security sector); the similarities in environment and social aspects of contracting to the military may delay access to formal services to address potential transition issues, as well as issues relevant to mental health and well-being. I have also reviewed the available data on the lack of eligibility of contractors for government transition services and VA healthcare for those injured during a contract or dealing with postmilitary health issues.

I discussed the data on the influences that motivate some veterans to replicate their military experience with civilian employment such as security contracting. Considerations include a perception of the probability of an individual's employability in civilian life and the extent to which provided preparations and transition services are adequate. Potential security contractors actively seek employment for which the barriers to entry are low, and when the probability of postcontract employability is somewhat risky. I showed how a career decision to become a security contractor immediately after military service may delay a successful transition to civilian life. This last issue is perhaps the most worrying, because it potentially creates a vulnerable population who will not have access to government-provided transition services within 180 days of separating from the military. Compounding this are mental health or well-being problems in many would-be contractors, because the duty of care for private security contractors remains a contested responsibility between the clients (governments or NGOs, etc.) and the PSCs themselves. I believe the high risks of security contracting may often be overlooked in veterans' career decisions.

The data indicate several positive attributes that U.S. veterans bring to private security contracting, such as professionalism, and motivations that include a high degree of patriotism. The accumulating evidence indicates that the security industry is a long-term career choice that may make reintegration into conventional civilian employment a nonissue, as long as the industry remains economically sustainable. Most important, the sample's demographics and stated reasons and motivations for becoming private security contractors indicated a perceived lack of transferable skills and lack of confidence in their ability and social skills to integrate back into civilian life. Research is urgently needed to address the social, psychological, medical, and employment challenges facing tens of thousands of U.S. veterans who have become security contractors since 2001 and to determine to what extent government-funded transition services should be developed and innovated to resolve these issues.

Notes

1. In order of importance, their data showed (1) "to face and meet new challenges 74.9 percent; (2) "to help others" 64.6 percent; (3) "to feel like my work makes a difference" 38 percent; (4) "to serve my country" 31.3 percent; (5) "to make more money than in my previous job" 25.2 percent; (6) "for personal growth" 22 percent; (7) "to seek adventure and excitement" 19.1 percent; (8) "to improve my chances of finding a better job" 13.1 percent; and (8) "to travel and visit new places" 11.3 percent.

2. Of the 1,516 survey respondents 1 percent were female (n = 18); 13 indicated UK nationality, 2 the United States; and the remaining 3 were from Latvia and South Africa.

3. This data collection was done using the Synchronized Predeployment and Operational Tracker (SPOT) platform. SPOT's purpose is to capture information on contractor movement in areas of operation, including number of personnel, geographic movement, and any incident reporting such as injury or death. SPOT, though, has been plagued by issues of software performance, cross-governmental buy-in, and inconsistent implementation in the field since its inception. As a result, the data collected on contractors in areas of operation by SPOT are largely not representative or reliable.

References

Abbott, Andrew. 1998. *The System of Professions: An Essay on the Division of Expert Labor*. Chicago: University of Chicago Press.

Abrahamsen, Rita, and Michael C. Williams 2007. "Securing the City: Private Security Companies and Non-State Authority in Global Governance." *International Relations* 21 (2): 237–253.

ASIS International. 2012. *Management System for Quality for Private Security Company Operations Requirements* (PSC.1). Alexandria, VA: ASIS.

Avant, Deborah D. 2005. *The Market for Force: The Consequences of Privatizing Security*. Cambridge, UK: Cambridge University Press.

Bergman, Beverly P., Howard Burdett, and Neil Greenberg. 2014. "Service Life and Beyond—Institution or Culture?" *RUSI Journal* 159: 60–68.

Berndtsson, Joakim. 2011. "Security Professionals for Hire: Exploring the Many Faces of Private Security Expertise." *Millennium Journal of International Studies* 40: 320–330.

Bruneau, Thomas. 2011. *Patriots for Profit: Contractors and the Military in U.S. National Security*. Stanford, CA: Stanford University Press.

Brunger, Helen, Jonathan Serrato and Jane Ogden. 2013. "No Man's Land: The Transition to Civilian Life." *Journal of Aggression, Conflict and Peace Research* 5: 86–100.

Burnett, Sandra E., and John Segoria. 2009. "Collaboration for Military Transition Students from Combat to College: It Takes a Community." *Journal of Postsecondary Education and Disability* 22: 53–58.

Chisholm, Amanda. 2014. "The Silenced and Indispensable: Gurkhas in Private Military Security Companies." *International Feminist Journal of Politics* 16 (1): 26–47.

Dickinson, Laura A. 2011. *Outsourcing War and Peace: Preserving Public Values in a World of Privatized Foreign Affairs*. New Haven, CT: Yale University Press.

Dunigan, Molly. 2011. *Victory for Hire: Private Security Companies' Impact on Military Effectiveness*. Stanford, CA: Stanford University Press.

Dunigan, Molly, Carrie M. Farmer, Rachel M. Burns, Alison Hawks, and Claude Messan Setodji. 2013. *Out of the Shadows: The Health and Well-being of Private Contractors Working in Conflict Environments*. Santa Monica, CA: RAND Corporation.

Dunsmuir, Lindsay. 2015. "Ex-Blackwater Guards Sentenced to Prison in Baghdad Killings." *Reuters*, April 13. Accessed May 13, 2016. http://www.reuters.com/article/2015/04/13/us-usa-blackwater-sentence-idUSKBN0N425320150413.

Eichler, Maya. 2013. "Gender and the Privatization of Security: Neoliberal Transformation of the Militarized Gender Order." *Critical Studies on Security* 1 (3): 311–325.

Feinstein, Anthony, and Maggie Botes. 2009. "The Psychological Health of Contractors Working in War Zones." *Journal of Traumatic Stress* 22 (2): 102–105.

Forces in Mind Trust. 2013. *The Transition Mapping Study: Understanding the Transition Process for Service Personnel Returning to Civilian Life*. August. Accessed January 16, 2016. http://www.fim-trust.org/wp-content/uploads/2015/01/20130810-TMS-Report.pdf.

Frank, Rex A. 1993. "Military Retirement in the Post-Cold War Era." In *The Military Family in Peace and War*, edited by Florence W. Kaslow, 214–240. New York: Springer.

Franke, Volker, and Marc von Boemcken. 2011. "Guns for Hire: Motivations and Attitudes of Private Security Contractors." *Armed Forces & Society* 37: 725–742.

Friedson, Eliot L. 1994. *Professionalism Reborn: Theory, Prophecy and Policy*. Cambridge, UK: Polity Press.

Fuller, Robert L., and David L. Redfering. 1976. "Effects of Preretirement Planning on the Retirement Adjustment of Military Personnel." *Work and Occupations* 3: 479–487.

Gowen, Mary A., Sonya Lee Solesbee Craft, and Raymond Zimmermann. 2000. "Response to Work Transitions by United States Army Personnel: Effects of Self-Esteem, Self-Efficacy and Career Resilience." *Psychological Reports* 84: 911–921.

Hall, Lynn K. 2011. "The Importance of Understanding Military Culture." *Social Work in Health Care* 50: 4–18.

Hammes, Thomas X. 2011. "Private Contractors in Conflict Zones: The Good, the Bad, and the Strategic Impact." *Strategic Forum* 260 (November). Accessed January 13, 2016. http://digitalndulibrary.ndu.edu/cdm/ref/collection/ndupress/id/43003.

Harris, Kira, Eyal Gringart, and Deidre Drake. 2013. "Military Retirement: Reflections from Former Members of Special Operations Forces." *Australian Army Journal* 10 (3): 97–112. Accessed January 13, 2016. http://works.bepress.com/kira_harris/5/.

Hatch, Stephani L., Samuel B. Harvey, Christopher Dandeker, Howard Burdett, Neil Greenberg, Nicola T. Fear, and Simon Wessely. 2013. "Life In and After the Armed Forces: Social Networks and Mental Health in the UK Military." *Sociology of Health & Illness* 35 (7): 1045–1064.

Hawks, Alison. 2014. "I've Got Soul but I'm Not a Soldier." *St. Antony's International Review* 9 (2): 71–88.

Hawks, Alison. 2015. "The Transition from the Military to Civilian Life: Becoming a Private Security Contractor After Military Service for US and UK Service Leavers." PhD thesis, King's College London.

Heron, John. 2010. *A Security Advisor in Iraq*. Milton Keynes, UK: Author House.

Higate, Paul. 2009. "Private Military Security Companies and the Problem of Men and Masculinities." Paper presented at the Annual Meeting of the ISA's 50th Annual Convention "Exploring the Past, Anticipating the Future," February.

Higate, Paul. 2011. "Cat-food and Clients: Gendering the Politics of Protection in the Private Militarised Security Company." Working Paper 08-11, School of Sociology, Politics and International Studies, University of Bristol. Accessed January 13, 2016. http://www.bristol.ac.uk/media-library/sites/spais/migrated/documents/higate-08-11.pdf.

Higate, Paul. 2012a. "Cowboys and Professionals: The Politics of Identity Work in the Private Military and Security Company." *Millennium Journal of International Studies* 40: 321–341.

Higate, Paul. 2012b. "Drinking Vodka from the 'Butt-Crack': Men, Masculinities, and Fratriarchy in the Private Militarized Security Company." *International Feminist Journal of Politics* 14 (4): 450–469.

Higate, Paul. 2012c. "In the Business of (In)Security? Mavericks, Mercenaries and Masculinities in the Private Security Company." In *Making Gender, Making War: Violence, Military and Peacekeeping Practices*, edited by Annica Kronsell and Erika Svedberg, 182–196. London: Routledge.

Higate, Paul. 2012d. "The Private Militarized and Security Contractor as Geocorporeal Actor." *International Political Sociology* 6 (4): 355–372.

Higate, Paul Richard. 2001. "Theorizing Continuity: From Military to Civilian Life." *Armed Forces & Society* 27 (3): 443–460.

Janowitz, Morris. 1964. *The New Military: Changing Patterns of Organization*. Vol. 1. New York: Sage.

Jocelyn, Ann. 2008. "Just How Much Are Contractors Paid?" *Feral Jundi* (blog). March 31. Accessed September 2015. http://feraljundi.com/36/industry-talk-just-how-overpaid-are-we/#more-36.

Jolly, Ruth A. 1996. *Changing Step: From Military to Civilian Life: People in Transition*. London: Brassey's.

Karoly, Lynn A., and Constantijn (Stan) Panis. 2004. "The Future at Work: Trends and Implications." Labor and Population Research Brief. Santa Monica, CA: RAND Corporation.

Kelty, Ryan, and Alex Bierman. 2013. "Ambivalence on the Front Lines: Perceptions of Contractors in Iraq and Afghanistan." *Armed Forces & Society* 39 (1): 5–27.

Kelty, Ryan D. 2005. "Civilianization of the Military: Social-Psychological Effects of Integrating Civilians and Military Personnel." PhD diss., University of Maryland.

Kelty, Ryan D. 2008. "The US Navy's Maiden Voyage: Effects of Integrating Sailors and Civilian Mariners on Deployment." *Armed Forces & Society* 34 (4): 536–564.

Kelty, Ryan D. 2009. "Citizen Soldiers and Civilian Contractors: Soldiers' Unit Cohesion and Retention Attitudes in the 'Total Force.'" *Journal of Political and Military Sociology* 37 (2): 1–33.

Kinsey, Christopher. 2006. *Corporate Soldiers and International Security: The Rise of Private Military Companies*. London: Routledge.

Kinsey, Christopher, and Mark Erbel. 2011. "Contracting out Support Services in Future Expeditionary Operations: Learning from the Afghan Experience." *Journal of Contemporary European Research* 7 (4): 539–560.

Krahmann, Elke. 2010. *States, Citizens and the Privatization of Security*. Cambridge, UK: Cambridge University Press.

Leander, Anna. 2005. "The Market for Force and Public Security: The Destabilizing Consequences of Private Military Companies." *Journal of Peace Research* 42 (5): 605–622.

Mandel, Robert. 2001. "The Privatization of Security." *Armed Forces & Society* 28 (1): 129–151.

McClure, Peggy. 1999. "The Transition to Civilian Life: The Case of Military Retirement." In *Pathways to the Future: A Review of Military Family Research*, edited by Peggy McClure, 303–326. Scranton, PA: The Military Family Institute. Accessed January 13, 2016. http://www.dtic.mil/dtic/tr/fulltext/u2/a364886.pdf.

McFate, Sean. 2015. *The Modern Mercenary: Private Armies and What They Mean for World Order*. Oxford: Oxford University Press.

Messenger, Katy, Lorna Farquharson, Pippa Stallworthy, Paul Cawkill, and Neil Greenberg. 2012. "The Experiences of Security Industry Contractors Working

in Iraq: An Interpretative Phenomenological Analysis." *Journal of Occupational and Environmental Medicine* 54: 859–867.
Miller, T. Christian. 2009a. "AIG Faces Inquiry over Medical Care for U.S. Contractors." *ProPublica*, April 22. https://www.propublica.org/article/aig-faces-inquiry-over-medical-care-for-u.s.-contractors-422.
Miller, T. Christian. 2009b. "Congressional Hearing: Officials Admit Major Flaws in Program to Aid Wounded War-Zone Workers." *ProPublica*, June 19. https://www.propublica.org/article/congressional-hearing-officials-acknowledge-program-to-treat-war-contra-619.
Miller, T. Christian. 2010. "This Year, Contractor Deaths Exceed Military Ones in Iraq and Afghanistan." *ProPublica*, September 23. https://www.propublica.org/article/this-year-contractor-deaths-exceed-military-ones-in-iraq-and-afgh-100923.
Milowe, Irvin D. 1964. "A Study in Role Diffusion: The Chief and the Sergeant Face Retirement." *Mental Hygiene* 48: 101–107.
Mockler, Anthony. 1970. *The Mercenaries*. London: Macmillan.
Percy, Sarah. 2007. *Mercenaries: The History of a Norm in International Relations*. Oxford: Oxford University Press.
"Protocol Additional to Geneva Conventions of 12 August 1949, and Relating to the Protection of Victims of International Armed Conflicts (Protocol I), 8 June 1977, Art. 47." n.d. In *The Geneva Conventions and Their Additional Protocols*. Accessed January 13, 2016. https://www.icrc.org/ihl.nsf/INTRO/470.
Ramio, David, Robert Ackerman, and Regina L. Mitchell. 2008. "From Combat to Campus: Voices of Student Veterans." *NASPA Journal* 45: 73–97.
Risen, James. 2007. "Contractors Back from Iraq Suffer Trauma from Battle." *New York Times*, July 5. http://www.nytimes.com/2007/07/05/us/05contractors.html?_r=0.
Rumann, Corey, and Florence A. Hamrick. 2010. "Student Veterans in Transition: Re-enrolling after War Zone Deployments." *Journal of Higher Education* 81: 432–458.
Schooner, Steven L., and Collin D. Swan. 2010. "Contractors and the Ultimate Sacrifice." GWU Legal Studies Research Paper No. 512.
Schwartz, Moshe. 2009. "Department of Defense Contractors in Iraq and Afghanistan: Background and Analysis." Congressional Research Service, CRS Report, August 13.
Schwartz, Moshe, and Jennifer Church. 2013. "Department of Defense's Use of Contractors to Support Military Operations: Background, Analysis, and Issues for Congress." Congressional Research Service, CRS Report No. R43074.
Schwartz, Moshe, and Joyprada Swain. 2011. "Department of Defense Contractors in Afghanistan and Iraq: Background and Analysis." Congressional Research Service, CRS Report No. R40764.
Shepherd, Bob. 2008. *The Circuit*. London: Macmillan.
Singer, Peter W. 2003. *Corporate Warriors: The Rise of the Privatized Military Industry and its Ramifications for International Security*. Ithaca, NY: Cornell University Press.

Stachowitsch, Saskia. 2013. "Military Privatization and the Remasculinization of the State: Making the Link Between the Outsourcing of Military Security and Gendered State Transformations." *International Relations* 27 (1): 74–94.

Stachowitsch, Saskia. 2014. "The Reconstruction of Masculinities in Global Politics Gendering Strategies in the Field of Private Security." *Men and Masculinities* (October 6). doi:10.1177/1097184X14551205.

Stanger, Allison. 2014. *One Nation Under Contract: The Outsourcing of American Power and the Future of Foreign Policy*. New Haven, CT: Yale University Press.

Thompson, Janice. 1994. *Mercenaries, Pirates, and Sovereigns*. Princeton, NJ: Princeton University Press.

U.S. Joint Forces Command. 2010. *Handbook for Armed Private Security Contractors in Contingency Operations*. Accessed February 1, 2016. http://www.dtic.mil/doctrine/doctrine/jwfc/apsc_hbk.pdf.

Vrdoljak, Anna Filipa. 2010. "Women and Private Military and Security Companies" In *War By Contract: Human Rights, Human Law and Private Contractors*, edited by Francesco Francioni and Natalino Ronzitti, 280–298. Oxford: Oxford University Press

Woodruff, Todd, Ryan Kelty, and David R. Segal. 2006. "Propensity to Serve and Motivations to Enlist Among American Combat Soldiers." *Armed Forces & Society* 32 (3): 353–366.

CHAPTER TWELVE

The Preferential Hiring of Military Veterans in the United States

Tim Johnson

Introduction

In March 2013 Brandon Friedman—a recipient of two Bronze Stars and the author of a well-regarded memoir on the Gulf War II conflicts—published a column in *Time* magazine dispelling the idea that military veterans suffer higher rates of unemployment than their nonveteran peers (Friedman 2013). Consistent with figures from the Bureau of Labor Statistics (2015), as well as research on potential mechanisms of employment discrimination against veterans (Kleykamp 2009), Friedman's article presented data suggesting that veterans' employment rates mirror those of comparable nonveterans, except in a small number of age cohorts. Moreover, for segments of the veteran population in which unemployment rates differ from those in the nonveteran population, Friedman proposed that these variances resemble the same labor market phenomena that nonveterans would face if they were in the midst of a career change. In sum, contrary to conventional wisdom, Friedman's article provided good reason to believe that the labor market experiences of veterans appear to be quite similar to those of nonveterans.

Friedman's article, however, did not mention an important difference between the labor market activities of veterans and nonveterans: only 2 percent of the nonveteran population works in the U.S. federal government, whereas 9 percent of all military veterans do so—and this latter figure grows to roughly 16 percent when considering veterans of the recent conflicts in Iraq and Afghanistan (National Center for Veterans Analysis and Statistics 2014). Just as the evidence in Friedman's article proved surprising because of the similarities it showed between the labor market outcomes of veterans and nonveterans, rates of federal government employment for veterans and nonveterans are surprising because of the stark differences they reveal.

The vast chasm between veterans' and nonveterans' rates of federal government employment likely results—at least in part—from a public policy known as *veterans' preference* (Lewis 2013; Johnson 2015).[1] In the U.S. federal service, veterans' preference supplements the scores veterans receive on their entry examinations, thus giving former military personnel a leg up on nonveterans in the hunt for federal jobs. Similar procedures have found their way into the hiring processes of myriad subnational governments (viz. Merit System Protection Board 2014; Lewis and Pathak 2014); also, recently a number of states have passed legislation that opens the door to the creation of veterans' preference programs in private enterprises (Sutton 2014).

How do these veterans' preference policies work, and how did they become common across sectors of the economy? How does veterans' preference comport with competing legal concepts that seek to ensure equal treatment and fairness in the employment process? How does veterans' preference affect the composition, qualifications, and performance of workplaces that adopt the policy? This chapter addresses these questions by depicting the workings, history, legal nuances, and practical implications of veterans' preference in the United States. Furthermore, by recounting what is known about veterans' preference, the chapter points to gaps in our current knowledge, thus highlighting areas where future research can continue to explore veterans' preference fruitfully.

How Does Veterans' Preference Work?

Imagine that a small business owner posts an advertisement for a position. For several weeks she has collected résumés and cover letters from job seekers, but recently one candidate has caught her eye. An honorably discharged veteran has applied for the job who possesses roughly the same qualifications as the rest of the applicant pool. Immediately the small business owner recalls popular press articles trumpeting the work-relevant talents and knowledge imparted via military service (e.g., Biro 2012). As a result, pending a successful interview, the owner plans to make a job offer: the candidate's veteran status has swayed her choice. One could say that the small business owner's heavy weighting of veteran status in the selection process indicates a *preference* for hiring veterans, but for the purposes of this chapter, it would not indicate that the employee was hired via *veterans' preference*.

In this chapter, veterans' preference refers to any policy that forces an employer to uniformly favor veterans or their close relatives when hiring, promoting, or firing employees. Favoring veterans or their close relatives can come in various forms, such as adding points to numerical scoring systems used in personnel management (e.g., entry exams or performance ratings), selecting veterans or their relatives in the event of "ties" (e.g., retaining a veteran during a reduction in force rather than coworkers laboring in the same job), or hiring/promoting/retaining preference-eligible individuals outright without consideration of the attributes of others in the labor pool. In other words, possessing an inclination to hire veterans, or merely considering veteran status in an evaluation of a candidate's biographical data, does not amount to implementing veterans' preference. Instead, veterans' preference involves policies that uniformly give employment advantages to veterans or their close relatives.

Even with this definition in place, veterans' preference policies vary widely. After all, veterans' preference figures into the management of personnel across all levels of government in the United States (Lewis and Pathak 2014). Also, recent legislation makes it possible for private sector organizations to create their own, customized veterans' preference policies (Sutton 2014). Across these jurisdictions and organizations, differences exist in (1) the criteria used to determine eligibility for veterans' preference, (2) the scope of personnel actions covered by veterans' preference, and (3) the administrative practices used to implement veterans' preference. By examining this variation, this section aims to shed light on how veterans' preference works.

Eligibility Criteria

Former military personnel are not the only individuals who are eligible for veterans' preference. In fact, many individuals who have served in the military are not eligible for veterans' preference at all, while some nonveterans are eligible. Consider, for example, the federal government's current eligibility criteria for veterans' preference (Office of Personnel Management 2015a), which are detailed in table 12.1 using language that is slightly truncated from the official OPM rules but retains important technical jargon. As table 12.1 indicates, different criteria apply for veterans and nonveterans seeking preference. For veterans, the eligibility criteria include, in broad terms, (1) the nature of an individual's discharge from

Table 12.1. Eligibility Criteria for Preference in the U.S. Federal Government.

0-Point Preference*
- Must have a passing exam score/rating.
- Must be an honorably discharged veteran.
- Must be the only surviving child in one's family.
- Must have had a father, mother, or sibling(s), who during his/her military service was either . . .
    - . . . killed . . .
    - . . . died as a result of wounds, accident, or disease . . .
    - . . . was designated captured or missing in action . . .
    - . . . was designated permanently 100 percent disabled and, thus, unemployable . . .
    - . . . is hospitalized on a continuing basis and, thus, unemployable . . .
        - . . . and the above condition did not occur because of intentional misconduct, willful neglect, or activity during a period of unauthorized absence.

5-Point Preference
- Must have a passing exam score/rating.
- Must be an honorably discharged veteran.
- Must have served during . . .
    - . . . a war
    - . . . the dates April 28, 1952, to July 1, 1955.
    - . . . the dates January 31, 1955, to October 15, 1976, for more than 180 consecutive days.
    - . . . the dates August 2, 1990, to January 2, 1992, in the Gulf War.
    - . . . the dates September 11, 2001, to August 31, 2010, for more than 180 consecutive days.
    - . . . a period in which one participated in a military action for which a campaign medal was awarded.

10-Point Preference (Disability)
- Must have a passing exam score/rating.
- Must be an honorably-discharged veteran, who . . .
    - . . . received a service-connected disability.
    - . . . received a Purple Heart.

10-Point Preference (Spouse)
- Must have a passing exam score/rating.
- Must be the spouse of an honorably discharged veteran, who . . .
    - . . . received a service related disability that is rated 100-percent disabled.
    - . . . is unemployable or cannot qualify for employment due to the possession of a service-connected disability.
    - . . . left, via retirement, separation, or resignation, a civil service job because of disability.

10-Point Preference (Widow/widower)
- Must have a passing exam score/rating.
- Must be a single (no remarriage) widow/widower of an honorably discharged veteran, who . . .
    - . . . either participated in or died in military service during a war, during the time period April 28, 1952, to July 1, 1955, or in a military action awarded a campaign medal.

10-Point Preference (Mother)
- Must have a passing exam score/rating.
- Must be the mother of an honorably discharged deceased or disabled veteran.
- Must be or have been married to the father of her veteran child.
- Must be either living with a partner who is no longer employable due to disability or she is no longer married.

---

*The 0-point preference does not add points to a recipient's exam scores, but ranks the recipient ahead of nonrecipients with the same score or rating in the hiring process. The table directly draws on information and quotes the exact technical terminology used in the Office of Personnel Management (2015a).

the military, (2) the period of an individual's service, (3) the possession of a service-connected disability, (4) the receipt of a Purple Heart, and (5) one's status as the only surviving child in a nuclear family in which other family members were substantially harmed in war. For nonveterans, the criteria, put broadly, include (6) an individual's relationship to a military veteran (whether one is the spouse, widow/widower, or mother of a veteran) and (7) whether the veteran to whom one is related has suffered detrimental service-related outcomes such as death or the acquisition of an incapacitating disability. These criteria determine whether an individual is eligible for veterans' preference in the federal service and, if so, which type of preference benefits the individual is to receive (a topic that we turn to in subsequent sections).

State governments often employ comparable eligibility criteria, as can be seen in table 12.2, which lists the laws underlying veterans' preference in state-level[2] public organizations. The column headed "Honorable Discharge" indicates whether a state uses honorable discharge in the determination of preference eligibility. According to the table, 86 percent of states do so. Furthermore, just as the federal government considers the acquisition of a service-connected disability as an event that can trigger preference eligibility or influence the type of preference awarded, 84 percent of state veterans' preference policies distinguish between individuals with a service-connected disability and those who do not possess such a disability. Table 12.2 also shows that 64 percent of states grant eligibility to a select set of veterans' relatives (e.g., mothers and spouses), and 72 percent of the states mention some baseline qualification that an employee must obtain to receive preference (e.g., a passing score on an entry exam). Thus, much like the federal government, state-level preference policies reserve preference to a subset of veterans and veterans' family members.

Unlike the criteria used by federal and state governments, the eligibility criteria for veterans' preference in private enterprises remain largely unknown. No systematic investigation has attempted to catalog which private employers have elected to implement veterans' preference, let alone which criteria those enterprises have used to assess eligibility for preference. However, it would be a mistake to assume that such eligibility criteria do not exist. For one, recent state laws enabling the use of veterans' preference in private employment include definitions of who constitutes an eligible veteran for private-sector preference and which close relatives can be given that preference (see discussion in Sutton 2014; also, e.g., Ark. Code Ann. §§ 11-15-101 to 105; Minn. Stat. Ann. § 197.4551). Furthermore, among the private-sector preference policies known to be in operation, some policies restrict preference in a manner similar to public-sector preference policies. For instance, in 2013 Walmart initiated a hiring program named the "Veterans Welcome Home Commitment"; the program recruited newly discharged veterans and prioritized their hiring (Walmart 2015). Although it does not use the term "veterans' preference," the program fits this chapter's definition of veterans' preference. The program is described as uniformly favoring veterans: "If you have been honorably discharged from the U.S. military since Memorial Day 2013 and meet our standard hiring criteria, there's a position for you at Walmart or Sam's Club" (Walmart 2015, para. 2). Also, the program uses eligibility criteria reminiscent of those employed in federal and state preference policies. That is, Walmart uses a veteran's discharge status, period of service, and satisfaction of baseline qualifications as criteria for determining whether "priority status" in hiring is awarded (Walmart 2015). Whether other private enterprises use similar criteria or other measures to assess eligibility remains unknown, due to the dearth of research on the topic. However, this single observation indicates that preference policies in the private sector have enumerated attributes—beyond, say, mere evidence of past military service—in order to specify who is eligible for preference, and these attributes constitute a subset of the criteria used in the public sector. As the next section indicates, similar overlap exists in the scope of personnel actions covered by veterans' preference in the public and private sectors.

Table 12.2. Veterans' Preference Policies across the United States.

	Eligibility Criteria				Scope of Covered Actions			Administrative Practices			
State	Honorable Discharge	Disability Status	Relative	Baseline Qualifications	Hiring	Promotion	Retention	Absolute	Point System	Tie Breaker	Vague
Alabama	1	1	1	0	1	0	1	0	1	1	0
Alaska	1	1	0	1	1	0	1	0	1	1	0
Arizona	1	1	1	1	1	0	0	0	1	1	0
Arkansas	1	1	1	1	1	1	1	0	1	1	0
California	1	0	1	1	1	0	0	0	1	0	0
Colorado	1	1	1	1	1	0	1	0	1	0	0
Connecticut	1	1	1	1	1	0	0	0	1	0	0
Delaware	0	1	1	1	1	0	0	0	1	0	0
Florida	1	1	1	1	1	0	0	0	1	0	0
Georgia	0	1	0	0	1	0	0	0	1	0	0
Hawaii	1	1	1	?	1	?	?	0	1	?	1
Idaho	1	1	0	0	1	0	0	0	1	0	1
Illinois	1	1	1	1	1	0	0	0	1	0	0
Indiana	1	1	0	1	1	0	0	0	0	0	1
Iowa	1	0	0	1	1	0	0	0	1	1	1
Kansas	1	0	0	1	1	0	0	0	0	0	1
Kentucky	1	1	1	0	1	0	0	0	1	0	0
Louisiana	1	1	1	1	1	0	1	0	1	1	0
Maine	1	1	1	1	1	0	0	0	1	0	0
Maryland	1	1	1	0	1	0	0	0	1	0	0

(Continued)

Table 12.2. Continued

State	Eligibility Criteria			Scope of Covered Actions			Administrative Practices			
	Honorable Discharge	Disability Status	Relative	Baseline Qualifications	Hiring	Promotion	Retention	Absolute	Point System	Tie Breaker	Vague
Massachusetts	1	1	0	1	1	1	0	1	1	0	0
Michigan	1	1	0	0	1	0	0	0	1	0	0
Minnesota	1	1	1	1	1	0	0	0	1	0	1
Mississippi	1	1	0	0	1	0	1	0	0	0	0
Missouri	1	1	1	0	1	0	0	0	1	0	0
Montana	1	1	1	1	1	0	0	0	1	0	0
Nebraska	0	1	1	1	1	0	0	0	1	1	0
Nevada	1	1	1	1	1	0	0	0	1	0	0
New Hampshire	1	0	0	1	1	0	0	0	0	1	0
New Jersey	0	1	0	1	1	0	0	1	1	0	0
New Mexico	1	1	0	1	1	0	0	0	1	0	0
New York	1	1	1	1	1	1	1	0	1	0	0
North Carolina	1	1	1	1	1	1	0	0	0	1	1
North Dakota	0	1	1	1	1	0	0	0	1	0	0
Ohio	1	0	0	1	1	0	0	0	1	0	0
Oklahoma	1	1	1	1	1	1	0	1	1	0	0
Oregon	0	1	0	1	1	1	1	0	1	0	0
Pennsylvania	0	1	1	1	1	0	1	1	1	0	0
Rhode Island	1	1	0	1	1	0	0	0	1	0	0
South Carolina	1	0	1	1	1	0	0	0	0	0	1
South Dakota	1	1	1	1	1	1	0	0	1	0	0

Tennessee	1	1	1	1	1	0	0
Texas	1	1	1	1	0	1	1
Utah	1	1	1	1	0	1	1
Vermont	1	1	0	1	1	0	0
Virginia	1	1	1	0	0	1	1
Washington	1	0	0	1	0	1	0
West Virginia	1	1	0	1	0	1	0
Wisconsin	1	1	0	1	0	1	0
Wyoming	1	1	0	1	0	1	0
TOTALS	43	42	32	36	50	11	9	4	43	12	9

Information derived from state statutes: Ala. Code § 36-26-15; Alaska Stat. Ann. § 39.25.159; Ariz. Rev. Stat. Ann. § 38-492; Ark. Code Ann. § 21-3-302; Cal. Gov't Code § 18973.1; Colo. Const. art. XII, § 15; Conn. Gen. Stat. Ann. § 5-224; Del. Code Ann. tit. 29, § 5935; Fla. Stat. Ann. § 295.08; Ga. Code Ann. § 43-1-9; Haw. Rev. Stat. § 76-103; Idaho Code Ann. § 65-503; 15 Ill. Comp. Stat. Ann. § 310/10b.7; Ind. Code Ann. § 5-9-3-1; Iowa Code Ann. § 35C.1; Kan. Stat. Ann. § 75-2955; Ky. Rev. Stat. Ann. § 18A.150; LA. Rev. Stat. Ann. § 33:2416(B); Maine Rev. Stat. Ann. tit. 5, § 7054; MD. Code Ann., State Gov't § 1-204; Mass. Gen. Laws Ann. ch. 31, § 3; Mich. Comp. Laws Ann. § 38.413; Minn. Stat. Ann. § 43A.11; Miss. Code Ann. § 71-5-121; Mo. Ann. Stat. § 36-220; Mont. Code Ann. § 39-29-101; Neb. Rev. Stat. Ann. § 48-227; Nev. Rev. Stat. Ann. § 284.260; N.H. Rev. Stat. Ann. § 283:4; N.J. Stat. Ann. § 11A:5-4; N.M. Stat. Ann. § 10-9-13.2; N.Y. Civ. Serv. Law § 85; N.C. Gen. Stat. Ann. § 128-15; N.D. Cent. Code Ann. § 37-19.1-02; Ohio Rev. Code Ann. § 124.23; Okla. Stat. Ann. tit. 74, § 840-4.14; Or. Rev. Stat. Ann. § 408.230; 51 Pa. Cons. Stat. Ann. § 7103; R.I. Gen. Laws Ann. § 36-4-19; S.C. Code Ann. § 1-1-550; S.D. Codified Laws § 3-3-1; Tenn. Code Ann. § 8-30-306; Tex. Gov't Code Ann. § 657.003(c); Utah Code Ann. § 71-10-2; Vt. Stat. Ann. tit. 20, § 1543; VA. Code Ann. § 2-2-2903; Wash. Rev. Code Ann. § 41.04.010; W. Va. Code Ann. § 6-13-1; Wis. Stat. Ann. § 66.0509; Wyo. Stat. Ann. § 19-14-102.

Scope of Covered Personnel Actions

What benefits can one expect after being deemed eligible for veterans' preference? As with eligibility criteria themselves, the answer to this question varies by jurisdiction and organization. However, the scope of personnel actions covered by veterans' preference appears to vary less across jurisdictions and organizations than do eligibility criteria. When considering the three primary personnel actions of hiring, promotion, and retention, veterans' preference appears to invariably apply to hiring, but only rarely does it apply to promotion and retention.

Hiring advantages are the most common form of preference benefit. The U.S. federal service focuses the bulk of its preference rules on the eligibility criteria and administrative practices associated with hiring advantages (Office of Personnel Management 2015a). All state statutes, furthermore, include hiring as one of the personnel actions covered by veterans' preference, as indicated in table 12.2. Likewise, when it comes to private-sector preference policies, hiring also appears to be at the forefront; to date, all laws enabling the creation of private-sector preference policies allow for hiring advantages (i.e., Wash Rev. Code Ann. § 73.16.110; Minn. Stat. Ann. § 197.4551; N.D. Cent. Code Ann. § 37-19.1-05; Ark. Code Ann. §§ 11-15-101 to 105; IA Code §35.3; 26 MRSA §876–78; Ch. 86 §2, E.H.B. 4023; FL ST 295.188; Michigan PA 508; Utah H.B. 232; Kansas H.B. 2154; Indiana S.B. 298). Thus, across all sectors of the economy, the scope of veterans' preference policies includes hiring advantages.

The ubiquity of hiring advantages can be contrasted with the rarity of promotion preferences. The U.S. Office of Personnel Management, which controls the bulk of employment matters in the U.S. federal service, unequivocally states that "[v]eterans' preference does not apply to promotion, reassignment, change to lower grade, transfer or reinstatement" (Office of Personnel Management 2015a, para. 9). State governments also appear reluctant to favor veterans or their kin in promotion decisions: only 22 percent of states maintain a veterans' preference policy that applies to promotions. Laws enabling private-sector preference policies are divided in regard to whether they include promotions within their scope. When considering the first four private-sector preference laws, Arkansas (Ark. Code Ann. §§ 11-15-101 to 105) and Minnesota (Minn. Stat. Ann. § 197.4551) explicitly mentioned promotions as a personnel action to which it is acceptable to apply preference, whereas Washington (Wash Rev. Code Ann. § 73.16.110) and North Dakota (N.D. Cent. Code Ann. § 37-19.1-05) only mentioned the application of preference to matters of "employment"—a vague term that implies hiring but may not include promotions. Furthermore, the dearth of systematic data collection concerning the use of veterans' preference in private enterprises means that researchers do not know whether employers implementing private-sector preference policies actually apply preference to promotion decisions.

Application of veterans' preferences to retention occurs in the federal government, but it rarely is included in the preference policies of state governments and private organizations. When the federal service reduces the size of its workforce, it sorts employees into "tenure groups" and then begins layoffs within each group (Office of Personnel Management 2015a). The order of layoffs within a group takes into account veterans' preference: ineligible employees are the first to be laid off; veterans without a service-connected disability and nonveterans who received preference due to their relationship with a veteran are laid off second; and finally, veterans with a service-connected disability are released from service (Office of Personnel Management 2015a). A small number of state governments also include retention provisions like these (see table 12.2). Nine out of the fifty states directly mention the inclusion of employee retention, during reductions in force, as falling within the scope of veterans' preference. Laws enabling veterans' preference in private employment also rarely include retention benefits within their scope. Again, when considering the first four states adopting private-sector preference, only Arkansas directly mentions the possibility of private employers creating a preference policy that applies to retention. Minnesota omits mention of retention, despite directly mentioning hiring and promotion, whereas the vague description of the scope of private-sector veterans' preference in North Dakota and Washington makes it unclear whether or not private-sector preferences apply to retention in those states.

Thus, although preferences in promotion and retention do exist, they are rare—especially compared to the inclusion of hiring preferences, which fall within the scope of veterans' preference across all levels of government and sectors of the economy. However, even with regard to widespread hiring preferences, variation in the administrative practices that implement preference can be found. These practices create noticeable differences between veterans' preference policies that would otherwise include the same set of personnel actions within their scope.

Administrative Practices

Subtle differences in the implementation of veterans' preference exist across organizations, and some of those differences—particularly as they concern *when* in the hiring process preference benefits are issued—have been the subject of debate within organizations.[3] However, those differences pale in comparison to the clearest form of variation: whether preference is implemented via a point system or whether it is "absolute."

Point systems are used to administer hiring preferences in the U.S federal government, as well as in the vast majority of states (see table 12.2). One can speculate that the prevalence of point systems relates to the ease with which they can be added to numerical rating methods such as exam scoring or performance rating. For example, the traditional method of appraising job candidates in the U.S. federal service involves scoring each candidate on an entry "exam." The exam need not be a written test, though in some instances it is or has been. Once a candidate receives a score, an official assesses whether or not the score meets or exceeds the score that officials have deemed a passing mark. For all of those candidates who receive a passing mark and meet the relevant eligibility criteria for veterans' preference, officials increase their exam scores by a set number of points. In the U.S. federal service, veterans who possess a service-connected disability or a Purple Heart receive an increase of 10 points on their applications, whereas veterans who do not satisfy those criteria, but who received an honorable discharge and served in qualifying service conditions, receive an increase of 5 points on their entry score; qualifying nonveterans receive an increase of 10 points. Furthermore, the 110th Congress created the 0-point preference, which does not add points to a recipient's exam scores, but ranks its recipient ahead of nonrecipients with the same score or rating in the hiring process (Public Law 110-317). Not all jurisdictions using point systems award these same point values, but the general contours of point administration remain the same.

Absolute forms of veterans' preference, on the other hand, give eligible individuals priority over other candidates, regardless of the attributes those other candidates possess. For instance, in Oklahoma, a veteran with a service-connected disability rating of 30 percent receives 10 additional points on her or his entry exam grade; these points, however, only influence the ranking of the veteran—in terms of hiring priority—when the veteran is compared to other veterans with service-connected disability ratings of 30 percent or more. When competing with other applicants—whether those applicants are veterans or nonveterans—the veteran with the service-connected disability rating of 30 percent or more is automatically placed at the top of the hiring register[4] and is hired unless an official can provide evidence of the veteran's inability to perform the job in question. Similar systems of preference exist in Massachusetts, New Jersey, and Pennsylvania (see table 12.2). One can also consider absolute preference to be the method used in the U.S. federal service when it comes to retention during reductions in force. Employees are placed in tenure groups, and regardless of individual attributes that might relate to an employee's deserving to be laid off, veterans with service-connected disabilities are the last to be laid off within each tenure group.

These two methods represent the most noticeable differences in how veterans' preference is administered. However, other approaches to administering preference exist. Some state statutes mention veterans' preference as serving a tie-breaking function, in which preference-eligible individuals are selected over candidates deemed equal in their employment-relevant traits (see table 12.2); interestingly, even when they have a point system in place, some states also mention a tie-breaking function or the importance of solely selecting preference-eligible candidates above equally qualified (as opposed to more-qualified) candidates. Finally, the statutory language enabling veterans' preference in some states does not specify the details of implementation, thus allowing administrative discretion to determine the nuances of executing preference policy.[5]

Similarly, laws facilitating private-sector veterans' preference policies have avoided, in large part, any effort to detail the methods that organizations need to employ when administering a preference policy. Once more considering the first four states to pass a private-sector preference law, Arkansas provides the most detail about administrative practices, but it is still quite minimal: its statute merely stipulates that any veterans' preference policy implemented by a private enterprise must be in writing and uniformly applied. All other states adopting such policies provide no discussion of the administrative practices used to implement veterans' preference.

Veterans' Preference in Practice: Summary

By elaborating upon the constituent attributes of preference (namely, eligibility criteria, the scope of personnel actions covered by the policy, and the administrative practices implementing preference), this section has explained how veterans' preference works. Across jurisdictions and organizations, much variation exists in these features of veterans' preference. This variation may have resulted from the scattered and uncoordinated emergence of veterans' preference, which the next section describes.

How Did Veterans' Preference Develop?

Since World War I, scholars and government officials have claimed that veterans' preference originated during the Civil War as a way to thank veterans for their military service (Breyer 1920; Civil Service Commission 1955; Public Law 98–330 1984; Ingraham 1996; State of North Carolina 2007; Lewis 2013). However, decades earlier, civil service reformers described veterans' preference as a method of patronage that George Washington resisted, but that early partisans adopted (Fish 1905, 5–12; Hunt 1896). To these earlier commentators, veterans' preference predated the Civil War and, implicitly, the Washington administration. Which account, if either, more accurately characterizes the historical emergence of veterans' preference? The current state of historical evidence merely *suggests* an answer to that question.

On the one hand, authoritative administrative histories, such as Leonard White's *The Federalists*, note that Washington's writings rejected the idea of using veteran status as a selection criterion for public employment (White 1948, 261). Communicating with a woman who sought government appointments to remedy the devastation her family had suffered from the Revolutionary War, Washington wrote that he could not accommodate her request; he intended "to nominate such persons alone to offices, as, in [his] judgment, shall be the best qualified to discharge the functions of the departments to which they shall be appointed" (Washington 1789a; also referenced in White 1948, 261). He had penned the same sentiment earlier in a letter to Benjamin Harrison, who sought a job from Washington on the premise that his service in the Revolutionary Army left him "some claim on America [*sic*] for assistance" (Harrison 1789, para. 3). Washington, however, told Harrison that "[f]or all recommendations for appointments, so far as they may depend upon or come from me, due regard shall be had to the fitness of characters, the pretensions of different candidates, and, so far as proper, to political considerations" (Washington 1789b, para. 2). In his administration, Washington signaled, veteran status would not sway personnel decisions.

Or maybe it would. White (1948, 304) acknowledged that "[i]n his appointments to the office of the collector, Washington was partial to former members of the Revolutionary Army." Likewise, Washington's thoughts about issuing land bonuses to Revolutionary War veterans hinted at an implicit veterans' preference policy. Bodenger (1971, 44–45) notes that Washington viewed land bonuses as a means to hire military veterans to, as he put it, "build a living wall against the Indians" (Bodenger 1971, 44–45, quoting Fitzpatrick 1938, 16). Thus, even though the gifting of land to Revolutionary War veterans primarily represented a nod of gratitude to those who fought the British (Freund 1946), the land bonuses functioned, in Washington's mind, as a policy that traded land for labor (viz. border security) without opening eligibility for that labor arrangement to nonveterans. This arrangement meets the definition of veterans' preference used in this chapter. Moreover, these passages suggest that, consistent with the civil service reformers' narrative, some form of veterans' preference may have existed prior to the Civil War. However, in contrast to the reformers' portrait, it is not clear that Washington resisted the preferential hiring of military veterans. In regard to his appointments to collector positions, he appears to have indulged in preference, and his strategic use of land bonuses borders on a policy that gives hiring preference to veterans.

But while civil service reformers may have overstated Washington's reluctance to participate in veterans' preference schemes, they were right to intimate that other political actors sought to initiate preference policies directly. Prior to the Washington administration, *The Journal of the Continental Congress* (Continental Congress 1776, 705; see also Bodenger 1971) recounts the passage of a policy stipulating that permanently injured Revolutionary War veterans would be given guard or garrison duty, if they could do so, in order to receive their military pensions. Although the pensions themselves served as a means of military recruitment and social welfare (National Archives 1974), the addendum to the pension policy requiring guard duty had the effect of distributing a government position to a veteran, even though a nonveteran could have performed that duty. In so doing, the policy can be regarded as an early and informal version of veterans' preference.

Accordingly, reformers appear to have been correct in noting that preference existed in the early days of the nation's history, albeit in an informal form with only the vaguest features of current preference policy. The first formal veterans' preference legislation emerged in a joint resolution of Congress on March 3, 1865 (Civil Service Commission 1955, 1). The law put forth eligibility criteria that consisted of honorable discharge, the acquisition of a disability during service, and "the business capacity necessary for the proper discharge of the duties [associated with the appointment]" (Civil Service Commission 1955, 1, quoting 13 Stat. 571). Furthermore, the scope of this formal preference policy solely included hiring, and it left unspecified the administrative practices involved in implementing the policy—except for the implicit requirement of providing some form of vetting to make sure that a candidate possessed the aforementioned "business capacity" necessary to perform the duties of the appointed position. As these details indicate, the 1865 legislation contained all of the elements that have come to define veterans' preference policies.

The specific content of those elements, however, differed markedly from current veterans' preference policy. The inaugural policy ignored veterans who did not have service-related disabilities, nor did it grant preference to veterans' close relatives. Furthermore, it did not specify the use of any point system, and it referred only to hiring. Thus, only in its broad outline did this initial legislation resemble the veterans' preference policy operating in today's federal service.

Over the subsequent half century, the attributes of contemporary preference policies emerged. Table 12.3 displays the birth of these provisions in legislation, legal opinions, and executive orders. As the table indicates, federal modifications to veterans' preference were frequent, and they

Table 12.3. Key Events in the Emergence of Post–World War II Veterans' Preference.

Date	Law, Rule, Opinion, or Other Formal Proceeding	Effect
1865	13 Stat. 571 (§ 1754 of the Revised Statutes)	First preference law. Creates hiring preference for honorably discharged veterans who acquired a service disability while fighting for the Union.
1876	19 Stat. 169	Extension of veterans' preference to include retention during a reduction in force for "those persons who may be equally qualified who have been honorably discharged from the military or naval service of the United States, and the widows and orphans of deceased soldiers and sailors."
1881	17 Op. Atty. Gen. 194	Attorney general publishes commentary maintaining that veterans' preference should only serve as a tie-breaking mechanism among equally qualified candidates.
1883	22 Stat. 403	Implements modern U.S. Civil Service system. Conspicuously protects veterans' preference by admonishing that "nothing herein shall be construed to take away from those honorably discharged from the military or naval service any preference conferred by the 1754th section of the Revised Statutes."
1900	*Keim v. U.S.*, 33 Ct. Cl., 174, 187 (1900)	Courts determine that administrative officials are to have discretion over what constitutes equal qualifications in assessing whether or not preference-eligible employees are to be retained during a reduction in force.

1906	Exec. Order 475	Grants honorably discharged veterans who apply for select positions in the War, State, and Navy Departments preference in appointment.
1910	28 Op. Atty. Gen. 298	Attorney General publishes commentary refuting the claim that veterans' preference is to act as a tie-breaking mechanism; instead, the Attorney General contends that eligible veterans are to be selected above all individuals ineligible for preference.
1910	28 Op. Atty. Gen. 298	Attorney General published commentary rejecting the notion that veterans' preference was limited by apportionment rules that specified the fraction of the federal service to be allotted to the residents of each state.
1912	37 Stat. 413	Creation of a new civil service rating system by Congress notes that "in the event of reduction being made in the force of any executive departments no honorably discharged soldier or sailor whose record in such department is rated good shall be discharged or dropped or reduced in rank or salary."
1919	40 Stat. 1293 (The Census Act)	Changes the criteria for preference eligibility; maintains that in hiring for federal positions, "preference shall be given to honorably discharged soldiers, sailors, and marines, and widows of such, if they are qualified to hold such positions."
1919	40 Stat. 1293 (The Deficiency Act)	Changes the criteria for preference eligibility once more; maintains that "preference shall be given to honorably discharged soldiers, sailors, and marines, and widows of such, and to the wives of injured soldiers, sailors, and marines, who themselves are not qualified, but whose wives are qualified to hold such positions."
1919	31 Op. Atty. Gen. 406	Attorney general publishes rule that determines that the methods of implementing the expanded preference statutes passed in 1919 were at the discretion of managers in the federal service
1919	Exec. Order 3152	Puts into operation the new preference statutes of 1919 and interprets the qualifications for preference eligibility to be a rating of 65 or higher.
1920	Exec. Order 3268	Preference applied to candidates applying for postmaster classes 1 to 3.

(Continued)

Table 12.3. Continued

Date	Law, Rule, Opinion, or Other Formal Proceeding	Effect
1921	Exec. Order 3560	Requires that 5 points be added to the entry exams of veterans of the Great War who applied for presidential postmaster positions. Represents the first use of a point system in the administration of preference.
1923	Letter of the Civil Service Commission to President Harding	Affirms political support for point system among American Legion and the public writ large. Recommends a 10-point preference for veterans who possess a service-related disability and sponsors the continuation of 5 points for other eligible veterans.
1923	Exec. Order 3801	Harding implements 10-point preference for all veterans with a service-related disability if they receive a grade of 60 or greater; other honorably discharged veterans, along with widows, receive 5-point preference pending an exam grade of 70 or greater. The order also requires that "an appointing officer who passes over a veteran eligible and selects a nonveteran with the same or lower rating shall place in the records of the department his reasons for doing so." Extends preference in retention to all classified civil service positions.
1929	Exec. Order 5068	Coolidge extends 10-point preference to widows and the spouses of veterans with disabilities that prevented them from obtaining preference.
1931	Exec. Order 5610	Coolidge clarifies the mechanisms for verifying veterans' claims of possessing service-connected disabilities. Specifies rules for administrators who pass over veterans in the selection process among candidates ranked among the top three on a list of applicants.
1944	Pub. L. No. 78-359, 58 Stat. 387	World War II–era legislation that provides the foundation of veterans' preference up to the present.

Information in the table, as well as quoted technical terminology used to describe the historical changes to veterans' preference policy and elements of the table itself, are drawn from Civil Service Commission (1955).

coincided with broader changes to the U.S. civil service, such as the advent of the merit system and exam-based personnel selection. Thus, haphazardly, these changes began to assemble today's federal veterans' preference policy.

The culmination of these changes was the Veterans Preference Act of 1944. The 1944 act tied together the changes to preference policy listed in table 12.3. According to the act, 5-point preference would be given to honorably discharged veterans who served full-time in military work that could not be deemed training or the assessment of physical fitness; moreover, this active-duty service had to have occurred during periods of war or in campaigns for which medals or ribbons were awarded (Civil Service Commission 1955). Under the 1944 law, veterans with a service-connected disability, the wives of disabled veterans, the widows of veterans, and the mothers of veterans were provided a 10-point preference. These provisions for the administration of preference in hiring were coupled with the specification of how preference would insulate individuals from reductions in force; as described in the previous section, it would prioritize the retention of preference-eligible employees, in a given ratings tier, above individuals ineligible for preference. Coupled with the end of World War II, the rollout of the 1944 act coincided with a rapid jump in the proportion of veterans employed in the federal service: one decade after the act was passed, 50 percent of all federal employees in the continental United States were veterans (Civil Service Commission 1955, 39).

The basic framework delineated in the 1944 act has persisted into the present (Office of Personnel Management 2015b), though subtle modifications of the policy were made in the aftermath of each foreign conflict (Johnson 2015). In 1952 legislation extended preference to military personnel serving on active duty during the conflict in Korea (Public Law 82-536, 66 Stat. 626); similar laws have been passed following the Vietnam and Gulf War conflicts to ensure that the veterans of those engagements remained eligible for preference (e.g., Executive Order 13518, November 9, 2009).

Perhaps the most significant change to veterans' preference since the 1944 act has resulted from the implementation of new hiring procedures in the U.S. federal government over the past decade. In 2010 President Barack Obama issued a memorandum titled, "Improving the Federal Recruitment and Hiring Process," which directed agencies to change their hiring methods (Obama 2010). Specifically, the memorandum replaced the practice of (1) conducting exams, (2) ranking candidates according to those exams, and then (3) selecting among the top-three highest-scoring candidates; in place of that procedure, the memorandum proposed the "category rating method," in which candidates were evaluated and then grouped into pools labeled "quality tiers." Managers could then select among candidates within the highest-rated pool. Within this system, preference-eligible applicants must be selected first within a given quality tier (Department of Labor 2015; Office of Personnel Management n.d.). That is to say, the category rating system implements something akin to an absolute preference system: within each quality tier, preference-eligible applicants must be selected first, regardless of within-tier differences in quality.

Furthermore, at roughly the same time that the category rating method was put forward, the Obama administration initiated a public relations program to encourage the employment of military veterans returning from conflicts in Iraq and Afghanistan (Executive Order 13518). This initiative encouraged the hiring of veterans, even though position papers of the Equal Employment Opportunity Commission (EEOC) had rejected the legality of veterans' preference schemes in private enterprises if they were not based on a formal statute (Equal Employment Opportunity Commission 1990; Black 2010). To protect private employers who sought to implement preference policies, states have begun to pass private-sector veterans' preference statutes that allow nonpublic employers to craft their own preference policies (Sutton 2014). These laws resulted from the creation of a legislative template drafted by David H. Black, an attorney who graduated from the University of Michigan Law School and served as a legislative director for chapters of the Society for Human Resource Management from 2008 to 2012 (see Black 2010; Dunlap 2013). Given Mr. Black's central role in the promulgation of private-sector preference statutes, I turned to him for information about the adoption of private-sector preference statutes over the past half decade, which he generously provided.[6] As he indicated and as legal documentation indicates, Washington blazed the trail in crafting legislation based on Black's template in 2011 (Wash Rev. Code Ann. § 73.16.110), with Minnesota passing legislation the following year (Minn. Stat. Ann. § 197.4551). Arkansas (Ark. Code Ann. §§ 11-15-101 to 105), North Dakota (N.D. Cent. Code Ann. § 37-19.1-05), Iowa (IA Code §35.3), Maine (26 MRSA §876–78), Oregon (Ch. 86 §2, E.H.B. 4023), Florida (FL ST 295.188), Michigan (PA 508), Utah (H.B. 232), Kansas (H.B. 2154), Indiana (S.B. 298), and Montana (S.B. 196) followed suit in passing private-sector preference legislation between 2013 and 2015. Also, in 2015 Alaska (S.B. 2; H.B. 6) introduced legislation that would allow the creation of private-sector veterans' preference statutes.[7] As discussed in the next section, these statutes resolved questions about the legality of veterans' preference—a topic debated for much of the past century.

How Can Veterans' Preference Be Legal?

Given that veterans' preference institutionalizes a biased hiring procedure favoring some veterans and their relatives, the legal foundation for it would appear to be dubious. How can a blatantly prejudicial policy be allowed to shape employment decisions? Furthermore, the U.S. federal government historically maintained policies that prevented various groups from participating in military service; therefore, the pool of candidates eligible for veterans' preference traditionally has consisted of a narrow demographic segment of the U.S. population (Campbell 1977; Lewis and Emmert 1984; Lewis 2013). Due to this correlation between preference eligibility and demographic characteristics, wouldn't veterans' preference be a pretext for gender or racial discrimination? These questions have permeated legal analyses of veterans' preference and have pressed the courts to determine whether veterans' preference violates concepts such as equal protection, due process, and nondiscrimination in employment. This section considers, in turn, how veterans' preference relates to each of these concepts.

Equal Protection

The equal protection clause of the U.S. Constitution's Fourteenth Amendment forbids states to maintain laws that unjustifiably discriminate against groups of individuals distinguished by a common attribute or "classification." Veterans' preference explicitly discriminates between preference-eligible individuals and individuals who are ineligible for preference. Thus, to assess the legality of veterans' preference laws, the courts have asked whether the inherent discrimination in veterans' preference is justifiable.

To understand the courts' views concerning the legality of veterans' preference in light of the equal protection clause, the U.S. Supreme Court case *Personnel Administrator of Massachusetts v. Feeney* (1979) is instructive. The case—whose details we derive from the court's opinion drafted by Justice Stewart—focused on the career of Helen B. Feeney, a Massachusetts resident who had worked in her state's government for over a decade, from 1963 to 1975, before she decided to file suit against it. During her career, Feeney experienced one upward move to a new position, transferring from the post of Senior Clerk Stenographer to Federal Funds and Personnel Coordinator. Ms. Feeney, however, wanted to be promoted more rapidly; throughout her career, she took a number of civil service examinations with the goal of securing better positions. Despite receiving high scores on those exams, even obtaining the second-best score on an exam in 1971,

Feeney consistently found herself passed over in favor of male military veterans, who, she learned, regularly scored worse than she did. These veterans benefited from Massachusetts's absolute veterans' preference policy, which ranked preference-eligible candidates above preference-ineligible candidates, regardless of the exam scores either party received. Accordingly, Feeney filed suit claiming that the Massachusetts statute granting absolute preference resulted in gender discrimination that violated the equal protection clause of the Fourteenth Amendment.

To assess whether the discrimination resulting from veterans' preference was illegal, the Supreme Court adapted a test regularly employed in assessing equal protection cases. First, the court asked, does the classification of individuals into the groupings of veterans and nonveterans have a "close and substantial relationship to important government objectives?" (*Personnel Administrator of Massachusetts v. Feeney* [1979]). The court then asked, does the classification discriminate based on gender, and is that discrimination intentionally aimed at disadvantaging women?

The Supreme Court's decision acknowledged that governments have several rational reasons to create discriminatory classifications between preference-eligible citizens and ineligible ones. Veterans' preference can be "justified as a measure designed to reward military veterans for the sacrifice of military service, to ease the transition from military to civilian life, to encourage patriotic service, and to attract loyal and well-disciplined people to civil service occupations" (*Personnel Administrator of Massachusetts v. Feeney* [1979], § C, ¶ 1; see also *Higgins v. Civil Service Commission* [1952]). Each of these functions can be seen as fulfilling a serious and significant government objective.

However, installing a preference for military veterans—according to the courts—will result in foreseeable gender discrimination. Though the Massachusetts statute emphasized the eligibility of both male and female veterans, the court acknowledged that the disproportionate rate of military participation among men—due in large part to formal restrictions on women's participation—would inevitably lead to gender discrimination. But according to the court, that gender discrimination was not imposed invidiously with the intention of creating worse outcomes for women. As Justice Stewart explained in the majority opinion, "[a]lthough few women benefit from the preference the nonveteran class is not substantially all female. To the contrary, significant numbers of nonveterans are men, and all nonveterans—male as well as female are placed at a disadvantage" (*Personnel Administrator of Massachusetts v. Feeney* [1979]).

In this decision, the court echoed sentiments from earlier decisions that had upheld veterans' preference in the face of equal protection claims (see

Branch v. Du Bois [1976]; *Higgins v. Civil Service Commission of New Bridgeport* [1952]). The court acknowledged a rational basis for preference legislation, thus indicating that it would meet the basic test of whether or not the discriminatory practice served a legitimate government interest. Also, the court noted that despite the unfavorable outcomes the law produced for women, it was not crafted such that it intentionally, exclusively, and invidiously imposed those outcomes on women. With this reasoning laid out by the Supreme Court, the equal protection clause has posed little threat to veterans' preference policies.

Due Process

When a government administers a veterans' preference program while simultaneously maintaining that it is legally required to select civil servants by merit, has the government violated the law? This is a question of due process. Due process is, in effect, a promise that a government itself will act within the confines of the law. Critics of veterans' preference have put forward questions, such as the one opening this paragraph, to claim that preference policies violate due process.

The case *Ballou v. State Department of Civil Service* (1978) involves one of the more widely cited instances in which a veterans' preference statute was pegged as a violation of due process, and we draw on the details of its opinion here to discuss how the courts have ruled on the legality of veterans' preference in regard to due process. Like *Feeney* (1979), *Ballou v. State Department of Civil Service* (1978) centered on a nonveteran, Ruth Ballou, whom New Jersey officials passed over in a hiring competition, despite the fact that Ballou had scored the highest grade on the entry exam for the position for which she applied. New Jersey officials passed over Ballou because a preference-eligible veteran had received the second highest score on the exam—a score of 82.5. New Jersey's veterans' preference law stipulated that any preference-eligible candidate in the top three scorers had to be selected regardless of the scores of ineligible candidates, such as Ballou, whose score was over 17 points higher than that of the selected candidate.

Ballou viewed these procedures as "gross and arbitrary" and conducive to a "veterans' preference system with exceptions allowing merit appointments to surface from time to time" (*Ballou v. State Department of Civil Service* [1978], ¶¶ 7 and 8). The New Jersey state constitution, after all, maintained that meritocratic selection should govern hiring and promotion in the New Jersey state government. Absolute preference, Ballou argued, therefore signified the New Jersey government was operating outside its constitutional bounds and, accordingly, in violation of due process.

The Supreme Court of New Jersey, in the *Ballou* decision, rejected the notion that an absolute preference violated due process. Agreeing with the lower appellate court, the court viewed the absolute preference as a reasonable means to achieve the goal of providing veterans with advantages in the pursuit of public employment. This goal, the court also observed, was inscribed alongside the state's merit principle; the state's constitution held that "[a]ppointments and promotions in the civil service of the state shall be made according to merit except that preference in appointments by reason of active service in any branch of the [armed services] may be provided by law" (NJ Const. 1947, art. VII, §1, ¶ 2). More generally, the decision postulated that the implementation of veterans' preference does not nullify legally mandated merit systems, even when preference policies take an extreme, absolute form. The statutory acknowledgment of veterans' preference, even if that statute describes an extreme form of the policy, protects against claims that due process has been violated.

Nondiscrimination in Employment

Title VII of the Civil Rights Act of 1964 outlaws workplace discrimination in enterprises with more than 15 employees working every day for 20 or more calendar weeks of the year (Equal Employment Opportunity Commission 2009). Recognizing that veterans' preference necessarily entails de jure discrimination in favor of military veterans, as well as de facto discrimination in favor of males, Title VII contained a caveat emphasizing that none of its stipulations should impede "any Federal, State, territorial, or local law creating special rights or preference for veterans" (§ 712, Title VII of the Civil Rights Act of 1964).

The courts have not challenged this section of Title VII. For instance, in *Skillern v. Bolger* (1984), William O. Skillern claimed that veterans' preference in Postal Service hiring violated Title VII. In its decision, the Seventh Circuit Court denied the basis of this logic, stating that "Skillern's invocation of Title VII to circumvent the veterans' preference of the Post Office would work exactly the sort of modification [of veterans' preference] that Congress did not intend the statute to bring about" (*Skillern v. Bolger* [1984], ¶ 6). Other cases, such as *Bannerman v. Department of Youth Authority* (1977), also have referred to this section to dispel claims that veterans' preference violates Title VII.

However, in a notice released in 1990, the EEOC presented policy guidance indicating that only mandatory veterans' preference policies, founded on statute, were protected under § 712 of Title VII. Voluntary, private-sector preference policies could not be protected by § 712. The emergence of private-sector veterans' preference statutes—also labeled "permissive veterans' preference"—is a response to this policy statement (Black 2010; Dunlap 2013; Sutton 2014). Grounding private-sector preference policies in statute insulates employers from Title VII violation.

Legal Issues: Summary

On its face, veterans' preference would appear to violate the legal principles of equal protection, due process, and nondiscrimination in employment. But the courts have upheld veterans' preference in the face of claims that it violates the aforementioned legal notions. A similar refutation of conventional wisdom about the implications of veterans' preference has occurred with respect to assessments of its practical implications for workplaces and employees.

How Does Veterans' Preference Affect Workplaces and Employees?

As veterans' preference became more common throughout the United States, and as courts came to protect veterans' preference, commentators and researchers increasingly questioned the effect that veterans' preference had on workplace diversity (Foster 1979; Keeton 1994; Mani 1999, 2001; Lewis 2013), as well as on employee qualifications and performance (Miller 1935; Ordway 1945; Lewis 2013). This work focuses entirely on the U.S. federal service; thus major effort needs to be directed toward studying the same issues in subnational U.S. governments and private workplaces. To provide a jumping-off point for such work, this section describes existing social science research on how veterans' preference affects workplace diversity, employee qualifications, and job performance.

Impact on Diversity

Although the U.S. armed forces have grown more diverse, they have historically been staffed predominantly by white males (Segal and Verdugo 1994). This fact prompted the litigation discussed in the last section, and it also encouraged academic research to consider the possibility that veterans' preference alters the demographic composition of workplaces that adopt the policy. Emmert and Lewis (1982) and Lewis and Emmert (1984) initiated this line of research by examining how veterans' preference influenced the composition of the U.S. federal service. They showed that veterans in the U.S. federal service are more likely to be male, white, and college educated than nonveterans entering the federal service. Furthermore, veterans are on average older, more experienced, better compensated, and more apt to enter the upper ranks of the federal service than are women. However, when controlling for their education and demographic characteristics, veterans appear to hold positions lower in the federal hierarchy, and they earn less (Lewis and Emmert 1984). Lewis and Emmert (1984) interpret these findings as providing evidence that veterans' preference alters the diversity of the federal workforce at the point of hire, but that veterans' advantages in terms of pay and placement in the federal hierarchy are due to their demographic characteristics, not their veteran status.[8]

A decade after Lewis and Emmert (1984) studied the broad effects of veterans' preference on the diversity of the federal service, Keeton (1994) considered the more narrow possibility that veterans' preference impedes the advancement of women in the federal service. Keeton (1994) examined rates of hiring and promotion among veterans from 1983 to 1992, relative to rates at which women were being hired and obtaining higher-grade positions in the federal service. Keeton (1994) found that veterans constituted a sizable portion of the federal service and were promoted at a substantial rate, whereas women's representation in the federal service was beneath that of the labor market writ large, and that representation took the form of lower-level positions. In a rather bold leap of logic, Keeton (1994) interpreted these summary statistics as evidence that veterans' preference was impeding women's advance in the federal service—a plausible hypothesis, albeit not with the data Keeton (1994) presented.

In a series of articles taking issue with Keeton (1994), Mani (1999, 2001) found that veterans' preference did not appear to improve the likelihood of promotion; thus, it might not be a factor influencing women's climb up the federal career ladder, be they veteran or nonveteran women. Mani (1999) modeled the likelihood of promotion via a federal employee's veteran status, sex, year of employment, and grade level. Her models showed that veteran status either has a negative or a null effect on promotion, thus suggesting that veterans' preference does not appear to stifle the promotion of females in the U.S. federal service as postulated by Keeton (1994). Reinforcing these findings, Mani (2001) shows that veterans' preference has come to play a smaller and smaller role in influencing the positions obtained by women in the federal civil service.

Yet both Keeton (1994) and Mani (1999, 2001) provide only broad evidence that veterans' preference distorts hiring, which appeared as a central insight of Lewis and Emmert (1984). As a result, Lewis (2013) examined census data during three periods—1990, 2000, and 2006–2009—to test whether veterans were more likely to staff federal jobs than nonveterans during those periods. Lewis (2013) found that veterans hold federal jobs at three times the rate of nonveterans, and they are slightly more likely to hold state/local government jobs than are nonveterans. Moreover, the veterans enjoying these posts were predominantly white, heterosexual males, thus suggesting that veterans' preference was impeding the hiring of individuals who did not identify with those attributes. Lewis's finding, in sum, reinforces the idea that veterans' preference reshapes the diversity of government by influencing who gets hired.

Qualifications

Even before concerns emerged about the effect of veterans' preference on workforce diversity, scholars had been worrying for decades that veterans' preference reduced the qualifications of employees in the U.S. federal service (Fish 1905; Miller 1935; Ordway 1945). Systematic investigations of this possibility, however, were slow to emerge, and only with the studies cited in the previous section was information about the qualifications of veterans' preference recipients put forward.

Studying a 1 percent sample of the U.S. federal government's primary employee database, the Central Personnel Data File (CPDF), Lewis and Emmert (1984) found that veterans were more likely to be college educated than nonveterans. Mani (1999, 2001), examining similar data, also found higher levels of education among veterans. However, decades later, Lewis (2013) found the opposite evidence; his study indicated that veterans had less education, on average, than their nonveteran peers.

All of these studies, however, ignore the possibility that veterans and nonveterans pursue different types of jobs, which require different levels of education, and thus any educational differences might be a function of position type, not veteran status. If that is the case, then preference recipients, say, might be educationally comparable to preference-ineligible employees in their same job, but not to ineligible employees working other jobs. Johnson and Walker (n.d.) consider this possibility and, indeed, find that when one controls for the jobs that employees enter, any differences in the educational attainment of preference recipients and nonrecipients largely disappear (in fact, in some instances, veterans' preference recipients appear to have higher educational attainment than nonveterans). Moreover, given that the analysis of Johnson and Walker (n.d.) is conducted on the complete U.S. Central Personnel Data File from 1973–1997, the results can be viewed as a definitive answer to the question of whether or not veterans' preference recipients held comparable educational credentials to individuals hired into their same positions during the period under study.

Performance

Given that veterans' preference partially circumvents screening procedures at the point of hire, conventional wisdom has long maintained that it leads to the selection of lower-performing employees (Miller 1935; Ordway 1945; Lewis 2013). Lewis and Emmert (1984, 341) provided brief evidence that veteran status leads to weaker performance, but Lewis (2013) provided the first systematic effort to test that hypothesis. Lewis (2013) compared the rate of General Schedule (GS) grade progress between veterans and nonveterans who began federal service at the same grade. Grade promotion correlates with job performance (Oh and Lewis 2013); therefore this dependent variable serves as a good proxy for performance. Lewis (2013) showed that nonveterans advanced roughly one-half to one-and-one-half grades faster than veterans who started service in their same grade (Lewis 2013, 263). This finding implied that veterans perform worse than nonveterans and thus that veterans' preference hurts the quality of the federal service by favoring the hiring of lower-performing employees.

Lewis (2013), however, ignored all potential confounding factors besides an employee's entry grade, thus creating the possibility that confounding factors were responsible for the relationship between veteran status and GS advancement. Johnson (2015) aimed to ferret out potential confounders by controlling for a wider range of job traits in his analysis. Johnson (2015, 669) compared employees who entered federal service in the same grade, occupation, year, agency, and duty station, and found that "recipients of veterans' preference hold grades greater than or statistically indistinguishable from the grades of non-recipients in 15 of the first 24 years of their careers" (669). Moreover, Johnson (2015) discovered that recipients of the maximal, 10-point preference climb the federal career ladder faster than any other employee group, including nonveterans, when one controls for their entry positions. Moreover, like Johnson and Walker (n.d.), Johnson (2015) studied the complete Central Personnel Data File from 1973 to 1997, thus making his results an authoritative, comprehensive portrait of how veterans' preference affected the performance of the federal service over the two decades under study.

Practical Implications: Summary

As these findings suggest, veterans' preference has implications for the diversity of the U.S. federal service, but it may have little, if any, effect on the qualifications and quality of employees. Ultimately, future research will need to examine whether these findings hold when examining veterans' preference outside the U.S. federal service. Presently, no studies have explored the effects of veterans' preference on state/local governments or private enterprises. Taking that step will provide a more complete view of how veterans' preference affects workplace and employee outcomes.

Conclusion

Veterans' preference represents a diverse range of policies that favor the hiring, promotion, and/or retention of military veterans and their close relatives. These policies emerged, informally, as far back as the Revolutionary War era, but they took tangible form between the final days of the Civil War and the end of World War II. After preference policies became formalized, they withstood legal challenges premised on the equal protection and due process clauses, as well as Title VII of the 1964 Civil Rights Act. With their legality established, researchers set about examining their practical implications, finding that veterans' preference reduces workplace diversity, yet it has no noteworthy effect on employee qualifications and quality. A promising direction for future research will be to examine whether comparable phenomena exist among state/local government and private-sector employers who adopt veterans' preference.

Future research might also consider asking a range of new questions about veterans' preference. For instance, does veterans' preference create a stigma for preference beneficiaries, as the Merit System Protection Board (2014) has implied? Also, what is the impact of veterans' preference on veterans' nonwork outcomes (e.g., their health, family stability, etc.)? What do the current politics of veterans' preference look like? Will private-sector companies actually adopt veterans' preference policies in states that have afforded them legal protection to do so? If so, which employers will take the step of crafting veterans' preference policies?

Ultimately, answering these questions will illuminate an important part of veterans' civilian lives. That is, when we think about the transition of veterans to the civilian sector, we often think about the employment transition. As this chapter indicates, an important part of the employment transition is veterans' preference. An immense number of veterans benefit from veterans' preference; thus, to understand veterans' employment transition involves an appreciation for veterans' preference, and future research would be well-served to continue illuminating that policy realm.

Notes

1. While past research claims that veterans' preference quite likely plays a role in driving veterans toward careers in government, it has not ruled out other mechanisms, such as the transferability of military skills and knowledge to the public

sector (Johnson 2015) or—as Jose Coll noted in his comments on this chapter—the fact that some government jurisdictions allow time in military service to accrue with civilian service for retirement purposes.

2. Some state laws stipulate that all lower levels of government, such as counties and municipalities, also must use the procedures that govern the application of veterans' preference in state-level public enterprises.

3. Long-standing debates have taken place, within the federal government as well as in some states, concerning *when* in the hiring process preference benefits should be applied. In some instances, officials have argued that preference benefits should be levied before entry exams or interviews are conducted, whereas others have asserted that preference benefits should be delivered immediately to ensure that preference-eligible candidates are not screened out of earlier rounds of personnel selection (see, e.g., Rowan 2011; Committee on Civil Service 1939).

4. Please note that a "hiring register" is simply a commonly employed synonym for a list of acceptable candidates from which to hire.

5. In fact, in Oregon administrative rules have altered not only the methods of implementing veterans' preference, but they have increased the scope of veterans' preference to include promotion. This extension, moreover, has occurred despite clear rules on how preference is to be administered (via a point system).

6. While any mistakes in the delivery of information about private-sector preference should be attributed to me, any accurate insights on that topic should be recognized as solely possible because of David H. Black's generous and thoughtful guidance.

7. Although the private-sector preference legislation extended the reach of veterans' preference, it does not represent the first time that U.S. laws have sought to promote private-sector veterans' preference. The first veterans' preference legislation at the federal level actually contained a provision encouraging private employers to preferentially hire military veterans (U.S. Revised Statute 1755), but this provision never held sway or offered employers in the private sector the same legal protections afforded by the new wave of private-sector statutes.

8. An interesting alternative hypothesis, raised by one of the editors of this volume, is that veterans might have limited experience negotiating a salary and labor contract, and this disadvantage shows up as a pay penalty once one controls for veteran status. Future research should examine that possibility.

References

Biro, Meghan B. 2012. "5 Reasons Leaders Hire Veterans." *Forbes*, November 4. Accessed May 27, 2016. http://www.forbes.com/sites/meghanbiro/2012/11/04/5-reasons-leaders-hire-veterans/.

Black, David H. 2010. "Permissive Veterans' Preference: A New Act to Permit Private Employers to Voluntarily Exercise a Preference for Veterans in Employment." *Veterans Today*, September 27. Accessed May 27, 2016. http://www.veteranstoday.com/downloads/BillDraftAppendices.pdf.

Bodenger, Robert G. 1971. *Soldiers' Bonuses: A History of Veterans' Benefits in the United States, 1776–1967.* Master's thesis, Pennsylvania State University.

Breyer, Adelbert John. 1920. "Veterans Preference for Civil Appointments." Master's thesis, University of Wisconsin, Madison.

Bureau of Labor Statistics (BLS). 2015. *Employment Situation of Veterans—2014.* Washington, DC: Department of Labor.

Campbell, Alan. 1977. *Statement Before the U.S. House of Representatives, Subcommittee on Civil Service of the Committee on Post Office and Civil Service, Veterans Preference Oversight Hearings.* Serial No. 95-43. 95th Cong. Washington, DC: Government Printing Office.

Civil Service Commission. 1955. *History of Veteran Preference in Federal Employment, 1865–1955.* Washington, DC: Government Printing Office.

Committee on the Civil Service. 1939. "Veteran Preference in Government Employment." *Hearing of the Committee on the Civil Service House of Representatives.* Washington, DC: U.S. Government Printing Office.

Continental Congress. 1776. *Journal of the Continental Congress, 1774–1789.* Vol. V, *1776.* Edited by W. C. Ford. Washington, DC: Government Printing Office.

Department of Labor. 2015. "Application of Veterans' Preference for Category Rating Jobs." Accessed May 27, 2016. http://www.dol.gov/oasam/doljobs/vetscategoryrating.htm.

DiPrete, Thomas A. 1987. "The Professionalization of Administration and Equal Employment Opportunity in the U.S. Federal Government." *American Journal of Sociology* 93: 119–40.

Dunlap, Thomas M. 2013. "ARSHRM Legislative Affairs Update—April 2013." Arkansas SHRM State Council, Inc. Accessed January 7, 2016. http://www.arshrm.com/arshrm-legislative-affairs-updateapril-2013_id219.html.

Emmert, Mark A., and Gregory B. Lewis. 1982. "Veterans Preference and the Merit System." In *Centenary Issues of the Pendleton Act of 1883*, edited by David H. Rosenbloom, 45–61. New York: Marcel Dekker, Inc.

Equal Employment Opportunity Commission. 1990. Notice No. N-915.056. Washington, DC: EEOC.

Equal Employment Opportunity Commission. 2009. "EEOC Compliance Manual, Section 2." Accessed January 7, 2016. http://www.eeoc.gov/policy/docs/threshold.html.

Fish, Carl Russell. 1905. *The Civil Service and the Patronage.* New York: Longmans, Green.

Fitzpatrick, John C. 1938. *The Writing of George Washington from the Original Manuscript Sources, 1745–1799,* 27:16–18. Washington, DC: Government Printing Office.

Foster, Gregory D. 1979. "The 1978 Civil Service Reform Act: Post-Mortem or Rebirth?" *Public Administration Review* 39 (1): 78–86.

Friedman, Brandon. 2013. "The Veterans' Jobless Crisis that Isn't." *Time*, March 12. Accessed January 7, 2016. http://nation.time.com/2013/03/12/the-veterans-jobless-crisis-that-isnt/.

Fruend, Rudolf. 1946. "Military Bounty Lands and the Origins of the Public Domain." *Agricultural History* 20 (January): 9–18.

Harrison, Benjamin. 1789. "To George Washington from Benjamin Harrison, 26 February 1789." In *The Papers of George Washington, Presidential Series*, Vol. 1, *24 September 1788–31 March 1789*, edited by Dorothy Twohig, 345–347. Charlottesville: University Press of Virginia. Accessed May 27, 2016. http://founders.archives.gov/documents/Washington/05-01-02-0256.

Hunt, Gaillard. 1896. "Office-Seeking During Washington's Administration." *America Historical Review* 1: 270–283.

Ingraham, Patricia Wallace. 1996. *The Foundations of Merit: Public Service in American Democracy*. Baltimore, MD: Johns Hopkins University Press.

Johnson, Tim. 2015. "Service after Serving: Does Veterans' Preference Diminish the Quality of the U.S. Federal Service?" *Journal of Public Administration Research and Theory* 25 (3): 669–696.

Johnson, Tim, and Robert W. Walker. n.d. "Veterans' Preference and Educational Qualifications." Working Paper.

Keeton, Kato B. 1994. "Women's Access to Federal Civil Service Management Positions: The Issue of Veterans' Preference." *Southeastern Political Review* 22 (1): 37–49.

Kleykamp, Meredith. 2009. "A Great Place to Start? The Effect of Prior Military Service on Hiring." *Armed Forces & Society* 35 (2): 266–285.

Lewis, Gregory B. 2013. "The Impact of Veterans' Preference on the Composition and Quality of the Federal Civil Service." *Journal of Public Administration Research and Theory* 23 (2): 247–65.

Lewis, Gregory B., and Mark A. Emmert. 1984. "Who Pays for Veterans' Preference?" *Administration & Society* 16 (3): 328–345.

Lewis, Gregory B., and Rahul Pathak. 2014. "The Employment of Veterans in State and Local Government Service." *State and Local Government Review* 46 (2): 91–105.

Mani, Bonnie G. 1999. "Challenges and Opportunities for Women to Advance in the Federal Civil Service: Veterans' Preference and Promotions." *Public Administration Review* 59 (6): 523–534.

Mani, Bonnie G. 2001. "Women in the Federal Civil Service: Career Advancement, Veterans' Preference, and Education." *American Review of Public Administration* 31 (3): 313–339.

Merit Systems Protection Board. 2014. *Veterans Hiring in the Civil Service: Practices and Perceptions*. Washington, DC: Merit Systems Protection Board.

Miller, John F. 1935. "Veteran Preference in the Public Service." In *Problems of the American Public Service*, edited by Carl Joachim Friedrich, William Carl Beyer, Sterling Denhard Spero, John Francis Miller, and George Adams Graham, 243–334. New York: McGraw-Hill.

National Archives and Record Administration. 1974. *Revolutionary War Pension and Bounty-Land-Warrant Application Files*. Washington, DC: NARA. Accessed May 27, 2016. http://www.archives.gov/research/microfilm/m804.pdf.

National Center for Veterans Analysis and Statistics. 2014. *Veterans Employment, 2000 to 2013*. Washington, DC: Department of Veterans Affairs.

Obama, Barack. 2010. "Presidential Memorandum—Improving the Federal Recruitment and Hiring Process." The White House, May 11. Accessed May 27, 2016. https://www.whitehouse.gov/the-pressoffice/presidential-memorandum-improving-federal-recruitment-and-hiring-process.

Office of Personnel Management. 2015a. "Veteran Services: VET GUIDE." Office of Personnel Management. Accessed January 7, 2016. https://www.opm.gov/policy-data-oversight/veteransservices/vet-guide/.

Office of Personnel Management. 2015b. "Documenting Veterans' Preference." In *Guide to Processing Personnel Actions*. Office of Personnel Management. Accessed May 27 2016. https://www.opm.gov/policy-data-oversight/data-analysis-documentation/personnel-documentation/processing-personnel-actions/gppa07.pdf.

Office of Personnel Management. n.d. "The President's Hiring Reform Initiative." Accessed May 27 2016. https://www.opm.gov/policy-data-oversight/human-capital-management/hiring-reform/reference/kick-off-presentation.pdf.

Oh, Seong Soo, and Gregory B. Lewis. 2013. "Performance Ratings and Career Advancement in the US Federal Civil Service." *Public Management Review* 15 (3): 740–761.

Ordway, Samuel H. 1945. "The Veteran in the Civil Service." *Annals of the American Academy of Political and Social Science* 238: 133–139.

Rowan, Dan. 2011. "A Salute to Veterans' Preference." *Local Focus* (November): 10–11. Accessed May 27, 2016. http://www.orcities.org/Portals/17/Publications/Newsletters/LF-Nov2011-FINAL.pdf.

Segal, David R., and Naomi Verdugo. 1994. "Demographic Trends and Personnel Policies as Determinants of the Racial Composition of the Volunteer Army." *Armed Forces & Society* 20 (4): 619–632.

State of North Carolina. 2007. "Chapter 128, Section 15: Veterans' Preference." In *State Human Resources Manual*. Raleigh: North Carolina Office of State Human Resources.

Sutton, Michael D. 2014. "Forging a New Breed: The Emergence of Veterans' Preference Statutes within the Private Sector." *Arkansas Law Review* 67: 1081–1109.

U.S. Senate. 1880. *Congressional Serial Set Reports of Committees: Proceedings of, and Testimony Before, the Committee on Civil Service and Retrenchment, United States Senate, in Relation to Alleged Violations in Rhode Island of Sections 1754 and 1755 of the Revised Statutes*. Washington, DC: Government Printing Office.

Walmart. 2015. "The Walmart Welcome Home Commitment." Accessed May 27, 2016. http://walmartcareerswithamission.com/why-walmart/veterans-welcome-home-commitment/.

Washington, George. 1789a. "George Washington to Mary Wooster, 21 May 1789." In *The Papers of George Washington, Presidential Series*, Vol. 2, *1 April 1789–15 June 1789*, edited by Dorothy Twohig, 361–362. Charlottesville: University Press of Virginia. Accessed May 27, 2016. http://founders.archives.gov/documents/Washington/05-02-02-0259.

Washington, George. 1789b. "George Washington to Benjamin Harrison, 9 March 1789." In *The Papers of George Washington, Presidential Series*, Vol. 2, *1 April 1789–15 June 1789*, edited by Dorothy Twohig, 375–377. Charlottesville: University Press of Virginia. Accessed May 27, 2016. http://founders.archives.gov/documents/Washington/05-01-02-0286.

White, Leonard D. 1948. *The Federalists: A Study in Administrative History*. New York: Macmillan.

CHAPTER THIRTEEN

The Retirement Patterns and Socioeconomic Status of Aging Veterans, 1995–2014

Christopher R. Tamborini, Patrick Purcell, and Anya Olsen

Introduction

This chapter examines trends in the relative socioeconomic status of aging veterans.[1] Using nationally representative data from the Current Population Survey from selected years from 1995 to 2014, we provide a demographic and economic portrait of older male veterans and nonveterans. To separate age and cohort effects, we stratify the analysis into three age groups: 55–61, 62–69, and 70 and older. Special attention is paid to veterans' labor and economic characteristics, including sources of income, reliance on Social Security benefits, and financial security. Together, the results document important changes in the older veteran population today in contrast to earlier periods and to nonveterans. Between 1995 and 2014, for example, male veterans aged 55–61 saw their labor force participation decline, family income fall, and poverty rates rise. These changes have arisen as veterans from the early part of the All-Volunteer Force (AVF) era have reached typical retirement ages.

Research on and policy interest in veterans and the effects of military service have grown dramatically over the past several decades. The extant literature has examined the possible role played by military service across an array of domains, such as health (Long, Polsky, and Metlay 2005; Teachman 2011; Wilmoth, London, and Heflin 2015b), the labor market (Angrist and Krueger 1994; Kleykamp 2013; Sampson and Laub 1996; Teachman and Tedrow 2004), and family (Teachman 2007b, 2008). Because much of the evidence has focused on working-age veterans, our understanding of the lives of older veterans remains limited (Wilmoth, London, and Heflin 2015a). This is surprising given the ongoing policy significance of older veterans' economic and social circumstances (Olsen and O'Leary 2011), coupled with the large size of veterans as a demographic group and the potential consequences of military service for later-life outcomes (MacLean and Elder 2007; Wilmoth and London 2011, 2013). One possibility is that individuals who served in the military have greater well-being in later life than nonveterans, possibly as a result of having dual entitlement to civilian and service-related benefits (Street and Hoffman 2013). Another possibility is that veterans face heightened vulnerabilities in later life, such as those stemming from poor health or labor market disruptions related to military service.

In this chapter we consider trends in the retirement patterns and socioeconomic status of U.S. veterans in later life, how they differ from nonveterans, and changes over the period 1995 to 2014. Drawing on nationally representative data from the Annual Social and Economic Supplement (ASEC) of the Census Bureau's Current Population Survey spanning the period from 1995 to 2014, our descriptive analysis examines a wide set of sociodemographic and economic measures. Special attention is paid to veterans' labor market and economic characteristics, including sources of income, reliance on Social Security, and financial security. To help disentangle age and cohort effects, we consider trends across three age groups that represent different stages of later life: 55–61, 62–69, and 70 and older. Because the older veteran population is overwhelmingly male, particularly in earlier service periods, our analysis focuses on men only.

The study's analysis extends the understanding of aging veterans (Street and Hoffman 2013; Wilmoth, London, and Heflin 2015a) by providing a sociodemographic and economic portrait of today's older male veterans in contrast to earlier periods and to older male nonveterans. Our results help identify important changes among the older male veteran population that play a role in their health and well-being, as well as their use of government programs. We find the strongest evidence of change in veterans' demographic traits and relative economic status among those currently nearing common retirement ages. These men served predominantly during the last years of the draft and the early part of the All-Volunteer Force (AVF) era. Understanding the scope of changes in the older veteran population may assist policy makers in considering the implications of taking different policy directions with regard to Social Security or veterans' programs (e.g., Government Accountability Office 2012). The results also highlight important life-course concepts related to the complex links between macro-historical context, earlier-life experiences, and late-life outcomes (Wilmoth and London 2013).

The Life Course of Veterans

Life-course perspectives offer a useful starting point for examining aging veterans. A central premise of a life-course approach is that earlier-life experiences shape individuals' life-course trajectories and later-life outcomes (Couch et al. 2013; Elder 1998). From this viewpoint, the relative status of aging veterans is seen as rooted in the accumulation of prior experiences, including those prior to military service, during military service, and in postservice civilian life (Wilmoth and London 2013). For some veterans, military service could represent a turning point that alters their life-course trajectories in ways that could benefit or harm their health, labor market opportunities, and economic status later in life (Sampson and Laub 1996; Wilmoth and London 2013).

Life-course concepts also focus on how historical context shapes individual trajectories (Tamborini, Couch, and Reznik 2015; Elder 1998). Historical forces have generated distinct periods of military service, which are associated with different types of individuals serving in the military, different military experiences, and whether service was primarily through conscription or was voluntary. Research has identified the historical context (i.e., period of service) as shaping a broad range of outcomes, including the age at service entry, the likelihood of seeing combat, and the effect of service on socioeconomic attainment (Teachman and Tedrow 2007; Teachman 2007a; Wilmoth and London 2013). Thus, we may expect that the socioeconomic status of aging veterans differs according to period of military service.

A number of other factors in early and midlife might underlie differences between older veteran and nonveteran populations. One dimension relates to socioeconomic attainment, which can have strong influences on late-life economic status. Some information can be gleaned from studies that have examined the effects of military service on labor market performance. Studies tend to show higher earnings among veterans of World War II and the Korean War than among nonveterans (MacLean and Elder 2007). These associations appear to be largely explained by selection into service during these eras based on health and education, rather than a positive effect of military service per se (Angrist and Krueger 1994; Teachman and Tedrow 2004). In contrast, military service has been associated with earnings disadvantages for men serving during the Vietnam War era. Angrist (1990) and Angrist, Chen, and Song (2011) indicate particularly sharp earnings losses in the later part of the 1970s and early 1980s for white men serving during the Vietnam era. However, among socially disadvantaged populations, such as African Americans and workers with limited skills, military service can act as a "bridging environment," leading to subsequent employment stability and improved economic well-being, including during the Vietnam and AVF eras (Kleykamp 2013; Sampson and Laub 1996; Teachman 2004; Teachman and Tedrow 2007).

Older veterans' economic status, as well as their early and midlife work trajectories, also depend on their prior educational attainment. Education has emerged as a key source of differences in economic status, including lifetime earnings and wealth (Tamborini, Kim, and Sakamoto 2015). Veterans' educational attainment when entering service, and how military service might have affected their subsequent schooling attainment, has implications for veterans' work trajectories, which in turn influence their circumstances in later life. Research has linked G.I. Bill benefits, which provided tuition and a monthly living allowance, with higher educational attainment among World War II veterans (Bound and Turner 2002; Stanley 2003). In contrast, individuals who served during the Vietnam and AVF eras had lower educational attainment than nonveterans (Teachman 2005, 2007b), although service-related educational benefits appear to have enhanced their schooling (Angrist 1993). Some evidence suggests that military service has a particularly positive effect on the human capital of men with a disadvantaged past (Teachman 2007a).

Health is also a powerful influence on later-life status. Considerable research has examined links between military service and health, as indicated by healthcare utilization (Long, Polsky, and Metlay 2005), receipt of Department of Veterans Affairs (VA) or Social Security Disability Insurance (SSDI) benefits (Wilmoth, London, and Heflin 2015b), military disability retirement (Niebuhr et al. 2011), later-life cognition (Brown, Wilmoth, and London 2014), mental health (Vogt et al. 2004), work limitations (Heflin, Wilmoth, and London 2012; Wilmoth, London, and Heflin 2015a), and self-assessed health (Teachman 2011). Much of the work in this area has found an association between military service and long-term health risks, particularly among those who experienced combat (Dobkin and Shabani 2009; MacLean and Elder 2007). Bedard and Deschênes (2006) found increased mortality among World War II and Korean War veterans, largely due to risky health behaviors (i.e., smoking) developed during years of service. Using the Health and Retirement Study (HRS), Wilmoth, London, and Parker (2010) found sharper age-related health declines after retirement age among veterans than nonveterans, especially among those serving during wartime. Among more recent military service periods, health impairment and problems such as substance abuse appear particularly acute among Vietnam veterans (Wilmoth and London 2011). Teachman (2011) found worse self-reported health among active-duty veterans from the AVF era at age 40 than among reserve-duty service members and nonveterans who had passed the military's physical entrance exam.

In addition, family patterns may shape veterans' retirement patterns and socioeconomic status in later life. Research tells us, for example, that marital history can have long-term impacts on men's health, as well as labor market outcomes (Couch, Tamborini, and Reznik 2015; Hughes and Waite 2009). A number of studies have linked military service with marriage and divorce outcomes. Research has shown a positive association between active-duty military service and the likelihood of first marriage (Teachman 2007b, 2009), and between military service and divorce among World War II veterans (Pavalko and Elder 1990). Teachman (2008) found a lower risk of divorce among black men serving in the U.S. Army. The extent to which these patterns shape veterans' work and health trajectories has relevance for their status later in life.

It is important to emphasize that observed differences between older veterans and men with no military experience could be driven, partly or entirely, by nonrandom selection into the military. Men who have military experience are not a random cross-section of the U.S. male population. Because the military rejects recruits who cannot pass the physical medical exam or the Armed Services Vocational Aptitude Battery (ASVAB, a timed, multiple-choice test that predicts occupational success in the military), selection bias affects any comparison of veterans with the general population. As an example, Angrist and Krueger (1994) showed that the earnings premium associated with military service in World War II was largely driven by nonrandom selection into service based on health and human capital characteristics rather than the effects of military service per se (see also Teachman and Tedrow 2004). Moreover, during the most recent AVF era, selection into the military also involved individual decisions, based on the weighing of personal costs and benefits of joining versus remaining in civilian life. Thus, differences between older veterans and nonveterans observed in this study should be viewed as highlighting the circumstances of veterans as a demographic group and changes in these circumstances over time, rather than as proof of a causal effect of military service on the outcomes examined. The latter would require accounting for selection into the military by using panel data in which individuals are followed over a long period of time.

In sum, events and experiences among veterans in early and midlife, including their background characteristics, period of military service, combat experience, education, marital status, and subsequent work trajectories, will affect veterans in their aging years. Once in their retirement years, veterans can also receive support from a variety of civilian and military-related government programs, which in turn may affect their economic status and other late-life outcomes. We summarize these below, in the context of the broader U.S. retirement system.

Veterans in Later Life, Retirement, and Military-Service-Related Programs

The economic status and retirement patterns of aging veterans are tied to the broader U.S. retirement system as well as to various veterans' programs. Retirement income in the United States is often thought of as a "three-legged stool" that is supported by Social Security, work-related pensions, and personal savings. Older veterans may depend on one or all of these sources in retirement, in addition to various pensions and programs associated with military service, which are further described below. Veterans may also depend on public assistance in their retirement years, based on their lack of retirement income from the "three-legged stool."

Like most Americans, the vast majority of veterans rely on Social Security income in retirement. Active-duty military service and active-duty training have been covered by the Social Security program since 1957. Individuals with at least 40 credits of earnings or 10 years of work in covered employment are entitled to Social Security retirement benefits starting at the earliest eligibility age, 62.[2] An individual earns one credit for every $1,220 in covered earnings up to a maximum of four credits per year. The amount of earnings needed for one credit is updated each year based on the average wage index. The size of Social Security's monthly cash payments is based on the highest 35 years of wage-indexed earnings, which include earnings during military service after 1956, and the age at which benefits are claimed.[3] Those who served between 1957 and 2001 also receive special credits (up to $1,200 a year) that augment the earnings used in computing their Social Security benefits.

Though their military service was not covered under Social Security, veterans who served between September 16, 1940, and December 31, 1956, may also receive special monthly military service credits. Military service credits, which were funded by the Department of Defense (DoD), were originally enacted because some military compensation, such as the value of food, shelter, and medical care, was not used in determining average earnings for computing Social Security benefits (Olsen and O'Leary 2011).

Veterans can receive Social Security retirement benefits and military retirement benefits (described below) simultaneously; they do not offset one another. Before age 62, veterans may be eligible for SSDI benefits if they are unable to work because they have a medical condition that is expected to last at least one year or to result in death.

In addition to Social Security, veterans may qualify for a range of government benefits and services related to military service. The military retirement system administered by the DoD provides retirement (and health) benefits to military retirees who remained on active duty or served in the Reserves or Guard for a sufficient period of time (usually a minimum of 20 years). Generally, a member of the military may be eligible for three types of nondisability retirement plans after 20 years of service, depending on when the veteran first entered active duty, his or her base pay at retirement, and years of service, among other factors.[4] A reserve retirement pension is also available for members who complete 20 qualifying years at age 60 or, in some instances, a lesser age. Retirement disability pensions may also be available for members who have been determined to be unfit for continued service and who have a disability rated by the military service as 30 percent or greater. Unlike Social Security retirement, members do not contribute a portion of their salary to help pay for military retirement benefits (which the vast majority of them never receive).

Veterans may also receive a range of benefits and services through the Department of Veterans Affairs (VA). Examples include education and training through the G.I. Bill or Reserve Educational Assistance Program (REAP), life insurance, home loans, veterans' compensation, and veterans' pensions. In contrast to DoD-based military pensions available to retired career members (i.e., those with at least 20 years on active duty), benefits provided by the VA extend to most veterans who served on active duty at some point in their lives. (Veterans can be denied benefits based on the type of their discharge from active duty, their length of service, or certain forms of involvement with the civilian criminal justice system.) Veterans' pensions are means-tested cash benefits for low-income aged or disabled veterans. These pensions are available from the VA for veterans with at least 90 days of active duty service, with at least one day during a wartime period. In addition, the veteran must be 65 years or older, or totally and permanently disabled, among other factors. The VA also provides veterans' compensation linked to service-related disability ratings. For those who qualify, monthly cash payments are provided in recognition of the effects of disabilities, diseases, or injuries incurred or aggravated during active duty military service. Unlike the VA's veteran pension program, veterans' compensation is not means-tested and provides cash benefits that increase based on the degree of the veteran's service-related disability, from 10 to 100 percent (for more information see Congressional Budget Office 2014; Department of Veterans Affairs 2014).

The availability and receipt of these government programs (civilian and military) shape veterans' economic status in later life and provide an additional layer of support to veterans (Wilmoth and London 2011). Prior work has indicated that career veterans have economic advantages in later life relative to noncareer veterans and nonveterans due to dual-entitlement to civilian (e.g., Social Security) and military pensions, as well as service-related health and other benefits (Street and Hoffman 2013). Against this background, this chapter examines trends in the retirement patterns and socioeconomic status of older American veterans.

Data and Methods

As mentioned previously, we analyze data from the ASEC of the Current Population Survey (CPS) from selected years between 1995 and 2014. The ASEC (i.e., the March CPS) is a nationally representative survey of around 75,000 households that provides information on demographic and economic characteristics of the resident civilian noninstitutionalized U.S. population, including earnings, labor force status, income sources, poverty, government program participation, and related variables.[5]

We use the 1995, 2005, and 2014 ASECs, which contain current-year demographic information and income information for the calendar year prior to the survey interview. Our analytical sample consists of men aged 55 or older. We divide the sample into veterans and nonveterans. A veteran is defined as an individual who reported previously serving on active duty in the U.S. armed forces. To help disentangle cohort and age effects, we provide estimates for three age groups within each selected year (55–61, 62–69, and 70 or older). We focus on men only because older veterans are much more likely to be men, and because we aim to compare older veterans across time. The number of women serving in the military has grown sharply since the AVF service era, particularly among the Gulf War–era cohorts and afterward (Olsen and O'Leary 2011).

We employ descriptive analysis to document trends in the status of aging veterans across several domains. The first area of interest contrasts the sociodemographic profiles of veterans and nonveterans. Sociodemographic indicators include period of military service, educational attainment, marital status, and race and ethnicity. We assigned the veteran's era of service according to the most recent period of active-duty service he reported on the CPS.[6]

The second domain of interest is the labor market. In particular, we assess indicators of respondents' employment status over the prior year, their main occupations, and industry. We also measure the prevalence of self-reported work-limiting disabilities, which are defined as a health problem or a disability that prevents work or limits the kind or amount of work.

The third area of interest explores income. We first examine individual sources and amounts of income, including earnings, Social Security, pensions (civilian and military), veteran benefits, and public assistance. Next we examine financial security by assessing family income relative to the federal poverty threshold. We also calculate Social Security reliance (total annual family Social Security income as a percentage of total annual family income) to gauge the respective role of Social Security in veterans' and nonveterans' household finances.

Note that all income is adjusted for inflation to 2013 dollars using the Consumer Price Index (CPI). The estimates reported here were weighted using the CPS survey weights to represent the population.[7]

Results

Sociodemographic and Educational Attainment Patterns

Tables 13.1a and 13.1b present estimates of the sociodemographic characteristics of older male veterans and nonveterans over the previous two decades across three age groups. In table 13.1a, the first row reveals a sharp decline in the proportion of men aged 55 to 61 who ever served on active duty in the armed forces. This decline coincided with the aging of men born between 1953 and 1959, few of whom were ever subject to the draft, which ended in 1973. In 1995, 49 percent of men aged 55 to 61 were veterans. These men were born between 1934 and 1940. The oldest reached age 18 in 1952, during the Korean War (1950–1953), and the youngest turned 18 in 1958. In the years 1952 to 1958, 1.7 million men were inducted into the armed forces via the draft.[8] In 2005, 41 percent of men aged 55 to 61 were veterans. These men were born between 1944 and 1950. The oldest reached age 18 in 1962, and the youngest turned 18 in 1968, during the war in Vietnam (1965–1975). In the years 1962 to 1968, 1.5 million men were drafted into the armed forces. In 2014, only 16 percent of men aged 55 to 61 were veterans. These men were born between 1953 and 1959. The oldest reached age 18 in 1971, and the youngest turned 18 in 1977. In the years 1971 to 1973, just 144,000 men were inducted into the armed forces, and none were drafted after 1973.

Alongside changes in the proportion of aging American men who are veterans, the data reveal shifts in the military service period represented by

Table 13.1a. Most Recent Military Service and Educational Attainment of Older Male Veterans and Nonveterans by Age, 1995–2014.

	1995						2005						2014					
	Veterans			Nonveterans			Veterans			Nonveterans			Veterans			Nonveterans		
	55–61	62–69	70 and older	55–61	62–69	70 and older	55–61	62–69	70 and older	55–61	62–69	70 and older	55–61	62–69	70 and older	55–61	62–69	70 and older
Share of age group (%)	49	65	59	51	35	41	41	43	64	59	57	36	16	36	51	84	64	49
Military service period (%)																		
1991–2014 (AVF)													16	5	1			
1976–1990 (AVF)							9						53	9	4			
1965–1975 (Vietnam)	16	5	1				91	36	3				32	84	23			
1956–1964 (Korea–Vietnam)	51	8	3			n/a		49	8			n/a		2	33			n/a
1950–1955 (Korean)	33	51	3					15	36						21			
Before 1950 (Includes WWII)	0	36	93						53						17			

Educational Attainment (%)																	
Did not finish high school	11	21	31	31	45	51	5	9	20	18	27	39	4	4	12	12	14	25
High school graduate	36	33	31	29	28	23	31	36	32	26	30	29	35	34	33	33	26	30
Some college	27	21	19	16	12	14	33	25	20	20	16	12	37	37	23	24	20	16
College graduate	26	24	19	24	15	12	30	30	27	35	27	19	24	25	32	31	40	29
Sample (N) Unweighted	1,944	2,705	2,919	2,093	1,462	2,085	2,702	2,115	3,775	3,965	2,835	2,205	863	1,670	2,271	4,592	2,966	2,388
Weighted (in thousands)	3,398	4,761	5,093	3,595	2,513	3,514	4,312	3,564	6,654	6,249	4,729	3,678	2,151	4,447	6,435	11,678	7,863	6,263

Source: March Supplement to the Current Population Survey. All data are weighted.
n/a = not applicable

Table 13.1b. Marital Status and Race/Ethnicity of Older Male Veterans and Nonveterans by Age, 1995–2014.

	1995 Veterans 55–61	1995 Veterans 62–69	1995 Veterans 70 and older	1995 Nonveterans 55–61	1995 Nonveterans 62–69	1995 Nonveterans 70 and older	2005 Veterans 55–61	2005 Veterans 62–69	2005 Veterans 70 and older	2005 Nonveterans 55–61	2005 Nonveterans 62–69	2005 Nonveterans 70 and older	2014 Veterans 55–61	2014 Veterans 62–69	2014 Veterans 70 and older	2014 Nonveterans 55–61	2014 Nonveterans 62–69	2014 Nonveterans 70 and older
Marital Status (%)																		
Married	81	81	77	79	77	70	78	80	73	73	77	69	63	75	71	70	73	74
Unmarried	19	19	23	21	23	30	22	20	27	27	23	31	37	25	29	30	27	26
Race-ethnicity (%)																		
White, non-Hisp.	90	90	91	75	71	80	86	87	91	72	73	71	70	83	88	74	72	71
Black, non-Hisp.	6	6	6	11	13	9	7	7	5	10	10	10	17	10	5	9	10	9
Hispanic	3	2	2	9	12	7	4	3	2	11	10	12	7	4	4	11	10	11
Other[a]	1	1	1	4	3	4	3	3	2	7	7	7	6	3	3	6	7	9

Source: March Supplement to the Current Population Survey. All data are weighted.
[a]"Other" consists mainly of persons of Asian or Native American heritage.

veterans. In 1995, the majority of older veterans had served in the Korean War or before 1950 (including World War II). By 2014, older veterans were more likely to have served during the Vietnam War and the AVF eras, particularly those aged 55 to 69. Among today's veterans 70 and older, the military service periods are more mixed. Naturally, as more recent cohorts age, the share of older veterans who served during the AVF era will continue to rise, which in turn has important implications for the socioeconomic status of older veterans.

Estimates of educational attainment are also summarized in table 13.1a. One noteworthy pattern is that older veterans today are more likely to have finished high school than in 1995 and also than nonveterans. This reflects, in part, the selective criteria of the military based on high school completion and the military's own aptitude tests. Importantly, the share of older veterans with at least a bachelor's degree showed substantial gains since 1995. Yet these gains lagged behind nonveterans over the same time period. In particular, among men aged 55 to 61, veterans were less likely to hold a bachelor's degree than nonveterans in 2014 (24 versus 31 percent) and in 2005 (30 versus 35 percent). In 2014, we also observe lower college attainment among male veterans aged 62 to 69 (25 percent had completed at least a bachelor's degree, compared to 40 percent of nonveterans). The story was much different in 1995. In that year, older veterans were more likely than, or just as likely as, nonveterans to hold at least a bachelor's degree across the age groups. This relative decline in older veterans' college attainment since 1995 compared with nonveterans highlights one pathway through which the aging of men from more recent military service periods (i.e., Vietnam and AVF eras) is changing the status of older veterans.

Marital status is also important for later-life well-being (Waite and Xu 2015), and table 13.1b reveals important changes in the marital status of older male veterans. Specifically, between 1995 and 2014, the proportion of veterans aged 55 to 61 who were unmarried increased from about 19 percent to 37 percent (compared with 21 percent to 30 percent among nonveterans). We also observe an increase in unmarried veterans in the two older age groups. This is a concern in part because poverty risk is higher among single older adults (Haveman et al. 2015; Tamborini 2007).

As for racial and ethnic patterns, table 13.1b reveals an increasingly diverse older veteran population. One notable pattern is the increase in the proportion of African American veterans. African Americans increased from 6 percent of veterans aged 55 to 61 in 1995 to 17 percent by 2014. Thus, although blacks were underrepresented among older veterans in earlier periods (relative to their share of the total population), they are

Table 13.2a. Labor Force Participation and Work-Limiting Disability among Older Male Veterans and Nonveterans by Age, 1995–2014.

	1995							2005							2014						
	Veterans			Nonveterans			Veterans			Nonveterans			Veterans			Nonveterans		
	55–61	62–69	70 and older	55–61	62–69	70 and older	55–61	62–69	70 and older	55–61	62–69	70 and older	55–61	62–69	70 and older	55–61	62–69	70 and older
Labor Force Participation (%)[a]
Year-round, Full-time	59	21	5	60	23	3	62	25	6	63	30	7	55	26	8	61	38	10
Year-round, Part-time	4	7	5	4	5	3	4	7	5	4	6	4	3	6	4	4	6	5
Part-year, Full-time	12	7	2	11	8	2	9	6	2	9	7	2	8	6	2	8	7	3
Part-year, Part-time	5	7	5	4	6	3	3	6	5	2	5	3	4	5	3	3	4	4
Did not work	20	58	83	22	58	88	23	55	83	22	52	84	30	57	83	24	46	78
Work-limiting Disability (%)	15	22	28	19	26	31	16	18	22	15	19	23	21	20	23	15	18	19

Source: March Supplement to the Current Population Survey. All data are weighted.
[a] Refers to employment in previous calendar year.

increasingly overrepresented. This is related to the aging of veterans from the AVF era. In addition, Hispanics increased their share of the older veteran population since 1995. This is related to the growth of Hispanics in the general U.S. population.

Labor Market Patterns

Labor market outcomes reflect another key domain of later life. One noteworthy pattern shown in table 13.2a is the decline in the labor market participation of older male veterans since 1995. Specifically, the percentage of veterans aged 55 to 61 years employed full-time, year-round fell from 59 percent in 1995 to 55 percent in 2014 (compared to 60 percent and 61 percent among nonveterans). Similarly, the percentage of veterans aged 55 to 61 who did not work in the past year was higher in 2014 (30 percent) than in 1995 (20 percent) and in 2005 (23 percent). By contrast, the percent who did not work at age 62 and older was about the same over the period.

Another important dimension is the incidence of work-limiting disabilities, and table 13.2a shows increasingly meaningful differences between older veterans and nonveterans in this outcome. In particular, among men aged 55 to 61 in 2014, a higher percentage of veterans reported a work-limiting disability (21 percent) compared with nonveterans (15 percent). This pattern diverges from past years, when older veterans had comparable or slightly favorable rates of work-limiting disabilities to those of nonveterans. Importantly, this pattern implies that veterans currently approaching typical retirement windows experience a higher prevalence of work limitations than previous cohorts at the same stage of life. The prevalence of work disability is likely to have critical implications for veterans' well-being and has been shown to be associated with a variety of material hardships (London, Heflin, and Wilmoth 2011).

Table 13.2b shows the occupational and industry profiles of older male veterans who were employed. Occupation and industry not only reflect the social context of work but also determine earnings and social standing. Our analysis shows many similarities in the occupational distributions of veterans and nonveterans. However, increasing divergence in the occupational experiences of veterans is evident in 2014. In particular, among employed men aged 55 to 61 years in 2014, a lower percentage of veterans held management and financial occupations (14 percent) than did nonveterans (21 percent). By contrast, in 1995 veterans of this age were more likely to hold management and financial occupations than were nonveterans. In addition, employed male veterans aged 55 to 61, particularly in

Table 13.2b. Occupation and Industry of Older Male Veterans and Nonveterans by Age, 1995–2014.

Occupation (% of employed sample)[a]	1995 Veterans 55–61	1995 Veterans 62–69	1995 Veterans 70 and older	1995 Nonveterans 55–61	1995 Nonveterans 62–69	1995 Nonveterans 70 and older	2005 Veterans 55–61	2005 Veterans 62–69	2005 Veterans 70 and older	2005 Nonveterans 55–61	2005 Nonveterans 62–69	2005 Nonveterans 70 and older	2014 Veterans 55–61	2014 Veterans 62–69	2014 Veterans 70 and older	2014 Nonveterans 55–61	2014 Nonveterans 62–69	2014 Nonveterans 70 and older
Management, business, and financial	20	16	16	17	14	16	20	21	23	20	20	25	14	23	25	21	22	23
Professional and related	5	6	5	6	4	4	7	5	4	7	6	2	7	7	6	7	8	4
Service	21	25	30	22	25	23	20	24	28	22	24	29	23	23	25	20	27	24
Sales and related	8	11	11	8	8	9	11	16	15	12	14	9	8	12	16	10	11	15
Office and administrative support	7	6	5	5	3	5	8	6	7	5	5	5	5	5	5	7	5	4
Farming, fishing, and forestry	4	7	10	6	10	20	1	1	1	1	2	2	0	1	1	1	1	2
Construction and extraction	6	5	4	6	7	2	8	6	4	8	8	5	9	5	4	10	6	5
Installation, maintenance, and repair	8	6	5	8	7	5	8	5	2	6	5	5	10	5	4	6	4	4
Production	10	7	6	12	9	8	9	6	3	10	8	5	8	7	3	8	6	6
Transportation and material moving	11	12	7	12	12	7	10	11	12	10	9	13	15	13	11	10	10	12

288

Industry (% of employed sample)[a]																					
Agriculture, forestry, fishing, mining	4	7	9	6	10	20	2	3	9	3	6	11	2	5	11	4	5	7
Construction	9	8	7	9	9	6	10	7	6	10	9	7	9	8	7	11	9	7
Manufacturing	15	9	5	15	10	8	17	12	9	17	14	10	17	11	9	18	12	10
Wholesale and Retail	8	6	2	10	7	5	13	18	19	14	16	18	9	15	17	12	14	16
Transportation and Utilities	11	7	4	9	7	1	11	8	5	8	7	4	13	9	6	9	7	4
Information	5	6	5	6	3	7	2	1	1	2	1	1	3	2	1	2	2	1
Financial activities	9	13	15	11	15	14	6	9	8	7	7	6	5	8	9	6	7	10
Professional and Business Services	6	8	7	5	6	9	11	12	15	11	10	10	11	14	11	13	12	15
Educational and Health Services	5	6	11	5	5	3	12	14	11	14	11	13	14	10	13	11	17	12
Leisure and Hospitality	2	4	3	2	2	3	3	4	5	5	6	8	4	5	6	5	5	7
Other Services	1	2	3	1	3	2	5	6	7	5	8	8	4	5	4	4	4	8
Public Administration	16	18	25	16	21	17	8	7	4	5	4	3	10	7	5	4	5	4
Armed Forces[b]	8	7	4	4	5	5	0	0	0	0	0	0	0	0	0	0	0	0

Source: March Supplement to the Current Population Survey. All data are weighted.
[a] Refers to employment in previous calendar year.
[b] Changes in distribution of "armed forces" from 1995 to 2014 reflects changes of industry classification from the standard industrial classification (SIC) to the North American Industrial Classifications System (NAICS).

2014, were more likely to be working in transportation and moving industries, as well as public administration, and less likely to work in manufacturing and wholesale trade.

Income Sources

Tables 13.3a and 13.3b look at several components of individual income and retirement benefits among older male veterans and nonveterans. In table 13.3a, the first set of rows shows the distribution of total individual income. In many cases, older men with military experience had modestly higher median individual income than nonveterans, such as those 70 years or older. The exception is veterans aged 55 to 61 in 2014, with modestly lower median individual income than nonveterans ($40,200 versus $44,000).

These data also reveal the extent to which veterans' own income comes from earnings. In 1995 and 2005, veterans were about as likely as, or more likely than, nonveterans to have earnings in their near retirement and retirement years. However, today's older veterans (aged 55 to 69) are less likely to derive income from paid work than are nonveterans. Specifically, a lower percentage of veterans aged 55 to 61 (70 percent) than nonveterans (76 percent) had labor income in 2014. In the same year, we also observe lower prevalence of labor income among veterans aged 62 to 69 (43 percent) than among nonveterans (54 percent).

Another critical source of income is Social Security. In general, older male veterans showed higher percentages with Social Security income than nonveterans. Veterans aged 55 to 61 saw gains in the share receiving Social Security income between 1995 and 2014 (7 percent to 12 percent, compared with 9 percent among nonveterans). Because Social Security retirement benefits cannot begin before age 62, most of these persons are Social Security disabled beneficiaries. Among veterans aged 62 to 69 in 2014, the data also reveal a higher prevalence of Social Security income (66 percent) compared with nonveterans (47 percent). This difference was narrower in 1995 and 2005. At this age range, higher percentages with Social Security income could imply that veterans increasingly choose to claim Social Security retirement benefits earlier than nonveterans and/or that receipt of disability benefits has increased at a faster rate among veterans between age 62 and their Social Security full retirement age than among nonveterans.

Table 13.3b contains information on employer-sponsored pensions, a key pillar of U.S. retirement income. Male veterans (aged 62 and older) generally had higher frequency of income from an employer-sponsored

Table 13.3a. Total Individual Income, Social Security, and Earnings among Older Male Veterans and Nonveterans by Age, 1995–2014.

	1995							2005							2014						
	Veterans			Nonveterans			Veterans			Nonveterans			Veterans			Nonveterans		
	55–61	62–69	70 and older	55–61	62–69	70 and older	55–61	62–69	70 and older	55–61	62–69	70 and older	55–61	62–69	70 and older	55–61	62–69	70 and older
Total individual income[a]																		
% with income	98	99	99	96	98	98	98	98	99	96	97	96	94	98	99	94	96	96
Median	51,134	32,860	25,141	43,584	24,091	19,010	54,252	38,789	26,641	49,320	32,446	19,279	40,200	38,459	28,369	44,000	36,000	23,799
75th percentile	81,115	55,718	40,463	77,028	40,834	29,348	83,228	65,731	45,372	49,320	59,184	33,016	68,000	61,736	48,899	75,723	65,202	43,016
25th percentile	26,526	19,620	16,998	20,829	13,074	12,722	29,696	21,282	17,261	24,660	16,295	12,689	19,259	22,892	18,563	22,343	19,000	15,184
Social Security[b]																		
% with income	7	73	93	9	68	92	9	70	92	9	61	87	12	66	90	9	47	85
Median	15,091	14,715	14,376	12,537	12,659	13,961	15,580	16,299	15,781	15,234	15,189	14,500	15,383	17,171	16,859	13,608	15,659	16,259
75th percentile	18,078	16,978	17,639	16,960	15,866	17,281	20,309	19,480	18,711	19,042	18,740	17,261	19,259	21,259	20,148	20,400	20,400	20,259
25th percentile	12,471	11,004	11,150	8,753	8,849	10,207	11,837	11,712	12,577	9,863	10,603	10,603	10,487	13,200	13,259	10,367	11,159	12,311
Earnings[c]																		
% with income	80	42	17	78	42	12	77	45	17	78	48	16	70	43	17	76	54	22
Median	50,304	27,510	13,079	47,160	24,759	12,563	55,485	37,423	16,646	50,553	36,990	18,495	48,000	41,600	26,700	50,000	42,000	28,000
75th percentile	78,600	62,880	36,156	78,600	50,304	31,440	83,844	70,281	46,854	86,310	66,588	49,320	70,000	65,000	63,000	80,000	76,200	60,000
25th percentile	26,724	9,432	4,716	25,152	9,432	3,144	30,825	14,796	6,165	28,852	15,413	7,398	28,300	16,000	10,000	28,000	20,800	11,500

Source: March Supplement to the Current Population Survey. All data are weighted.

Note: Income amounts are based on those with positive values. Amounts refer to previous calendar year and are indexed to 2013 dollars.

[a] Sum of individual's income from all sources in previous calendar year.
[b] Includes disabled worker, retired worker, spouse, and survivor benefits.
[c] Wages, salaries, and income from self-employment.

(nonmilitary) pension than nonveterans over the selected years, particularly in 1995 (46 percent of veterans aged 62 to 69 reported income from a civilian, job-related pension, compared with 30 percent of nonveterans). This later-life income advantage may have reflected the socioeconomic advantages of veterans from military service periods prior to the AVF and Vietnam eras.

Income sources especially relevant to older veterans are military pensions and veterans' benefits. A notable pattern shown in table 13.3b is that the overall percentage of older veterans receiving a military pension is actually quite low, due to the length of service requirement (20 years). Thus, around 5 percent of veterans (aged 55 or older) in 2014 received income from a military pension. Over the time examined, the prevalence was roughly similar, ranging from 3 to 8 percent across the different age groups. For those receiving military pensions, however, the typical annual amount (e.g., $20,000) was substantial and therefore likely plays a key role in improving the well-being and quality of life for those veterans receiving them.

Persons with any military service, as well as their spouses and widows, may also qualify for an array of other service-related benefits, such as means-tested veterans' compensation and veterans' pensions administered by the VA. The data show increasing receipt of these benefits since 1995. Among veterans in 2014, 13 percent aged 55 to 61, 18 percent aged 62 to 69, and 11 percent aged 70 and older received veterans' benefits of some type. In 1995 the respective rates were 6 percent, 8 percent, and 11 percent. This growth in the percentage receiving such benefits since 1995, especially among those aged 55 to 61, could be associated with the characteristics of recent cohorts of veterans, including their background (e.g., educational attainment) and military experiences (service period), or it could relate to changes to these programs over time, or both (Congressional Budget Office 2014). The typical annual amount of these benefits was fairly substantial. In 2014, the median amount was $6,000 for veteran beneficiaries 55 to 61 years old, $14,400 for those 62 to 69 years old, and around $11,000 for those 70 or older.

Table 13.3b also contains information on the prevalence of public assistance (e.g., Supplemental Security Income, Temporary Assistance for Needy Families, and other cash welfare). In earlier decades (1995 and 2005), smaller shares of older male veterans than nonveterans relied on public assistance income for near-retirement and retirement income. However, by 2014 about the same percent of veterans and nonveterans aged 55–61 relied on public assistance (4 percent).

Table 13.3b. Civilian and Military Pensions, Veterans' Benefits, and Public Assistance among Older Male Veterans and Nonveterans by Age, 1995–2014.

	1995							2005							2014						
	Veterans			Nonveterans			Veterans			Nonveterans			Veterans			Nonveterans		
	55–61	62–69	70 and older	55–61	62–69	70 and older	55–61	62–69	70 and older	55–61	62–69	70 and older	55–61	62–69	70 and older	55–61	62–69	70 and older
Civilian Pensions[a]																		
% with income	19	46	51	14	30	38	17	39	50	13	29	36	9	36	45	9	25	35
Median	22,788	15,091	12,104	21,128	12,865	7,546	23,674	18,184	14,796	24,660	18,495	11,097	20,520	16,800	14,400	26,379	19,128	14,400
75th percentile	37,728	28,296	23,580	34,747	22,712	15,902	40,881	29,634	28,112	40,689	32,058	23,674	31,788	30,000	27,600	38,400	31,500	26,400
25th percentile	9,432	7,300	5,282	10,187	6,917	3,773	10,653	9,055	6,412	10,712	8,313	4,439	11,500	8,000	6,108	9,408	7,400	6,000
Military Pensions[b]																		
% with income	8	5	4	1	n/a	n/a	3	6	3	1	n/a	n/a	6	5	4	1	n/a	n/a
Median	22,637	18,864	17,292				23,422	20,714	20,137				20,400	20,000	24,000			
75th percentile	33,955	27,126	39,520				34,031	27,126	38,223				32,400	38,400	36,000			
25th percentile	17,058	15,091	13,362				16,029	16,276	13,938				12,000	15,684	17,076			
Veterans' Benefits[c]																		
% with income	6	8	11	1	1	1	10	7	9	1	1	2	13	18	11	1	1	1
Median	7,357	3,999	3,131	12,576	3,961	3,131	12,413	9,764	5,976	16,126	6,805	5,917	6,000	14,400	10,920	10,800	7,200	14,160
75th percentile	15,720	12,576	7,546	14,903	11,318	7,602	31,070	20,713	14,795	35,509	17,754	13,315	14,364	33,384	24,000	15,840	29,280	29,280
25th percentile	1,572	1,641	1,585	1,415	1,572	1,377	3,032	3,313	2,218	3,685	4,438	1,597	2,400	5,280	3,360	4,960	1,560	3,600

(Continued)

Table 13.3b. Continued

	1995							2005							2014						
	Veterans			Nonveterans			Veterans			Nonveterans			Veterans			Nonveterans		
	55–61	62–69	70 and older	55–61	62–69	70 and older	55–61	62–69	70 and older	55–61	62–69	70 and older	55–61	62–69	70 and older	55–61	62–69	70 and older
Public Assistance[d]
% with income	1	1	1	4	6	6	3	2	1	4	4	5	4	1	1	4	4	4
Median	7,451	4,452	3,150	7,074	5,471	3,792	8,878	4,439	3,418	8,286	8,345	5,711	8,400	11,436	7,200	8,640	8,520	7,596
75th percentile	10,743	9,036	7,772	8,659	9,036	8,413	14,796	9,233	7,398	9,617	11,097	10,357	12,000	15,576	13,200	10,800	11,436	9,000
25th percentile	3,999	2,905	2,072	1,717	2,905	1,717	7,280	2,663	1,480	4,128	2,787	1,776	6,000	4,326	2,892	4,000	5,520	4,800

Source: March Supplement to the Current Population Survey. All data are weighted.
Note: Income amounts are based on those with positive values. Amounts refer to previous calendar year and are indexed to 2013 dollars.
[a] Private-sector, and public-sector pensions.
[b] Military retired pay and survivor pensions.
[c] Veterans' Compensation and Veterans' Pensions. Veterans' pensions are means-tested cash benefits for low-income aged or disabled veterans.
[d] Supplemental Security Income, Temporary Assistance for Needy Families and other cash welfare.

Financial Security and Reliance on Social Security

Table 13.4 explores trends in aging veterans' financial security using the family unit, rather than individual, as the primary level of analysis. One useful indicator is family income, measured as the annual income of all family members in the same household. Older male veterans had higher median family income than older male nonveterans in the earlier years examined in our study (1995 and 2005) across the three age groups (though the discrepancies were bigger at the older ages). However, the pattern among today's older veterans is more mixed. Among those 55 to 61 years old in 2014, median family income was lower among veterans ($62,000) than among nonveterans ($70,600) and compared to similarly aged veterans in 2005 ($80,000) and 1995 ($77,000). These patterns highlight a downward shift in the economic status of aging veterans, relative to earlier periods and to nonveterans.

Table 13.4 also presents family income in relation to official poverty thresholds, which helps capture the extent of material hardship in households (Haveman et al. 2015). Several patterns stand out. In most instances, older male veterans were better off than nonveterans. At advanced ages (70 or older), about 5 percent of veterans were classified as poor, compared with around 10 percent of nonveterans. Among those aged 62 to 69, veterans also had significantly lower poverty rates than nonveterans in all three of the selected years. Veterans aged 62 or older also were slightly less likely than nonveterans to be living in deep poverty (family income less than 50 percent of the official poverty threshold).

A striking exception is exhibited among male veterans aged 55 to 61 years. Among this group, poverty increased sharply, from around 7 percent in 1995 and 2005 to 14 percent in 2014. These veterans also were worse off than nonveterans, in that they had greater percentages living in deep poverty (6 percent versus 4 percent). This rise in material hardship is likely a consequence of changes in military service periods comprising the older veteran population, namely the aging of AVF-era veterans, who exhibit more disadvantaged characteristics than veterans from earlier military service periods. Recall that these veterans (aged 55 to 61 in 2014) had lower labor force participation, marriage rates, and college attainment, as well as higher prevalence of work-limiting disabilities, as shown in tables 13.1a, 13.1b, and 13.2a.

Table 13.4 also shows the respective role that Social Security plays in the financial status of older veterans and their families. Overall, Social Security represents a key source of income for older veterans and nonveterans alike. Generally, when all sources of family income are added together, the

Table 13.4. Family Income, Poverty, and Reliance on Social Security Income, Older Veterans and Nonveterans by Age, 1995–2014.

	1995 Veterans 55–61	62–69	70 and older	1995 Nonveterans 55–61	62–69	70 and older	2005 Veterans 55–61	62–69	70 and older	2005 Nonveterans 55–61	62–69	70 and older	2014 Veterans 55–61	62–69	70 and older	2014 Nonveterans 55–61	62–69	70 and older
Total Family Income (median)[a]	76,714	50,798	39,063	67,634	40,872	30,297	80,029	59,184	40,195	75,583	53,018	32,221	62,010	60,400	44,010	70,577	59,940	40,026
Poverty Rate (%)	7	6	5	11	12	11	7	6	4	9	9	12	14	5	5	11	9	9
Family Income Relative to Poverty Threshold (%)																		
300% or more	70	57	45	62	43	30	72	63	48	67	56	34	60	66	52	64	60	46
200% to 299%	14	20	26	14	20	26	12	17	24	13	16	22	13	15	21	13	15	20
150% to 199%	5	10	14	7	13	18	5	8	14	6	8	16	7	8	14	6	9	12
100% to 149%	5	7	10	6	12	15	4	6	10	5	10	15	6	6	8	6	8	13
50% to 99%	4	4	4	7	10	9	3	4	3	5	6	9	8	3	3	7	5	6
Less than 50%	3	2	1	4	2	2	3	2	1	4	4	3	6	2	2	4	4	3
Median Family Income Reliance on Social Security (%)[b]	22	38	52	27	43	67	23	37	55	30	39	66	38	36	55	35	41	61

Source: March Supplement to the Current Population Survey. All data are weighted.
Note: Income amounts are based on those with positive values. Amounts refer to previous calendar year and are indexed to 2013 dollars.
[a] Sum of income from all sources of all family members.
[b] Median reliance among individual families

typical veteran family (with a beneficiary) had slightly lower reliance on Social Security than nonveterans, but this difference has narrowed over time. For example, among men 70 or older in 2014, the typical veteran family with a beneficiary had about 55 percent of income from Social Security, compared with 61 percent among nonveterans (in 1995, these estimates were 52 percent and 67 percent, respectively). This narrowing of differences reflects, in part, changes across military service periods. For example, older veterans in 1995 were more likely to report income from an employer-sponsored pension. This would naturally reduce reliance on Social Security income in retirement.

Conclusion

The economic and social well-being of veterans has ongoing policy and scholarly significance. This is evident from the large investment of public resources in establishing and maintaining a system of benefits, including cash transfers, educational assistance, and health benefits for which only veterans are eligible. The changing demographic profile of veterans approaching retirement age has implications for their economic security in retirement, and these changes could result in a larger proportion of veterans making use of these services even as the overall number of living veterans declines.

In this chapter we used large, nationally representative data spanning the last 20 years to better understand key trends in the retirement patterns and socioeconomic status of aging veterans. Contrasting today's older male veterans with veterans of earlier periods and with nonveterans, our study helps clarify important continuities and also highlights changes in relevant sociodemographic, educational, and economic outcomes. We find that the aging of men who served during the AVF and the Vietnam War eras, particularly those currently nearing common retirement ages (i.e., aged 55 to 61 in 2014), have contributed the sharpest changes to the older veteran population. This pattern, we emphasize, has resulted in increasing heterogeneity in the older veteran population.

One important area of change revealed by our analysis relates to sociodemographic and educational characteristics. Older veterans are more likely to have a bachelor's degree today than they were 20 years ago, but their progress in college attainment fell short of the gains experienced by nonveterans over the same period. As a result, college attainment is now *less common* among veterans than nonveterans among older men aged 55 to 69. Our analysis also shows an increase in older veterans who were unmarried. In 2014, more than one in three veterans aged 55 to 61 was unmarried, a possible cause of concern given that marriage is positively associated with income and health in later life (Couch, Tamborini, and Reznik 2015; Hughes and Waite 2009; Umberson and Montez 2010). Another sociodemographic change highlighted by our estimates is the increase in African American and Hispanic older veterans.

The results also indicate declines in older veterans' labor force participation over the past two decades, particularly those aged 55 to 61 in 2014. These patterns could reflect the more disadvantaged backgrounds of men serving in the AVF and Vietnam eras relative to earlier military service periods. Another factor to consider is the higher prevalence of work-limiting disabilities among veterans aged 55–61 in 2014. Less paid work could also be a function of the availability of military and service-related pensions, in combination with Social Security retirement and disability benefits.

Our results also point to important income disparities between older veterans and nonveterans and across military service periods. One advantage of having veteran status in later life is potential access to military pensions, with an annual median value in our sample of around $20,000–$24,000. However, the percentage of older veterans receiving military pensions is relatively low, because most veterans served for less than the 20 years required to earn a DoD military pension. A larger share of older veterans, however, did receive benefits from the VA (i.e., veterans' compensation and veterans' pensions). Receipt of these benefits has increased among older veterans over time.

Despite access to these benefits, the results also highlight increasing economic disadvantages among older veterans, namely among those who served in the Vietnam era and earlier part of the AVF period (i.e., veterans aged 55 to 61 in 2014). This is evident in their lower individual median income relative to earlier periods and compared with similarly aged nonveterans. It is also evident in a higher incidence of receipt of Social Security prior to the retirement earliest eligibility age, which implies increasing use of Social Security disability benefits. Importantly, male veterans aged 55 to 61 saw their real family income fall and their poverty rates rise between 1995 and 2014. These patterns, particularly the increase in poverty, raise questions about the extent to which veterans currently approaching common retirement windows experience material hardship and other disadvantages relative to nonveterans.

In addition, our analysis highlights the crucial importance of Social Security for veterans and their families during a time of policy discussion about possible reforms to retirement and disability programs. For the typical male veteran 70 or older, Social Security makes up more than half of total family income. Moreover, as previously noted, an increasing share of veterans receive income from Social Security prior to age 62, likely related to disability benefits. Today's veterans aged 62 to 69 are also more likely than nonveterans of the same age to receive income from Social Security.

Several limitations of our study are important to mention. First, our analysis did not adjust for complex interactions and relationships among the variables examined. Further work using multivariate regression is needed. Second, we did not examine diversity within the aging veteran population. Grouping veterans together can conceal important differences within the veteran population, such as by race and ethnicity and by educational attainment. A third limitation is that our analysis sample was limited to men, because female representation among older veterans is quite low, particularly in earlier periods. The need to investigate the status of aging female veterans is increasingly important as more recent cohorts age into their retirement years.

In addition, we caution readers not to draw inferences about the causal impact of military service on later-life outcomes based on the descriptive analysis presented here. Examining the causal impact of military service on subsequent outcomes requires accounting for selectivity into military service, which can be more readily undertaken using panel data. Finally, our analysis does not capture the full range of indicators that has relevance for older veterans. The inclusion of measures related to wealth, retirement timing, and health, among other measures, would be valuable additions to this analysis. Further research is also needed to determine the types of service-connected compensation received by older veterans (e.g., veteran pension versus veteran compensation) and how these payments affect veterans' household finances. Despite these limitations, this study provides a valuable step in clarifying our understanding of trends in the retirement patterns and relative status of veterans in later life. The aging of men who served during the AVF period appears to be an important contributor to further changes on the horizon among the older veteran population.

Notes

1. This chapter was created by the authors as part of their duties as federal government employees. Thus, it is in the public domain and no copyright claim over it is made.

2. *Covered employment* refers to a job in which the employers and employees pay Social Security taxes on their earnings.

3. Although Social Security retired worker benefits are first available at age 62, benefits claimed before the full retirement age (FRA) are actuarially reduced. The FRA depends on year of birth. For persons born in 1937 or earlier, FRA was 65. For those born from 1943 to 1954, FRA is 66. For persons born in 1960 or

later, FRA will be 67. Benefits claimed after FRA are actuarially increased up to age 70.

4. These are Final Pay plan, High-36 Month Average plan, and Military Retirement Reform Act of 1986 (more commonly referred to as REDUX) plan.

5. Like all surveys, the CPS is subject to both sampling error and nonsampling error. Sampling error occurs if the sample selected to be interviewed is not representative of the population. Nonsampling error occurs when respondents answer questions incorrectly or when errors are introduced during the process of editing the data and imputing answers in cases of item nonresponse.

6. In both the March 2005 and March 2014 CPS, veterans could report more than one period of service. In the March 1995 CPS, only a single period of service is recorded for each veteran.

7. Estimates based on the CPS are subject to both sampling and nonsampling error. Caution is urged when interpreting small differences between estimates over time or between veteran and nonveteran populations.

8. For more information, see https://www.sss.gov/About/History-And-Records/Induction-Statistics.

References

Angrist, Joshua D. 1990. "Lifetime Earnings and the Vietnam Era Draft Lottery: Evidence from Social Security Administrative Records." *American Economic Review* 80: 313–336.

Angrist, Joshua D. 1993. "The Effect of Veterans Benefits on Education and Earnings." *Industrial and Labor Relations Review* 46: 637–652.

Angrist, Joshua D., Stacey H. Chen, and Jae Song. 2011. "Long-Term Consequences of Vietnam-era Conscription: New Estimates Using Social Security Data." *American Economic Review* 101: 334–338.

Angrist, Joshua D., and Alan B. Krueger. 1994. "Why Do World-War-II Veterans Earn More Than Nonveterans?" *Journal of Labor Economics* 12: 74–97.

Bedard, Kelly, and Olivier Deschênes. 2006. "The Long-term Impact of Military Service on Health: Evidence from World War II and Korean War Veterans." *American Economic Review* 96: 176–194.

Bound, John, and Sarah Turner. 2002. "Going to War and Going to College: Did World War II and the G.I. Bill Increase Educational Attainment for Returning Veterans?" *Journal of Labor Economics* 20: 784–815.

Brown, Maria T., Janet M. Wilmoth, and Andrew S. London. 2014. "Veteran Status and Men's Later-Life Cognitive Trajectories Evidence from the Health and Retirement Study." *Journal of Aging and Health* 26: 924–951.

Congressional Budget Office (CBO). 2014. "Veterans' Disability Compensation: Trends and Policy Options." Washington, DC: CBO. Accessed July 28, 2015. https://www.cbo.gov/sites/default/files/45615-VADisability_2.pdf.

Couch, Kenneth A., Christopher R. Tamborini, and Gayle Reznik. 2015. "The Long-Term Health Implications of Marital Disruption: Divorce, Work Limits, and Social Security Disability Benefits Among Men." *Demography* 52: 1487–1512.

Couch, Kenneth A., Christopher R. Tamborini, Gayle Reznik, and John W. R. Phillips. 2013. "Divorce, Women's Earnings and Retirement over the Life Course." In *Lifecycle Events and Their Consequences: Job Loss, Family Change, and Declines in Health*, edited by Kenneth A. Couch, Mary Daly, and Julie Zissimopoulos, 133–157. Stanford, CA: Stanford University Press.

Department of Veterans Affairs. 2014. *Federal Benefits for Veterans, Dependents and Survivors*. 2014 online ed. Washington, DC: Office of Public Affairs. Accessed July 28, 2015. http://www.va.gov/opa/publications/benefits_book.asp.

Dobkin, Carlos, and Reza Shabani. 2009. "The Health Effects of Military Service: Evidence from the Vietnam Draft." *Economic Inquiry* 47: 69–80.

Elder, Glen H. 1998. "The Life Course as Developmental Theory." *Child Development* 69: 1–12.

Government Accountability Office (GAO). 2012. *Veterans' Pension Benefits: Improvements Needed to Ensure only Qualified Veterans and Survivors Receive Benefits*. GAO 12-540. Washington, DC: U.S. Government Printing Office.

Haveman, Robert, Rebecca Blank, Robert Moffitt, Timothy Smeeding, and Geoffrey Wallace. 2015. "The War on Poverty: Measurement, Trends, and Policy." *Journal of Policy Analysis and Management* 34: 593–638.

Heflin, Colleen M., Janet M. Wilmoth, and Andrew S. London. 2012. "Veteran Status and Material Hardship: The Moderating Influence of Work-Limiting Disability." *Social Service Review* 86: 119–142.

Hughes, Mary Elizabeth, and Linda J. Waite. 2009. "Marital Biography and Health at Mid-Life." *Journal of Health and Social Behavior* 50: 344–358.

Kleykamp, Meredith. 2013. "Unemployment, Earnings and Enrollment among Post 9/11 Veterans." *Social Science Research* 42: 836–851.

London, Andrew S., Colleen M. Heflin, and Janet M. Wilmoth. 2011. "Work-Related Disability, Veteran Status, and Poverty: Implications for Family Well-Being." *Journal of Poverty* 15: 330–349.

Long, Judith A., Daniel Polsky, and Joshua P. Metlay. 2005. "Changes in Veterans' Use of Outpatient Care from 1992 to 2000." *American Journal of Public Health* 95: 2246–2251.

MacLean, Alair, and Glen H. Elder Jr. 2007. "Military Service in the Life Course." *Annual Review of Sociology* 33: 175–196.

Niebuhr, David W., Rebekah L. Krampf, Jonathan A. Mayo, Caitlin D. Blandford, Lynn I. Levin, and David N. Cowan. 2011. "Risk Factors for Disability Retirement among Healthy Adults Joining the U.S. Army." *Military Medicine* 176: 170–175.

Olsen, Anya, and Samantha O'Leary. 2011. "Military Veterans and Social Security: 2010 Update." *Social Security Bulletin* 71: 1–15.

Pavalko, Eliza K., and Glen H. Elder. 1990. "World War II and Divorce: A Life-Course Perspective." *American Journal of Sociology* 95: 1213–1234.

Sampson, Robert J., and John H. Laub. 1996. "Socioeconomic Achievement in the Life Course of Disadvantaged Men: Military Service as a Turning Point, Circa 1940–1965." *American Sociological Review* 61: 347–367.

Stanley, Marcus. 2003. "College Education and the Midcentury GI Bills." *Quarterly Journal of Economics* 118: 671–708.

Street, Debra, and Jessica Hoffman. 2013. "Military Service, Social Policy, and Later-life Financial and Health Security." In *Life Course Perspectives on Military Service*, edited by Janet M. Wilmoth and Andrew S. London, 221–242. New York: Routledge.

Tamborini, Christopher R. 2007. "Never-Married in Old Age: Projections and Concerns for the Near Future." *Social Security Bulletin* 67: 25–40.

Tamborini, Christopher R., Kenneth A. Couch, and Gayle L. Reznik. 2015. "Long-term Impact of Divorce on Women's Earnings across Multiple Divorce Windows: A Life Course Perspective." *Advances in Life Course Research* 26: 44–59. doi:10.1016/j.alcr.2015.06.001.

Tamborini, Christopher R., ChangHwan Kim, and Arthur Sakamoto. 2015. "Education and Lifetime Earnings in the United States." *Demography* 52: 1383–1407.

Teachman, Jay. 2004. "Military Service during the Vietnam Era: Were there Consequences for Subsequent Civilian Earnings?" *Social Forces* 83: 709–730.

Teachman, Jay. 2005. "Military Service in the Vietnam Era and Educational Attainment." *Sociology of Education* 78: 50–68.

Teachman, Jay. 2007a. "Military Service and Educational Attainment in the All-Volunteer Era." *Sociology of Education* 80: 359–74.

Teachman, Jay. 2007b. "Race, Military Service, and Marital Timing: Evidence from the NLSY-79." *Demography* 44: 389–404.

Teachman, Jay. 2008. "Divorce, Race, and Military Service: More than Equal Pay and Equal Opportunity." *Journal of Marriage and Family* 70: 1030–1044.

Teachman, Jay. 2009. "Military Service, Race, and the Transition to Marriage and Cohabition" *Journal of Family Issues* 30: 1433–1454.

Teachman, Jay. 2011. "Are Veterans Healthier? Military Service and Health at Age 40 in the All-Volunteer Era." *Social Science Research* 40: 326–335.

Teachman, Jay, and Lucky M. Tedrow. 2004. "Wages, Earnings, and Occupational Status: Did World War II Veterans Receive a Premium?" *Social Science Research* 33: 581–605.

Teachman, Jay, and Lucky M. Tedrow. 2007. "Joining Up: Did Military Service in the Early All Volunteer Era Affect Subsequent Civilian Income?" *Social Science Research* 36: 1447–1474.

Umberson, Debra, and Jennifer Karas Montez. 2010. "Social Relationships and Health: A Flashpoint for Health Policy." *Journal of Health and Social Behavior* 51: 54–66.

Vogt, Dawne S., Daniel W. King, Lynda A. King, Vincent W. Savarese, and Michael Suvak. 2004. "War-Zone Exposure and Long-Term General Life Adjustment Among Vietnam Veterans: Findings From Two Perspectives." *Journal of Applied Social Psychology* 34: 1797–1824.

Waite, Linda J., and Janet Xu. 2015. "Aging Policies for Traditional and Blended Families." *Public Policy & Aging Report* 25: 88–93.

Wilmoth, Janet M., and Andrew S. London. 2011. "Aging Veterans: Needs and Provisions." In *Handbook of Sociology of Aging*, edited by Richard A. Settersten, Jr. and Jacqueline L. Angel, 445–461. New York: Springer.

Wilmoth, Janet M., and Andrew S. London, eds. 2013. *Life Course Perspectives on Military Service*. New York: Routledge.

Wilmoth, Janet M., Andrew S. London, and Colleen M. Heflin. 2015a. "Economic Well-being among Older-Adult Households: Variation by Veteran and Disability Status." *Journal of Gerontological Social Work* 58: 399–419.

Wilmoth, Janet M., Andrew S. London, and Colleen M. Heflin. 2015b. "The Use of VA Disability Compensation and Social Security Disability Insurance among Working-Aged Veterans." *Disability and Health Journal* 8: 388–396.

Wilmoth, Janet M., Andrew S. London, and Wendy M. Parker. 2010. "Military Service and Men's Health Trajectories in Later Life." *Journal of Gerontology: Social Sciences* 56: 744–755.

CHAPTER FOURTEEN

Military Expatriates: U.S. Veterans Living Abroad

*Yvonne McNulty, Kelly L. Fisher,
Louis Hicks, and Tim Kane*

Introduction

As a young man, Warren Johnson was deployed to West Germany in the late 1960s as part of U.S. Army Europe (USAREUR), the main ground force bulwark against the USSR's Group Soviet Forces Germany (GSFG). He married his German sweetheart, Karin, in 1969 in Sycamore, Illinois. He attended college and graduate school thanks to the G.I. Bill. He and Karin returned to West Germany in 1974, and he taught college courses, mostly to American service members and their families, throughout Western Europe for 40 years. He still lives in Bavaria. Johnson is but one of the many thousands of U.S. service members whose military service overseas led them to become expatriate veterans.

American service members are sent all over the globe. This has been true certainly since the entry of the United States into World War II in 1941 (Gartner 2006, 82–119). Even before then, in the early part of the 20th century, significant numbers of U.S. service members were sent to such locations as the Philippines and the Dominican Republic (Chew 2014, 31). A surprising number of these veterans take up life as expatriates, some of them forever. How many of them are there? Where exactly are they living? What are they like? What challenges do they face? Why do they go abroad? Do they indeed go forever, or do they return? These are questions that have no readily available answers. In fact, we contend that veterans living abroad are an understudied population about which we know very little. Despite there being approximately 22 million U.S. veterans (National Center for Veterans Analysis and Statistics 2015), almost nothing is known about those who choose to live permanently or semipermanently outside the territory of the United States. They are left out of the surveys and studies that provide most of our information about U.S. veterans. Indeed, their absence sometimes isn't even noticed. When Westat (2010, 45) noted the major subgroups left out of its magisterial 2010 survey of veterans (e.g., homeless and institutionalized veterans), expatriate veterans were not mentioned. Many expatriate veterans are thought to be concentrated in or near locations where the U.S. military has had a long-term deployment and/or basing presence, notably Germany, Great Britain, the Philippines, Italy, Vietnam, Japan, Spain, and South Korea. They are thought to fall into clear categories of either having been stationed there while on active duty or having ties to a particular country that predates their U.S. military service. There is, however, no empirical research that systematically explores the locations of expatriate U.S. veterans.

Private military companies are particularly active in recruiting healthy ex-U.S. military personnel with backgrounds in strategic planning, intelligence, and logistics (see chapter 11, on veterans as private security contractors) to live and work abroad (see, for example, the numerous jobs available at DynCorp [2016]). Thus, nonretired expatriate veterans represent a potentially important but insufficiently tapped and underresearched component of the global talent agenda for these, and other, companies (Beechler and Woodward 2009; Findlay 2006; Tarique and Schuler 2010). While this gap in the literature may be explained by a lack of access to, or interest in, studying this unique cohort of veterans, we contend (based on anecdotal evidence) that a significant pool of veteran expatriates is already engaged in global mobility. Furthermore, for veterans who do engage in expatriation, a duty of care exists to ensure they are getting appropriate mental health screenings and other healthcare support. In addition, it is in the national security interest to track veterans who choose to sign up as mercenaries working for other countries.

In this chapter we provide a synthesis of what is known about U.S. veterans living abroad, with detailed information about their "lived experiences." Our aim is (1) to address the gap in research that has largely ignored this trajectory of military-influenced life courses, (2) to understand the unique needs of expatriate veterans and the factors that may lead to higher levels of successful living abroad, and (3) to propose a future research agenda to guide more scholarly work on this topic. We draw on data from a sample of 27 U.S. veterans who are living or have previously lived abroad, plus information from three expert commentators, and various secondary data sources. We address the following research questions:

1. How many U.S. veterans live abroad as expatriates, and where do they reside?
2. Why do U.S. veterans live abroad?
3. What factors influence U.S. veterans to remain abroad or return to the United States?
4. What interactions do expatriate veterans have with the U.S. Department of Veterans Affairs (VA)?

Our objective is not to reinvent theories about U.S. veterans that engage in global mobility (if there is such a theory). Rather, it is to use an empirical approach that explores the actual lived experiences of some U.S. veterans. When combined with others' perceptions, we can then explore the ways in which U.S. federal government policy and practice regarding this unique cohort of veterans can be enhanced.

The chapter begins by defining our unit of analysis, i.e., U.S. veterans living abroad and their characteristics. Next, we position our study within the broader context of demographic theory by providing a brief overview of the theory of human migration, particularly in the past half century. We then explain our methods, noting that the data we present for the remainder of the chapter are explained almost entirely through the methods we used to collect and interpret them. This is then followed by the findings of the study, which are presented in relation to the research questions. We conclude with a detailed discussion of the implications arising from our study, including directions for further study on U.S. veterans living abroad.

Characteristics of U.S. Veterans' Expatriation

Who Is a U.S. Expatriate Veteran?

By statute, a veteran is defined as a "person who served in the active military, naval, or air service, and who was discharged or released therefrom under conditions other than dishonorable" (Szymendera 2015). An expatriate is any individual who lives outside his or her home country and does not acquire citizenship of the host country or (in the case of dual citizenship) does not officially reside in the host country using a passport of that country (McNulty and Brewster forthcoming). An expatriate veteran is thus defined as a U.S. military veteran who chooses to live outside the states, territories, and possessions of the United States, and intends to continue residing outside the United States indefinitely (38 U.S.C. pt. 1, ch. 1, ¶ 101). This *excludes* U.S. veterans living, for example, in Puerto Rico and Guam, whose residency and employment are within (and not outside) the jurisdiction of the U.S. federal government. The definition we use is guided by the VA's web page "Veterans Living Abroad" (Department of Veterans Affairs 2015e), which describes expatriate U.S. veterans as including (1) people who spent a short period of time in the military and then went to work overseas for a military contractor and/or (2) immigrants who return "home" after their period of service. The definition encompasses those who relocate abroad permanently as well as those who do so temporarily.

Demographic Theory of Expatriate Veterans

Demographers have been intensely interested in human migration since the earliest days of the discipline (Demeny 1988; Greenhalgh 1996; Keyfitz 1993). Migration is one of the three fundamental processes of demographic change (the others being birth and death; Poston and Bouvier 2010; Skeldon 2013). A general theory of migration decision making holds that potential migrants weigh push and pull factors for their current and their potential homes (De Jong 2000; De Jong and Gardner 1981). To this basic structure of pluses and minuses is added consideration of intervening obstacles, such as immigration laws, and personal factors, such as being married or having children (Daugherty and Kammeyer 1995). The situation of deployed military personnel is a curious one from the standpoint of demographic theory. First, they are not, in general, voluntary migrants to the theater of operations in which they find themselves. Second, having arrived in a country strange to them, the cognitive availability of an alternative home is suddenly and dramatically increased. That is to say, they aren't reading about different countries or seeing different countries on television—they are actually living there, sometimes for years. In the sections below, we generally interpret our findings about U.S. expatriate veterans in terms of these standard demographic ideas about push and pull factors, obstacles, and personal situations.

Military Deployments, 1950–2015

The deployment of U.S. armed forces over, under, and around the globe during the past 65 years is the greatest organized dispersal and recall of human beings ever in history. No empire of the past—and no other organization in the present—has deployed its people in such large numbers and in so many places. When space exploration is included—all but 1 of the 24 people who have ever ventured beyond low Earth orbit were U.S. military personnel or veterans (National Aeronautics and Space Administration 2016)—the volume of space within which the U.S. military has deployed people is thousands of times larger than the volume of space within which all other human associations have operated.

It is possible to think of the American military establishment over time as consisting of "billets," where a "billet" is one service member for one year. There have been a total of 139,729,204 person-years of U.S. military personnel on active duty from 1950 to 2015. Of these person-years, 32,572,505 were deployed outside of the United States. Put another way, on average, 23 percent of all U.S. service members were stationed on foreign soil during the period from 1950 to 2015. In 2015, 16 percent of U.S. service members were deployed, which is near the low points in the post–Cold War era. The low point in percentage terms was 14 percent in 1995, with the high points being about 32 percent in 1951 and 31 percent in 1968 (for details, see Kane 2016).

American military personnel have been deployed to 203 countries since 1950. The country that received the most person-years of deployment was (West) Germany, with a total of 11.2 million. Several countries received only a handful. The distribution of these countries according to the total number of deployed person-years is shown in table 14.1. The distribution of American military personnel fluctuated throughout the post–World War II era, as can be seen in tables 14.2, 14.3, and 14.4.

The propensity of U.S. veterans to live abroad could be explained by the frequency with which U.S. military personnel are stationed around the world, including conflicts in World War II and the Korean, Vietnam, and Persian Gulf Wars (Department of Veterans Affairs 2015e). World War II (WWII) was the most widespread war in history, with more than 8.91 million U.S. military personnel serving abroad (Department of Veteran Affairs 2015e). Approximately 5.7 million personnel served in the Korean War conflict from 1950 to 1955, while approximately 2.7 million American men and women served in Vietnam. The Persian Gulf War (1990–1991) saw an estimated 694,550 U.S. service members deployed to the theater of operations there. The number of U.S. military service members deployed abroad during the more than 10 years since the Global War on Terror (GWOT) began now exceeds 2 million (White House 2011). In 2015 there were just over 200,000 U.S soldiers, sailors, airmen, and marines deployed worldwide (Kane 2016).

Various parts of the U.S. armed services—U.S. Army, U.S. Air Force, U.S. Navy, U.S. Marine Corps, the National Guard and Reserve, and the

Table 14.1. Total Deployment of U.S. Military Personnel in Person-Years (Billets), 1950–2015, in 20 Largest Receiving Countries.

Country	Total Billets 1950–2015
Germany	11,208,999
Japan	4,526,509
South Korea	3,786,510
Vietnam	2,636,655
United Kingdom	1,427,354
Iraq	1,341,736
Italy	744,019
Afghanistan	738,071
France	686,060
Philippines	685,949
Panama	485,752
Kuwait	463,671
Spain	390,914
Thailand	383,096
Turkey	315,604
Canada	257,327
Qatar	193,848
Cuba/Guantanamo	183,500
Iceland	160,411
Taiwan	152,365

Source: Author (Kane) calculations from quarterly reports by the Defense Manpower Data Center.

Table 14.2. U.S. Military Deployed Personnel by 20 Largest Receiving Countries, Cold War Era, 1950–1989.

1950–1989	Annual Average	Percent of All Deployed Personnel
Germany	232,678	38.1
Japan	86,737	14.2
South Korea	73,348	12.0
Vietnam	65,909	10.8
United Kingdom	27,882	4.6
France	17,107	2.8
Philippines	16,226	2.7
Italy	11,350	1.9

Panama	10,228	1.7
Thailand	9,476	1.6
Spain	8,116	1.3
Canada	6,293	1.0
Turkey	6,125	1.0
Taiwan	3,808	0.6
Morocco	3,698	0.6
Cuba / Guantanamo	3,663	0.6
Greece	3,316	0.5
Iceland	3,167	0.5
Greenland	2,296	0.4
Bermuda	2,222	0.4

Source: Author (Kane) calculations from quarterly reports by the Defense Manpower Data Center.

Table 14.3. U.S. Military Deployed Personnel by 20 Largest Receiving Countries, Gulf War I Era, 1990–2001.

1990–2001	Annual Average	Percent of All Deployed Personnel
Germany	101,360	38.9
Japan	42,755	16.4
South Korea	36,997	14.2
United Kingdom	14,804	5.7
Italy	12,162	4.7
Saudi Arabia	6,491	2.5
Panama	6,366	2.4
Bosnia and Herzegovina	3,727	1.4
Turkey	3,613	1.4
Spain	3,507	1.3
Kuwait	2,303	0.9
Iceland	2,283	0.9
Cuba / Guantanamo	2,103	0.8
Philippines	2,030	0.8
Belgium	1,810	0.7
Afghanistan	1,749	0.7
Haiti	1,677	0.6
Serbia and Montenegro	1,466	0.6
Egypt	1,345	0.5
Netherlands	1,304	0.5

Source: Author (Kane) calculations from quarterly reports by the Defense Manpower Data Center.

Table 14.4. U.S. Military Deployed Personnel by 20 Largest Receiving Countries, Post-9/11 Era, 2002–2015.

2002–2015	Annual Average	Percent of All Deployed Personnel
Iraq	95,803	26.7
Afghanistan	51,184	14.3
Germany	48,970	13.6
Japan	38,856	10.8
Kuwait	31,123	8.7
South Korea	29,188	8.1
Qatar	13,816	3.8
Italy	10,290	2.9
United Kingdom	9,601	2.7
Bahrein / Bahrain	5,083	1.4
Kyrgyzstan	2,756	0.8
United Arab Emirates	2,529	0.7
Djibouti	2,143	0.6
Turkey	1,948	0.5
Spain	1,727	0.5
Belgium	1,303	0.4
Saudi Arabia	1,171	0.3
Philippines	896	0.2
Cuba / Guantanamo	839	0.2
Serbia and Montenegro	773	0.2

Source: Author (Kane) calculations from quarterly reports by the Defense Manpower Data Center.

Coast Guard—have their own policies regarding the frequency and length of the rotation and assignment of their members between overseas and the continental United States (Groysberg, Hill, and Johnson 2010; Office of the Deputy Chief of Staff 2010). These policies and practices have fluctuated dramatically since the end of World War II.

Deployment and Expatriate Veterans

It is widely thought that a large proportion of expatriate U.S. veterans choose to live abroad after living in a foreign country where they were stationed while on active duty. This suggests that military deployments may affect veterans' decision to expatriate. Tharenou (2013) describes organizationally assigned expatriates as those individuals tasked by their employing organizations to work and live for a fixed period in a country of the organization's choosing. As so defined, "military expatriates" are a type of organizationally assigned employee, similar to the thousands of Americans sent abroad by corporations such as General Motors and Hershey Foods.

When military expatriates return to the United States after deployment abroad, they may be drawn to expatriate again, as veterans, under many conditions. First, they can find civilian employment in a business or country they came to know in the service and thus engage in organizationally assigned expatriation once more. Second, they can self-initiate their expatriation abroad without the promise of employment and find a job once there of their own volition. This may be especially suited to veterans with preexisting ties to another country, such as Mexican immigrants who serve in the U.S. military and then eventually return to Mexico, or defectors. Third, they may decide that their retirement dollars will go further in a foreign country, which may or may not be a country to which they had been deployed. Finally, while personal ties formed during deployment may be the basis for remaining in or returning to the country or region of past deployment, the reality is that many possibilities exist as reasons for veterans to expatriate, including marrying abroad and returning to their partner's homeland after retirement or discharge.

Military veterans of the United States can be found in many countries of the world. Many groups of expatriate veterans are a legacy of deployments in various parts of the world. Others are veterans returning to countries where they had ties before joining the U.S. military. Human beings are socially sticky; that is, they form attachments to people, places, and things. When millions of veterans are sent all around the world, some of them stick. They may come back to the United States after their deployment, but then the attachment takes over and they go back. Alternatively, some expatriate veterans will never have been deployed outside the United States; they perhaps simply decided that their military retirement dollars or VA disability compensation would afford them a much better lifestyle in some foreign land. The two reasons may also overlap: a formerly deployed service member who moves back to a foreign country to live may share his or her satisfaction with former military friends, who sell everything and move overseas as a result.

Method

As this is an underresearched topic about which little (if anything) is known, we use primary and secondary data to address our research questions. Our overall research design utilizes a qualitative, inductive approach to draw on U.S. veterans' lived experiences as expatriates. Marshall and

Rossman (2006) assert that when a topic is underresearched (such as the current one), and the researcher is not fully aware of the details of the phenomenon under investigation, qualitative research is often a better choice when new theoretical perspectives are required. Qualitative research may therefore uncover as yet unspecified or undiscovered variables. In other words, because so little is known about expatriate veterans, this study raises more questions than it answers.

Primary Data

Primary data were obtained using a qualitative approach to explore the research questions through "vignettes." Our approach is justifiable on several grounds. First, it addresses the need for more research of understudied expatriate populations (e.g., Fee and Gray 2011; McNulty 2015; McPhail and McNulty 2015; Wilkinson and Singh 2010), including those in military communities (e.g., Fisher and Hutchings 2013; Fisher, Hutchings, and Pinto 2015; Fisher 2016). Second, the growing number of veterans who choose to expatriate requires a greater degree of understanding about their motivations for doing so and the challenges they face in accessing VA benefits from abroad, if they choose to use VA benefits at all. Thus, laws pertaining to VA benefits in the overseas locations where veterans live require more detailed analysis than questionnaires or surveys alone can provide. The case study method allows us to explore the lived experiences in relation to these challenges in detail and facilitates access to information that heretofore has been difficult to obtain and publish. While we acknowledge our method is not a typical case approach, in that we did not focus on one particular case, but instead on 27 lived experiences, each with different military backgrounds, industries, sectors, ranks, and host countries, our approach is valuable because it allows us to distill themes emerging across all of the cases into the three case studies that best exemplify issues that are common to all 27 U.S. veterans' stories, taking into account additional perspectives expressed by the three expert commentators. A third justification is that case studies are sufficiently flexible to allow for iterative inquiry to occur (Eisenhardt 1989), from which theory can eventually be developed in future studies of expatriate veterans. The study was approved by the Institutional Review Board of St. Mary's College of Maryland on July 9, 2015.

We collected information from three expert commentators familiar with the topic of U.S. veterans living abroad (see table 14.5) and 27 male expatriates who identify as U.S. veterans who are currently living abroad, of which 26 were surveyed, 1 participated in an interview only, and 5 completed both the survey and an interview (see table 14.6). In-depth interviews allowed for core themes to be explored, with enough flexibility to give participants an opportunity to identify issues that they considered important and to elaborate on critical incidents (Creswell and Clark 2007). The participants had a range of occupational backgrounds, including being fully retired. We note that differences in participants' age, current employment status, rank at time of discharge, and length of service impact the diversity of the findings and need to be considered in each participant's responses.

Semistructured interviews with nine of the respondents (three expert commentators and six U.S. veterans living abroad) were conducted over a five-month period between August and December 2015. Two interviews were conducted by e-mail, while the other seven were conducted using a combination of e-mail, Skype, and telephone. There were 26 online survey respondents who participated over the same period. Interview and survey questions were identical, to allow for thematic analysis and core themes to emerge, with enough flexibility to allow participants to identify issues that they considered important and to elaborate on critical incidents (i.e., by asking respondents to either "tell me more" or by inserting in the online survey a "further comments" section after key questions; Creswell and Clark 2007).

Using a theoretical sampling approach (Creswell 2003), the nine interview participants were personally invited to join the study, having been identified as an expatriate veteran or expert commentator through the authors' personal networks. The 26 survey respondents were sourced using a combination of personal networks, social media, and snowball sampling approaches (i.e., via participants who contacted other U.S. veteran expatriates in their network to suggest they also participate; Marshall and Rossman 2006). Once we had developed the survey instrument using the same questions used in the interviews, we created a questionnaire using online survey software (at https://surveymonkey.com) and placed a link online

Table 14.5. Sample Characteristics of Expert Commentators.

Name	Position	Location	Type of Interview
	Expert Commentators (n = 3)		
1 Nissa Rhee	Journalist	Vietnam	Phone
2 Mark Leach	Sociologist with Census Bureau	Washington, DC	E-mail
3 Dawn McCarty	RSO	Benelux	E-mail

Table 14.6. Characteristics of Participants (n = 30).

U.S. Veterans Living Abroad (Interviews and Online Survey)

Number	Name	Gender	Age	Marital Status	Child(ren)	Living where	Branch	Employed / Retired	Rank	Race	Countries Lived in (Other Than USA)
1	Adam	M	30	Married	0	UK	Marines 2002–06	FT Employed	E1-E9	Caucasian	UK
2	Milt	M	40	Married	3	Philippines	Marines 1992–96	FT Employed	E1-E9	Caucasian / Indian	Philippines
3	Nick	M	50	Married	3	Thailand	Air Force 1985–93	Retired	E1-E9	Caucasian	Thailand, Panama, Philippines
4	Jeb	M	50	Married	0	Belgium	Army 1983–11	Retired	E1-E9	Caucasian	Belgium, South Korea, Germany
5	Joey	M	50	Married	3	Italy	Navy 1985–11	FT Employed	E1-E9	Caucasian	Italy, Belgium, Malaysia, Yemen, South Africa
6	Tyron	M	50	Married	1	Germany	Air Force 1975–97	Retired	E1-E9	Caucasian	Germany, Turkey, South Korea, Saudi Arabia
7	Scott	M	50	Married	1	Belgium	Army 1982–05	FT Employed	E1-E9	African American	Belgium, Germany
8	Aron	M	60	Married	4	Belgium	Army 1970–90	Retired	E1-E9	Asian	Belgium, Netherlands
9	James	M	70	Married	2	Belgium	Air Force 1960–62	Retired	O1-O10	Caucasian	Belgium
10	Fred	M	70	Married	0	Belgium	Army 1962–82	Retired	E1-E9	Caucasian	Belgium, Austria, Germany, Japan, Korea, Vietnam
11	Felix	M	70	Married	2	Ireland	Navy 1960–64	Retired	E1-E9	Caucasian	Ireland, England
12	Sly	M	40	Married	3	Ireland	Navy 1988–92	PT Employed	E1-E9	Caucasian	Ireland
13	Eddy	M	40	Defacto	2	Mexico	Army 1984–97	VA Disabled	E1-E9	Caucasian	Mexico, Honduras, Costa Rica
14	Derek	M	60	Married	2	Mexico	Navy 1967–71	Retired	E1-E9	Caucasian	Mexico
15	David	M	70	Re-married	2	Mexico	Navy 1960–63	Retired	E1-E9	Caucasian	Mexico

16	Lyle	M	60	Married	4	Mexico	Army 1965–68	Retired	E1-E9	Caucasian	Mexico
17	Abe	M	70	Married	2	Mexico	Air Force 1966–86	Retired	E1-E9	Caucasian	Belize, Mexico
18	Ringo	M	70	Married	0	Mexico	Army 1966–68	Retired	E1-E9	Caucasian	Mexico
19	Philip	M	70	Unknown	Unknown	Mexico	Army 1965–80	Retired	Unknown	Caucasian	Mexico
20	Arup	M	50	Married	1	Germany	Army 1977–80	FT Employed	E1-E9	Caucasian	Germany
21	Fritz	M	50	Married	2	Germany	Army 1982–86	Self-employed	E1-E9	Caucasian	Germany
22	Kevin	M	70	Widower	1	Germany	Army 1954–80	Retired	E1-E9	Caucasian	Germany, Vietnam
23	Giles	M	60	Separated	2	Vietnam	Marines 1966–68	Retired	E1-E9	Caucasian	Vietnam
24	Bob	M	50	Divorced	0	Switzerland	Navy 1983–96	FT Employed	O1-O10	Caucasian	Switzerland
25	Roy	M	60	Married	1	Vietnam	Marines 1968–72	Self-employed	E1-E9	Caucasian	Germany, Vietnam
26	Tim	M	60	Divorced	0	Cambodia	Army 1967–69	Retired	E1-E9	Caucasian	Vietnam, Cambodia
27	Greg	M	70	Married	0	USA	Unknown	Retired	Unknown	Caucasian	Latin America, SE Asia

at http://expatresearch.com. We then posted an invitation on Facebook, LinkedIn, and Google Plus to source participants and used memberships in military Web sites and associations (e.g., https://facebook.com/VFW Fans, https://facebook.com/ALDeptFrance, http://americanlegion-ireland.com) to make contact with U.S. veterans living abroad. This included liaising with local Veterans of Foreign Wars (VFW), American Legion, and Disabled American Veteran associations in select cities/countries via national chapters; sending out e-mails to United Services Organizations (USOs) to solicit information and to promote the study; connecting in person with veterans during trips abroad by the authors themselves; and inviting the survey participants to be interviewed. As a result, 30 respondents (27 + 3) were recruited in total. Using a "small-N" case study approach (see Blatter and Haverland 2012), 3 of the 27 U.S. veterans' stories are reported here in richly detailed vignettes as best representing the lived experiences of the broader cohort of expatriate veterans. We further elaborate key findings by using quotes from the remaining participants.

Estimates of the size of the U.S. veteran expatriate population vary so widely that it is not reasonable for us to determine a sampling rate. We consider our sample of 27 U.S. veterans and 3 expert commentators (N = 30) to be a good result of our sample-gathering efforts, with the online survey facilitating anonymity for those who felt uncomfortable with being identified. Expatriate veterans in this study comprise those who are currently company-assigned as well as self-initiated. While women were not intentionally excluded as respondents, only men were included as participants, because only they volunteered to take part in the study.

Questions asked during the interviews were developed from a number of prior studies on expatriates in general (e.g., Haslberger and Brewster 2009; Haslberger and Vaiman 2013; Hippler 2009; Vance and McNulty 2014), as well drawing on the second author's expertise as a retired military expatriate. An interview guide was subsequently developed and pilot tested with a former military expatriate who had repatriated back to the United States. We adopted Yin's (2003) advice to use multiple case studies to uncover what is common among respondents but also what is unique in certain contexts (e.g., by industry, branch, or ethnicity). Each participant was advised that the research was conducted in accordance with approved ethical protocols, that participation was voluntary, and that all responses would be treated in confidence, with anonymity assured by pseudonyms to be utilized in any published research.

Interviews ranged from one to two hours in length and were recorded and transcribed. Surveys and interview transcripts were then manually coded using computer-aided qualitative analysis software. Hierarchical categories were used to reduce, sort, and cluster the data and derive key themes (Denzin and Lincoln 2000), as well as content analysis to determine how strongly the themes are manifested (Miles and Huberman 1994). Although participants provided a single-rater response, they can be viewed as expert informants.

Secondary Data

Secondary data were drawn from a number of sources via e-mail, phone, and/or social media (Facebook, LinkedIn); print material; and online databases, and included the following:

1. The National Center for Veterans Analysis and Statistics (NCVAS), whose mission is to act as the "authoritative clearinghouse for the Department of Veterans Affairs (VA) to collect, validate, analyze, and disseminate key statistics on the Veteran population and VA programs." The NCVAS does not seem to provide any public data on the expatriate veteran population and was unresponsive to e-mail or phone call requests.
2. The Foreign Medical Program (FMP) Office is the official federal organization that oversees the healthcare benefits program for U.S. veterans who are residing or traveling abroad and have VA-rated, service-connected disabilities (Department of Veterans Affairs 2015c). As such, we expected it to have a rich repository of demographic data on the population that it serves; however, we discovered that this information is not available to the public, including access to testimony and annual reports.
3. Nationally known civilian organizations that work closely with veterans, such as
    a) Veterans of Foreign Wars (VFW), established in 1899 to secure rights and benefits for veterans in early wars. Membership in the VFW and its auxiliaries is estimated at more than 1.7 million. The organization currently has services officers who act as points of contact in three large regional areas: Europe, Pacific Areas, and Latin America/Caribbean.
    b) American Legion, chartered by Congress in 1919 as a patriotic veterans' organization, with approximately 2.4 million members (American Legion 2016), it currently has one or more posts in 11 countries: the Philippines (5), Portugal (1), Spain (1), Mexico (5), Ireland (3), Greece (1), Germany (10), France (2), Costa Rica (3), Canada (6), and Australia (2).
    c) United Services Organizations (USO), established by Franklin D. Roosevelt in 1941 to serve military members and their families, with over 160 centers worldwide, supported by thousands of volunteers.
4. Blogs and online groups administered by expatriate veterans, for example, Military Anthropology listserv (http://Mil_Ant_Net@yahoogroups.com), Facebook groups, American Legion Service Officers (http://legion.org/serviceofficers), and

military retirement overseas offices (https://soldierforlife.army.mil/retirement/rso/oconus).
5. Articles in newspapers such as *Stars and Stripes*.
6. Expert commentators; we contacted the authors of articles about U.S. veterans (e.g., Rhee 2013, 2014a, 2014b, 2015) to gain greater insight into their findings and to secure additional information. We also contacted military veteran and retiree support services, found on most U.S. bases and the larger army, navy, and air force overseas bases. These support services typically comprise an office that is manned by volunteers who are also veterans. These "retirement service officers" (RSOs) are a central source of expert information on current programs, policies, and regulations on living and working in the host country, along with general advice that is tailored to retiree or veteran status (as access to benefits may vary). They are generally well known and connected within their community and have an "insider's" understanding of the motivations that drive veterans to reside abroad or to return stateside.

How Many U.S. Veterans Live Abroad?

The number of service members who have chosen to retire or remain overseas after discharge from active duty (as U.S. veterans) is either not known to the government or is not released to the general public, despite our attempts to obtain it. There are, however, good reasons for thinking that the number is not small. First, there are a lot of U.S. veterans alive today—about 21.6 million. Of these, about 46 percent, or about 9.9 million, are veterans aged 65 or older (National Center for Veterans Analysis and Statistics 2015). Veterans who are 65 or older are almost universally eligible for Social Security and other age-based government benefits. The sheer number of millions of American boots on foreign soil over the past 65 years hints at the potential number of expatriate veterans living abroad. Once they leave active-duty service, these veterans may open up their own small businesses, seek employment at a multinational firm, or choose to work for private, quasi-military security contractors for a more lucrative paycheck (Maieli 2014). This also includes veterans working at American embassies and consulates abroad or those who do so by choice for family reasons. Irrespective of an expatriate veteran's particular circumstances, his or her VA benefits are payable regardless of place of residence or nationality (Department of Veterans Affairs 2015a).

Veterans living abroad are generally eligible for a wide range of benefits available to all U.S. military veterans. Benefits from the VA may include disability compensation, pension, education and training, healthcare, home loans, insurance, vocational rehabilitation and employment, and burial (Department of Veterans Affairs 2015a). The Foreign Medical Program

(FMP) Office is responsible for determining eligibility for reimbursed medical treatment while residing abroad (with the exception of veterans living in the Philippines). The VA will reimburse veterans for treatment of VA-rated and service-connected conditions if the treatment is medically necessary and recognized by the VA and/or the U.S. medical community. For veterans living in the Philippines, the VA maintains a regional office through which they may access medical care via the local VA outpatient clinic.

It appears that neither the Department of Defense (DoD) nor the VA formally tracks the number of veterans who live abroad, nor where they are located. In our study, we used mainly secondary sources to obtain anecdotal information on the size of the expatriate veteran population. We focused our search for contacts in regions that would most likely have a significant U.S. veteran population. For example, Germany currently has 21 active U.S. military bases, and Vietnam had a large build-up of American troops in Vietnam during the conflict. Other regional factors that might support a sizable veteran population were also considered, such as the existence of a military healthcare facility, commissary, and postal services that were accessible to military retirees and/or veterans. These types of benefits are governed by local status of forces agreements (SOFA), which vary widely from country to country, and sometimes over time within a country. The U.S. has SOFA agreements with over 100 countries. These include comprehensive agreements with-long standing U.S. allies and partners such as Australia, Israel, Japan, and Korea, and a variety of less comprehensive agreements with other nations (Department of State 2015b). By accessing data related to VA benefits and by contacting various VA offices, officers, and other VA associations abroad, we have been able to gain a potentially clearer picture of the numbers of expatriate veterans living abroad, which we outline below.

In a newsletter published by the VA, an article on the FMP stated that in 2005 the Denver office had received VA claims from 131 countries, with most claims coming from Germany, Panama, and Costa Rica (Johnson 2005). The Veterans Benefits Administration (VBA) has identified more than 15,000 veterans who live overseas and receive disability compensation.

According to the VA, 4.17 million out of 21.7 million veterans were receiving VA disability compensation on September 30, 2015 (National Center for Veterans Analysis and Statistics 2015). In other words, 19.2 percent of veterans were receiving disability compensation. If the proportion of veterans receiving disability compensation is the same among veterans living inside the United States as it is among veterans living overseas (a big assumption, to be sure), it is possible to estimate the number of the expatriate veterans at 78,058 in 2015.

According to data collected by the VA's Office of the Actuary, in Puerto Rico and Guam there were an estimated 93,240 and 9,453 veterans, respectively, as of September 2014. When the Virgin Islands is included, the given estimate for veterans living in "Islands + Foreign" is 117,113 (Office of the Actuary 2014). Subtracting Puerto Rico and Guam from the total gives a figure of 14,420 veterans living in foreign countries. This is obviously much too low, because it is lower even than the number of veterans living overseas who are receiving VA disability compensation.

Another crude approach to estimating the number of U.S. veterans living abroad is to apply the U.S. veteran percentage of the population to the number of U.S. citizens living abroad. The Department of State (2015a) estimates that about 8.7 million U.S. citizens live abroad. The Census Bureau (2015) estimates the resident population of the United States on January 1, 2016, to be 322,761,807. Multiplying the number of Americans living abroad by the proportion of veterans in the U.S. resident population (21,681,000/322,761,807) gives an estimate of 584,410 veterans living outside the United States.

This estimate is almost an order of magnitude larger than the extrapolation made from the number of veterans living abroad who are receiving VA disability compensation. It is clear from this wide gap that considerable uncertainty exists as to the precise number of expatriate veterans, but it also must be said that they are not a negligibly small group.

Where Do U.S. Veterans Live Abroad?

If little is known about how many U.S. veterans live abroad, even less is known about how they are distributed. Two ideas point toward reasonable guesses: that they live where U.S. military personnel have been deployed and/or where U.S. citizens (including nonveterans) are thought to be residing. The top 10 countries for U.S. deployments during the 1950–2015 time frame were (in decreasing order) Germany, Japan, South Korea, Vietnam, the United Kingdom, Iraq, Italy, Afghanistan, France, and the Philippines (see table 14.1; Kane 2015). The top 10 countries for U.S. citizens living abroad can be estimated in various ways, which produce a much less reliable number than we have for the deployment countries. One approach to estimating where Americans live abroad is to consider the foreign countries to which the Social Security Administration (SSA) sends payments. These payments include retirement, survivors', disability, and spousal benefits. The total amount sent to beneficiaries outside the United States in 2014 was $4.845 billion (Social Security Administration 2015, table 5J1). While not all of these recipients are U.S. citizens, many are. In

December 2015 the SSA sent payments to 639,097 people living outside the United States and its territories. The top 10 countries in decreasing order of the number of recipients were Canada, Japan, Mexico, Germany, United Kingdom, Philippines, Italy, Poland, Greece, and France (Social Security Administration 2016). Six of these countries are also among the top 10 countries for U.S. deployments since 1950.

The Philippines is the only host country that has a regional VA healthcare facility. According to the director of the Manila Regional Benefit Office of the VA, benefits available to American veterans include disability compensation, pension, education, and vocational rehabilitation. The outpatient clinic provides a full range of outpatient medical services for eligible veterans and other beneficiaries. In 2012 the clinic had an annual budget of $13 million and had 30,000 clinical visits annually (Department of Veteran Affairs 2015d). The Regional Office itself administers benefits to 16,000 beneficiaries and disburses approximately $17.5 million every month. This unique office is partly a legacy of the Philippines' years as a U.S. colony and partly due to the large number of Filipinos who served in the U.S. armed forces in the Far East during World War II.

A retirement services officer (RSO) in Belgium (D. McCarty, personal communication) responded to a request for information by reporting that approximately 350 military retirees and over 100 veterans live in Belgium, with a small minority still working but most retired. McCarty also estimates that there are 300 veterans in France, 400 in the Netherlands and Northern Germany, and over 100 in Luxembourg. The RSO explained that veterans' quality of life may be influenced by their level of access to military retiree benefits and entitlements as allowed under that country's SOFA with the United States. For example, France and Luxembourg do not have a SOFA agreement with the United States, so any military retiree who chooses to live in one of those countries may not go to Belgium and use the commissary and exchange, have access to the bases, and have ration cards (i.e., to purchase fuel on base at much cheaper prices), even though he or she holds a DoD-issued retiree ID card.

A few hundred former service members are thought to have moved to Vietnam, but it is difficult to get an accurate count of the Vietnam-era veterans who live there permanently. Nissa Rhee, an expert commentator and field researcher in Vietnam, informed us:

> I have no precise number of U.S. veterans living in Vietnam to share with you. The numbers I always tell people—hundreds of vets living in Vietnam and thousands who have returned as tourists since the war's end—are based on interviews I've done with vets in Vietnam and researchers in the United

States. I've talked to people at the U.S. embassy in Vietnam before about this and while they can tell you how many Americans are living in Vietnam they can't tell you how many of these are veterans. Complicating this matter is the fact that many vets are living in Vietnam under the radar of both the Vietnamese and American government authorities. For example, they may tell the U.S. government that they are living in the U.S. so they can continue to collect VA checks. Or they may only have a temporary visa in Vietnam and do a visa run to Cambodia or Laos every 3 months, even though they own a house or work in Vietnam. So it's a difficult question. (Nissa Rhee, personal communication, November 12, 2015)

Why Do U.S. Veterans Live Abroad?

Data in our study show that there are a number of motives for veterans to live abroad. Many are thought to fall into clear categories, such as those (1) who continue to live abroad after living in a country where they were stationed; (2) who found civilian employment in a business or country they came to know in the service; (3) with preexisting ties to another country, such as Mexican immigrants who serve in the U.S. military; and (4) with dramatic stories, such as defectors to North Korea or the USSR. As one respondent from the Military Anthropology listserv explained:

One category are nationals of other countries who serve in the U.S. military and then return to the home country, or retire in the U.S. A case in point is that Native Americans in Canada apparently serve in the U.S. Marines to the consternation of Canada. In fact Native Americans in general may be an example of vets who live in foreign countries that are within the U.S. given that reservations are sovereign, not to mention natives of Alaska, American Samoa, and Hawaii. Citizens of Texas who return to Texas, or vets who now live in Texas would be a different issue. One thing that you may find is that in the military, "foreign" does not have the same meaning as in general usage, indeed in many ways the military is a foreign country inside and outside the U.S. and its overseas (OCONUS) bases. Also, in the U.S. military foreigners are called civilians or locals. (Mil_Ant_Net@yahoogroups.com, June 13, 2015)

Another respondent on the same listserv explained that

the reasons to be an expat have changed. . . . It isn't easier to be an expat now, due to domestic and international laws, financial scrutiny, health care and insurance, suspicious of foreign intelligence and security services, etc. But the attraction is at least as strong as ever. Some reasons that occur to me currently: (1) I think financial lures are significant, as is cost of living. There has always been a "tax avoidance" element to expats. (2) Escape from politics and policies—mostly at the U.S. national level. This has components of ideology, personal values, and self-interest (professionally and politically). (3) For the newer generations of expats, travel is easier, and return visits much more feasible in terms of time and cost. (4) Earlier "final" retirements—this has great appeal to the Boomers and those younger. For vets, retirement from their post-military period is an aspect. (5) Language training or learning is now very available in modes not existing decades ago. The MILANT [military anthropology list serve] members appreciate more than most that language is probably the most powerful window on any given culture. (6) The private military companies are plentiful, and a big draw for operators, intelligence folks, planners, and logisticians. This MAY be a major finding for you: Blackwater, Triple Canopy, EX Solutions, XYZ . . . ABC . . . have a huge draw for those in good health, with enough working years in front of them, based on adventure, compensation, etc. (7) There are more women now than before as expats. I suspect the reasons are generational, and more complex. (Mil_Ant_Net@yahoogroups.com, June 14, 2015)

Other respondents on the Military Anthropology listserv suggest that some military personnel retire early as a means of facilitating a life abroad. We found that, given the number of expatriate veterans residing in Costa Rica and Belize, the possibility of living in a developing country could be a significant incentive to retire early. This idea is supported by the existence of numerous Web sites that provide advice about expatriate life (e.g., http://retire-asia.com) and that often describe particular destinations as especially popular with former U.S. military personnel (i.e., the Philippines, Vietnam).

Personal motives for living abroad emerged as significant. They include, for example, "falling in love with a Vietnamese woman" and "because they are married to a foreign national" (McCarty 2015; Rhee 2015). But unlike veterans who were based in Europe and then stayed for a better quality of life, the chance to travel widely, or to work for a multinational company (in addition to marrying a local), motivations for choosing to return and live in particular countries, such as Vietnam, can be more complex. According to the Vietnamese government, 400,000 Americans visit the country annually, with most experts putting the figure of returning veterans in the tens of thousands (Rhee 2013). Anecdotal reports suggest that many veterans are looking for closure and healing from their experiences during the Vietnam conflict. In her interviews with veterans who choose to remain in Vietnam, Rhee (2015) states that for some it is about "wanting to make amends for the massacre at My Lai."

There is a voluntary group of professors from the University of Maryland University College (UMUC) named "Overseas Marylanders." Of the roughly 350 members, about 90 report having been in the military:

> [M]ore than [a] few of those were recruited or, as in my case, self-initiated expats based on their military experience and knowledge that they could get jobs with UMUC. In general, those who have stayed overseas have done so because they preferred the intellectual freedom they enjoyed. . . . Due to drawdowns everywhere, I suspect there are lots of "abandoned" expats who originally had ties to their local military communities. There are about 400 Americans in Augsburg, counting family members. Perhaps half were formerly employed by the Army and half of those 'retired' too soon when the Army pulled out in 1998. (Warren Johnson, personal communication, December 18, 2015)

Vignettes

In this section we use narrative analysis and develop vignettes about the lived experiences of U.S. veterans living abroad to explain their motives for doing so. The narrative analysis is applied to 3 of the 27 U.S. veterans' stories as best representing the motives, opportunities, and challenges that expatriate veterans face when they relocate abroad. From the remaining three respondents (expert commentators), we draw insights and aggregated data to further convey key themes. We use narrative analysis as a methodological perspective that recounts the lived experience (Favell, Feldblum, and Smith 2006; Marshall and Rossman 2006), in this case through stories of those engaged in expatriation as U.S. veterans. A key feature of narrative analysis in this study is to focus on the as yet "unheard voices" of U.S. veteran expatriates.

Vignette 1—Daniel in Mexico: Urban Villagers in Puerto Vallarta

In the first vignette we meet Daniel, an expatriate veteran and native of California who is living in Puerto Vallarta, Mexico. Daniel's main reason for living abroad (among others) is that the facilities and services that can be found overseas are far more extensive than in the town where he was living in the United States. Daniel's story illustrates that the motives for living abroad are complex, and the decision to do so is not without challenges.

Daniel is a white male in his seventies who spent three years as a soldier during the Vietnam conflict. He currently resides in Puerto Vallarta with his second wife, after retiring as a California highway patrolman. He has lived there for 12 years after hearing the call of the Lord to do missionary work at age 62. Like many other local expats, the couple's life there began with a short visit to the area, but unlike other veterans who decide to split their time between the United States and Mexico, they quickly felt comfortable and began to extend their visits until they made it their permanent home. Being a "residente permanente," Daniel and his wife have almost all of the same privileges as citizens. Daniel loves the friendliness of the locals, and that people are always smiling and welcoming.

Daniel supports his family with his Social Security benefits and with additional support from his church back in the United States. He is a chaplain for the local American Legion post and is heavily involved in both the expat veteran and local host communities, including the Navy League. He and his wife volunteer to teach English at the local high school and orphanage, provide community services such as picking up people for appointments, and act as a liaison with visiting U.S. and other national military ships.

While Daniel states that his main reason for choosing to reside in Mexico is that they "were chosen by our Lord to become missionaries in Mexico," he mentions that he is able to stretch his limited financial resources much further in Mexico than in the United States, having lost his state police pension to his ex-wife when they divorced. "I think the motivation of most of the gringos here in PV that are permanent, including the vets, is that it is a much safer, friendly, cheaper, and more weather-friendly place to live," he says. "Most of the normal benefits of the U.S. are here, i.e., two Walmarts, Sam's Club, Costco, Home Depot, MacDonald's, Burger King, Wendy's, The Outback, Domino's, KFC, Office Max, Office Depot, Auto Zone, etc.

"Plus we are much like San Francisco in that we have hundreds of great restaurants, but cheaper. And PV is rated the #5 most desirable place for tourists to visit. We get as many as 5 cruise ships in at a time."

Daniel says he came to love living in the area because he felt safer there than he did in cities like Chicago. He feels that the United States has lost its "moral compass" and "become too socialistic." As a retired highway patrolman, Daniel occasionally works with local police to help them identify and capture U.S. citizens on the run from American law. This includes U.S. veterans, who often come to PV to escape criminal conviction in the United States.

Although he will mostly likely live out his days in Mexico, Daniel intends to remain a U.S. citizen. As a serviceman during a time of war, he feels a strong bond with his fellow U.S. veterans, with some of whom he has close personal relationships. This requires that he and his wife travel back and forth to the United States on a regular basis to visit them, as well as their children and grandchildren and their sponsoring church. Last year they put 8,300 miles on their vehicle and traveled all the way to Canada. Although his wife's daughter has visited them in PV, Daniel's children have yet to do so due to lack of funds.

One of the few criticisms Daniel makes about his expat lifestyle is ongoing frustration with the VA. He would like to use the services, but they are not available in his area. Instead, both he and his wife have had several small surgeries locally, and while they are quite satisfied with the quality and cost of care, it remains a source of frustration to be cut off from VA access because they are abroad. When they do travel to the United States, they like to use VA benefits as a matter of convenience via Medicare. Daniel is puzzled that the VA does not realize how much cheaper it is to pay for medical services overseas than to have vets return to the continental United States for medical access.

Vignette 2—Alan in London: The Time Zone Bind

In the second vignette we look at the experiences of Alan. Here we see that a key motivation for living abroad is work-life balance. This seems to apply to younger veterans who leave active duty after one or two tours and are still raising their families.

Alan is an army veteran who signed on for one tour of active duty before leaving the service. He decided to go abroad as a trailing partner when his girlfriend was offered a job in London that offered good pay and benefits. Both Alan and his (now) wife feel that living overseas has presented them with "huge" opportunities for travel around Europe, especially "before the kids come." Alan has been in the United Kingdom for just over a year and believes that the quality of life there is better than in the United States. He cites examples such as the greater health benefits, bonuses, time off, and overall work-life balance, including generous holiday leave of five to six weeks annually.

"There's no comparison between being a corporate expat in comparison to military life," he says, "which grants only 30 days of leave annually, but demands many additional hours and days of extra work including multiple rotations, training requirements, and deployments." While on active duty, Alan felt that he had no work-life balance and that staying in the military put too much stress on a young family. He and his wife have discussed staying in Europe and raising their family in Germany or the Netherlands, because they provide greater support for families, and the cost of living in London is too expensive. Alan would like to remain in Europe for the next several years, because there is the possibility of his wife getting an EU passport through her company. With an EU passport, they would have many other possibilities to live, travel, and work in Europe without having to be sponsored by a corporation.

Alan feels quite strongly that he will keep his U.S. citizenship status. It is "part of my identity," he stated, and "I have family, friends, colleagues back in the U.S." The only reason he and his wife would return to the United States would be for "something catastrophic" such as a death or serious illness, or if one of them lost his or her job for an extended time. Currently, they return to the United States approximately once a year, but find it too expensive to return more often. Also, the visit is stressful with the "hustle and bustle" of traveling to see family and close friends across three or four states.

For the time being, Alan is content to remain abroad, although he and his wife admit that once they have children they might consider returning to the United States to allow them the opportunity to grow up around U.S. relatives (i.e., cousins and aunts), at least for some unknown length of time. The other possibility is to remain in Europe while raising their family and return to the United States if their kids decide to go to American colleges. Their long-term plan is nonetheless to retire in Europe.

Vignette 3—Ken in Germany: The Strength of Family Ties

Our third vignette focuses on a combat veteran who created a satisfying and happy life with his German wife in her home country, highlighting another common theme: family ties that result from overseas deployment. As with most of the participants' stories though, Ken's journey illustrates that the ability to cope with small things can escalate into the need to face bigger challenges.

Ken is now a retired army widower who, in the early 1960s, fell in love with a German woman while stationed in Ansbach, Germany. Since then he has lived in Bad Windsheim, Germany, for 54 years. Ken holds a permanent visa in his adopted country, but has retained his U.S. citizenship. Despite almost six decades of life as an expatriate, Ken is still strongly patriotic. He stated, "I am an American citizen. I fought and bled for this country." During active duty, he was "a good soldier" who did what was required by his chain of command. For Ken, this meant three combat tours in Vietnam, in 1962, 1967–1968, and 1971. He described the war as "not a nice time" and reflected that he "learned to do what is best for your life." Although he traveled back and forth to the United States from Germany every three years while his mother was alive, he considers Germany "home" and would like to be buried next to his German wife. Over the course of their marriage, Ken and his wife had a daughter. When his wife died, Ken inherited the family farm that his wife had owned. He now lives with his daughter, her German husband, and his grandchild on the property.

While Ken is retired, he still has strong ties in both the local host-country community and expat community, socially and professionally. He is involved with the local VFW and German-American Friendship Club and is the commanding officer (CO) of the 1982 American Legion Ansbach Germany, where he frequently assists the German widows of the American expat veterans in navigating the complex VA paperwork, assuring that they continue receiving their rightful benefits. Ken remarked that many retirees simply don't prepare for death, despite a concerted effort by the American Legion to educate its members through a variety of outreach programs. He remarks that the widows and widowers often "don't know who to call." Ken remains heavily involved with active-duty service members and their families who are stationed in the area.

In the past he has used only local healthcare resources through his medical insurance, which he acquired through his 21 years working for the Army and Air Force Exchange Services (AAFES). In the future he hopes to access VA benefits to help pay for his hearing aids. Ken has dealt with a number of physical challenges associated with his time in Vietnam. However, when he retired he did not receive a thorough physical from the VA, which would have provided him with substantial benefits through overseas VA-affiliated healthcare facilities. He is currently dealing with significant paperwork in order to have his past wartime injuries be recognized by the VA.

Perspectives from the Vignettes

An important contribution of this study is the focus on the lived experiences of expatriate veterans, whereby the context within which their expatriation experiences unfold underscores the important role that the VA plays in shaping their experiences living abroad. The use of both surveys and semistructured interviews has provided an opportunity to identify some of the environmental challenges that veterans navigate while living and working abroad and to focus on the concrete nature of their lived experience by capturing the complexity of their lives as former U.S. military personnel. An important consideration in this study is undoubtedly the international context within which expatriation occurs, which may pose problems for some veterans more than others in terms of access to VA benefits. It is worth noting, however, that all of the participants at some point during their expatriation could have opted out of their life abroad and moved back to the United States. That many of them are successful in negotiating expatriation as U.S. veterans, despite some not having access to VA benefits, is telling. More research is nonetheless needed to understand the indirect barriers that may prevent veterans from accessing VA benefits in a timely manner. Central to our study is the idea that veteran status can be viewed as both a disabler *and* enabler to expatriation, whereby some veterans see their military experience as essential to gaining civilian employment, while others view a lack of access to benefits from the VA as restricting their employment opportunities abroad.

Limitations and Future Research

A limitation of the study is undoubtedly the scarcity of research on expatriate veterans, which precludes interpretation of the results in light of existing theory. Thus, the findings raise more questions than they answer. Further limitations include the fact that all of the survey participants are men. It would be interesting to examine a larger cohort of expatriate veterans that includes more women. Employer experiences of employing ex-U.S. military personnel would further enable greater triangulation of data by analyzing the policies used to support them. Especially needed are in-depth studies that examine specific types of expatriate veterans according to age (preretirement, semiretired, and fully retired/65+) so as to better understand how to support each age group at the policy level in terms of accessing VA benefits while living abroad. For example, virtually nothing is known about expatriate veterans with special needs, of which there are likely to be many, given that many have served in conflict zones. Two important questions are: (1) What are the available local resources for veterans who suffer from reduced mental and/or physical well-being due to their combat experiences (e.g., PTSD)? and (2) How can the VA better meet the needs of older veterans?

Future studies also need to consider the context in which expatriation unfolds for expatriate veterans, taking into account significant variability in host-country cost of living, access to VA benefits, and host-country SOFA. On this basis, studies could examine more homogeneous samples of expatriate veterans, for example, separate studies of those employed by military contractors, those who have started their own business, and so forth. Similarly, studies that examine the different motives for expatriating among, for example, officers and enlisted veterans, or among categories of race, could be useful if there are patterns of race/ethnicity associated with the different motivations. Doing so might also shed light on the link between education and civilian income potential. The rationale for these studies is twofold: (1) while expatriate veterans share common characteristics and challenges, each nonetheless has a unique set of circumstances that warrants attention from both practical and policy points of view as well, as theoretically in terms of the personally relevant elements and behaviors that drive their success while living abroad, and (2) a single interview of, for example, a military contractor may not be generalizable across an entire population of veterans, thus providing poor representation of the actual life experiences of the different types of expatriate veterans.

Conclusion

Much of the literature to date on expatriate management has focused on traditional corporate assignees, to the exclusion of expatriates in other communities (see McNulty and Hutchings 2016 review). This study is one of the first to examine military expatriates (see also Fisher 2016), and in particular, U.S. veterans living abroad. In this chapter we have departed from established norms to explore a relatively underresearched segment of the global talent pool—U.S. veterans—who choose to live abroad. In doing so, we have examined their motives for doing so and their perceptions of the opportunities, barriers, and challenges they face when choosing to live abroad either temporarily or permanently, including how they overcome and deal with medical and other issues away from U.S. territories. Our study is significant in suggesting that traditional ideas about migration (push and pull factors, barriers, and personal situations) are relevant to U.S. expatriate veterans. Our respondents gave accounts of their lives and situations that could be framed in these ways. They spoke of factors pushing them out of the United States (e.g., cost of living); factors pulling them back to the United States (e.g., children living there); factors pulling them to migrate (e.g., an easygoing lifestyle); factors pushing them away from migration (e.g., difficulty with VA benefits); barriers such as immigration issues; and their personal situations, including striving to balance the time demands of marriage, busy careers, and small children.

While this study represents promising research about military expatriates, among other studies (e.g., Fisher and Hutchings 2013; Fisher, Hutchings, and Pinto 2015; Fisher forthcoming) and studies that focus on nontraditional expatriates (e.g., Gedro 2010; Gedro et al. 2013; McNulty 2015; McPhail et al. 2016) as well as expatriates in different communities (Davoine et al. 2013; Fee and Gray 2011; Merlot and De Cieri 2011; Oberholster and Doss forthcoming; Patel et al. 2000; Quigley, Claus, and Dothan 2015), it remains important for the international human resource management (IHRM) field in general to engage in a more fundamental discussion about expatriate veterans (i.e., how they are defined, the complexity of their experiences, and the extent of their acculturation) in order to increase the potential for veterans to expand the ex-U.S. military international labor pool. These elements are worth exploring further to prompt the development of a range of new perspectives about expatriation, which in turn is likely to help advance the field of global staffing in general, both for the military community and in other communities in which veterans can be employed.

References

American Legion. 2016. "About Us." Accessed January 26, 2016. http://www.legion.org/presscenter/about.

Beechler, Schon, and Ian C. Woodward. 2009. "The Global 'War for Talent.'" *Journal of International Management,* 15 (3): 273–285.

Blatter, Joachim, and Markus Haverland. 2012. *Designing Case Studies: Explanatory Approaches in Small-N Research.* Hampshire, UK: Palgrave Macmillan.

Census Bureau. 2015. "Population Estimates, National Totals, Vintage 2015." Accessed December 29, 2015. http://www.census.gov/popest/data/national/totals/2015/index.html.

Chew, Emrys. 2014. "How Big Powers Fight Small Wars: Contending Traditions of Asymmetry in the British and American Ways of War." *Armed Forces & Society* 40 (1): 17–48.

Creswell, John W. 2003. *Research Design: Qualitative, Quantitative, and Mixed Methods Approaches.* 2nd ed. Thousand Oaks, CA: Sage.

Creswell, John W., and Vicki L. Plano Clark. 2007. *Designing and Conducting Mixed Methods Research.* Thousand Oaks, CA: Sage.

Daugherty, Helen Ginn, and Kenneth C. W. Kammeyer. 1995. *An Introduction to Population.* 2nd ed. New York: Guilford Press.

Davoine, Eric, Claudia Ravasi, Xavier Salamin, and Christel Cudré-Mauroux. 2013. "A 'Dramaturgical' Analysis of Spouse Role Enactment in Expatriation: An Exploratory Gender Comparative Study in the Diplomatic and Consular Field." *Journal of Global Mobility,* 1 (1): 92–112.

De Jong, Gordon F. 2000. "Expectations, Gender, and Norms in Migration Decision-Making." *Population Studies* 54 (3): 307–319.

De Jong, Gordon F., and Robert W. Gardner. 1981. *Migration Decision Making: Multidisciplinary Approaches to Multilevel Studies in Developed and Developing Countries.* New York: Pergamon Press.

Demeny, Paul. 1988. "Social Science and Population Policy." *Population and Development Review* 14: 451–479.

Denzin, Norman K., and Yvonna S. Lincoln. 2000. "Introduction: The Discipline and Practice of Qualitative Research." In *Handbook of Qualitative Research.* 2nd ed., edited by Norman Denzin and Yvonna Lincoln, 1–28. Thousand Oaks, CA: Sage.

Department of State. 2015a. "By the Numbers: Passports, International Travel, Visas." Accessed December 29, 2015. http://travel.state.gov/content/dam/travel/CA percent20bypercent20thepercent20Numbers-percent20Maypercent202015.pdf.

Department of State. 2015b. *Report on Status of Forces Agreements (SOFA)*. Washington, DC: Department of State.

Department of Veterans Affairs. 2015a. "About the National Center for Veterans Analysis and Statistics." Accessed December 28, 2015. http://www.va.gov/vetdata/About_Us.asp.

Department of Veterans Affairs. 2015b. "Elderly Veterans." Accessed December 28, 2015. http://www.benefits.va.gov/persona/veteran-elderly.asp.

Department of Veterans Affairs. 2015c. "Foreign Medical Program." Accessed December 28, 2015. http://www.va.gov/purchasedcare/programs/veterans/fmp/.

Department of Veterans Affairs. 2015d. "Manila Regional Benefit Office." Accessed December 28, 2015. http://www.va.gov/directory/guide/facility.asp?ID=681.

Department of Veterans Affairs. 2015e. "Veterans Living Abroad." Accessed December 28, 2015. http://www.benefits.va.gov/persona/veteran-abroad.asp.

DynCorp. 2016. "Careers with DI." Accessed January 26, 2016. http://www.dyn-intl.com/careers/overview/.

Eisenhardt, K. 1989. "Building Theories from Case Study Research." *Academy of Management Review*. 14 (4): 532–550.

Favell, Adrian, Miriam Feldblum, and Michael Peter Smith. 2006. "The Human Face of Global Mobility: A Research Agenda." In *The Human Face of Global Mobility: International Highly Skilled Migration in Europe, North America and the Asia-Pacific*, edited by Michael Peter Smith and Adrian Favell, 1–27. New Brunswick, NJ: Transaction Publishers.

Fee, Anthony, and Sidney J. Gray. 2011. "Fast-tracking Expatriate Development: the Unique Learning Environments of International Volunteer Placements." *The International Journal of Human Resource Management* 22 (3): 530–552.

Findlay, Allan M. 2006. "Brain Strain and Other Social Challenges Arising from the UK's Policy on Attracting Global Talent." In *Competing for Global Talent*, edited by Christiane Kuptsch & Pang Eng Fong, 65–86. Geneva, Switzerland: International Institute for Labor Studies.

Fisher, Kelly. Forthcoming. "Military Expatriates." In *The Research Handbook of Expatriates*, edited by Yvonne McNulty and Jan Selmer. Cheltenham, UK: Edward Elgar.

Fisher, Kelly, and Kate Hutchings. 2013. "Making Sense of Cultural Distance for Military Expatriates Operating in an Extreme Context." *Journal of Organizational Behavior* 34: 791–812.

Fisher, Kelly, Kate Hutchings, and Luisa Helena Pinto. 2015. "Pioneers across War Zones: The Lived Acculturation Experiences of US Female Military Expatriates." *International Journal of Intercultural Relations* 49: 265–277.

Gartner, Scott Sigmund. 2006. "Selected Characteristics of the Armed Forces—Personnel, Draftees, Medical Care, and Military Pay, By War: 1861–1975." In

Historical Statistics of the United States, Earliest Times to the Present, millennial Ed., edited by Susan B. Carter, Scott Sigmund Gartner, Michael R. Haines, Alan L. Olmstead, Richard Sutch, and Gavin Wright, 5:363 (Table Ed82–119). Cambridge, UK: Cambridge University Press.

Gedro, Julie. 2010. "The Lavender Ceiling Atop the Global Closet: Human Resource Development and Lesbian Expatriates." *Human Resource Development Review* 9 (4): 385–404.

Gedro, Julie, Robert C. Mizzi, Tonette S. Rocco, and Jasper van Loo. 2013. "Going Global: Professional Mobility and Concerns for LGBT Workers." *Human Resource Development International* 16 (3): 282–297.

Greenhalgh, Susan. 1996. "The Social Construction of Population Science: An Intellectual, Institutional, and Political History of Twentieth-Century Demography." *Comparative Studies in Society and History* 38: 26–66.

Groysberg, Boris, Andrew Hill, and Toby Johnson. 2010. "Which of These People Is Your Future CEO? The Different Ways Military Experience Prepares Managers for Leadership." *Harvard Business Review* 88 (11): 80–85.

Haslberger, Arno, and Chris Brewster. 2009. "Capital Gains: Expatriate Adjustment and the Psychological Contract in International Careers." *Human Resource Management* 48 (3): 379–397.

Haslberger, Arno, and Vlad Vaiman. 2013. "Self-Initiated Expatriates: A Neglected Source of the Global Talent Flow." In *Talent Management of Self-initiated Expatriates*, edited by Vlad Vaiman and Arno Haslberger, 1–15. London: Palgrave Macmillan.

Hippler, Thomas. 2009. "Why Do They Go? Empirical Evidence of Employees' Motives for Seeking or Accepting Relocation." *The International Journal of Human Resource Management* 20 (6): 1381–1401.

Johnson, Glenn A. 2005. "Caring for Veterans Worldwide." *VAnguard* 51 (1): 11–13.

Kane, Timothy. 2016. *The Decline of American Engagement: Patterns in U.S. Troop Deployments*. Economics Working Paper 16101. Stanford, CA: Hoover Institution. Accessed June 6, 2016. http://www.hoover.org/sites/default/files/research/docs/16101_-_kane_-_decline_of_american_engagement.pdf.

Keyfitz, Nathan. 1993. "Thirty Years of Demography and *Demography*." *Demography* 30: 533–549.

Maieli, Steven. 2014. "Private Security Contractor Jobs: Good Money with Risks." Army Times, July 14, 23–23.

Marshall, Catherine, and Gretchen B. Rossman. 2006. *Designing Qualitative Research*, 4th edition. Thousand Oaks, CA: Sage.

McNulty, Yvonne. 2015. "Acculturating Non-Traditional Expatriates: A Case Study of Single Parent, Overseas Adoption, Split Family, and Lesbian Assignees." *International Journal of Intercultural Relations* 49: 278–293.

McNulty, Yvonne, and Kate Hutchings. 2016. "Looking for talent in all the right places: A critical literature review of non-traditional expatriates." *International Journal of Human Resource Management* 27 (6): 699–728.

McNulty, Yvonne, and Chris Brewster. Forthcoming. "The 'Meanings' of Expatriate." In *The Research Handbook of Expatriates*, edited by Yvonne McNulty and Jan Selmer. Cheltenham, UK: Edward Elgar.

McPhail, Ruth, and Yvonne McNulty. 2015. "'Oh, the Places You Won't Go as an LGBT Expatriate!' A Study of HRM's Duty of Care to Lesbian, Gay, Bisexual and Transgender Expatriates in Dangerous Locations." *European Journal of International Management* 9 (6): 737–765.

McPhail, Ruth, Yvonne McNulty, and Kate Hutchings. 2016. "Lesbian and Gay Expatriation: Opportunities, Barriers, and Challenges for Global Mobility." *International Journal of Human Resource Management* 27 (3): 382–406.

Merlot, Elizabeth, and Helen De Cieri. 2011. "The Challenges of the 2004 Indian Ocean Tsunami for Strategic International Human Resource Management in Multinational Nonprofit Enterprises." *International Journal of Human Resource Management* 23 (7): 1303–1319.

Miles, Matthew B., and A. Michael Huberman. 1994. *Qualitative Data Analysis: An Expanded Sourcebook*. 2nd ed. Thousand Oaks, CA: Sage.

National Aeronautics and Space Administration (NASA). 2016. "Biographies of Apollo 11 Astronauts." Accessed on January 21, 2016. http://history.nasa.gov/ap11ann/astrobios.htm.

National Center for Veterans Analysis and Statistics. 2015. "At-A-Glance Pocket Card. FY 2016 1st Quarter." Accessed December 28, 2015. http://www.va.gov/vetdata/docs/pocketcards/fy2016q1.pdf.

Oberholster, Braam, and Cheryl Doss. Forthcoming. "Missionary (Religious) Expatriates." In *The Research Handbook of Expatriates*, edited by Yvonne McNulty and Jan Selmer. Cheltenham, UK: Edward Elgar.

Office of the Actuary. 2014. *VetPop 2014*. Washington, DC: Department of Veteran Affairs.

Office of the Deputy Chief of Staff. 2010. *Assignments, Details, and Transfers: Overseas Service*. Washington, DC: Department of the Army.

Patel, Dipti, Charles J. Easmon, Carol Dow, David C. Snashall, and Paul T. Seed. 2000. "Medical Repatriation of British Diplomats Residents Overseas." *Journal of Travel Medicine* 7 (2): 64–69.

Poston, Dudley L., Jr., and Leon F. Bouvier. 2010. *Population and Society: An Introduction to Demography*. Cambridge, UK: Cambridge University Press.

Quigley, Robert, Lisbeth Claus, and Michael Dothan. 2015. "Medical Requests for Assistance from Globally Mobile Populations: Contrasting International Assignees from Different Sectors." *European Journal of International Management* 9 (6): 712–736.

Rhee, Nissa. 2013. "Why US Veterans Are Returning to Vietnam." *Christian Science Monitor*, November 10. Accessed December 28, 2015. http://www.csmonitor.com/USA/Society/2013/1110/Why-US-veterans-are-returning-to-Vietnam.

Rhee, Nissa. 2014a. "The Soldier Who Needed 'Nam.'" Accessed December 29, 2015. http://narrative.ly/american-dreamless/the-soldier-who-needed-nam/.

Rhee, Nissa. 2014b. "The Things They Carried Back." *University of Chicago Magazine* (March/April). Accessed June 6, 2016. https://nissarhee.files.wordpress.com/2012/12/rhee_alumni_essay.pdf.

Rhee, Nissa. 2015. "Back to War." *Guernica*, April 15. Accessed December 29, 2015. https://www.guernicamag.com/daily/nissa-rhee-back-to-war/.

Skeldon, Ronald. 2013. *Global Migration: Demographic Aspects and Its Relevance for Development*. Technical Paper No. 2013/6. New York: United Nations Department of Economic and Social Affairs, Population Division.

Social Security Administration. 2015. *Annual Statistical Supplement, 2015*. Washington, DC: Social Security Administration.

Social Security Administration. 2016. "Payments to Beneficiaries Outside the U.S." Accessed on January 21, 2016. https://socialsecurity.gov/deposit/GIS/data/Reports/ALLCTRYWEB.htm.

Szymendera, Scott D. 2015. *Who Is a "Veteran"? Basic Eligibility for Veterans' Benefits*. CRS Report No. R42324. Washington, DC: Congressional Research Service. Accessed December 29, 2015. https://www.fas.org/sgp/crs/misc/R42324.pdf.

Tarique, Ibraiz, and Randall S. Schuler. 2010. "Global Talent Management: Literature Review, Integrative Framework, and Suggestions for Further Research." *Journal of World Business* 45 (2): 122–133.

Tharenou, Phyllis. 2013. "Self-Initiated Expatriates: An Alternative to Company-Assigned Expatriates?" *Journal of Global Mobility* 1 (3): 336–356.

Vance, Charles, and Yvonne McNulty. 2014. "Why and How Women and Men Acquire Expatriate Career Development Experience: A Study of American Expatriates in Europe." *International Studies of Management and Organization* 44 (2): 34–54.

Westat. 2010. *National Survey of Veterans, Active Duty Service Members, Demobilized National Guard and Reserve Members, Family Members, and Surviving Spouses*. Rockville, MD: Westat.

White House. 2011. *Strengthening Our Military Families: Meeting America's Commitment*. Washington, DC: White House. Accessed January 26, 2016. http://www.dol.gov/dol/milfamilies/strengthening_our_military_families.pdf.

Wilkinson, Amanda, and Gangaram Singh. 2010. "Managing Stress in the Expatriate Family: A Case Study of the State Department of the United States of America." *Public Personnel Management* 39 (2): 169–181.

Yin, Robert K. 2003. *Case Study Research: Design and Methods*. 3rd ed. Thousand Oaks, CA: Sage.

CHAPTER FIFTEEN

Veterans' Families

Jasmine Strode-Elfant, Paul Hemez, Lucky Tedrow, and Jay Teachman

Introduction

Both the military and families have long been considered greedy institutions, in that both demand exclusive time and energy from the individuals involved in them (Segal 1986).[1] Participating in the military and maintaining a family are often thought of as largely incompatible roles, yet individuals are frequently part of both; over 60 percent of service members on active duty in 2013 were married or had children (Department of Defense 2013). The demands of these greedy institutions are historically greater for women, as women typically bear a larger burden of time and energy within families, and the military has been slow to support the families of female service members.

Military policies concerning families have evolved across eras to increasingly support family formation for service members; however, these policies have not always promoted military families and have not been applied equally to men and women. Prior to World War II, married men were actively discouraged from joining the military, and even throughout World War II, the military provided insufficient support and housing for married members (Albano 1994). Despite the preference for unmarried men, in the early 1940s the military began providing benefits to service members with families, such as a monthly allowance to male service members with wives and children (Bell and Iadeluca 1988). These benefits, however, were not extended to female service members, and until the mid-1970s enlisted women could be dishonorably discharged for marriage or pregnancy (Albano 1994). With the inception of the All-Volunteer Force (AVF) in 1973, the military began increasing the benefits provided to families in order to bolster the appeal of military service and remain competitive with civilian occupations. In 1979 the military first recognized the importance of familial support for military success (Albano 1994). More recently, military policies have become progressively more family-friendly; including expanding the definition of family covered by benefits and providing increased compensation to spouses, such as assistance with tuition (Wadsworth and Southwell 2011).

Although policies that govern active-duty service members do not dictate behaviors once members become veterans, these policies do influence the family composition of veterans. Veterans from eras with limited support for families may have been discouraged from forming families, whereas increased benefits may encourage family formation among veterans. In this chapter, we examine the composition of veterans' families. In particular, we compare marital status, household composition, and presence of children between veterans and nonveterans. Furthermore, we make these comparisons by historical era and sex.

Literature Review

Although findings regarding families of veterans are largely era-dependent, several findings remain consistent across eras. Veterans of all eras are more likely to marry than nonveterans (Department of Veterans Affairs 2011; Teachman 2009; Settersten 2008; Call and Teachman 1991, 1996; Frey-Wouters and Laufer 1986; Laufer and Gallops 1985). Regardless of era, veterans also have fewer children than nonveterans (Department of Veterans Affairs 2011; Card 1983; Teachman, Tedrow, and Anderson 2015).

Studies of families of World War II– and Korean War–era veterans are limited in number. Veterans of the World War II (WWII) era are more likely to marry than nonveterans (Settersten 2008; MacLean and Elder 2007). The findings in terms of divorce are mixed: some research finds that veterans of that era are more likely to be divorced than nonveterans (Settersten 2008; Pavalko and Elder 1990), whereas other studies find that those veterans are at a lower risk for divorce than nonveterans (Ruger, Wilson, and Waddoups 2002). Most of the research examining veterans of the WWII era does not consider children or household composition. Researchers looking at veterans of this era primarily focus on veterans themselves, not on differences between veterans and nonveterans. Furthermore, the majority of this literature utilizes the same few databases, particularly the Oakland

Veterans' Families

and Berkeley Guidance Studies and the Stanford-Terman Longitudinal Survey, reducing the generalizability of these conclusions. Limited findings for veterans of the Korean War appear similarly to WWII veterans (Settersten 2008; MacLean and Elder 2007); however, this similarity is potentially due to the lack of an in-depth study of the Korean War era (see Ruger, Wilson, and Waddoups 2002).

The most study on veterans and their families has been of those in the Vietnam era. Nearly all research indicates that Vietnam-era veterans are more likely to marry than nonveterans (Department of Veterans Affairs 2011; Call and Teachman 1996; Call and Teachman 1991; Frey-Wouters and Laufer 1986; Laufer and Gallops 1985; but see Card 1983 for a contrary view). Prior studies do not reach a consistent conclusion about divorce. Some studies find no difference between Vietnam veterans and nonveterans in terms of divorce (Cohen and Segal 2009; Call and Teachman 1991; Card 1983), whereas other studies find that Vietnam veterans are less likely to divorce than nonveterans (Heerwig and Conley 2013; Ruger et al. 2002; Laufer and Gallops 1985), and yet other studies find that divorce rates depend on when in the life course the veterans were enlisted or married (Call and Teachman 1996; Frey-Wouters and Laufer 1986). Vietnam veterans who saw combat are more likely to marry and more likely to divorce (Ruger et al. 2002; Gimbel and Booth 1994; Laufer and Gallops 1985). Veterans of the Vietnam era appear to have fewer children (Card 1983). The limited findings available on household composition, number of times married, and number of times divorced indicate that Vietnam veterans do not differ from nonveterans with respect to these variables (Card 1983).

There are few studies on veterans of the AVF and post-9/11 eras, partly due to the limited time these individuals have been veterans. Both male and female veterans of the AVF era are more likely to marry than nonveterans (Usdansky, London, and Wilmoth 2009; Cooney et al. 2003), especially white veterans (Teachman 2007, 2009). White veterans of this era are similarly more likely to cohabit than white nonveterans (Teachman 2009). For male AVF veterans, there is no difference in divorce rates compared to nonveterans (Teachman and Tedrow 2008). However, female veterans of these eras are more likely to be divorced than female nonveterans (Cooney et al. 2003). Veterans of the AVF have fewer children than nonveterans (Teachman, Tedrow, and Anderson 2015).

Gaps in the Literature

The primary gap in the literature is the limited number of studies investigating demographic trends in families of veterans. Most studies look at qualitative family outcomes for veterans, such as the quality of relationships with children or spouses, or the impact of families on the mental health of veterans. Few studies look at measures of demographic differences between veterans and nonveterans, such as how many children veterans have or how many times they marry. Quantitative topics in the study of veterans and families that researchers have overlooked include household composition of veterans from all eras, number of times married and divorced for veterans of all eras, rates of cohabitation for veterans of all eras before the AVF era, and number of children for veterans of the WWII and Korean War eras. Furthermore, there are few quantitative studies on veterans from the AVF era onward.

A second gap in the literature is the lack of studies that include female veterans. The majority of studies on veterans' families disregard female veterans due to the small number of cases, especially in early eras. Furthermore, studies that do consider women in the military primarily focus on enlisted personnel and the issues female active-duty members experience with families, such as pregnancy and relocation with young children. Female veterans are approximately 9 percent of all U.S. veterans (Department of Veterans Affairs 2014), therefore that they are consistently overlooked is problematic, and research into their family formation patterns is valuable.

A third flaw in prior research is the focus on post-traumatic stress disorder (PTSD) in conjunction with marriage and divorce of veterans, especially how spouses, partners, or families handle veterans with PTSD (Orcutt, King, and King 2003; Dekel et al. 2005; Lyons 2001; Riggs et al. 1998; Roberts et al. 1982). These studies consider the impact of PTSD on family members, including secondary stress (Franciskovic et al. 2007), intergenerational stress (Dekel and Goldblatt 2008), and caregiver burden (Calhoun, Beckham, and Bosworth 2002; Beckham, Lytle, and Feldman 1996). Similarly, there is a large focus in the extant body of literature on the impacts of exposure to combat on the families of veterans (Ruger, Wilson, and Waddoups 2002; Call and Teachman 1996; Gimbel and Booth 1994; Laufer and Gallops 1985). Although PTSD is a tragedy in the lives of veterans, and research into the effect it has on families is valuable, such research ignores the much larger group of veterans who do not have PTSD.

Finally, within the prior literature there is a sizable focus on military service in the life course of veterans themselves. These studies tend to consider the sequencing of key life events, such as marriage, divorce, and birth of children. Although these studies contain important information on how military service can interrupt the life course, researchers largely consider these differences within populations of veterans and therefore

Veterans' Families

provide few comparisons between veterans and nonveterans (Elder, Shanahan, and Clipp 1994; Jordan et al. 1992; Elder 1987). From these studies, it is difficult to attribute life-course trends among veterans to military service itself.

We address these gaps in the prior literature in multiple ways. First, our data include veterans of all eras from World War II onward, allowing us to make comparisons across eras. Second, we consider the family compositions of both veterans and nonveterans. Third, we consider both male and female veterans and nonveterans. Finally, we include many variables that encompass a wide variety of family-related measures.

Data and Methods

We use data gathered in the 2013 one-year American Community Survey (ACS). The ACS is conducted annually by the Census Bureau and provides nationally representative data on a wide variety of topics, including veteran status (Census Bureau 2015). The 2013 one-year ACS includes information on 2,459,182 men and women over age 18, including 193,354 veterans of active-duty military service (7.86 percent of the sample).

From these data, we created six subsamples, each corresponding to a historical era representing potential military service. The six historical eras are shown in table 15.1: World War II, the Korean era, the period between the Korean era and the Vietnam era (BKV), the Vietnam era, the All-Volunteer Force (AVF) era, and the post-9/11 era. We constructed an indicator of whether a respondent was a veteran of these eras using a measure of period of service provided in the ACS. Veterans of the AVF were considered to be respondents who served during the first Gulf War (August 1990 to August 1991) and those who were on active service in the period between the Vietnam War and the first Gulf War. If veterans served in multiple eras, they were assigned to their first era of service in order to maintain consistent cohort comparisons. Eras of service for veterans are therefore exclusive. For each era, we then selected birth cohorts of nonveteran men and women who were between the ages of 18 and 24 during that era. Accordingly, we can compare veterans to nonveterans of comparable ages across the six different historical eras. The eras of service for nonveterans are nonexclusive. Some nonveterans can be compared to veterans of multiple eras, as they were of military age (18–24 years old) during multiple eras. For example, a nonveteran respondent born in 1942 can be compared to veterans of both BKV and the Vietnam era. Although there are many ways of allocating nonveterans to eras for comparison, we chose to include all individuals between 18 and 24 years of age because

Table 15.1. U.S. Veterans by Birth Cohort, Age in 2013, and Historic Era.

Historic Era	War Years	Birth Cohort	Age in 2013
World War II (WWII)	1942–1945	1918–1927	86–95
Korea	1950–1953	1926–1935	78–87
Between Korea and Vietnam (BKV)	1954–1963	1930–1945	68–83
Vietnam	1964–1975	1940–1957	56–73
All-Volunteer Force (AVF)	1976–2000	1952–1982	31–61
Post-9/11	2001–2013	1977–1995	18–36

they represent the majority of individuals at risk of enlistment (for another method, see Landes et al. forthcoming).

To compare veterans and nonveterans, we constructed a set of doubly robust treatment effects models (Funk et al. 2011; Morgan and Harding 2006) in version 13 of STATA. In essence these models equate veterans and nonveterans with respect to a number of important characteristics (e.g., age, education, race/ethnicity, region of residence) when making comparisons on the variable of interest. These models allow the calculation of the average treatment effect (ATE), which is the effect of the treatment if the entire population had been treated. Here, the treatment is active-duty military service, and the ATE values shown in our results indicate the effect of such service if everyone had served. The estimates help to reduce, but do not eliminate, biases that may occur due to the selectivity of military service. Tests of traditional statistical significance are also shown, but with the very large sample sizes available in the ACS, even small differences between veterans and nonveterans can be statistically significant. It is more prudent, therefore, to pay attention to the magnitude of reported differences.

The most straightforward comparisons that can be made are between veterans and nonveterans within eras. It is possible to compare results for veterans across different eras, but such comparisons are sometimes confounded by strong life-course differences in an outcome that is not necessarily linked to military service. For example, it is much more likely that the more recent cohorts of veterans will have children living at home than earlier cohorts of veterans simply because the children of the latter group will be much older.

Variables

We use indicators of marital status and household composition provided by the ACS 2013 to compare the families of veterans and nonveterans throughout the historical military eras. The dependent variables measuring marital status (married, widowed, divorced, separated, and never married) were recoded into mutually exclusive dichotomous variables from a question asking respondents "What is this person's marital status?," with 1 meaning the condition applies to the respondent and 0 indicating that the condition does not apply. We reverse coded "never married" to create an indicator of "ever married," where 1 indicates the respondent has ever married. We also make use of the question "How many times has this person been married?" to create a dummy variable indicating multiple marriages. Respondents were coded 1 if they had married two or more times, otherwise 0. Cohabitation was coded as a 1 if the respondent lived with an unmarried partner and 0 if there were no unmarried partners in the household. The presence of the respondents' biological child in the household was coded 1, 0 otherwise.

We also constructed an "ever divorced" dichotomous variable, using three variables: the respondents' marital status, an indicator of a divorce in the past 12 months, and the previously described indicator of multiple marriages. If respondents reported being currently divorced, divorced in the past 12 months, or married more than once, they were coded as a 1; otherwise, respondents were coded as a 0. This variable could inadvertently capture individuals whose first marriage ended in the death of a spouse; however we believe it is suitable in our analysis because the majority of cases with multiple marriages ended the first marriage with a divorce.

Our final dependent variables are indicators of household type. These variables include "Living in a married couple household" (0 = no, 1 = yes); "Living in a family household with a male householder and no wife" (0 = no, 1 = yes); "Living in a family household with a female householder and no husband" (0 = no, 1 = yes); "Living in a non-family household alone" (0 = no, 1 = yes); "Living in a nonfamily household, not alone" (0 = no, 1 = yes).

Indicators of service era were used as our primary independent variables. For the purpose of this study, veterans were coded into one of six eras, as explained previously.

Finally, we include multiple control variables in our treatment effects model to reduce the likelihood of spuriousness associated with selectivity into the military. These include dichotomous variables indicating race (white, black, Hispanic), dichotomous variables of the respondents' residential region in the United States (Northeast, Midwest, South, and West), the respondents' age; and their total number of years of schooling.

Table 15.2. Descriptive Statistics for Female Veterans and Nonveterans, by Era, in 2013.

Females: Percentages of Marital Status, Children in the Home, and Cohabitation

Era		Currently Married	Ever Married	Currently Divorced	Ever Divorced	Currently Separated	Widowed	Married 2+ Times	Currently Cohabiting	Live with Own Child
All Eras	Veterans	51	83	21	28	28	8	31	6	27
	Nonveterans	52	77	12	44	22	11	19	6	28
WWII	Veterans	20	92	8	25	0	63	20	1	1
	Nonveterans	13	95	7	23	0	75	18	1	1
Korea	Veterans	46	94	13	34	1	34	17	2	1
	Nonveterans	32	96	9	27	1	54	21	1	2
BKV	Veterans	56	96	17	40	1	21	29	2	1
	Nonveterans	48	95	13	34	1	33	26	1	2
Vietnam	Veterans	53	90	25	52	2	10	38	4	2
	Nonveterans	61	93	17	41	2	13	30	3	4
AVF	Veterans	56	88	25	54	4	3	39	7	32
	Nonveterans	64	86	15	33	3	3	22	6	39
Post-9/11	Veterans	43	59	11	20	4	0	11	8	40
	Nonveterans	36	42	4	8	2	0	4	11	44

Table 15.3. Descriptive Statistics for Male Veterans and Nonveterans, by Era, in 2013.

Males: Percentages of Marital Status, Children in the Home, and Cohabitation

Era		Currently Married	Ever Married	Currently Divorced	Ever Divorced	Currently Separated	Widowed	Married 2+ Times	Currently Cohabiting	Live with Own Child
All Eras	Veterans	68	91	13	39	2	2	32	4	13
	Nonveterans	54	67	9	22	2	2	15	7	29
WWII	Veterans	56	97	4	25	0	37	23	1	1
	Nonveterans	51	94	6	25	1	37	21	1	2
Korea	Veterans	70	97	7	29	1	18	27	2	1
	Nonveterans	67	96	7	31	1	20	25	2	2
BKV	Veterans	75	96	10	38	1	10	33	2	1
	Nonveterans	74	95	10	36	1	10	30	2	2
Vietnam	Veterans	73	95	16	47	2	5	38	3	3
	Nonveterans	72	91	14	38	2	4	30	4	6
AVF	Veterans	63	87	20	46	3	1	33	7	32
	Nonveterans	65	80	12	27	2	1	18	7	37
Post-9/11	Veterans	43	53	7	13	2	0	6	8	32
	Nonveterans	28	32	3	5	1	0	2	10	33

Results

Descriptive Statistics

Tables 15.2 and 15.3 show the descriptive statistics for some of the primary variables used in our analysis, separated by gender, veteran status, and military conflict era. Across all eras, white men are overrepresented in the veteran population, whereas black and Hispanic men are underrepresented. A similar trend occurs for female veterans, although black females are overrepresented in the veteran population during more recent eras (AVF and post-9/11). Male veterans have the highest likelihood of marriage (90 percent across all eras), followed by female veterans (83 percent across all eras). Both male and female veterans have higher rates of ever divorcing than their nonveteran counterparts (39 percent and 44 percent, respectively). Mean number of years of schooling increases across all groups as eras become more recent. Veterans report more years of schooling than their nonveteran counterparts, with female veterans generally having the most education of all groups.

Multivariate Results

Marital Statuses: Women

For marital status, we compare veteran and nonveteran women in terms of the following statuses: married, ever married, divorced, ever divorced, widowed, and separated. In examining the marital status of veteran women compared to nonveteran women, we find that results are similar in direction across the six eras for the divorced and ever divorced marital statuses (see table 15.4). Female veterans are more likely than nonveterans to be divorced and ever divorced in all eras. However, the findings vary by era for the marital status categories of married, ever married, and widowed. We find that female veterans are more likely than female nonveterans to be presently married, except for the Vietnam (–8 percentage points) and AVF (–7 percentage points) eras, where we find veteran women less likely than nonveteran women to be married. Female veterans during the post-9/11 era are both more likely to be married (8 percentage points) and considerably more likely to be ever married (17 percentage points) than respective nonveteran women. For other eras, female veterans do not differ greatly or significantly from female nonveterans in terms of ever married comparisons. For the WWII and Korea eras, female veterans are less likely to be widowed than nonveteran

Table 15.4. Differences between Female Veterans and Female Nonveterans in Marital Status, Cohabitation, and Children: Treatment Effects.

Era	Married	Ever Married	Divorced	Ever Divorced	Separated	Widowed	Married 2+ Times	Cohabitation	Own Child
World War II	9.06*	–	–	9.30*	–	-13.16*	8.74*	–	–
Korean War	14.58*	-1.62	2.8	5.4	0.37	-19.14*	4.24	–	-0.37
Between Korea & Vietnam	6.28*	-0.12	3.6	5.22*	–	9.58*	3.33	–	-0.86
Vietnam War	-8.17*	-2.86*	7.11*	9.64*	0.26	-1.85	7.02*	1.69*	-1.21*
All-Volunteer Force	-7.24*	1.96*	8.71*	19.88*	0.7	0.16	16.33*	2.32*	0.18
Post-9/11	8.37*	16.59*	7.73*	14.07*	1.99*	0.19	8.08*	-1.61*	-1.69

–Insufficient cases
*Significant at the 0.01 alpha level

women (−13 and −19 percentage points, respectively). However, during the BKV era, female veterans are more likely (by 10 percentage points) to be widowed than nonveteran women. The differences between veteran and nonveteran women in terms of separated marital status are small and predominantly insignificant.

Marital Statuses: Men

The same marital status categories used for women are used to compare male veterans with male nonveterans (see table 15.5). First, we discuss the presently divorced and ever divorced statuses. The WWII era is the only period of the 12 comparisons for which veterans are significantly less likely than nonveterans to be presently divorced. For the other five era divorce comparisons and all six eras for ever-divorced comparisons, we find that male veterans are more likely than male nonveterans to be divorced and to be ever divorced. The Korean War era is the only era without significant differences in terms of divorce.

Male veterans are significantly more likely to be presently married than male nonveterans for the post-9/11 era. At 13.4 percentage points, the post-9/11 era represents the largest difference in marriage between the veteran and nonveteran men. World War II–era male veterans are significantly more likely than male nonveterans to be married as well. Male veterans of the BKV, Vietnam, and AVF eras are less likely than male nonveterans to be married. The findings for Vietnam and AVF eras, although less than negative two percentage points, are significant. We find male veterans significantly more likely than nonveterans to be ever married in all eras, with the most striking percentage point difference of 19 for the post-9/11 era. Male veterans are more likely than male nonveterans to be widowed in the most recent four eras and separated in the most recent three eras; however these differences are small.

Married More Than Once: Men and Women

In all six eras, both male and female veterans are more likely than nonveterans to be married more than once (see tables 15.4 15.5). Both male and female veterans have similar ranges of differences over the eras. Of note is that the largest difference between veterans and nonveterans for both men and women is for the AVF era. For the 12 veteran versus nonveteran comparisons, 6 each for women and men, the only nonsignificant differences are for women during the Korean War and BKV eras.

Table 15.5. Differences between Male Veterans and Male Nonveterans in Marital Status, Cohabitation, and Children: Treatment Effects.

Era	Married	Ever Married	Divorced	Ever Divorced	Separated	Widowed	Married 2+ Times	Cohabitation	Own Child
World War II	3.67*	4.05*	-1.15*	2.43*	-0.04	1.57	3.48*	0.09	-0.43*
Korean War	0.8	1.76*	0.3	3.07*	-0.17	1.02	3.22*	0.04	-0.89*
Between Korea & Vietnam	-0.42	1.77*	1.93*	6.35*	0.09	0.78*	6.06*	0.21	-0.79*
Vietnam War	-1.86*	2.67*	4.08*	10.62*	0.26*	0.75*	9.35*	0.38*	-1.86*
All-Volunteer Force	-1.92*	5.73*	7.35*	17.72*	0.77*	0.26*	13.71*	0.94*	2.05*
Post-9/11	13.41*	18.46*	5.07*	9.65*	1.26*	0.18*	5.44*	1.41*	0.08

*Significant at the 0.01 alpha level

Cohabitation: Men and Women

Female veterans of the Vietnam and AVF eras are slightly more likely to cohabit than nonveterans (see table 15.4). Veteran women are less likely than nonveteran women to cohabit during the post-9/11 era. Although these differences are significant for all three periods (Vietnam, AVF, and post-9/11), the percentage point differences are small, around two percentage points. The veteran and nonveteran comparisons for men are both significant and positive for the same three periods (see table 15.5). Similar to the women, these era-dependent comparisons between veterans and nonveterans are based on small differences of less than two percentage points in all eras.

Married Couple Household: Men and Women

Next we examine veterans' families in terms of married couple households separately for women and men (see tables 15.6 and 15.7). Female veterans of the early eras of WWII and Korea are significantly more likely than nonveteran women to live in a married couple household. During the later eras of Vietnam and AVF, female veterans are significantly less likely than female nonveterans to live in married couple households. Overall, the magnitude of the differences between veterans and nonveterans is lower for men than for women. This pattern suggests an important shift in the impact of military service on family life. We find significant differences for veteran males compared to nonveteran males during the three most recent eras (Vietnam, AVF, and post-9/11). However, the highest percentage point change of five, found during the post-9/11, era is considerably lower than the four larger differences for women.

Other Family Households for Men and Women

In this section we compare veterans and nonveterans for the category other family households. For women, these households include women living in households with female householders and no husband present and women living in households with a male householder and no wife present (see table 15.6). For female householders with no husband present, only very low percentage point differences are evident, with the highest difference between veteran and nonveterans at less than four points for those in the AVF era. For women living in households with a male householder, no wife present (see table 15.6), we find very low percentage point differences between veterans and nonveterans across the eras. Female veterans are less

Table 15.6. Differences between Female Veterans and Female Nonveterans in Household Type: Treatment Effects.

	Other Family Household			Nonfamily Household	
Era	Married Couple Household	Female Householder; No Husband	Male Householder; No Wife	Lives Alone	Lives with Others
World War II	9.22*	–	–	-5.88	–
Korean War	10.64*	-0.66	0.72	-13.36*	2.24
Between Korea & Vietnam	2.87	–	–	-3.57	–
Vietnam War	-8.56*	1.56	0.47	3.83*	2.16*
All-Volunteer Force	-7.38*	3.79*	-0.56	2.52*	1.99*
Post-9/11	-1.6	-0.05	-1.27*	4.50*	-0.95

—Insufficient cases.
*Significant at the 0.01 alpha level.

Table 15.7. Differences between Male Veterans and Male Nonveterans in Household Type: Treatment Effects.

	Other Family Household			Nonfamily Household	
Era	Married Couple Household	Female Householder; No Husband	Male Householder; No Wife	Lives Alone	Lives with Others
World War II	0.66	-1.15*	-0.03	0.43	0.2
Korean War	-0.7	-0.42*	0.02	1.37*	-0.21
Between Korea & Vietnam	0.91	-0.36*	0.2	1.25*	-0.04
Vietnam War	1.68*	-0.18	0.14	1.64*	0.08
All-Volunteer Force	-2.26*	0.51*	0.92*	1.43*	-0.31
Post-9/11	4.53*	-4.95*	-1.70*	2.69*	0.77

*Significant at the 0.01 alpha level.

likely to live in male households with no wife present during the post-9/11 era, but even this is only a one percentage point difference.

For men, other family households include men living in households with a female householder and no husband present and men living in households with a male householder and no wife present. Examining men residing in households with a female householder and no husband present (see table 15.7, column 2), veterans are significantly less likely than nonveterans to live in this type of residence in five of the six eras, while being slightly more likely in the AVF era. Next we focus on male householders with no wife present (see table 15.7). We find significant differences between veterans and nonveterans for the AVF and post-9/11 eras, with the veterans being more likely in the former era and less likely in the latter to live in this type of household.

Nonfamily Households for Women and Men

We compare female veterans with nonveterans for two types of nonfamily households that have a female householder: women living alone and women not living alone (see table 15.6). In terms of nonfamily households with women living alone, veteran women are significantly different from nonveterans in four eras. In the Korea era, female veterans are 13 percentage points less likely than female nonveterans to live in this type of household. In the most recent three eras, Vietnam, AVF, and post-9/11, female veterans are all more likely than female nonveterans to live alone in nonfamily households, although by small percentages. For the second category of nonfamily households, those not living alone, we find little difference between veteran women and nonveteran women. Insufficient cases prevent comparison for the WWII era and the era between Korea and Vietnam. Female veterans of the Vietnam and the AVF eras are slightly and significantly more likely to be not living alone.

For men, we compare veterans with nonveterans for the same two types of nonfamily households as women: men living alone and men not living alone (see table 15.7). Veteran men are consistently more likely to live alone than nonveteran men in all eras, as indicated by the positive percentage point differences in all eras. The difference is significant for all eras except for the WWII era. No consistent pattern exists between male veterans and nonveterans not living alone in nonfamily households.

Children: Men and Women

Only small differences (two percentage points or less) are found between nonveterans and veterans for both men and women when it comes to the presence of own minor children (see tables 15.4 and 15.5). The AVF era is the only time veterans are more likely to have children. This is evident for both male and female veterans. Female veterans are significantly different from nonveterans for the Vietnam era only. For male veterans, the differences were significant for all eras except the post-9/11 period.

Discussion

Prior literature overwhelmingly indicates that veterans of all eras are more likely to marry than nonveterans. We find this holds true for male veterans but not female veterans. Further, male veterans in each separate era are more likely than male nonveterans to marry. Likewise, female veterans of the AVF and post-9/11 eras are more likely to marry than their nonveteran counterparts; however, female veterans of the Vietnam era are less likely than nonveterans to marry, and we find no difference between female veterans and nonveterans of earlier eras. This finding that male and female veterans differ with regard to the likelihood of marriage is significant, because women are largely overlooked in research regarding veterans. In terms of prior research regarding divorce, there is no consistent pattern both within and between eras. We find that both male and female veterans of all eras are more likely to have ever divorced than nonveterans. These results correspond to our finding that veterans are more likely to ever marry. In addition, we find that female veterans of the latter three eras (Vietnam, AVF, and post-9/11) and male veterans of the latter four eras (between Korea and Vietnam, Vietnam, AVF, and post-9/11) are more likely to be presently divorced than nonveterans.

Prior literature reports that WWII veterans are more likely to marry than nonveterans, and our results support this finding. We find that both male and female WWII veterans are more likely to be presently married than nonveterans, and that male WWII veterans are more likely than nonveterans to ever marry. In addition, similar to MacLean and Elder (2007) and Settersten (2008), we find that both male and female WWII veterans are more likely to ever divorce. We also find that male WWII veterans are less likely to be presently divorced than nonveterans, and that both male and female WWII veterans are more likely to marry more than once. These findings indicate that WWII veterans are more likely to marry, divorce, and remarry than nonveterans. Female veterans of WWII are much less likely than female nonveterans to be widowed, likely because they remarry after the death of their spouse, whereas nonveterans are less likely to remarry and therefore stay widowed.

Most studies that consider Korean War veterans include them with WWII veterans, assuming that they behave similarly; however, our findings indicate that this assumption is incorrect. Our results for Korean War veterans differ from those for WWII veterans. Similar to WWII veterans, female Korean War veterans are more likely than nonveterans to be presently married and less likely to be widowed. However, we find no difference between female veterans and nonveterans in terms of likelihood of marriage, divorce, or marriage more than once. In other words, female Korean War veterans behave fairly similarly to nonveterans. Male Korean War veterans, like WWII veterans, are more likely than nonveterans to ever divorce, ever marry, and marry more than once, but unlike WWII veterans, are no more likely than nonveterans to be presently married or presently divorced. This difference between WWII and Korean War veterans is possibly due to the relatively smaller, more selective number of veterans of the Korean War compared to WWII.

In addition, prior research on veterans of the era between the Korean War and the Vietnam War remains virtually nonexistent. We find that, similar to the prior two eras, female veterans of the BKV era are more likely than nonveterans to be presently married. However, unlike the prior two eras, female BKV veterans are more likely to be widowed than nonveterans. It is possible that these veterans are at an age where their spouses are more likely to die and, unlike WWII and Korean War veterans, they may not yet have had a chance to remarry. Male veterans of the BKV era are more likely than nonveterans to be ever married, presently divorced, ever divorced, and married more than once.

Although prior studies consistently indicate that Vietnam era veterans are more likely to marry than nonveterans, we find this only holds true for male veterans. Female Vietnam veterans are less likely to ever marry than nonveterans, and both male and female Vietnam veterans are less likely than nonveterans to be presently married. Given that studies of Vietnam era veterans do not distinguish between male and female veterans, it is not surprising that our findings regarding female veterans differ from prior findings. Furthermore, although there is little consensus among prior literature regarding likelihood of divorce for Vietnam veterans, none of the studies report that Vietnam veterans are more likely to divorce than nonveterans. We find that male and female Vietnam veterans are more likely to be presently divorced and to ever divorce than nonveterans. However, because we do not control for selectivity, our findings are most similar to those in Heerwig and Conley's (2013) first model, which likewise does not control for selectivity. In this model, Heerwig and Conley find that Vietnam veterans are more likely to divorce than nonveterans. Therefore, although their conclusions indicate that Vietnam veterans are less likely to divorce than nonveterans, these differences can likely be attributed to selectivity. That is, before entering military service, veterans may have higher propensity to divorce than nonveterans. Thus, the observed differences in risk of divorce may not be attributable to military service itself. In addition, prior studies have found no difference between Vietnam veterans and nonveterans in terms of number of times married and household composition (Card 1983). Contrary to these results, we find that Vietnam era veterans are more likely than nonveterans to marry more than once, and are more likely to live alone.

Prior research finds that veterans of the AVF are more likely to marry than nonveterans, and our findings reflect this. We find that both male and female AVF era veterans are more likely than nonveterans to ever marry. However, they are less likely than nonveterans to be presently married. In addition, prior literature finds that male AVF era veterans are no different from nonveterans in terms of divorce (Teachman and Tedrow 2008), whereas female AVF era veterans are more likely than nonveterans to divorce (Cooney et al. 2003). We find this holds true for female veterans but not male veterans. Both male and female veterans of AVF era are more likely than nonveterans to be presently divorced and to ever divorce. Veterans of the AVF era are also more likely than nonveterans to cohabit and to marry more than once. These findings indicate that both male and female AVF veterans are more likely than nonveterans to marry, divorce, and remarry, although they are less likely to be presently married.

Finally, there is limited literature on the families of post-9/11 era veterans for which to compare our results, likely due to the limited time these individuals have been veterans. We find that veterans of the post-9/11 era are more likely to be presently married and to ever marry. For male veterans, this is one of the two eras where they are significantly more likely to be presently married than nonveterans (the other being WWII). Furthermore, for both male and female veterans, the coefficients for ever married are large, indicating that these veterans are much more likely than nonveterans to ever marry. This difference may, in part, be due to the age of this cohort, which limits the amount of time they have had to marry. Given that military service increases the likelihood of marrying at a younger age (Teachman 2007), it is possible that as this cohort ages, the nonveterans will marry equally or more so than their veteran counterparts. Furthermore, post-9/11 era veterans are more likely than nonveterans to be presently divorced, to ever divorce, and to marry more than once. Because nonveterans are so much less likely to have ever married than veterans of the post-9/11 era, it follows that they are less likely to divorce and to remarry.

Our data are not without limitations that should be considered for future research. The first is the lack of a question in the ACS regarding respondents' total number of children. Our data include a question about the "household presence and age of own children," but there is no indication of children that no longer live with respondents. This is especially frustrating when analyzing the outcomes of older respondents, as their children will likely have moved out of the parental home and are not captured by the survey. As such, we provide minimal description of the results for children, because the differences between veterans and nonveterans are small or insignificant. A second limitation is that the ACS does not sample homeless populations. Homelessness rates among veterans also vary by era, with Vietnam War veterans having the highest rates (National Coalition for the Homeless 2009). It is estimated that about 57,849 veterans were homeless on any given night in 2013, accounting for over 12 percent of all homeless adults (Department of Housing and Urban Development 2013). Because homelessness can create additional stressors, we expect that family outcomes of homeless veterans would differ from the outcomes of their nonhomeless counterparts.

Another limitation to our study is the use of cross-sectional data. Although the ACS is unique in that we can discern specific eras in which respondents served, we are unable to track changes in the respondents' behavior due to participation in the military. Being able to do so, using longitudinal data and a fixed-effects regression model, for example, would allow for better controls of selectivity into the military during nondraft eras. A fourth limitation is the potential error in our variable measuring if the respondent has ever divorced. As previously mentioned, this variable could capture respondents who had a preceding marriage end because of the death of their spouse. Future research on the families of veterans should consider using surveys that ask respondents if they have ever divorced. Finally, our data give a low number of female respondents who served in the WWII and BKV eras (636 and 671, respectively), limiting our analyses. This is not surprising, as many of these service members have died since the wars, and predominantly men served during these eras. A data set with an oversample of women and/or veterans of pre-Vietnam eras would help to attain more statistically significant results for these groups (although we are not aware of any such survey).

Conclusion

Overall, we find similar general trends for marital statuses across eras for both male and female veterans. In terms of marriage, we find that female veterans of the WWII, Korea, BKV, and post-9/11 eras are more likely than nonveterans to be presently married, whereas female veterans of the

Vietnam and AVF eras are less likely to be presently married. This pattern holds true for male veterans as well; however, the differences between veterans and nonveterans are of smaller magnitudes. Male veterans of all eras and female veterans of AFV and post-9/11 eras are more likely than nonveterans to have ever been married. In terms of divorce, we find that male and female veterans of all eras are more likely than nonveterans to ever divorce, and that male and female veterans of the latter eras are more likely to be presently divorced. This finding is partially supported by our findings that veterans of all eras are more likely to be ever married. Along with this trend, we find that male and female veterans of all eras are more likely than nonveterans to be married more than once.

Our findings regarding household composition are similar to our marital status findings. Female veterans of the Vietnam and AVF eras are less likely than female nonveterans to live in married-couple households, which corresponds with our finding that female veterans of these two eras are less likely to be presently married. Furthermore, female veterans of the Vietnam, AVF, and post-9/11 eras are more likely to live alone. We also find that veteran men of all eras are more likely to live alone than nonveteran men. Given that we find that male veterans are more likely than nonveterans to have ever been divorced and to be presently divorced, it is not surprising that male veterans are more likely to live alone.

Note

1. This research was supported by grant no. R15 HD069958 from the National Institute of Child Health and Human Development (NICHD). Any opinions, findings, and conclusions expressed in this material are those of the authors and do not necessarily reflect the views of NICHD.

References

Albano, Sondra. 1994. "Military Recognition of Family Concerns: Revolutionary War to 1993." *Armed Forces & Society* 20 (2): 283–302.

Beckham, Jean C., Barbara L. Lytle, and Michelle E. Feldman. 1996. "Caregiver Burden in Partners of Vietnam War Veterans with Posttraumatic Stress Disorder." *Journal of Consulting and Clinical Psychology* 64 (5): 1068–1072.

Bell, Bruce, and Robert Iadeluca. 1988. "The Origins of Volunteer Support for Army Family Programs." *Minerva* 6 (3): 26–43.

Calhoun, Patrick, Jean Beckham, and Hayden Bosworth. 2002. "Caregiver Burden and Psychological Distress in Partners of Veterans with Chronic Posttraumatic Stress Disorder." *Journal of Traumatic Stress* 15 (3): 205–212.

Call, Vaughn R. A., and Jay Teachman. 1991. "Military Service and Stability in the Family Life Course." *Journal of Military Psychology* 3 (4): 233–250.

Call, Vaughn R. A., and Jay Teachman. 1996. "Life-course Timing and Sequencing of Marriage and Military Service and Their Effects on Marital Stability." *Journal of Marriage and the Family* 58 (1): 219–226.

Card, Josefina J. 1983. *Lives after Vietnam: The Personal Impact of Military Service*. Lexington MA: Lexington Books.

Census Bureau. 2015. American Community Survey. Accessed April 14, 2015. http://www.census.gov/acs/www/.

Cohen, Jere, and Mady Segal. 2009. "Veterans, the Vietnam Era, and Marital Dissolution: An Event History Analysis." *Armed Forces & Society* 36 (1): 19–37.

Cooney, Richard, Mady Segal, David Segal, and William Falk. 2003. "Racial Differences in the Impact of Military Service on the Socioeconomic Status of Women Veterans." *Armed Forces & Society* 30 (1): 53–86.

Dekel, Rachel, and Hadass Goldblatt. 2008. "Is There Intergenerational Transmission of Trauma? The Case of Combat Veterans' Children." *American Journal of Orthopsychiatry* 78 (3): 281–289.

Dekel, Rachel, Hadass Goldblatt, Michal Keidar, Zahava Solomon, and Michael Polliack. 2005. "Being a Wife of a Veteran with Posttraumatic Stress Disorder." *Family Relations* 54 (1): 24–36.

Department of Defense. 2013. "2013 Demographics: Profile of the Military Community." Office of the Deputy Assistant Secretary of Defense. Accessed May 17, 2016. http://download.militaryonesource.mil/12038/MOS/Reports/2013-Demographics-Report.pdf.

Department of Housing and Urban Development, Office of Community Planning and Development. 2013. "The 2013 Annual Homeless Assessment Report (AHAR) to Congress: Part1, Point-in-Time Estimates of Homelessness." Accessed May 17, 2016. https://www.hudexchange.info/resources/documents/ahar-2013-part1.pdf.

Department of Veterans Affairs. 2011. "Annual Benefits Report: Fiscal Year 2010." Accessed May 27, 2016. http://www.vba.va.gov/REPORT/abr/2010_abr.pdf.

Department of Veteran Affairs. 2014. "Women Veteran Profile." Accessed May 27, 2016. http://www.va.gov/VETDATA/docs/SpecialReports/Women_Veteran_Profile5.pdf.

Elder, Glen. 1987. "War Mobilization and the Life Course: A Cohort of World War II Veterans." *Sociological Forum* 2 (3): 449–472.

Elder, Glen, Michael Shanahan, and Elizabeth Clipp. 1994. "When War Comes to Men's Lives: Life-Course Patterns in Family, Work, and Health." *Psychology and Aging* 9 (1): 5–16.

Franciskovic, Tanja, Aleksandra Stevanovic, Ilijana Jelusic, Branka Roganovic, Miro Klaric, and Jansa Grkovic. 2007. "Secondary Traumatization of Wives of War Veterans with Posttraumatic Stress Disorder." *Croatian Medical Journal* 48: 177–184.

Frey-Wouters, Ellen, and Robert Laufer. 1986. *Legacy of a War: The American Soldier in Vietnam*. New York: M. E. Sharpe, Inc.

Funk, Michele, Daniel Westreich, Chris Wiesen, Til Sturmer, M. Alan Brookhart, and Marie Davidian. 2011. "Doubly Robust Estimation of Causal Effects." *American Journal of Epidemiology* 173 (7): 761–767.

Gimbel, Cynthia, and Alan Booth. 1994. "Why Does Military Combat Experience Adversely Affect Marital Relations?" *Journal of Marriage and the Family* 56 (3): 691–703.

Heerwig, Jennifer, and Dalton Conley. 2013. "The Causal Effects of Vietnam-Era Military Service on Post-War Family Dynamics." *Social Science Research* 42 (2): 299–310.

Jordan, B. Kathleen, Charles Marmar, John Fairbank, William Schlenger, Richard Kulka, Richard Hough, and Daniel Weiss. 1992. "Problems in Families of Male Vietnam Veterans with Post-Traumatic Stress Disorder." *Journal of Consulting and Clinical Psychology* 60 (6): 916–926.

Landes, Scott, Andrew London, Alair MacLean, and Janet Wilmoth. Forthcoming. "Appendix A: Recommendations Regarding the Measurement Periods of Military Service and Corresponding Age 18 Birth Cohorts." In *Long-Term Outcomes of Military Service*, edited by Ron Spiro, Richard Settersten and Carolyn Aldwin. American Psychological Association.

Laufer, Robert S., and Mark S. Gallops. 1985. "Life-Course Effects of Vietnam Combat and Abusive Violence: Marital Patterns." *Journal of Marriage and the Family* 47 (4): 839–853.

Lyons, Margaret. 2001. "Living with Post-Traumatic Stress Disorder: The Wives'/Female Partners' Perspective." *Journal of Advanced Nursing* 34(1): 69–77.

MacLean, Alair, and Glen Elder. 2007. "Military Service in the Life Course." *Annual Review of Sociology* 33: 175–96.

Morgan, Stephen, and David Harding. 2006. "Matching Estimators and Causal Effects: Prospects and Pitfalls in Theory and Practice." *Sociological Methods and Research* 35 (1): 3–60.

National Center for Veterans Analysis and Statistics. 2011. "America's Women Veterans: Military Service History and VA Benefit Utilization Statistics." Accessed May 27, 2016. http://www.va.gov/vetdata/docs/specialreports/final_womens_report_3_2_12_v_7.pdf.

National Center for Veterans Analysis and Statistics. 2015. "VA Benefits and Health Care Utilization Pocket Card." Accessed May, 27, 2016. http://www.va.gov/vetdata/docs/pocketcards/fy2015q2.pdf.

National Coalition for the Homeless. 2009. "Homeless Veterans." Accessed June 22, 2015. http://www.nationalhomeless.org/factsheets/veterans.html.

Orcutt, Holly, Linda A. King, and Daniel W. King. 2003. "Male-Perpetrated Violence among Vietnam Veteran Couples: Relationships with Veteran's Early Life Characteristics, Trauma History, and PTSD Symptomatology." *Journal of Traumatic Stress* 16 (4): 381–90.

Pavalko, Eliza K., and Glen Elder. 1990. "World War II and Divorce: A Life-Course Perspective." *American Journal of Sociology* 95 (5): 1213–1234.

Riggs, David S., Christina A. Byrne, Frank W. Weathers, and Brett T. Litz. 1998. "The Quality of the Intimate Relationships of Male Vietnam Veterans: Problems Associated with Posttraumatic Stress Disorder." *Journal of Traumatic Stress* 11 (1): 87–101.

Roberts, William R., Walter E. Penk, Milton L. Gearing, Ralph Robinowitz, Michael P. Dolan, and Erika T. Patterson. 1982. "Interpersonal Problems of Vietnam Combat Veterans with Symptoms of Posttraumatic Stress Disorder." *Journal of Abnormal Psychology* 91 (6): 444–450.

Ruger, William, Sven Wilson, and Shawn Waddoups. 2002. "Warfare and Welfare: Military Service, Combat, and Marital Dissolution." *Armed Forces & Society* 29 (1): 85–107.

Segal, Mady. 1986. "The Military and the Family as Greedy Institutions." *Armed Forces & Society* 13 (1): 9–38.

Settersten, Richard. 2008. "When Nations Call: How Wartime Military Service Matters for the Life Course and Aging." *Research on Aging* 28 (1): 12–36.

Teachman, Jay. 2007. "Race, Military Service, and Marital Timing: Evidence from the NLSY-79." *Demography* 44 (2): 389–404.

Teachman, Jay. 2009. "Military Service, Race, and the Transition to Marriage and Cohabitation." *Journal of Family Issues* 30 (10): 1433–1454.

Teachman, Jay, and Lucky Tedrow. 2008. "Divorce, Race, and Military Service: More Than Equal Pay and Equal Opportunity." *Journal of Marriage and Family* 70 (4): 1030–1044.

Teachman, Jay, Lucky Tedrow, and Carter Anderson. 2015. "The Relationship between Military Service and Childbearing for Men and Women." *Sociological Perspectives* 58:595–608.

Usdansky, Margaret L., Andrew S. London, and Janet M. Wilmoth. 2009. "Veteran Status, Race-Ethnicity, and Marriage among Fragile Families." *Journal of Marriage and Family* 71 (3): 768–786.

Wadsworth, Shelley, and Kenona Southwell. 2011. "Military Families: Extreme Work and Extreme 'Work Family.'" *Annals of the American Academy of Political and Social Science* 638: 163–183.